Sexual Harassment in the Workplace
Second Edition

Sexual Harassment in the Workplace
Second Edition

by

ARJUN P. AGGARWAL

M.A., LL.M., J.S.D.

Butterworths
Toronto and Vancouver

Sexual Harassment in the Workplace
© Butterworths Canada Ltd. 1992

All rights reserved. No part of this publication may be reproduced, stored in a retrieval system, or transmitted, in any form or by any means (photocopying, electronic, mechanical, recording, or otherwise) without the prior written permission of the copyright holder.

Printed and bound in Canada by John Deyell Company Limited

The Butterworth Group of Companies

Canada
  Butterworths Canada Ltd., 75 Clegg Road, MARKHAM, Ont., L6G 1A1 and 409 Granville St., Ste. 1455, VANCOUVER, B.C. V6C 1T2

Australia
  Butterworths Pty Ltd., SYDNEY, MELBOURNE, BRISBANE, ADELAIDE, PERTH, CANBERRA and HOBART

Ireland
  Butterworths (Ireland) Ltd., DUBLIN

New Zealand
  Butterworths of New Zealand Ltd., WELLINGTON and AUCKLAND

Puerto Rico
  Equity de Puerto Rico, Inc., HATO REY

Singapore
  Malayan Law Journal Pte. Ltd., SINGAPORE

United Kingdom
  Butterworth & Co. (Publishers) Ltd., LONDON and EDINBURGH

United States
  Butterworth Legal Publishers, AUSTIN, Texas; BOSTON, Massachusetts; CLEARWATER, Florida (D & S Publishers); ORFORD, New Hampshire (Equity Publishing); ST. PAUL, Minnesota; and SEATTLE, Washington

Canadian Cataloguing in Publication Data

Aggarwal, Arjun P. (Arjun Prakash), 1929–
  Sexual harassment in the workplace

2nd ed.
Includes index.
ISBN 0-409-90670-0

1. Sexual harassment - Canada. 2. Sexual harassment of women - Law and legislation - Canada. I. Title.

KE8928.A44 1992   344.71'01133   C92-093261-4
KF9325.A9356 1992

Sponsoring Editor: Mary Anne Logan
Editor: Anne Lynas Shah
Cover Design: Brant Cowie
Production: Kevin Skinner
Typesetting: Video Text Inc.

To My Wife Mithilesh

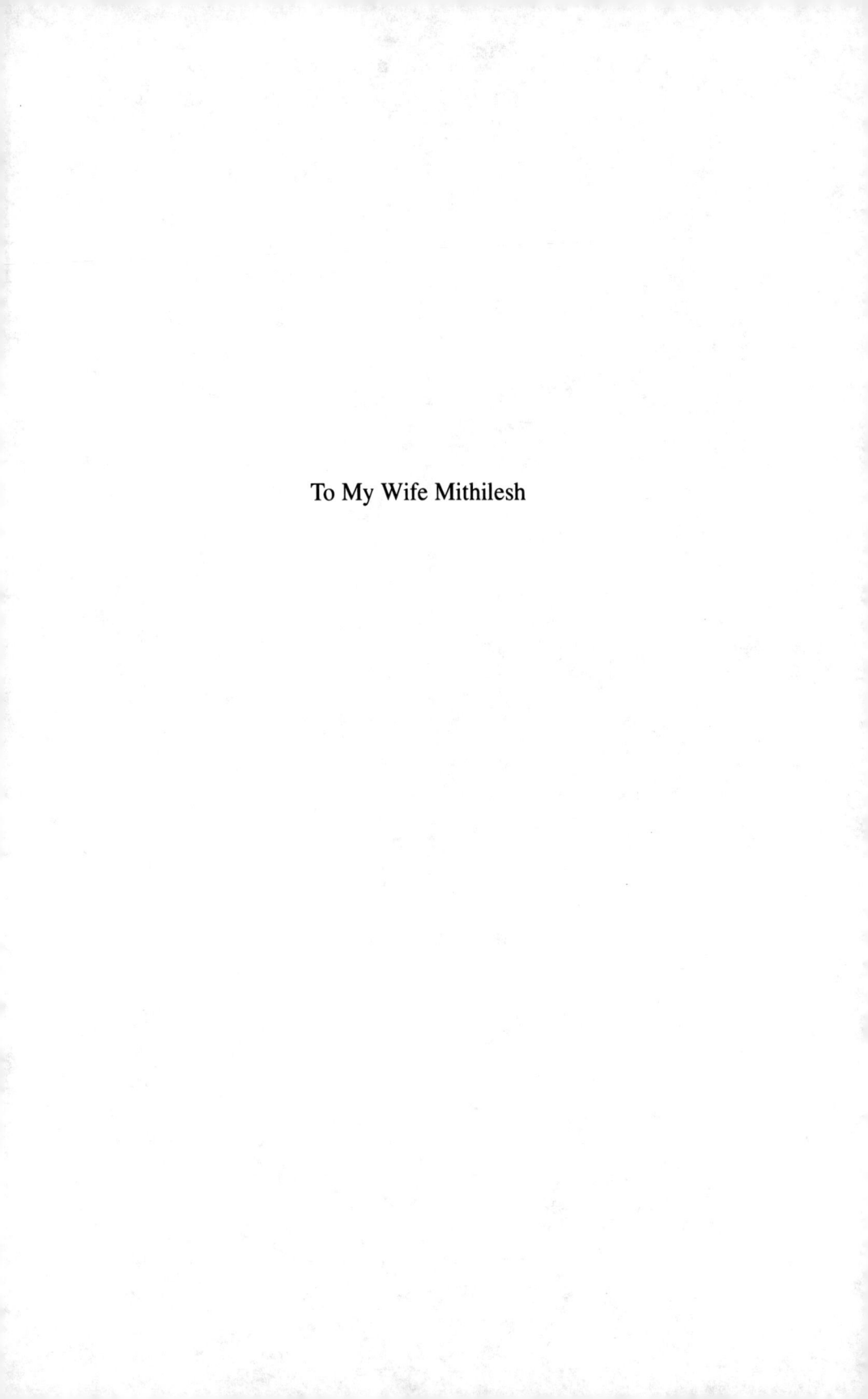

Preface to the Second Edition

At the time of publication of the first edition of *Sexual Harassment in the Workplace* in 1987, the question was frequently raised of whether there was a need for a book on this topic. Was the issue of sexual harassment important enough to deserve that much attention? Since then it has become obvious that sexual harassment in the workplace has emerged as a major societal, legal and economic issue. Nonetheless, even today a large number of employers have difficulty accepting and comprehending the gravity and impact of sexual harassment on the working environment and its consequences for working people, particularly women.

Since the publication of the first edition, the Supreme Court of Canada had the opportunity to review the growth of sexual harassment law. The court delivered its verdict in two important sexual harassment cases: *Robichaud v. Treasury Board* in 1987 and *Janzen v. Platy Enterprises Ltd.* in 1989. The decisions of the highest court were very significant and had serious implications for employers as well as for the future development of sexual harassment law. An analysis of the ramifications of those decisions has been incorporated in the new edition.

Moreover, some other developments as well as some legal issues have emerged during the past five-year period, for example, the issues of *res judicata*, delays in adjudication, remedies for the victims under the *Workers' Compensation Act*, entitlement to Unemployment Insurance benefits on being fired or leaving a job due to sexual harassment, obligations of the employer to the alleged harasser, application of arbitral jurisprudence to sexual harassment cases, and the extent of a union's liability for sexual harassment of employees. These issues are quite significant for all concerned parties including victims, employers, alleged harassers, lawyers, human rights tribunals and the courts. I have attempted to explain these issues in the second edition.

In addition to the persons named in the first edition, I would like to thank Professor William Pentney, General Counsel of the Canadian Human Rights Commission, and Mr. Aaron Berg, Counsel for the Manitoba Human Rights Commission, for their valuable suggestions in connection with the second edition. As well, I thank Ms. Lisa Gagliardi and Mr. George Smith for assisting me in the preparation of the index.

I also want to thank the editorial, production and marketing staff at Butterworths for their professionalism and co-operation. In particular, I am indebted to Ms. Marie Graham, Managing Editor (Legal and Academic Texts), for her expert guidance and support throughout this project, as well as to Ms. Anne Lynas Shah. Also I would like to thank Ms. Mary Sakel for her enthusiasm and efforts in the promotion of this book.

Finally, I would like to pay tribute to my wife Mithilesh who has endured my obsession with the revision of this book. Without her support, encouragement and patience the revision would never have occurred.

I hope the second edition proves useful, as was the first edition, in the handling and prevention of sexual harassment in the workplace.

Thunder Bay, Ontario Arjun P. Aggarwal
February 1992

Preface to the First Edition

Prior to 1980 sexual harassment was virtually unknown in Canadian jurisprudence. In the *Cherie Bell* case (Ontario 1980), for the first time it was recognized that sexual harassment amounts to sex discrimination prohibited by the Ontario *Human Rights Code*. From this point onwards, the meaning and scope of sexual harassment and its legal ramficiations began to unfold in various Canadian jurisdictions through successive "harassment cases". Every new case tended to expand on one or more aspects of this problem. Gradually, the issue of sexual harassment in the workplace became a public concern, and changes in public policies and legislative amendments began to emerge in many Canadian jurisdictions.

My intention in writing this book has been to examine and analyze decided sexual harassment cases, legislative provisions and public policies. This analysis focusses on the development of legal norms relating to various aspects of sexual harassment such as the nature and scope of prohibited behaviour, rights of the victims, liabilities of the harasser and the employer and the ways and means to combat sexual harassment. These principles of law and practice have been presented for the benefit of lawyers, employers, personnel managers, affirmative and equal opportunity administrators, union representatives, women's organizations and all others who are involved in the practice or administration of human rights legislation.

Laws are not only a declaration of rights and obligations, but can also be an instrument of social change. The development of sexual harassment law clearly demonstrates such changes. In this respect, the boards of inquiry have frequently suggested that sexual harassment can be combatted better through prevention rather than litigation. With this in mind, one chapter has been devoted exclusively to the prevention of sexual harassment, with some specific suggestions on how to develop and enforce a sexual harassment policy.

In the preparation of this book, I am thankful to the chairpersons of the boards of inquiry and human rights tribunals whose thought provoking and enlightened deliberations in their sexual harassment decisions greatly inspired me to undertake this study. I also wish to acknowledge my gratitude to earlier writers on this topic, particularly Professor Constance Backhouse, Leah Cohen, and Lin Farley for providing me with a deeper appreciation and insight into the concept of sexual harassment.

I am also thankful to Professor Peter Cumming, Osgoode Hall Law School, who has chaired many boards of inquiry, for encouraging me to write this book. In addition, I had the benefit of comments and advice from a number of people, especially Professor Harish C. Jain of McMaster University, who read the first and second draft of the manuscript.

I am deeply indebted to my colleague Thomas Joseph, without whose continuous encouragement, support and generous assistance I would not have completed this book.

Thanks are also due to Lorne Kenney, Director, Industrial Relations Information Service, Labour Canada, John Ford of the Ontario Ministry of Labour Library and to the library staff of the Confederation College for their cooperation and assistance in securing the research materials.

Finally, I would like to thank my family for their continuous support and encouragement.

It is needless to say that I alone am responsible for any errors, omissions or shortcomings.

Thunder Bay, Ontario
January 1987

Arjun P. Aggarwal

Table of Contents

Preface to the Second Edition... vii
Preface to the First Edition.. ix
Table of Cases... xvii

Introduction: Sexual Harassment: An Issue for the 1990s............ 1

Chapter 1: Sexual Harassment and Human Rights Legislation....... 7
  A. What Behaviour Constitutes Sexual Harassment?.............. 7
    1. Verbal Behaviour...................................... 11
    2. Gestures and Other Non-Verbal Behaviour............... 12
    3. Visual Sexual Harassment.............................. 12
    4. Physical Behaviour.................................... 13
    5. Psychological Sexual Harassment....................... 13
  B. Does Sexual Harassment Amount to Sex Discrimination........ 14
  C. Development of Sexual Harassment Law in the United States.. 16
    1. E.E.O.C. Guidelines................................... 25
    2. Quality of Working Environment........................ 27
  D. Development of Sexual Harassment Law in Canada............. 32
  E. Statutory Amendments to Ban Sexual Harassment.............. 47

Chapter 2: Characteristics of Sexual Harassment................. 57
  A. Sexual Harassment Definition............................... 57
    1. Unsolicited and Unwelcome............................. 63
      (a) "Unwelcome" versus "Voluntarily"................. 63
      (b) Complainant's Past Conduct....................... 65
      (c) "No" Does Not Mean "No".......................... 68
      (d) Verbal Protest Not Necessary..................... 69
      (e) Constructive Knowledge — Standard of Reasonable Person 70
      (f) Consensual Relationships......................... 73
    2. Coerced and Forced.................................... 76
    3. Persistent and Repeated............................... 80
    4. Deliberate and Intentional............................ 85
    5. Sexually Stereotyping Behaviour....................... 89
      (a) Crude and Bad Jokes.............................. 89
      (b) Visual Jokes, Cartoons of Sexual Nature, or Nudity 96
      (c) Dress and Grooming Requirements.................. 98
    6. Job-Related Consequences............................. 102
      (a) Reward or Punishment............................ 102

            (i) Dismissal..103
            (ii) Constructive Dismissal.........................107
            (iii) Other Job-Related Consequences................110
            (iv) Favours for Submission.........................111
        (b) Poisonous and Offensive Work Environment.............112
    7. Sex-Based Harassment.....................................116
 B. Summary and Analysis..121

Chapter 3: Taking Legal Action — A Predicament for the Victim....127
 A. Victim's Reluctance to Complain.............................127
 B. Burden of Proof in Sexual Harassment Cases..................130
 C. Nature of Proof...137
    1. Evidentiary Problems.....................................139
    2. Credibility of Witnesses.................................140
    3. Hearsay Evidence...145
    4. Similar Fact Evidence....................................147
 D. Plaintiff Must Plead and Prove..............................154
 E. Application of Res Judicata to Proceedings Before Human Rights
    Tribunals...156
    1. Decision by Board of Arbitration.........................157
    2. Prior Proceedings Under the *Criminal Code*..............164
        (a) Were the Issues the Same?..........................165
        (b) Were the Parties the Same?.........................165
    3. Paramountcy of Human Rights Legislation..................166
 F. Delays in Adjudication......................................168
    1. Criteria for Determining Unreasonable Delay..............170
    2. Delays Prejudicial to the Defendant......................171
    3. Delays Prejudicial to Society (Community Interest).......172

Chapter 4: Employer's Liability for Sexual Harassment of Employees 181
 A. The Basis of Employer Liability for the Discriminatory Conduct
    of Its Employees..183
    1. Vicarious Liability......................................183
    2. Organic Theory of Corporate Responsibility...............186
    3. Statutory Liability......................................189
        (a) Background to the *Robichaud* case.................190
        (b) Implications of the Federal Court Decision.........192
        (c) Implications of the Supreme Court Decision.........193
        (d) Implications for Public Policy.....................195
        (e) Employer Policy and Procedures.....................198
        (f) Conclusions..199

Table of Contents

- B. Employer's Liability for Sexual Harassment by its Supervisory Personnel...201
  - 1. Employer's Liability on the Principle of Agency.............211
    - (a) In Quid Pro Quo Cases..............................211
    - (b) In Hostile Environment Cases........................212
- C. Sexual Harassment by Co-Workers..........................213
- D. Employer's Liability for Sexual Harassment by Non-Employees...218
- E. Employer's Liability to the Alleged Harasser.................224
  - 1. Wrongful Dismissal of Supervisory Personnel (in a Non-Union Setting)..228
  - 2. Discipline of a Co-Worker Harasser (in a Union Setting).......232

Chapter 5: Remedies Available to the Victim....................235
- A. Employer's Internal Complaint Procedure....................235
- B. Remedies for Sexual Harassment...........................237
  - 1. Tort Remedies..237
  - 2. Civil Action for Breach of Fiduciary Duty.................240
- C. Remedies Under the Human Rights Statutes...................242
  - 1. Compensatory Damages — Philosophy and Purpose.........243
    - (a) Damages for Loss of Earnings......................246
    - (b) Damages for Loss of Job Opportunity................250
  - 2. Determination of Loss of Earnings.......................251
    - (a) Do Earnings Include Indirect Benefits?................251
    - (b) Deduction of Welfare Benefits......................253
    - (c) Damages for Loss of Dignity and Humiliation..........254
    - (d) Punitive Damages................................258
    - (e) Interest on Compensatory Damages..................260
    - (f) Legal Costs.....................................262
    - (g) Costs Against the Respondent......................266
  - 3. Reinstatement of the Victim............................268
  - 4. Apology...270
  - 5. Prevention of Future Violations.........................271
- D. Workers' Compensation Benefits...........................273
- E. Unemployment Insurance Benefits..........................279

Chapter 6: Arbitral Review of Sexual Harassment Cases...........285
- A. Grievances by the Victims................................286
- B. Grievances by Alleged Harassers..........................290
  - 1. Discharge for Sexual Harassment.......................291
    - (a) Reduction of Discharge Penalty.....................295
  - 2. Alleged Harasser Exoneration..........................297
    - (a) Do Arbitral Standards Differ?......................299

3. Severe or Mild Harassment..................................301
C. The Choices Involved...302
D. Ramifications of Reinstatement.............................303

Chapter 7: Prevention of Sexual Harassment — A Necessity.........307
A. Organization's Ability to Adapt..............................307
B. Implications of Sexual Harassment for Employers..............308
C. Economic Cost of Sexual Harassment..........................309
   1. Back Pay..309
   2. Consequential Damages....................................309
   3. Hidden Cost of Sexual Harassment.........................309
   4. Prospect of Aggressive Unionism..........................311
D. Should Employers Put a Complete Ban on Sexual Behaviour?.....311
E. Can Employers Afford to be Passive?.........................313
F. Remedial and Preventive Action — A Legal Obligation..........317
   1. Remedial Action..317
      (a) Employer's Appropriate Response — An Example........319
G. What Can Employers Do?......................................320
H. Essential Elements of a Sexual Harassment Policy..............321
   1. Policy Statement...321
   2. Purpose..322
   3. Definition of Sexual Harassment..........................323
   4. Application and Scope of the Policy......................325
      (a) Employees at All Levels.............................325
      (b) Prospective Employees...............................325
      (c) Non-Employees.......................................325
   5. Consensual Relationships.................................326
   6. Redress Mechanism..327
      (a) Reporting of Complaints.............................327
      (b) Protection Against Retaliation......................328
      (c) Availability..328
      (d) Confidentiality.....................................329
      (e) Complaint Procedure.................................329
      (f) Investigation Procedure.............................330
      (g) Penalties for the Harasser..........................331
      (h) Remedies to the Victim..............................331
      (i) Appeals...332
   7. False Accusation...332
   8. Implementation and Prevention............................332
      (a) Communication.......................................333
      (b) Education...333
      (c) Training..333

9. Conclusion..334
Example of Sexual Harassment Policy and Procedure in a
   Unionized Setting.......................................335
Example of Sexual Harassment Policy and Procedure in a Non-
   Union Professional Setting..............................336

Chapter 8: Unions and Sexual Harassment......................353
   A. Unions' Attitude Towards Sexual Harassment..................354
   B. Unions Face a Challenge....................................355
   C. Legal Obligations of Unions................................359
      1. Unions' Liability......................................360
   D. Union's Duty of Fair Representation........................366
   E. Sexual Harassment Clauses in Collective Agreements..........367
   F. Highlights of Sexual Harassment Clauses....................368

Index..375

Table of Cases

A

Abihsira v. Arvin Automotive et al. (Ont. 1981), 2 C.H.R.R. D/271
    (Hunter) 159, 160
Abouna v. Foothills Provincial General Hospital Bd., [1977] 5 W.W.R.
    75, 77 D.L.R. (3d) 220 (Alta. S.C.); varied [1978] 2 W.W.R. 130, 83
    D.L.R. (3d) 333 (Alta. C.A.) 228
Acadia University (1981), unreported (Kimball) 292, 302
Alberta and A.U.P.E., Re (1982), 5 L.A.C. (3d) 268 (Jolliffe) 233, 272, 296
Alberta and A.U.P.E., Re (1983), 8 L.A.C. (3d) 1 (Jolliffe) 293, 302
Alberta and A.U.P.E., Re (1983), 10 L.A.C. (3d) 179 (Larson) ... 85, 134, 233, 298
Alberta and A.U.P.E. (Harding Grievance), Re (1988), 34 L.A.C. (3d)
    204 (McFetridge) 293
Aleem v. General Felt Industries, 661 F. 2d 135, 27 FEP 569 (9th Cir.
    1981) 168
Alexander v. Gardner-Denver Co., 415 U.S. 36, 7 FEP 81, 94 S. Ct. 101
    (1974) 167, 168
Allan v. Riverside Lodge (Ont. 1985), 6 C.H.R.R. D/2978 (Hunter) 98, 100,
                                                                    101, 144, 221
Amber v. Leder (Ont. Bd. of Inquiry 1970), unreported (Tarnopolsky) 244, 263
Anthony v. B.C. (Council of Human Rights) (B.C. 1990), 11 C.H.R.R.
    D/58 (S.C.) 253, 254
Aragona v. Elegant Lamp Co. Ltd. (Ont. 1982), 3 C.H.R.R. D/1109
    (Ratushny) 57, 62, 89, 90, 114, 141
Aronoff v. Hawryluk (Que. 1981), 2 C.H.R.R. D/534 (Que. Prov. Ct.) 261, 263
Assn. (The) of Professors of The University of Ottawa v. The University
    of Ottawa (1979), unreported (O'Shea) 1, 129, 229
A.-G. Alta. v. Gares (1976), 67 D.L.R. (3d) 635, 76 CLLC 14,016 (Alta.
    S.C.) 86, 260
A.-G. Can. v. Can. Human Rights Commn. (Can. 1980), 1 C.H.R.R. D/
    91 (Fed. Ct.) 263
A.-G. Can. v. McAlpine, [1989] 3 F.C. 530, 99 N.R. 221 (C.A.) 252

B

Ballantyne v. Molly 'N' Me Tavern (Ont. 1982), 4 C.H.R.R. D/1191
    (McCamus) 17, 98
Barbetta v. Chemlawn Services Corp., 669 F. Supp. 569, 45 E.P.D. para.
    37,568 (W.D.N.Y. 1987) 95
Barnes v. Costle. See Barnes v. Train

Barnes v. Train, 13 FEP 123 (D.D.C. 1974); revd (*sub nom.* Barnes v. Costle),
561 F. 2d 983 (D.C. Cir. 1977) 18, 20, 21, 63, 209
Barrett v. Omaha National Bank, 584 F. Supp. 22, 35 FEP 585 (D. Neb.
1984); affd 726 F. 2d 424, 33 E.P.D. para. 34, 132 (8th Cir. 1984) ..... 84,'319
Base-Fort Patrol Ltd. v. Alberta Human Rights Commn. (Alta. 1983),
4 C.H.R.R. D/1200, 23 Alta. L.R. (2d) 372, [1983] 2 W.W.R. 752,
143 D.L.R. (3d) 334, 83 CLLC 17,010 (Q.B.) 131, 132
Bell v. The Flaming Steer Steak House Tavern Inc. (Ont. 1980), 1 C.H.R.R.
D/155, 27 L.A.C. (2d) 227 (*sub nom.* Re Bell and Korczak) (Shime)
.... 8, 32, 33, 34, 46, 56, 61, 81, 98, 114, 121, 130, 138, 141, 148, 150, 151, 201
Bell and Korczak, Re. See Bell v. The Flaming Steer Steak House Tavern
Inc.
Bellemare and Treasury Board (C.E.I.C.) (1977), P.S.S.R.B. 166-2-2341
(Descoteaux) 292
Bellieau v. District No. 13 School Bd. (N.B. 1981), 2 C.H.R.R. D/263 (Savioe) 2
Bennet v. Treasury Bd. (1991), P.S.S.R.B. File No. 166-2-21123 (Wexber) 8
Bennett v. Corron & Black Corp., 845 F. 2d 105 (5th Cir. 1988) 31
Bhadauria v. Seneca College of Applied Arts and Technology Bd. of Gov.
(1979), 27 O.R. (2d) 142, 105 D.L.R. (3d) 707, 9 B.L.R. 117, 11 C.C.L.T.
121, 80 CLLC 14,003 (C.A.); revd (Can. 1981), 2 C.H.R.R. D/468,
[1981] 2 S.C.R. 181, 124 D.L.R. (3d) 193, 37 N.R. 455, 14 B.L.R. 157,
17 C.C.L.T. 106, 81 CLLC 14,117, 22 C.P.C. 130 .... 238, 239, 240, 366
Bhinder v. C.N.R. (Can. 1981), 2 C.H.R.R. D/546 (Cumming) 130
Bishop v. Hardy (Ont. 1987), 8 C.H.R.R. D/3868, 86 C.L.L.C. 17,022
(Soberman) 94, 153
Blair v. Progressive Products Ltd. (B.C. 1990), 11 C.H.R.R. D/130 (Barr) .. 164, 165
Bowe v. Colgate-Palmolive, 272 F. Supp. 322, 1 FEP 201 (S.D. Ind. 1967);
revd 416 F. 2d 711, 2 FEP 121 (7th Cir. 1969) 167
Broomfield v. Treasury Bd. (1989), P.S.S.R.B. File No. 166-2-18516 (Young) ... 287
Brown v. City of Guthrie, 30 E.P.D. para. 33,031, 22 FEP 1631 (W.D.
Okla. 1980) 26, 27
Brown v. Fidinam (Canada) Ltd. (1980), 23 A.R. 608 (Q.B.) 228
Bundy v. Jackson, 641 F. 2d 934 (D.C. Cir. 1981) 26, 27, 28, 29, 36, 113, 236
Burridge v. Katsiris (Sask. 1989), 11 C.H.R.R. D/427 (Katzman) 94, 250, 262
Button v. Westsea Construction Co. (B.C. 1991), 13 C.H.R.R. D/1
(Powell) 94, 105, 248

C

Calgary (City) and A.T.U., Loc. 583, Re (1988), 35 L.A.C. (3d) 279
(Jones) 293, 302
Canada Cement Lafarge Ltd. and Energy & Chemical Workers Union,
Loc. 219, Re (1986), 24 L.A.C. (3d) 202 (Emrich) 296
Canada Post Corp. and Canadian Union of Postal Workers (C.U.P.W.),
Re (1983), 11 L.A.C. (3d) 13 (Norman) 82, 205, 288, 299, 300, 315

Table of Cases   xix

Canada Post Corp. and Canadian Union of Postal Workers (Gibson), Re
  (1987), 27 L.A.C. (3d) 27 (Swan) 65, 85, 96, 118, 295, 299, 300, 302
Can. Football League v. Can. Human Rights Commn. (Can. 1980), 1 C.H.R.R.
  D/45 (Fed. Ct.) 263
Can. National Ry. Co. v. Can. Human Rights Commn. (Can. 1988), 8 C.H.R.R.
  D/4210, [1987] 1 S.C.R. 1114, 87 CLLC 17,022, (*sub nom.* Action
  Travail des Femmes v. C.N.R. Co.) 76 N.R. 161 .... 124, 198
Can. National Ry. Co. and Can. Brotherhood of Railway, Transport &
  General Workers (1989), 1 L.A.C. (4th) 183 (Picher) 294, 302
C.P. Express v. Transportation Communications Union (1989), unreported
  (Picher) 294, 302
Can. Safeway Ltd. and Steel et al., Re (Man. 1984), 27 Man. (2d) 79, [1984]
  4 W.W.R. 390, 9 D.L.R. (4th) 330, 84 CLLC 16,157 (Q.B.); affd 29
  Man. R. (2d) 154, [1985] 1 W.W.R. 479, 13 D.L.R. (4th) 314 (C.A.).
  Leave to appeal to S.C.C. dismissed Feb. 11/85 B.S.C. Feb. 15/85 p.
  163 .... 87, 100
Can. Union of Public Employees (C.U.P.E.) and Office and Professional
  Employees' Int'l. Union, Loc. 491, Re (1982), 4 L.A.C. (3d) 385
  (Swinton) 74, 122, 287, 301
Carignan v. Master Craft Publications (B.C. 1984), 5 C.H.R.R. D/2282
  (Rankin) 109, 247, 261, 266
Cashin v. Can. Broadcasting Corp. (Can. 1986), 7 C.H.R.R. D/3203 (Tribunal
  — Ashley) 263, 270
Cassidy v. Sanchez (B.C. 1988), 9 C.H.R.R. D/5278 (Wilson) 8
Chelsea v. Sportman's Motel (B.C. 1981), 2 C.H.R.R. D/424 (Flood) 262
Christie v. Central Alberta Dairy Pool (Alta. 1984), 6 C.H.R.R. D/2488
  (Johanson) 86
Chu v. Persichilli (Ont. 1988), 9 C.H.R.R. D/4617 (Hovius) 67
Chuba v. Can. Employment and Immigration Commn. See Kotyk v. Can.
  Employment Immigration Commn.
Civil Services Assn. of Alta. v. Foothills Provincial General Hospital (Alta.
  Bd. of Inquiry 1977), unreported (Hill) 261
Commodore Business Machines Ltd. v. Ont. Minister of Labour. See Olarte
  et al. v. Commodore Business Machines Ltd.
Consolidated Coal Co., 79 LC 940 (1982) 234
Continental Can Co. v. State of Minnesota, 22 FEP 1809, 23 E.P.D. para.
  30,997, 297 N.W. 2d 241 (Minn. S. Ct. 1980) 32, 218
Corne v. Bausch & Lomb Inc., 390 F. Supp. 161, 10 FEP 345, 9 E.P.D.
  para. 10,093 (D. Ariz. 1975) 18, 20, 209
Coutroubis v. Sklavos Printing (Ont. 1981), 2 C.H.R.R. D/457 (Ratushny),
  82 CLLC 17,001 .... 34, 35, 77, 107, 202, 247, 249, 255, 272
Cox v. Jagbritte Inc. (Ont. 1982), 3 C.H.R.R. D/609 (Cumming) 17, 36, 37, 57,
                                                              108, 114, 130, 202
Cuff v. Gypsy Restaurant (Ont. 1987), 8 C.H.R.R. D/3972 (Bayefsky) 124, 262
Currie v. China Town Restaurant (N.S. 1982), 3 C.H.R.R. D/1085 (Oliver) 131

D

Daigle v. Hunter (N.B. 1989), 10 C.H.R.R. D/5670 (Ruben) 66, 67
Dantu v. North Vancouver District Fire Dept. (B.C. 1986), 8 C.H.R.R.
  D/3649 (Elliot) 250, 251
Dartmouth District School Bd. and Nova Scotia Union of Public Employees,
  Unit No. 2, Re (1983), 12 L.A.C. (3d) 425 (Flemming) 296, 300
Dayton Power Ltd. Co., 80 LA 19 (1982) 233
Decision No. 918 (1988), 9 W.C.A.T.R. 48 .... 276, 277
Decision No. 1018/87 (1989), 10 W.C.A.T.R. 82 277
Decision 145/89 (1990), 14 W.C.A.T.R. 74 277
Decision No. 684/89 (1990), 16 W.C.A.T.R. 132 278
Decision No. 980/89 (1990), 13 W.C.A.T.R. 304 277
Deisting v. Dollar Pizza (1978) Ltd. (Alta. 1982), 3 C.H.R.R. D/898
  (Clarke) 46, 57, 115, 247, 257, 265, 272
Deiwick v. Frid, 11 *The Lawyers Weekly*, No. 28, p. 4 (Nov. 22, 1991) 241
Dennis v. Family and Children's Services of London and Middlesex (Ont.
  1990), 12 C.H.R.R. D/285 (Backhouse) 159, 161, 162, 163, 175
Derken v. Flyer Industries (Man. 1977), unreported (London) 159, 160
Dhillon v. F.W. Woolworth Ltd. (Ont. 1982), 3 C.H.R.R. D/743
  (Cumming) 113, 271
Doherty v. Lodger's Int'l. Ltd. (N.B. 1982), 3 C.H.R.R. D/628, 38 N.B.R.
  (2d) 217, 100 A.P.R. 217, 82 CLLC 17,006 (Goss) 46, 98, 221, 222
Dornhecker v. Malibu Grand Prix Corp., 828 F. 2d 307, 44 E.P.D. para.
  37, 557 (5th Cir. 1987) 110
Douglas v. Saskatchewan (Human Rights Commn.) (Sask. 1990), 11 C.H.R.R.
  D/240, 79 Sask. R. 44, [1990] 1 W.W.R. 455, 90 CLLC 17,002, 28
  C.C.E.L. 207 (Q.B.) 169, 174, 175
Downes v. Federal Aviation Administration 775 F. 2d 288, 38 E.P.D. 35,590
  (D.C. Cir. 1985) 84
Duncan v. Afoakwah (B.C. 1991), 13 C.H.R.R. D/9 (Barr) 105, 248
Durham College of Education v. O.P.S.E.U., Loc. 354 (1987), unreported
  (Samuel) 298
Dyson v. Louie Pasin Plaster & Stucco Ltd. (B.C. 1990), 11 C.H.R.R. D/
  495 (Joe) 67

E

Edmonton (City) and A.T.U., Loc. 569, Re (1985), 23 L.A.C. (3d) 84
  (Thomas) 295, 296
Elmore v. Today's Market Line (1987) Inc. (B.C. 1989), 10 C.H.R.R. D/
  5861 (Hughes) 84, 251
E.E.O.C. v. Hacienda Hotel, 881 F. 2d 1504, 51 E.P.D. 39, 250 (9th Cir.
  1989) 212
E.E.O.C. v. Sage Realty Corp., 507 F. Supp. 599, 25 E.P.D. para. 31,529
  (S.D.N.Y. 1981) 98, 220, 221

Erickson v. Canadian Pacific Express and Transport Ltd. (Can. 1987),
    8 C.H.R.R. D/3942 (Fetterly) 159

F

Famz Foods Ltd. (Swiss Chalet) and Can. Union of Restaurant Employees,
    Loc. 88, Re (1988), 33 L.A.C. (3d) 435 (Roberts) 297, 299, 302
Faryna v. Chorny, 4 W.W.R. (N.S.) 171, [1952] 2 D.L.R. 354 (B.C.C.A.) 144
Fazal v. Chinook Tours (Alta. 1981), 2 C.H.R.R. D/472 (McGowan) 262
Ferguson v. E.I. Dupont de Nemours & Co., 560 F. Supp. 1172, 33 E.P.D.
    para. 34,141 (D. Del. 1983) 66
Fields v. Willie's Rendezvous Inc. (B.C. 1985), 6 C.H.R.R. D/3074 (Powell);
    new hearing (B.C. 1985), 6 C.H.R.R. D/2711 (B.C.S.C.) 70, 71, 145, 257
Fisher v. Flynn, 598 F. 2d 663, 19 E.P.D. para. 9204 (1st Cir. 1979) 216
Foisy v. Bell Canada (Que. 1985), 6 C.H.R.R. D/2817, 18 D.L.R. (4th)
    222, 85 CLLC 17,008 (S.C.) 46, 92, 104, 207, 208, 240, 355
Foreman et al. v. Via Rail Canada, Inc. (Can. 1980), 1 C.H.R.R. D/233
    (Review Tribunal — Gibson) 245, 246
Frame v. Smith, [1987] 2 S.C.R. 99, 23 O.A.C. 84, 42 D.L.R. (4th) 81,
    78 N.R. 40, 42 C.C.L.T. 1, 9 R.F.L. (3d) 225 240
Friesen v. Regina (City) Commrs. of Police (Sask. 1991), 13 C.H.R.R.
    D/11 (Sproule) 251
Fuller v. Candur Plastics Ltd. (Ont. 1981), 2 C.H.R.R. D/419 (Kerr) 148

G

Gabbidon v. S. Golas (Ont. Bd. of Inquiry 1973), unreported (Lederman) 259
Gadowsky, Re. See Gadowsky v. Two Hills, No. 21 School Committee.
Gadowsky v. Two Hills, No. 21 School Committee (Alta. Bd. of Inquiry,
    1979), unreported (McLaren); affd 1 C.H.R.R. D/184, [1981] 1 W.W.R.
    647 (*sub nom.* Re Gadowsky), 120 D.L.R. (3d) 516, 81 CLLC 14,092
    (Alta. Q.B.) 249
Garber v. Saxon Business Products, 552 F. 2d 1032 (4th Cir. 1977) 21
Gervais v. Agriculture Canada (Can. 1988), 9 C.H.R.R. D/5002, 88 CLLC
    71,014 (Review Tribunal — Fleck) 84, 201, 250
Gibson v. Longshoremen, Loc. 40, 543 F. 2d 1259, 13 FEP 997 (9th Cir.
    1976) 167
Gilardi v. Schroeder, 672 F. Supp. 1043, 45 FEP 283 (N.D. Ill. 1986) 84
Giouvanoudis v. Golden Fleece Restaurant & Tavern Ltd. (Ont. 1983),
    5 C.H.R.R. D/1967 (Cumming) 17, 57, 58, 77, 98, 106
Gohm v. Domtar Inc. (No. 4) (Ont. 1990), 12 C.H.R.R. D/161
    (Pentney) 262, 362, 363, 364, 365
Governors (The) of Acadia University v. The Acadia University Faculty
    Assn. (1981), unreported (Kimball) 1
Graesser v. Porto (Ont. 1983), 4 C.H.R.R. D/1569 (Zemans) 108, 246, 258, 273

Graham v. Sunrise Poultry Processors Ltd. (B.C. 1988), 9 C.H.R.R. D/4771 (Barr) 94, 97
Green v. 709637 Ontario Inc. (Ont. 1988), 9 C.H.R.R. D/4749 (Plaut) 93, 262
Guyette v. Stauffer Chemical Co., 518 F. Supp. 521, 27 E.P.D. para. 32,139 (1981) 216

H

Hadley v. City of Mississauga (Ont. Bd. of Inquiry 1976), unreported (Lederman) 263
Haight v. Tantrum (B.C. 1990), 12 C.H.R.R. D/250 (Wilson) 318
Haight v. W.W.G. Management Inc. (B.C. 1990), 11 C.H.R.R. D/124 (Hughes) 93, 94, 95
Hall v. Int'l. Firefighters' Assn., Loc. 1137 (Ont. 1977), unreported (Dunlop) 161, 359
Hall v. Sonap Canada (Ont. 1989), 10 C.H.R.R. D/6126 (Plaut) 153, 262
Hamilton v. Appleton Electric Co., E.R.D. Case 7301025 (S. Wisc. 1976) 32
Hartling v. City of Timmins Bd. of Police Commrs. (Ont. 1981), 2 C.H.R.R. D/487 (Cumming) 185, 186, 271
Heelan v. Johns-Manville Corp., 451 F. Supp. 1382, 20 FEP 251 (D.C. 1978) 22
Hendry v. Liquor Control Bd. of Ont. (Ont. 1980), 1 C.H.R.R. D/160 (Soberman) 245
Henson v. City of Dundee, 682 F. 2d 897, 29 E.P.D. para. 32,993 (11th Cir. 1982) 26, 29, 63, 134, 139
Herman v. Rodin (Sask. 1989), 10 C.H.R.R. D/5798, 73 Sask. R. 169 (*sub nom.* Rodin v. Herman), [1989] 2 W.W.R. 709, 56 D.L.R. (4th) 180, 89 CLLC 17,007; affg 9 C.H.R.R. D/5375 (Wiebe) 93, 138
Hewes v. City of Etobicoke, *The Globe and Mail*, October 4, 1991, p. 9A (Ont. Gen. Div.) 230
Highlander v. K.F.C. National Management Co., 805 F. 2d 644, 41 E.P.D. para. 36,675 73
Hotel, Restaurant and Cafeteria Employees Union, Loc. 75 v. Constellation Hotel Corp. Ltd. (1981), 82 CLLC 16,150 (O.L.R.B.) 233, 292
Howard v. Lemoignan (Alta. 1982), 3 C.H.R.R. D/1150 (Welsh) 57, 90
Huebschen v. Department of Health & Social Services, 30 E.P.D. para. 33,124 (W.D. Wisc. 1982) 1
Hufnagel v. Osama Enterprises Ltd. (Man. 1982), 3 C.H.R.R. D/922 (Teskey) 46, 57, 61, 73, 270
Hughes v. Dollar Snack Bar (Ont. 1982), 3 C.H.R.R. D/1014 (Kerr) 35, 103, 202, 255
Huhn v. Hunter's Haus of Burgers (B.C. 1987), 8 C.H.R.R. D/4157 (Wilson) 93
Humble v. K. Parsad & Co. (B.C. 1988), 9 C.H.R.R. D/5057 (Hughes) 93
Hyman v. Southam Murray Printing and Int'l Brotherhood of Teamsters, Loc. 419 (Ont. 1982), 3 C.H.R.R. D/617 (McCamus) 159

Table of Cases xxiii

I

Imberto v. Coiffure (Ont. 1981), 2 C.H.R.R. D/392 (McCamus) 245
Insce. Corp. of B.C. v. Heerspink (Can. 1982), 3 C.H.R.R. D/1163, [1982]
2 S.C.R. 145, 39 B.C.L.R. 145, [1983] 1 W.W.R. 137, 137 D.L.R. (3d)
219, 43 N.R. 168 166
Int'l. Assn. of Machinists and Aerospace Workers, Loc. 2413 v. Wardair
Canada (1975) Ltd. (1980), unreported (O'Shea) 272
Irving v. Medland (Man. 1985), 6 C.H.R.R. D/2842 (Leland Berg) 58, 97,
248, 257, 258
Ives v. Palfy (B.C. 1990), 12 C.H.R.R. D/483 (Joe) 143, 248

J

Jain v. Acadia University (N.S. 1984), 5 C.H.R.R. D/2123 (Atton) 94
Janzen v. Platy Enterprises (Man. 1985), 6 C.H.R.R. D/2735 (Henteleff);
revd in part (Man. 1986), 7 C.H.R.R. D/3309, 38 Man. R. (2d) 20,
[1986] 2 W.W.R. 273, 24 D.L.R. (4th) 31, 86 CLLC 17,008 (Q.B.);
revd (Man. 1986), 8 C.H.R.R. D/3831, 43 Man. R. (2d) 293, [1987]
1 W.W.R. 385, 33 D.L.R. (4th) 32, 87 CLLC 17,014 (C.A.); revd (Man.
1989), 10 C.H.R.R. D/6205, [1989] 1 S.C.R. 1252, 58 Man. R. (2d)
1, [1989] 4 W.W.R. 39, 59 D.L.R. (4th) 352, 89 CLLC 17,011, 25
C.C.E.L. 1 .... 58, 59, 60, 63, 83, 108, 118, 120, 123, 124, 136, 143, 166,
206, 207, 208, 216, 236, 248, 256, 258, 288, 317
John v. Goodyear Tire and Rubber Co., 491 F. 2d (5th Cir. 1974) 359
Johnstone c.o.b. as Wessex Inn v. Zarankin. See Zarankin v. Johnstone
c.o.b. as Wessex Inn

K

Kahlon v. Treasury Bd. (Solicitor General) (1991), P.S.S.R.B. File No. 166-
2-20871 (Kwavnick) 93, 94, 226, 227
Karlenzig v. Chris' Holdings Ltd. (Sask. 1991), 91 CLLC 17,015 318
Katz v. Dole, 709 F. 2d 251, 32 E.P.D. para. 33,639 (4th Cir. 1983) 65
Kennedy v. Mohawk College Board of Governors (Ont. 1973), unreported
(Borins) 137
Kodellas v. Sask. Human Rights Commn. (Sask. 1989), 10 C.H.R.R. D/
6305, 77 Sask. R. 94, [1989] 5 W.W.R. 1 (*sub nom.* Sask. Human Rights
Commn. v. Kodellas), 60 D.L.R. (4th) 143 (C.A.); revg in part (Sask.
1987) 8 C.H.R.R. D/3712, 52 Sask. R. 139, [1987] 2 W.W.R. 195, 34
D.L.R. (4th) 30, 87 CLLC 17,006 (Q.B.) 139, 166, 169-179
Korda v. PK and JP Enterprises Ltd. (B.C. 1990), 12 C.H.R.R. D/201 (Barr) 94
Kotyk v. Can. Employment Immigration Commn. (Can. 1983), 4 C.H.R.R.
D/1416, 83 CLLC 17,012 (Ashley); affd (*sub nom.* Chuba v. Can. Employment
and Immigration Commn.) (Can. 1983), 5 C.H.R.R. D/1895, (*sub nom.*

Chuba v. Kotyk) 84 CLLC 17,005 (Review Tribunal — Lederman) .. 43, 44, 45, 58, 68, 69, 75, 79, 81, 114, 142, 193, 203, 225, 256, 273, 308, 315

L

Lamers v. Pacific Building Maintenance Ltd. (Sask. 1991), 13 C.H.R.R. D/235, 91 CLLC 17,014 (Boryski) 266, 267
Landry v. Richmond Fisheries Ltd. (N.S. 1991), 13 C.H.R.R. D/4 (N.S. Bd. of Inquiry) 365
Langevin v. Engineered Air Division of Air Tex Industry Ltd. (B.C. 1985), 6 C.H.R.R. D/2552 (Powell) 105, 144, 248, 256
Larouche v. Emergency Car Rental (Que. 1980), 1 C.H.R.R. D/119 (Que. Prov. Ct.) 261
Lavoie v. Treasury Bd. (Solicitor General) (1989), P.S.S.R.B. File No. 166-2-18953 (Galibeault) 97
Leclair v. Paquet (Que. 1981), 2 C.H.R.R. D/444 (Que. Prov. Ct.) 263
Leith v. Community Bingo (Wetaskiwin) Ltd. (Alta. 1988), 9 C.H.R.R. D/5165 (Manning) 93
Lennard's Carrying Co. Ltd. v. Asiatic Petroleum Co. Ltd., [1915] A.C. 705, [1914-15] All E.R. Rep. 280 (H.L.) 187
Libitka v. Treasury Bd. (1980), P.S.S.R.B. File No. 166-2-8128 (Ramsay) .. 272, 291
Lipsett v. University of Puerto Rico, 864 F. 2d 881, 48 E.P.D. para. 38,393 (1st Cir. 1988) 70

M

McCaskill v. Treasury Bd. (Indian and Northern Affairs) (1990), P.S.S.R.B. File No. 166-2-19524 (Chodos) 93
MacDonald v. 283076 Ont. Inc. (1979), 23 O.R. (2d) 185, 95 D.L.R. (3d) 723, 10 C.P.C. 242 (H.C.); revd 26 O.R. (2d) 1, 102 D.L.R. (3d) 383, 8 B.L.R. 193 (C.A.) 237, 238
Mackie v. Genesio Canada Ltd., 11 *The Lawyers Weekly*, No. 21, p. 16 (October 4, 1991) 231, 232
McPherson v. "Mary's Donuts" (Ont. 1982), 3 C.H.R.R. D/961 (Cumming) 108, 123, 202, 256, 272
Macklin v. Spector Freight Systems Inc., 478 F. 2d 979 (D.C. Cir. 1973) 359
Makara v. Osama Enterprises Ltd. (Man. 1985), 6 C.H.R.R. D/2935 (Henteleff) 58, 61, 75, 76, 132, 133
Makin v. A.-G. for New South Wales, [1894] A.C. 57, [1891-94] All E.R. Rep. 24 (P.C.) 148
Man. Food and Commercial Workers Union v. Can. Safeway Ltd. (Man. 1983), 4 C.H.R.R. D/1495 (Steel) 99, 166
Marcotte v. Rio Algom Ltd. (Can. 1983), 5 C.H.R.R. D/2010 (Review Tribunal — Hesler) 86
Mears v. Ont. Hydro (Ont. 1984), 5 C.H.R.R. D/1927 (Zemans) 261, 262

Mehta v. MacKay (1991), 100 N.S.R. (2d) 319, 272 A.P.R. 319, 91 CLLC
  17,013 (C.A.) 147, 153
Mehta v. Mackinnon et al. (N.S. 1985), 6 C.H.R.R. D/2861, 67 N.S.R.
  (2d) 112, 155 A.P.R. 112, 85 CLLC 17,015 (S.C.), affd 67 N.S.R. (2d)
  429, 155 A.P.R. 429, 19 D.L.R. (4th) 148 (C.A.). Leave to appeal to
  S.C.C. dismissed Nov. 21/85, 69 N.S.R. (2d) 450*n*, 163 A.P.R. 450*n*,
  64 N.R. 240*n* 46, 47
Mengel Co. and the Employees Union of Mengel Co., 61-2 ARB #8352 233
Meritor Savings Bank v. Vinson, 106 S. Ct. 2399, 40 E.P.D. para. 36,159
  (1986), 89 L. Ed. (2d) 567; (*sub nom.* Vinson v. Taylor) 753 F. 2d 141,
  36 E.P.D. para. 34,946, denied a hearing 760 F. 2d 1330, 37 E.P.D.
  35, 232 (D.C. Cir. 1985); revg 22 E.P.D. para. 30,708 (D.D.C. 1980) ... 23, 24,
               25, 26, 30, 63, 64, 124, 125, 199, 210, 211, 317, 327
Miller v. Bank of America, 418 F.Supp. 233 (N.D. Cal. 1976) 18, 19
Mitchell v. Nobilium Products (Ont. 1981), 3 C.H.R.R. D/641 (Kerr) 148
Mitchell v. Traveller Inn (Sudbury) Ltd. (Ont. 1981), 2 C.H.R.R. D/590
  (Kerr) 37, 84, 140, 151, 202, 251, 257, 270, 273
Mohammad v. Mariposa Stores Ltd. (B.C. 1990), 14 C.H.R.R. D/215
  (Barr) 222, 223, 224
Morgan v. Hertz Corp., 27 FEP 990 (W.D. Tenn. 1981) 26
Morrison v. Phung (B.C. 1988), 9 C.H.R.R. D/5282 (Hughes) 93
Moylan v. Maires County, 792 F. 2d 746, 40 E.P.D. para. 36,228 (8th
  Cir. 1986) 84
Munford v. James T. Barnes & Co., 441 F. Supp. 459 (E.C. Mich. 1977) 209
Myers v. Gilman Paper Co., 544 F. 2d 837 (5th Cir. 1977); modified on
  rehearing 556 F. 2d 758 (5th Cir. 1977), cert. denied, 434 U.S. 801
  (1977) 359

N

Nanticoke (City of) and C.U.P.E., Loc. 246, Re (1980), 29 L.A.C. (2d)
  64 (Barton) 272, 295, 302
Neigum v. Wilkie Co-operative Assn. Ltd. (1987), 55 Sask. R. 210 (Q.B.) 231
Neilson (William) Ltd. v. U.F.C.W. (1987), unreported (Deom) 297, 301
Nelson v. Byron Price & Associates. See Nelson v. Gubbins.
Nelson v. Gubbins (1979), 17 B.C.L.R. 259, 106 D.L.R. (3d) 486 (S.C.);
  affd (*sub nom.* Nelson v. Byron Price & Associates Ltd.) (1981), 2 C.H.R.R.
  D/385, 27 B.C.L.R. 284, 122 D.L.R. (3d) 340, 81 CLLC 14,107
  (C.A.) 184, 185, 193
Nelson v. Reisher (4th Cir. 1989), 88-1133 32
Nesvog v. Rutschmann (B.C. 1988), 9 C.H.R.R. D/5293 (Powell)) 93, 97
Newfoundland Assn. of Public Employees v. Treasury Bd. (1986), unreported
  (Fagon) 287
Newfoundland (Newfoundland Farm Products Corp.) and Newfoundland
  Assn. of Public Employees, Re (1988), 35 L.A.C. (3d) 165 (Dicks) 288, 289

Noffke v. McClaskin Hot House (Ont. 1990), 11 C.H.R.R. D/407 (Zemans) 94, 124

O

Olarte et al. v. Commodore Business Machines Ltd. (Ont. 1983), 4 C.H.R.R. D/1705, 83 CLLC 17,028 (Cumming); affd (*sub nom.* Commodore Business Machines Ltd. v. Ont. Minister of Labour) (Ont. 1985), 6 C.H.R.R. D/2833, 49 O.R. (2d) 17, 6 O.A.C. 176, 14 D.L.R. (4th) 118, 84 CLLC 17,028, 13 C.R.R. 338 (Div. Ct.) 38, 39, 40, 47, 58, 74, 75, 79, 80, 106, 112, 116, 140, 142, 146, 147, 152, 153, 154, 188, 189, 204, 205, 241, 259, 260, 261, 262, 269, 272

Ont. Human Rights Commn. et al. v. Borough of Etobicoke (Ont. 1982), 3 C.H.R.R. D/781, [1982] 1 S.C.R. 202, 40 N.R. 159, 132 D.L.R. (3d) 14 .... 87, 133, 263, 354, 360

Ont. Human Rights Commn. v. Simpsons-Sears Ltd. (Ont. 1985), 7 C.H.R.R. D/3102, [1985] 2 S.C.R. 536, 52 O.R. (2d) 799, 12 O.A.C. 241, 23 D.L.R. (4th) 321, 64 N.R. 161, 86 CLLC 17,002 .... 87, 88, 124, 166, 198, 301

Oram v. Pho (B.C. 1975), unreported (Wood) 184

Osborne v. Inco Ltd. (Man. 1984), 5 C.H.R.R. D/2219, 28 Man. R. (2d) 199, [1984] 5 W.W.R. 228, 10 D.L.R. (4th) 239 (Q.B.); revd 31 Man. R. (2d) 17, [1985] 2 W.W.R. 577, 15 D.L.R. (4th) 723, 85 CLLC 17,005 (C.A.) 87

Ostifichuk and Corrington v. C.A.M. Janitorial Ltd. (Man. 1986), 7 C.H.R.R. D/3331 (Steel) 93, 94

Ottawa Board of Education and Ottawa Board of Education Employees' Union, Re (1989), 5 L.A.C. (4th) 171 (Bendel) 72, 298, 300

Ouimette v. Lily Cups Ltd. (Ont. 1990), 12 C.H.R.R. D/19 (Baum) 265

P

Pachouris v. St. Vito Italian Food (Ont. 1984), 5 C.H.R.R. D/1944 (Dunlop) ... 142

Peck v. Blank and Bunster (1981), *Ms. Magazine*, p. 68 .... 129, 229

Pham v. Beach Industries Ltd. (Ont. 1987), 8 C.H.R.R. D/4008 (Hubbard) 264

Phillips v. Hermiz (Sask. 1985), 5 C.H.R.R. D/2450 (Katzman) ... 46, 78, 111, 140, 257, 258

Piazza v. Airport Taxi Cab (Malton) Assn. (Ont. 1986), 7 C.H.R.R. D/3196 (Zemans) 257, 258

Pilon v. Peugeot Canada Ltd. (1980), 29 O.R. (2d) 711, 114 D.L.R. (3d) 378, 12 B.L.R. 227 (S.C.) 228

Porcelli v. Strathclyde Regional Council (1985), 1 C.R. 177 (EAT-Scot.); affd (1986), 1 C.R. 564 (Ct. of Sess.) 56

Potapczyk v. MacBain (Can. 1984), 5 C.H.R.R. D/2285 (Lederman) 1, 45, 70, 71, 79, 83, 88, 116, 129, 263

Potvin v. Treasury Bd. (1985), P.S.S.R.B. File No. 166-2-14871 (Galipeault) 301

Purdy v. Marwick Manufacturing Co. (Ont. 1987), 9 C.H.R.R. D/4840
(Simmons) 84, 97

R

Rabidue v. Osceola Refining Co., 805 F. 2d 611, 41 E.P.D. para. 36,643
(6th Cir. 1986) 30, 73, 95
Rack v. The Playgirl Cabaret (B.C. 1985), 6 C.H.R.R. D/2857
(Verbrugge) 91, 92, 105
Rajput v. Algoma University College (Ont. Bd. of Inquiry — 1976), unreported
(Tarnopolsky) 249
Rand v. Sealy Eastern Ltd. (Ont. 1981), 3 C.H.R.R. D/938 (Cumming) 86
Renaud v. School District No. 23 (Central Okanagan) (B.C. 1987), 8 C.H.R.R.
D/4255 (Verbrugge) 270, 361, 362
Richelieu Inn Hotel, Restaurant and Cafeteria Employees Union, Loc.
75 (1983), unreported (Barton) 287
Richman v. Bureau of Affirmative Action, 536 F. Supp. 1149, 30 FEP
1644 (M.D. Pa. 1982) 66
Robichaud v. Brennan (Can. 1982), 3 C.H.R.R. D/977, 82 CLLC 17,012
(Abbott); revd (Can. 1983), 4 C.H.R.R. D/1272, 83 CLLC 17,008 (Review
Tribunal — Dyer); affd in part (*sub nom.* Treasury Board v. Robichaud)
(Can. 1985), 6 C.H.R.R. D/2695, [1984] 2 F.C. 799, 57 N.R. 116; revd
(*sub nom.* Robichaud v. Treasury Bd.) (Can. 1987), 8 C.H.R.R. D/4326,
[1987] 2 S.C.R. 84, 40 D.L.R. (4th) 577 (*sub nom.* Robichaud v. R.)
87 CLLC 17,025, 75 N.R. 303 .... 40, 41, 42, 47, 57, 62, 81, 111, 113,
114, 116, 124, 165, 189-201, 203, 208, 215, 225, 279, 317
Robinson v. Company (The) Farm Ltd. (Ont. 1984), 5 C.H.R.R. D/2243
(Cumming) 84, 105, 106, 139
Robinson v. Lorillard Corp., 444 F. 2d 791 (4th Cir. 1971) 359
Rodin v. Herman. See Herman v. Rodin
Rocca Group Ltd. and Muise, Re (1979), 22 Nfld. & P.E.I.R. 1, 58 A.P.R.
1, 102 D.L.R. (3d) 529 (S.C.). Leave to appeal to S.C.C. denied 24
Nfld. & P.E.I.R. 90, 65 A.P.R. 90, 30 N.R. 613n, 102 D.L.R. (3d) 529n
(S.C.C.) 86
Rochester Telephone Corp. v. Communication Workers of America, 65-
2 ARB #8701 234
Romman v. Sea-West Holdings Ltd. (Can. 1984), 5 C.H.R.R. D/2312
(Jones) 1, 8, 107
Roosma v. Ford Motor Co. (Ont. 1988), 9 C.H.R.R. D/4743 (Mercer);
affd (Ont. 1989), 10 C.H.R.R. D/5761, 66 O.R. (2d) 18, 29 O.A.C.
84, 53 D.L.R. (4th) 90, 89 CLLC 17,013 (Div. Ct.) 360, 361
Ross v. Gendall (Sask. 1989), 10 C.H.R.R. D/5836 (Piche) 38, 84, 251

S

St. Joseph's Health Centre v. C.U.P.E. Loc. 1144 (1983), unreported (Roberts) 233, 272, 293
Sardigal v. St. Louis National Stockyard Co., 41 E.P.D. para. 36, 613 (S.D. Ill. 1986) 66
Sask. Human Rights Commn. v. The Engineering Students' Soc. (Sask. 1984), 5 C.H.R.R. D/2074 (Havemann) 97
Sask. Human Rights Commn. v. Kodellas. See Kodellas v. Sask. Human Rights Commn.
Sask. Human Rights Commn. v. Sask. Dept. of Social Services (Sask. 1989), 10 C.H.R.R. D/6434 (Q.B.) 262
Schechter Poultry Corp. v. United States, 295 U.S. 495, 79 L. Ed. 1570 (1935) 198
Scott v. Sears Roebuck Co., 798 F. 2d 210, 41 E.P.D. para. 36, 439 (7th Cir. 1986) 84
Seneca College of Applied Arts and Technology Bd. of Gov. v. Bhadauria. See Bhadauria v. Seneca College of Applied Arts and Technology Bd. of Gov.
Seneca College of Applied Arts and Technology and Ont. Public Service Employees Union, Re (1983), 10 L.A.C. (3d) 315 (Brown) 158, 286
Seritis v. Lane, 22 E.P.D. para. 30,747 (Cal. Sup. Ct. 1980) 32
Shack v. London Drive-Ur-Self (Ont. Bd. of Inquiry — 1974), unreported (Lederman) 244
Shaffer v. Treasury Board (Can. 1984), 5 C.H.R.R. D/2315 (Review Tribunal — Mullins) 214
Sharp v. Seasons Restaurant (Ont. 1987), 8 C.H.R.R. D/4133 (Springate) 93
Shaw v. Levac Supply Ltd. (Ont. 1991), 14 C.H.R.R. D/36, 91 CLLC 17,007 (Hubbard) 117, 118, 200, 318
Shiels v. Sask. Govt. Insce. (1988), 67 Sask. R. 220, 51 D.L.R. (4th) 28, 20 C.C.E.L. 55 (Q.B.) 227, 229, 230, 285
Simms v. Ford Motor Co. of Canada (Ont. 1979), unreported (Krever) 186, 213
Sing v. Security and Investigation Services Ltd. (Ont. 1977), unreported (Cumming) 86
Singh v. Domglas (Ont. 1980), unreported (Kerr) 36
Skelly v. Assist Realty Ltd., 11 *The Lawyers Weekly*, No. 30, p. 20 (December 6, 1991) 224
Smith v. Rust Engineering Co., 18 E.P.D. para. 8698 (N.D. Ala. 1978) 216
Spears v. Antoniadis (Que. 1980), 1 C.H.R.R. D/188 (Que. Prov. Ct.) 263
Splett v. Sum's Family Holdings Ltd. (Alta. 1991), 13 C.H.R.R. D/119 (McManus) 109, 116, 266
Steele v. Offshore Shipbuilding Inc., 867 F. 2d 1311, 49 E.P.D. para. 38,839 (11th Cir. 1989) 31
Swentek v. U.S. Air Line Inc., 830 F. 2d 552, 44 E.P.D. para. 37,457 (4th Cir. 1987) 65

Table of Cases

T

Tellier v. Bank of Montreal (1987), 17 C.C.E.L. 1 (Ont. Dist. Ct.) 231, 285
Texas Department of Community Affairs v. Burdine, 450 U.S. 248 (1981) 131
Thessaloniki Holdings Ltd. v. Saskatchewan Human Rights Commn. (Sask. 1991), 91 CLLC para. 71,029 (Q.B.) 216
Tomkins v. Public Service Electric and Gas Co., 422 F. Supp. 533 (D.N.J. 1977); revd (*sub nom.* Tomkins II), 568 F. 2d 1044, 16 FEP (3rd Cir. 1977) 18, 19, 20, 21, 22, 209
Toronto Hydro Electric System and C.U.P.E., Loc. 1, Re (1989), 2 L.A.C. (4th) 169 (Davis) 294, 301, 302
Torres v. Royalty Kitchenware Ltd. (Ont. 1982), 3 C.H.R.R. D/858 (Cumming) 89, 103, 104, 202, 246, 249, 255, 257, 259, 269, 272, 273
Treasury Board v. Robichaud. See Robichaud v. Brennan.
Treasury Bd. (Employment and Immigration) and Gaudreau, Re (1988), 34 L.A.C. (3d) 419 (Wexler) 291

U

United States v. City of Buffalo, 457 F. Supp. 612, 19 FEP 776 (W.D.N.Y. 1978) 317
University of Manitoba and Canadian Assoc. of Industrial, Mechanical & Allied Workers, Loc. 9, Re (1989), 6 L.A.C. (4th) 182 (Chapman); revd by Man. Q.B., unreported (1989); affd (1990), 63 Man. R. (2d) 56, 68 D.L.R. (4th) 412 (C.A.) 119, 120
University of Ottawa (1979), unreported (O'Shea) 292, 302

V

Vinson v. Taylor. See Meritor Savings Bank v. Vinson
Voeller v. Kingfisher Sales Inc. (B.C. 1990), 11 C.H.R.R. D/433 (Powell) 93, 94

W

Walter v. KFGO Radio, 518 F. Supp. 1309, 28 E.P.D. para. 32,497 (D.N.D. 1981) 26, 30
Waltman v. International Paper Co., 875 F. 2d 468, 50 E.P.D. para. 106 (5th Cir. 1989) 31
Wan et al. v. Greygo Gardens (Ont. 1982), 3 C.H.R.R. D/812 (Kerr) 149, 264
Ward Air (1980), unreported (O'Shea) 291
Watt v. Regional Municipality of Niagara (Ont. 1984), 5 C.H.R.R. D/2453 (McCamus) 16, 83, 84, 91, 115, 143
Webb v. Cyprus Pizza (B.C. 1985), 6 C.H.R.R. D/2794 (Wilson) 78, 134, 257
Wilgan v. Wendy's Restaurants of Canada Inc. (B.C. 1990), 11 C.H.R.R. D/119 (Barr) 124, 214, 215
Williams v. Civiletti, 23 E.P.D. para. 30,916 (D.D.C. 1980) 313

Williams v. Saxbe, 413 F. Supp. 654, 12 FEP. 345, 11 E.P.D. para. 10,840
(D.D.C. 1976) 20, 209
Winnipeg School Division No. 1 v. Craton (Man. 1985), 6 C.H.R.R. D/
3014 (S.C.C.) 166

Y

Yargeau v. Treasury Board (1981), P.S.S.R.B. File No. 166-2-8614 (Galipeault)
.... 291
Yates v. Avco Corp., 819 F. 2d 630, 43 E.P.D. para. 37,086 (6th Cir. 1987)
.... 31, 212

Z

Zarankin v. Johnstone c.o.b. as Wessex Inn (B.C. 1984), 5 C.H.R.R.
D/2274 (Smith); affd (B.C. 1985), 6 C.H.R.R. D/2651, 85 CLLC 17,022
(B.C.S.C.) 17, 46, 47, 57, 58, 69, 82, 116, 134, 146, 153, 256, 266

INTRODUCTION

Sexual Harassment: An Issue for the 1990s

Sexual harassment is a complex issue involving men and women, their perceptions and behaviour, and the social norms of the society. Sexual harassment is not confined to any one level, class, or profession. It can happen to executives as well as factory workers. It occurs not only in the workplace and in the classroom,[1] but even in parliamentary chambers[2] and churches.[3] Sexual harassment may be an expression of power or desire or both. Whether it is from supervisors, co-workers, or customers, sexual harassment is an attempt to assert power over another person.

Sexual harassment is any sexually oriented practice that endangers an individual's continued employment, negatively affects his/her work performance, or undermines his/her sense of personal dignity. Harassment behaviour may manifest itself blatantly in forms such as leering, grabbing, and even sexual assault. More subtle forms of sexual harassment may include sexual innuendos, and propositions for dates or sexual favours.

Although there are cases where men have been sexually harassed,[4] the majority of victims are women. Women are especially vulnerable to sexual harassment because, for the most part, they are employed in low-status, low-paying jobs. Most work in the clerical and service

---

[1] See L. Middleton, "Sexual Harassment by Professors: An Increasingly Visible Problem", *The Chronicle of Higher Education* (September 15, 1980), pp. 3-5; and arbitration cases: *The Assn. of Professors of The University of Ottawa v. The University of Ottawa* (1979), unreported (O'Shea); *The Governors of Acadia University v. The Acadia University Faculty Association* (1981), unreported (Kimball). See also K. Wilson and L. Kraus, "Sexual Harassment in the University" (1983), 24 *Journal of College Students Personnel*, No. 3.

[2] See *Potapczyk v. MacBain* (Can. 1984), 5 C.H.R.R. D/2285 (Lederman).

[3] *The United Church Observer* (May 1984), pp. 35-36.

[4] See *Huebschen v. Department of Health & Social Services*, 30 E.P.D. para. 33,124 (W.D. Wisc. 1982), where a female supervisor was found liable for the harassment of a male state employee whom she demoted after he ended a sexual relationship with her. In *Romman v. Sea-West Holdings Ltd.* (Can. 1984), 5 C.H.R.R. D/2312 (Jones), the Canadian Human Rights Tribunal for the first time found a male supervisor guilty of sexually harassing a male employee.

areas of the employment sector, and are usually supervised by male bosses. Because of the fear of losing their jobs, many women have silently endured sexual harassment in the workplace, considering it to be a "normal" occupational hazard. Until recent years, the practice of sexual harassment was virtually unchallenged.

However, the social and political climate on women's issues has begun to change. This social change has encouraged women's groups and organizations to discuss women's issues openly and demand equity, fairness, and justice in the workplace and in their social life. The Universal Declaration of Human Rights proclaimed by the United Nations in 1948, and the subsequent enactment of human rights laws have affirmed the equality of women before the law. This has given them the impetus to carry on their struggle for equality and dignity in day-to-day life. Moreover, the statutory protection[5] to the complainants of discrimination and sexual harassment from discharge or disciplinary action by their employers has enabled women to fight for their self-respect and dignity.

The issue of sexual harassment, once a hidden and ignored problem, has in recent years prompted much concern and study. Prior to 1976, few reliable statistics on the incidence of sexual harassment were available. However, recent studies confirm that sexual harassment is one of the most serious and widespread problems facing women in employment today. One of the earliest North American studies on

---

[5] See for example s. 8 of the Ontario *Human Rights Code*, R.S.O. 1990, c. H.19. It provides: "Every person has a right to claim and enforce his or her rights under this Act, to institute and participate in proceedings under this Act and to refuse to infringe a right of another person under this Act, without reprisal or threat of reprisal for so doing." See also s. 8 of the New Brunswick *Human Rights Act*, R.S.N.B. 1973, c. H-11, which provides:

> No person shall discharge, refuse to employ, exclude, expel, suspend, deny, evict, or otherwise discriminate against any person because he has made a complaint or given evidence or assisted in any way in respect of the initiation, inquiry or prosecution of a complaint or other proceeding under this Act.

In the case of *Bellieau v. District No. 13 School Board* (N.B. 1981), 2 C.H.R.R. D/263 (Savioe), the New Brunswick Board of Inquiry concluded that the school board refused to employ the complainant as a supply bus driver after November 1978, because she had earlier made a complaint to the Human Rights Commission against the respondent school board. The Board awarded her $5,000 as compensation for financial losses and damages and ordered that she be reinstated without loss of seniority.

In the United States, section 704 of Title VII of the *Civil Rights Act*, 1964, prohibits employers from retaliating against employees who initiate complaints under Title VII.

sexual harassment was conducted among U.N. employees by the Ad Hoc Group on Equal Rights for Women, in 1975.[6] The study was based on a questionnaire distributed to 875 women and men in both professional and general service (clerical) occupations. Half of the women and 31 per cent of the men respondents reported that they either had at some time personally experienced sexual harassment or were aware of such actions occurring within the organization.

In 1980, a landmark survey of sexual harassment was conducted by the U.S. Merit Systems Protection Board among U.S. federal government employees.[7] After studying a sample group of 23,000 male and female employees, the Board found that 42 per cent of women and 15 per cent of men were victims of incidents of overt sexual harassment over a two-year period. Such incidents ranged from sexual teasing, jokes, remarks and questions to actual or attempted rape or sexual assault.

In 1988, an update survey by the U.S. Merit Systems Protection Board concluded that some 36,000 employees in the U.S. Federal Government quit their job because of sexual harassment during a two-year period between 1985 and 1987. The Board estimated that it cost the U.S. Federal Government $267 million in paying sick leave to employees who missed work because of harassment, in replacing employees who left their job and in reduced productivity.

Further, a 1988 survey by *Working Woman* magazine of Fortune 500 manufacturing and service companies in the United States revealed that about 24 per cent of harassed women use leave time in order to avoid the situation. About 5 per cent of women who experience sexual harassment quit, 10 per cent resign giving sexual harassment as one reason for their departure, and 50 per cent try to ignore it. Among this 50 per cent, there is a 10 per cent productivity drop in the work of the victim.[8] Analysis of the survey shows that at least 15 per cent of female employees have been sexually harassed in the last 12-month period of their employment with the employer surveyed.

---

[6] M. Kelber: "Sexual Harassment: The U.N.'s Dirty Little Secret", *Ms Magazine*, (November 1977), p. 51. See also C. Safran, "What Men Do to Women on the Job", *Redbook Magazine* (November 1976), pp. 149, 217-221.

[7] *Sexual Harassment in the Federal Workplace, Is it a Problem?*, A report of the U.S. Merit Systems Protection Board, March 1981. See also E.G.C. Collins and T.B. Blodgett: "Sexual Harassment... Some See it... Some Won't" (1981), 59 *Harvard Business Review* 77.

[8] Ronni Sandroff, "Sexual Harassment in the Fortune 500", *Working Woman* (December 1988), p. 69.

The *Working Woman* study found that sexual harassment cost a typical Fortune 500 company $6.7 million per year in absenteeism, employee turnover, low morale and low productivity.[9] Further, the cost of settling sexual harassment suits has climbed steadily. For example, in 1987 K-Mart Corporation of the United States paid a record of $3.2 million in fines and penalties to settle a single case.[10]

A 1989 survey of women in large law firms in the United States conducted by *National Law Journal* and West Publishing Company concluded that 60 per cent of these women had experienced some form of sexual harassment. These incidents included unwanted sexual teasing, jokes, remarks or questions, unwanted sexual looks or gestures and unwanted deliberate touching, leaning over, cornering or pinching, as well as pressure for sex.[11]

A telephone poll conducted in the United States during the week of October 7, 1991 by the National Association for Female Executives found that 53 per cent of female professionals have been sexually harassed at least once in their career or know of someone who has been, and 64 per cent among those did not report the incident.

In 1982, the Equal Pay and Opportunity Commission in Britain reported a continued increase in the number of sexual harassment cases referred to it. The majority of these cases involved harassment on the part of an employer, usually the owner or manager of a small business. Although women are now more willing to confront the problem of sexual harassment and are lodging more complaints, the surveys reveal that at least 50 per cent of victims deal with the problem by leaving their jobs.[12]

Surveys conducted in Canada testify to the fact that sexual harassment is a widespread problem in the workplace. A study conducted among women union members by the British Columbia Federation of Labour and Women's Research Centre in 1980[13] revealed

---

[9] Freada Klein, *The 1988 Working Woman Sexual Harassment Survey* (1988), pp. 29-35.
[10] Ronni Sandroff, "Sexual Harassment in the Fortune 500", *Working Woman* (December 1988), p. 69 at 70.
[11] Emily Couric, "Women in the Large Firms: A High Price of Admission?" 12 *National L.J.*, No. 14, December 11, 1989, p. S2.
[12] "Working Conditions: Sexual Harassment" (September 1983), *Labour Research*, vol. 72, No. 9, pp. 233-235. See also M. Rubenstein, "The Law of Sexual Harassment at Work" (1983), 12 *Industrial L.J.* 1-18.
[13] *Sexual Harassment in the Workplace: A Discussion Paper* (Van.: British Columbia Federation of Labour Women's Rights Committee and The Vancouver Women's Research Centre, March 1980).

the 90 per cent of the respondents had experienced it themselves, and over half saw it as a problem for working women and/or knew of incidents happening to others.

In 1983, the Canadian Human Rights Commission published its survey on unwanted sexual attention and sexual harassment.[14] The survey was based on a sample of 2,004 persons, including both women and men. The results showed that 49 per cent of the women and 33 per cent of the men had experienced unwanted sexual attention. In addition, three-quarters of the respondents agreed that sexual harassment is a serious problem among working women. According to this survey, 1.2 million women in Canada believe that they have been sexually harassed.

A telephone poll survey was conducted by Angus Reid and Southam News in October 1991, shortly after the highly publicized charges of sexual harassment against U.S. Supreme Court nominee (now confirmed) Judge Clarence Thomas by his former aide Professor Anita Hill. The survey found that 37 per cent of women and 10 per cent of men believe that they have suffered some form of sexual harassment on the job. Among young women, 44 per cent believe that they have been victimized. But of those who feel they have been harassed, 59 per cent, both men and women, said they never did anything about it. A 1988 Quebec study found that 75 per cent of victims are female and under the age of 30, and 57 per cent were under the age of 25.

Among the professional groups, a survey was conducted in 1991 by the Law Society of Upper Canada of lawyers called to the bar in Ontario between 1975 and 1990. The findings of that survey have been published in *Transitions in the Ontario Legal Profession*. According to *Transitions* 70 per cent of the female respondents surveyed indicated that they had suffered some kind of sexual discrimination on the job at their law firms. Some of the women lawyers were vocal about their experiences of sexual harassment. Those experiences are an eye-opener:

> In the (number) years I practised law I came to believe that for the most part the legal profession is a men's club. Misogyny, sexism and sexual harassment are often the norm and, surprisingly perhaps, not the preserve of older members of the profession. I suppose that eventually the profession will improve, but when I think of the disadvantage and pain that women have suffered, I know

---

[14] *Unwanted Sexual Attention and Sexual Harassment: Results of a Survey of Canadians* (Ottawa: Canadian Human Rights Commission, 1983).

that any change has been purchased by women who have put their careers on the line and who often as not will never recoup for themselves what they have personally lost.

> When I was in private practice sexual harassment was a major issue. Some was overt, but most was of the undermining type, e.g., stereotyping, "sweetie" and "dear" in front of the clients, attention brought to one's dress, lack of general respect as an equal. At my firm, a partner once fired a receptionist because he thought she wasn't pretty enough and then boasted about it. When I reviewed my personnel file prior to leaving I read the hiring partner's notes on my original resume — "Easy on the eyes." I guess that was the basis upon which I was hired...[15]

Even people working in the churches are not immune from sexual harassment. Surveys conducted among women ministers also show that sexual harassment is a problem.[16] The Division of Ministry Personnel and Education of the United Church conducted a survey which showed that 35 per cent of respondent women in the ministry had been victims of sexual harassment. Another survey, conducted by Rev. Charlotte Caran, professor at St. Andrew's College in Saskatoon, showed that 39 per cent of the respondent women in the professional ministry in the three prairie provinces experienced overt physical harassment.

Many people are surprised and shocked to learn how widespread and deep-rooted the practice of sexual harassment is in the workplace. These studies confirm that sexual harassment, even in the 1990s, is a most serious and pressing problem facing women in employment.

---

[15] *Transitions in the Ontario Legal Profession: A Survey of Lawyers Called to the Bar Between 1975 and 1990*, A Report of the Law Society of Upper Canada (Toronto, 1991), pp. 84-85.
[16] *The United Church Observer* (May 1984), pp. 35-36.

CHAPTER 1

Sexual Harassment and Human Rights Legislation

A. WHAT BEHAVIOUR CONSTITUTES SEXUAL HARASSMENT?

There is a wide divergence of perceptions in our society as to what words or actions constitute sexual harassment. Because of the complexity of human behaviour, it is difficult to pinpoint what exact behaviour will be perceived as harassment by any particular individual. Because sexist attitudes and behaviours are highly persistent in our society, it is often difficult to draw the line between what is "acceptable" and what is "unacceptable" behaviour in the workplace. To one person, an arm around the shoulder may be perceived as a gesture of affection; to another person the same gesture may be offensive and harassing.

Sexual behaviour that a person finds personally offensive may be considered sexual harassment. Such behaviour may be subtle or obvious, verbal or non-verbal. Its scope may cover a wide range of behaviour that runs the gamut from patting women's bottoms when they walk down the hall; to pinching; to repeated, intrusive, insistent arms around the shoulder, couched in friendliness, but with a hidden agenda underneath; to an atmosphere contaminated with degrading comments, jokes, or innuendoes, and/or reference to women's bodies, to male prowess, and questions about women's sex lives; to public displays of derogatory images of women; to the requirement that women dress in costumes that leave them the target of sexual comments and propositions from the general public; all the way to the explicit propositions that require women to engage in sexual relations or be terminated or lose deserved promotions.

Sexual harassment in this context is employment discrimination by means of sexual blackmail, being a comprehensive pattern of hostile behaviour meant to underscore women's difference from and, by implication, inferiority with respect to the dominant male group. It is closely analogous in form and in effect to race discrimination. It is a systemic, arbitrary abuse of male power and authority used to extract sexual favours, remind women of their inferior ascribed status, and deprive women of employment opportunities and equality.

Sexual harassment in this context is an infringement of an employee's right to work in an environment free from sexual pressure of any kind. While sexual harassment need not necessarily involve a male supervisor and a female subordinate, this has been the most common situation in which the problem arises. But pressure can come from a person of either sex against a person of the opposite or same sex,[1] and from peers as well as supervisors.

With their legislative mandate, Human Rights Commissions in Canada have attempted to curb harassing conduct and to provide all employees equal opportunities. Initially human rights statutes in Canada have prohibited sex discrimination in employment without any specific reference to sexual harassment in the workplace. However, the Boards of Inquiry and the Tribunals have since given a broader interpretation to sex discrimination to include sexual harassment.[2] Subsequently in some jurisdictions, human rights statutes were amended to specifically prohibit sexual harassment.

Until 1978, the term "sexual harassment" was not in use and such behaviour was referred to as "sexual misconduct", "sexual advances", or "sexual molestation". However, during the last decade concern for women's rights has grown. Consequently, government agencies,[3]

---

[1] See *Romman v. Sea-West Holdings Ltd.* (Can. 1984), 5 C.H.R.R. D/2312 (Jones). Rodney Romman was employed as a deckhand on a tugboat owned by Sea-West Holdings Ltd. During his employment, he claims that he was sexually harassed by Douglas McDonald, skipper of the vessel. Mr. Romman complained that Mr. McDonald grabbed his genitals and patted him in the genital area and these advances would be made at least twice during each of the boat's 36-hour trips. Despite Mr. Romman's protests to the tugboat owner, Mr. McDonald's conduct continued. In September 1981, three months after he started working for the company, he was fired for refusing to report to work when he learned that Mr. McDonald would be the skipper of the voyage. The tribunal awarded the 20-year-old Vancouver sailor more than $3,700 for lost wages and hurt feelings. See also *Cassidy v. Sanchez* (B.C. 1988), 9 C.H.R.R. D/5278 (Wilson); *Bennet v. Treasury Board* (1991), P.S.S.R.B. File No. 166-2-21123 (Wexber).

[2] See for example *C. Bell v. The Flaming Steer Steak House Tavern Inc.* (Ont. 1980), 1 C.H.R.R. D/155 (Shime) (hereinafter cited as the *Cherie Bell* case).

[3] The foremost guardian of civil rights in the United States, the *Equal Employment Opportunity Commission*, defined "sexual harassment" in its guidelines issued on November 10, 1980, as follows:

> Unwelcome sexual advances, requests for sexual favours, and other verbal or physical conduct of a sexual nature constitute sexual harassment when (1)

Boards of Inquiry, Human Rights Tribunals, and the courts have attempted to define and describe "sexual harassment". Many Human Rights Commissions' guidelines now include references to "sexual harassment". For example, the British Columbia Human Rights Commission describes the term "sexual harassment" as:

> ...harassment, intimidation, coercion or threats to suspend, impose a penalty, or discriminate against any person because of that person's refusal to engage in sexually related interaction while applying for work, during work, or after work.[4]

The Alberta Human Rights Commission has defined it as follows:

> Sexual harassment is an unwanted sexual solicitation or advance made by a person who knows or ought to know that it is unwelcome.
>
> A reprisal or threat by someone in a position of authority, after a sexual advance is rejected constitutes sexual harassment.
>
> An employer or a person in a position of authority, after becoming aware of an occurrence of sexual harassment, and who fails to take appropriate action, may be held liable.[5]

Guidelines issued by the Canadian Human Rights Commission on February 1, 1983, describes sexual harassment as:

1. verbal abuse or threats;
2. unwelcome remarks, jokes, innuendoes or taunting;
3. displaying of pornographic or other offensive or derogatory pictures;
4. practical jokes which cause awkwardness or embarrassment;
5. unwelcome invitations or requests, whether indirect or explicit, or intimidation;
6. leering or other gestures;

> submission to such conduct is made either explicitly or implicitly a term or condition of an individual's employment, (2) submission to or rejection of such conduct by an individual is used as the basis for employment decisions affecting such individual, or (3) such conduct has the purpose or effect of unreasonably interfering with an individual's work performance or creating an intimidating, hostile, or offensive working environment.

See Equal Employment Opportunity Commission, *Sex Discrimination Guidelines* (1980), 29 C.F.R. 1604.11. On December 30, 1980, the Office of Federal Contract Compliance adopted the same definition in its Sex Discrimination Guidelines which took effect on January 29, 1981.

[4] *Report of the British Columbia Human Rights Commission* (1983) p. 43.
[5] *Your Rights — Under the Individual Rights Protection Act*, p. 19 (Edmonton: The Alberta Human Rights Commission, 1982).

7. unnecessary physical contact such as touching, patting, pinching, punching; or
8. physical assault.[6]

It should be noted that the above definitions and descriptions of "sexual harassment" are not included in the *Canadian Human Rights Act*, but a statutory definition of "sexual harassment" is found in the *Canada Labour Code*. It defines "sexual harassment" as:

> [A]ny conduct, comment, gesture or contact of a sexual nature
> (a) that is likely to cause offence or humiliation to any employee; or
> (b) that might, on reasonable grounds, be perceived by that employee as placing a condition of a sexual nature on employment or on any opportunity for training or promotion.[7]

These identified descriptions of "sexual harassment" appear to indicate that such behaviour can be divided into two categories: sexual coercion and sexual annoyance.[8] Sexual coercion is sexual harassment that results in some direct consequence to the worker's employment status or some gain or loss of tangible job benefits. Sexual harassment of this coercive kind can be said to involve an "employment nexus". The classic case of sexual harassment falls in this "nexus" category: a supervisor, using his power over salary, promotions, and employment itself, attempts to coerce a subordinate to grant sexual favours. If the worker accedes to the supervisor's request, tangible job benefits follow: if the worker refuses, job benefits are denied.

Sexual annoyance, the second type of sexual harassment, is sexually related conduct that is hostile, intimidating, or offensive to the employee, but nonetheless has no direct link to any tangible job benefit or harm. Rather, this annoying conduct creates a bothersome work environment and effectively makes the worker's willingness to endure that environment a term or condition of employment.

This second category contains two subgroups. Sometimes an employee is subjected to persistent requests for sexual favours and persistently refuses. Although that refusal does not cause any loss in

---

[6] See (1983), 4 C.H.R.R. at p. ND/8.
[7] *Canada Labour Code*, R.S.C. 1985, c. 9 (1st Supp.), s. 17. See also the definition of "sexual harassment" in S.N.S. 1991, c. 12, s. 1.
[8] J. W. Waks and M. G. Starr, "The 'Sexual Shakedown' in Perspective: Sexual Harassment in its Social and Legal Contexts" (1982), 7 *Employee Relations L.J.* 567 at 572.

job benefits, the very persistence of the demands creates an offensive work environment, which the employee should not be compelled to endure. The second subgroup encompasses all other conduct of a sexual nature that demeans or humiliates the person addressed and in that way also creates an offensive work environment. This includes sexual taunts, lewd or provocative comments and gestures, and sexually offensive physical contact.

In summary, sexual harassment can manifest itself both physically and psychologically. In its milder form it may be confined to verbal innuendoes and inappropriate affectional gestures. Sexual harassment can, however, escalate to extreme behaviour amounting to attempted or actual rape.

1. Verbal Behaviour

Listed below are examples of unacceptable verbal behaviours that may constitute sexual harassment. The behaviours listed below do not necessarily have to be specifically directed at the victim to constitute sexual harassment:

— continuous idle chatter of a sexual nature and graphic sexual descriptions;
— offensive and persistent risqué jokes or jesting and kidding about sex or gender-specific traits;
— suggestive or insulting sounds such as whistling, wolf-calls, or kissing sounds;
— comments of a sexual nature about weight, body shape, size, or figure;
— pseudo-medical advice such as "You might be feeling bad because you didn't get enough" or "A little tender loving care (TLC) will cure your ailments";
— staged whispers or mimicking of a sexual nature about the way a person walks, talks, sits, etc;
— derogatory or patronizing name calling;
— innuendoes or taunting;
— unwelcome remarks;
— rough and vulgar humour or language;
— jokes that causes awkwardness or embarrassment;
— gender-based insults or sexist remarks;
— comments about person's looks, dress, appearance or sexual habits;

Ch. 1 - Sexual Harassment and Human Rights Legislation

— inquiries or comments about an individual's sex life and/or relationship with sex partner;
— remarks about a woman's breasts, buttocks, vagina, and her overall figure;
— speculations about a woman's virginity, her choice of sexual partner or practices;
— verbal threat or abuse;
— telephone calls with sexual overtones.

2. Gestures and Other Non-Verbal Behaviour

Gesture are movements of the body, head, arms, hands and fingers, face and eyes that are expressive of an idea, opinion or emotion. Non-verbal behaviours are actions intended for an effect or as a demonstration. Gestures and non-verbal behaviours generally do not involve physical contact. Some gestures are intended only to get the attention of the victim, while others are intended to provoke a reaction from the receiver.

Listed below are examples of unacceptable gestures and non-verbal behaviours that may constitute sexual harassment:

— sexual looks such as leering and ogling with suggestive overtones;
— licking lips or teeth;
— holding or eating food provocatively;
— lewd gestures, such as hand or sign language to denote sexual activity;
— persistent and unwelcome flirting.

3. Visual Sexual Harassment

This includes:

— display of pornographic or other offensive, derogatory and/or sexually explicit pictures, photographs, cartoons, drawings, symbols and other material;
— display of girlie magazines;
— showing of pornographic or sexually explicit movies or slides;
— sexual exposure, such as dropping down pants in view of female employees.

4. Physical Behaviour

Unwanted physical contact can range from offensive conduct to criminal behaviour. One employee may feel that the physical contact is sexual harassment, while another may dismiss it as an annoyance.

The examples of behaviours listed below involve *actual physical contact* with the victim. Some of these behaviours are explicitly sexual in nature, some may be accidental:

— touching that is inappropriate in the workplace such as patting, pinching, stroking or brushing up against the body;
— hugging;
— cornering or mauling;
— invading another's "personal space";
— attempted or actual kissing or fondling;
— physical assaults;
— coerced sexual intercourse;
— attempted rape or rape.

5. Psychological Sexual Harassment

This includes:

— repeated unwanted social invitations, for dinner, drinks, or movies;
— relentless proposal of physical intimacy beginning with subtle hints which may lead to overt requests for dates and/or sexual intercourse;
— sexual favours;
— propositioning;
— requiring to wear "sexist and revealing" or suggestive uniforms, material or buttons.

All working women, regardless of their age, physical appearance, social status, and job security, may encounter sexual harassment. The only difference is that women working at the bottom of the economic scale are subject to the more gross expression of sexual harassment. They often encounter crude suggestive comments and crass physical assaults. Professional and managerial women, on the other hand, receive more subtle treatment. Instead of the outright physical abuse, they are subject to psychological intimidation. They receive offers for after-work drinks, expensive lunches and dinners, and business trips with the implicit message that sexual favours are expected.

Thus, sexual harassment may be described as a sexual encounter imposed upon a female employee against her wishes as a trade-off or condition of employment, normally by a supervisor[9] or a person with authority. The female employee is left with no alternative except either to concede to unwanted sexual advances or to face humiliation and/or adverse employment consequences.

B. DOES SEXUAL HARASSMENT AMOUNT TO SEX DISCRIMINATION?

All of the provinces and the federal government in Canada have enacted human rights statutes that prohibit "sex discrimination" in employment.[10] However, prior to the 1981 amendments to the *Ontario Human Rights Code*, sexual harassment on the job was not specifically prohibited by any human rights statute in Canada. In the absence of a specific provision in the statutes great uncertainty and confusion continued to hang over the issue of whether or not sex discrimination included sexual harassment. Prior to the 1981 amendments, the *Ontario Human Rights Code* had stated that:

4(1) No person shall,
  (b) dismiss or refuse to employ or to continue to employ any person;
        . . .

---

[9] It is sometimes questioned whether or not sexual encounters should be made by the supervisor or person in authority to constitute "sexual harassment". For example, the Alberta Human Rights Commission has recently deleted the expression "person in a position of authority" from its definition of sexual harassment. However, the new Ontario *Human Rights Code* provides "a sexual solicitation or advance *made by a person in a position to confer, grant or deny a benefit or advancement...*" [emphasis added].

[10] In British Columbia, *Human Rights Act*, S.B.C. 1979, c. 22; in Alberta, *Individual's Rights Protection Act*, R.S.A. 1980, c. I-2; in Saskatchewan, *Saskatchewan Human Rights Code*, S.S. 1979, c. S-24.1; in Manitoba, *Human Rights Code*, S.M. 1987, c. 45 (C.C.S.M., H175); in Quebec, *Charter of Human Rights and Freedoms*, R.S.Q. 1977, c. C-12; in New Brunswick *Human Rights Act*, R.S.N.B. 1973, c. H-11; in Nova Scotia, *Human Rights Act*, R.S.N.S. 1989, c. 214; in Prince Edward Island, *Human Rights Act*, R.S.P.E.I. 1988, c. H-12; in Newfoundland, *Human Rights Code*, S.N. 1988, c. 62; and in the federal jurisdiction, *Canadian Human Rights Act*, R.S.C. 1985, c. H-6.

(g) discriminate against any employee with regard to any term or condition of employment because of ... sex ... of such person or employee.[11]

The relevant provision in the *Canadian Human Rights Act* provides:

7. It is a discriminatory practice, directly or indirectly,

. . .

(b) in the course of employment, to differentiate adversely in relation to an employee, on a prohibited ground of discrimination.[12]

Section 3 of the Act designated "sex" as a prohibited ground for discrimination.

All other provinces in Canada have a similar provision prohibiting discrimination in relation to employment on the basis of "sex". Thus, the issue of whether or not the legislatures intended to outlaw sexual harassment in the workplace remained uncertain, unclear and unresolved for many years.

It appears that the Human Rights Commissions (the agencies responsible for administering the human rights laws in their respective jurisdictions) had difficulty in comprehending the meaning and scope of "sex discrimination", as well as the legislative intent with regard to sexual harassment. They were not convinced that the human rights statutes prohibited "sexual harassment". Initially, they took a narrow view of sex discrimination and on that basis discouraged or turned down complaints of sexual harassment. Women who lodged complaints of sexual harassment were told that the human rights legislation did not prohibit this behaviour.[13] It was argued that when the legislation said no discrimination on the basis of sex, "sex" meant biological status and not sexual intercourse.[14] Where a man was harassing only one woman, it might have been a result of her personality rather than sex itself.[15] The earlier attitudes and views of the Human Rights Commissions in this regard are evident from the letter the Chairperson of the Alberta Human Rights Commission, Mr. Max Wyman, wrote to the Calgary Status of Women Action Committee. He stated:

---

[11] *Ontario Human Rights Code*, R.S.O. 1980, c. 340 [repealed and replaced by the *Human Rights Code, 1981*, S.O. 1981, c. 53; now R.S.O. 1990, c. H.19].
[12] *Canadian Human Rights Act*, R.S.C. 1985, c. H-6, s. 7.
[13] See C. Backhouse and L. Cohen: *The Secret Oppression: Sexual Harrassment of Working Women* (1978), p. 118.
[14] *Ibid.*
[15] *Ibid.*

Sexual harassment does not necessarily involve discrimination. In a one-man, one-woman office, either could be guilty of sexual harassment but it is difficult to see how a discriminatory practice is involved.[16]

In recent years, however, the Human Rights Commissions have changed their stand on sexual harassment and have begun to include it in the sex discrimination provision of the statute. They have become convinced about the seriousness of this problem and its impact on legislative policy on the one hand and on the women employees on the other. They have begun to attack this problem on two fronts. They have been strongly urging their respective governments to clarify and specifically prohibit sexual harassment in human rights legislation.[17] At the same time they have been vigorously and confidently pursuing the sexual harassment complaints with a view to expanding judicially the scope of "sex discrimination" to cover sexual harassment.

C. DEVELOPMENT OF SEXUAL HARASSMENT LAW IN THE UNITED STATES

The movement towards considering sexual harassment as "sex discrimination" under the existing legislation actually began in the United States in the mid 1970s. In the absence of Canadian jurisprudence on this subject, the Canadian Boards of Inquiry, Tribunals and courts have frequently examined or referred to, and even adopted, U.S. court cases and other authorities.[18] In view of this fact, it would be desirable to discuss briefly the development of sexual harassment law in the United States.

---

[16] *Ibid*, at p. 119.

[17] See for example *The Report of the B.C. Human Rights Commission on Extensions to the Code* (February 1983), p. 45 where it states:

> The Commission recommends: 'That protection against sexual harassment be made explicit in the Human Rights Code.'

It was ironic that on July 7, 1983, the Government of British Columbia introduced Bill 27, an Act to amend the present British Columbia *Human Rights Code*. Bill 27 abolished the B.C. Human Rights Commission and the B.C. Human Rights Branch and replaced them with a five member Human Rights Council

[18] See for example *Watt v. Regional Municipality of Niagara* (Ont. 1984), 5 C.H.R.R. D/2453 (McCamus). The learned chairperson acknowledged at p. D/2455 (para. 20339) that "the concept of 'sexual harassment' was first given a clear recognition

In the United States, Title VII of the *Civil Rights Act* of 1964 and various state legislation prohibits sex discrimination. The Equal Employment Opportunity Commission (E.E.O.C.), the agency responsible for the administration of the *Civil Rights Act*, investigates complaints brought under this Act. In the United States there is no system of Boards of Inquiry. Instead, if cases are not settled through conciliation, they are ultimately taken before the courts by the complainant or the Equal Employment Opportunity Commission.

Like Canadian human rights statutes, Title VII of the *Civil Rights Act*, 1964, prohibits sex discrimination in employment but makes no specific mention of sexual harassment.[19] The American courts were

---

by an American court interpreting provision of Title VII of the *Civil Rights Act* of 1964 (42 U.S.C. Paras. 2000 E-2000 E17)". See also: *Cox v. Jagbritte Inc.* (Ont. 1982), 3 C.H.R.R. D/609 (Cumming); *Giouvanoudis v. Golden Fleece Restaurant* (Ont. 1983), 5 C.H.R.R. D/1967 (Cumming); *Ballantyne v. Molly 'N' Me Tavern* (Ont. 1982), 4 C.H.R.R. D/1191 (McCamus); *Zarankin v. Johnstone c.o.b. as Wessex Inn* (B.C. 1984), 5 C.H.R.R. D/2274 (Smith).

[19] *The Civil Rights Act*, 1964, Title VII, sections 701-718, 42 U.S.C. section 2000e-2(a). Title VII of this legislation deals with equal employment opportunities. Although Title VII is broad in its coverage and content, its core is section 703(2), which provides:

It shall be unlawful employment practice for an employer — (1) to fail or refuse to hire or to discharge any individual, or otherwise to discriminate against any individual, with respect to his compensation, terms, conditions, or privileges of employment, because of such individual's race, colour, religion, sex or national origin: or
(2) to limit, segregate, or classify his employees or applicants for employment in any way which would deprive or tend to deprive any individual of employment opportunities or otherwise adversely affect his status as an employee, because of such individual's race, colour, religion, sex, or national origin.

To effectuate Title VII's purpose of providing a safe and effective means for resolving complaints of employment discrimination, Congress included section 704, which prohibits employers from retaliating against employees who initiate complaints under Title VII. In 1972, Congress added section 717 to extend the coverage of Title VII to federal employees.

These are the crucial provisions of Title VII. Although the legislative history of Section 703 reveals that the provisions prohibiting discrimination based on sex were added in a last-minute attempt to prevent passage of Title VII, the legislative history of the 1972 addition to section 717 evidences Congress's commitment to eliminating employment discrimination based on sex:

Discrimination against women is no less serious than other forms of prohibited employment practices and is to be accorded the same degree of social concern given to any type of unlawful discrimination.

faced with the issue of whether or not sexual harassment constitutes gender-based discrimination within the definition of "sex discrimination" and thereby amounts to a violation of laws prohibiting discrimination. The initial response of the courts, in the earlier sexual harassment cases which alleged a violation of the Title VII, was negative.[20]

Ten years after the enactment of Title VII, the federal judiciary confronted its first case in which sexual harassment was the primary allegation. In *Barnes v. Train*,[21] a woman hired as the administrative assistant to the male director of the Environment Protection Agency's Equal Opportunities Division filed a suit in the District Court alleging that her job was abolished because she refused to engage in sexual relations with the director. The District Court dismissed the case, arguing that *although Barnes was discriminated against, the discrimination was not because she was a woman, but because she refused to engage in sexual behaviour with her supervisor*. Thus, the District Court decided that sexual harassment was not treatment based on sex within its legal meaning.

The leading case denying recourse to a harassed employee under Title VII is *Corne v. Bausch & Lomb Inc.*[22] In this case, two women sued stating that their male supervisor had taken unsolicited and unwelcome sexual liberties with them and that they had to resign their jobs to avoid their supervisor's verbal and physical sexual advances. The District Court in Arizona dismissed the case on the ground that sex discrimination cases had always been founded on company policies, not on the "personal proclivity" of a supervisor. Further, there was no sex discrimination *per se* in the Court's opinion since, if males had also been victims of harassment, there would be no grounds for a suit. The court went on to say:

The legislative history further reveals that Title VII is not confined to explicit acts of discrimination nor to discrimination based solely on sex. Any decision in which sex is a factor is discriminatory, even if other, legitimate, factors also motivated the decision. In essence, sex is to be treated like any other prohibited ground for discrimination.

[20] See for example *Barnes v. Train*, 13 FEP 123 (D.D.C. 1974); revd *sub nom. Barnes v. Costle*, 561 F. 2d 983 (D.C. Cir. 1977); *Corne v. Bausch & Lomb Inc.*, 390 F. Supp. 161, 9 E.P.D. para. 10,093 (D. Ariz. 1975); *Miller v. Bank of America*, 418 F. Supp. 233 (N.D. Cal. 1976); and *Tomkins v. Public Service Electric and Gas Co.*, 422 F. Supp. 533 (D. N.J. 1977); revd (*sub nom. Tomkins II*), 568 F. 2d 1044 (3rd Cir. 1977).

[21] *Supra*, note 20.

[22] *Supra*, note 20.

An outgrowth of holding such activity to be actionable under Title VII would be a potential federal lawsuit every time an employee made amorous or sexually oriented advances toward another. The only sure way an employer could avoid such charges would be to have employees who were asexual.[23]

In *Miller v. Bank of America*,[24] the District Court for Northern California determined that sexual harassment was an isolated misconduct not attributable to employer policy. In this case, a black woman charged that her white male supervisor promised her a better job if she would be "sexually co-operative." She refused and was fired. The court phrased the issue as to whether Title VII was intended to hold an employer liable for what is essentially the isolated and unauthorized sexual misconduct of one employee to another. The District Court dismissed the complaint, stating that Miller should have filed a complaint with the Employee Relations Department of the bank which would have conducted an "appropriate investigation".

In *Tomkins v. Public Service Electric and Gas Co.*,[25] Tomkins, an office worker, complained to the company that her supervisor made physical sexual advances, had told her that a sexual relationship was essential to an effective working relationship, had threatened her with work-related reprisals when she refused, and had physically restrained her. Fifteen months after her complaint was filed, she was fired. The New Jersey Federal District Court rejected the argument that sexual harassment could constitute an offence under Title VII. The court, rather than viewing sexual harassment as being discrimination against an individual because of her sex, viewed it as being discrimination because of an individual's refusal to engage in sexual activity. The court stated:

> Title VII was enacted in order to remove those artificial barriers to employment which are based upon unjust and long encrusted prejudice. Its aim to make careers open to talents irrespective of race or sex. It is not intended to provide a federal tort remedy for what amounts to physical attack motivated by sexual desire on the part of the supervisor and which happened to occur in a corporate corridor rather than in a back alley.[26]

The court further stated that "sexual harassment is neither employment related nor sex-based, but a personal injury properly pursued in state court".

---

[23] *Ibid.*, at 163.
[24] *Supra*, note 20.
[25] *Supra*, note 20.
[26] *Ibid.*

us as demonstrated in the above cited cases, the courts refused to rule that sexual harassment constituted sex discrimination prohibited by Title VII of the *Civil Rights Act*. The courts gave a narrow interpretation to the term "sex discrimination" and viewed inappropriate sexual conduct in the workplace as an issue to be decided under criminal law. The courts' logic behind these restricted interpretations of Title VII, (*i.e.*, that sexual harassment is not sex discrimination) was based on various factors,[27] including:

1. Sexual harassment does not constitute "sex discrimination" within the definitional purview of Title VII because it is discrimination based upon willingness versus non-willingness to engage in sexual activity, as opposed to discrimination based upon gender. Further, that such was not an arbitrary barrier to employment, but the result of an "inharmonious personal relationship" between the supervisor and the subordinate.[28]
2. The employer cannot be held liable for the personal actions and conflicts of its employees and that such an activity as sexual harassment is not within the scope of employment. Further, the activity was "nothing more than personal proclivity, peculiarity, or mannerism" and that "by his alleged sexual advances", the defendant supervisor "was satisfying a personal urge".[29]
3. In the *Tomkins* case, the District Court reiterated the concern that a broad interpretation of Title VII to include sexual harassment would open courtroom doors to a potentially massive class of new litigation which would require "4,000 federal trial judges instead of some 400".[30]

The first case in which sexual harassment was clearly said to be "treatment based on sex" under Title VII was *Williams v. Saxbe*.[31] For the first time, a female victim of sexual harassment in the United States was successful in winning an action against her employer, who in this case happened to be none other than the U.S. Department of Justice. Williams, an employee, asserted that her supervisor "engaged in a continuing pattern and practice of harassment and humiliation...". The U.S. District Court for the District of Columbia, in taking an

---

[27] See R. Schupp, J. Windham and D. Draughn, "Sexual Harassment Under Title VII: The Legal Status" (1981), 32 *Labour L.J.* 238.
[28] *Barnes v. Train, supra*, note 20.
[29] *Corne v. Bausch & Lomb Inc., supra*, note 20.
[30] *Tomkins v. Public Service Electric and Gas Co., supra*, note 20.
[31] 413 F. Supp. 654, 11 E.P.D. para. 10,840 (D.D.C. 1976).

expansive interpretation of Title VII, held that retaliatory actions taken by a male supervisor against a female employee because of her refusal to submit to his sexual advances constituted sex discrimination under Title VII of the *Civil Rights Act*.[32] The court reasoned that violations of Title VII could be found whenever a supervisor approached only members of one sex, but that no violation of Title VII would occur if a supervisor made advances to subordinates of both genders.

Although in 1976 the Federal District Court for the District of Columbia in *Williams v. Saxbe* took an expansive view of "sex discrimination" by holding that sexual harassment is discrimination on the basis of sex for the purpose of Title VII, the real change in the American judicial opinion on sexual harassment did not take place until 1977. In that year alone, three federal Courts of Appeal[33] held that sexual harassment amounts to sexual discrimination under Title VII of the *Civil Rights Act, 1964*.

In *Garber v. Saxon Business Products Inc.*,[34] the U.S. Court of Appeals for the Fourth Circuit in a *per curiam* judgement ruled that an employer who has a policy or acquiesces in a practice of compelling female employees to submit to the sexual advances of male supervisors is in violation of Title VII.[35]

In *Barnes v. Costle*,[36] the plaintiff was an employee of the Environment Protection Agency. She alleged that because she rebuffed her director's repeated sexual advances and his intimations that an affair would enhance her career, he abolished her job. The Court of Appeals found that retention of the plaintiff's job was conditioned upon sexual co-operation with her supervisor, a condition which her supervisor did not apply to male employees.

The Circuit Court ruled that women cannot be denied promotion or employment because they refuse to give sexual favours to superiors, *i.e.* retaliation is sex discrimination. The court held that sexual harassment is actionable under Title VII as sex-based discrimination. Furthermore, an employer is vicariously liable for the acts of its

---

[32] *Ibid.*, at 659. The court made it clear that it would also be a case of sex discrimination if a female supervisor imposed upon a male employee or if a homosexual imposed upon a worker of the same sex.

[33] *Barnes v. Costle*, 561 F. 2d 983 (D.C. Cir. 1977); *Garber v. Saxon Business Products*, 552 F. 2d 1032 (4th Cir. 1977); and *Tomkins v. Public Service Electric and Gas Co. (Tomkins II)*, 568 F. 2d 1044 (3rd Cir. 1977).

[34] *Supra*, note 33.

[35] *Ibid.* However, the court's opinion implied that sexual harassment would not have been considered discrimination if both men and women were harassed.

[36] *Supra*, note 33.

supervisory personnel. However, if a supervisor contravenes the employer's policy without the employer's knowledge, and the consequences are rectified when discovered, the employer may be relieved from responsibility under Title VII. The court read the *Civil Rights Act* as a general prohibition against all sex-based discrimination. As such, it was held that it should be construed liberally in its application to novel employment circumstances.

In *Tomkins II*,[37] the Third Circuit reversed the lower court decision and ruled that:

> ... Title VII is violated when a supervisor with the actual or constructive knowledge of the employer makes sexual advances or demands towards a subordinate employee and conditions that employee's job status — evaluation, continued employment, promotion, or other aspects of career development — on a favourable response to those advances or demands, and the employer does not take prompt and appropriate remedial action after acquiring such knowledge.[38]

In this case, the court devised a two-part test to establish a claim of sexual harassment under Title VII. A complaint of sexual harassment must first constitute a condition of employment, and it must show that this condition was imposed by the employer on the basis of sex.

There is an underlying concern in these cases about possible legal intervention into what may be essentially personal relationships, even though the relationships took place in the workplace. In *Heelan v. Johns-Manville Corp.*,[39] Finesilver D.J. stated:

> Title VII should not be interpreted as reaching into sexual relationships which may arise during the course of employment, but which do not have a substantial effect on that employment.[40]

The court, however, pointed out that an employer is responsible for the discriminatory acts of its agents, even if it does not have a policy of endorsing sexual harassment.

Thus, the U.S. courts were willing in these cases to interpret the words "discrimination against individual ... because of such individual's sex" in section 2 of the *Civil Rights Act* in a broad way.

---

[37] *Tomkins v. Public Service Electric and Gas Co. (Tomkins II), supra*, note 33.
[38] *Ibid.*
[39] 451 F. Supp. 1382, 20 FEP 251 (D.C.1978).
[40] *Ibid.*, at 1388.

The early sexual harassment cases that reached appellate courts had all concerned female employees who were denied promotions or were discharged or forced to resign after refusing a supervisor's sexual advances. However, a more restrictive interpretation was placed on the words "term, conditions or privileges of employment" in section 2 of the Act. For the plaintiff to succeed, the courts in these cases insisted that she must prove that her continued employment was contingent on her acceptance of a supervisor's sexual advances. Where the harasser was not in a position to affect the plaintiff's "employment opportunities" or where such deprivations could not be proved, the court generally had difficulty in reaching the conclusion that Title VII's jurisdiction extended to such cases. The issue, then, is whether or not a case would fall within the scope of Title VII if sexual harassment is not followed by job-related consequences.

However, the U.S. Supreme Court in 1986, in the landmark case *Meritor Savings Bank v. Vinson*,[41] confirmed in no uncertain terms that sexual harassment constitutes sex discrimination prohibited by Title VII of the *Civil Rights Act*. The court rejected the employer's contention that Title VII prohibits only discrimination that causes "economic" or "tangible" injury. The court held that a plaintiff may establish a violation of the Title VII "by providing that discrimination based on sex has created a hostile or abusive work environment".[42]

The *Vinson* case posed three questions for the Supreme Court:

1. Does unwelcome sexual behaviour that creates a hostile working environment constitute employment discrimination on the basis of sex?
2. Can a Title VII violation be shown when the District Court found that any sexual relationship that existed between the plaintiff and her supervisor was a "voluntary one"?
3. Is an employer strictly liable for an offensive working environment created by a supervisor's sexual advances when the employer does not know of, and could not reasonably have known of, the supervisor's misconduct?

---

[41] 106 S. Ct. 2399, 40 E.P.D. para. 36,159 (1986). This was the first time that the High Court directly addressed the issue of sexual harassment. Initially, women's groups and organized labour had expressed fears that the Supreme Court might reject the theory that hostile environment claims of sexual harassment were a form of sex discrimination actionable under Title VII. However, the court has seen fit to give credence to these claims.

[42] See R.K. Robinson, K. Delany and E.C. Stephens: "Hostile Environment: A Review of the Implications of *Meritor Savings Bank v. Vinson*" (1987), 38 *Labour L.J.* 179.

In this case, the plaintiff had alleged that her supervisor constantly subjected her to sexual harassment both during and after business hours, on and off the employer's premises; she alleged that he forced her to have sexual intercourse with him on numerous occasions, fondled her in front of other employees, followed her into the women's restroom and exposed himself to her, and even raped her on several occasions. She alleged that she submitted for fear of jeopardizing her employment. She testified, however, that this conduct had ceased almost a year before she first complained in any way, by filing a Title VII suit; her E.E.O.C. charge was filed later. The supervisor and the employer denied all of her allegations and claimed they were fabricated in response to a work dispute.

The District Court found that the plaintiff was not the victim of sexual harassment and was not required to grant sexual favours as a condition of employment or promotion.[43] The District Court found that if a sexual relationship had existed between the plaintiff and her supervisor, it was a "voluntary one ... having nothing to do with her continued employment". The court, nonetheless, went on to hold that the employer was not liable for its supervisor's actions and had no notice of the alleged sexual harassment; although the employer had a policy against discrimination and an internal grievance procedure, the plaintiff had never lodged a complaint.

On appeal, the Court of Appeals for the District of Columbia reversed and remanded, holding that the lower court should have considered whether the evidence established a violation under the "hostile environment" theory.[44] The court ruled that a victim's "voluntary" submission to sexual advances has "no materiality whatsoever" to the proper inquiry: whether "toleration of sexual harassment (was) a condition of her employment". The court further held that an employer is absolutely liable for sexual harassment committed by a supervisory employee, regardless of whether the employer actually knew or reasonably could have known of the misconduct, or would have disapproved of and stopped the misconduct if aware of it.

In June 1986, the U.S. Supreme Court issued its opinion on *Meritor* in a landmark decision that established the principle of employer liability and sexual harassment while simultaneously limiting the extent of that liability. The Supreme Court agreed that the case should be remanded for consideration under the "hostile environment" theory

---

[43] *Vinson v. Taylor*, 22 E.P.D. para. 30,708 (D.D.C. 1980).
[44] *Vinson v. Taylor*, 753 F. 2d. 141, 36 E.P.D. para. 34,946, *denied a hearing* 760 F. 2d. 1330, 37 E.P.D. para. 35, 232 (D.C.Cir. 1985).

and held that the proper inquiry focuses on the "unwelcomeness" of the conduct rather than the "voluntariness" of the victim's participation. But the court held that the Court of Appeals erred in concluding that employers are always automatically liable for sexual harassment by their supervisory employees.

The court further held that for harassment to violate Title VII, it must be "sufficiently severe or pervasive 'to alter the conditions of (the victim's) employment and create an abusive working environment'".

Citing the E.E.O.C.'s guidelines, the court said the gravamen of sexual harassment claim is that the alleged sexual advances were "unwelcome". Therefore, "the fact that sex-related conduct was 'voluntary', in the sense that the complainant was not forced to participate against her will, is not a defense to a sexual harassment suit brought under Title VII. ... The correct inquiry is whether (the victim) by her conduct indicated that the alleged sexual advances were unwelcome, not whether her actual participation in sexual intercourse was voluntary".[45] Evidence of a complainant's sexually provocative speech or dress may be relevant in determining whether she found particular advances unwelcome, but should be admitted with caution in light of the potential for unfair prejudice.

Thus, the Supreme Court in *Vinson* put the stamp of its approval on the argument that sexual harassment constitutes sex discrimination (whether or not that causes economic and tangible injury) and is prohibited under Title VII of the *Civil Rights Act*.

1. E.E.O.C. Guidelines

In 1980, the Equal Employment Opportunity Commission (E.E.O.C.) published in the *Federal Register* final guidelines on discrimination because of sexual harassment.[46]

These guidelines, effective as of November 10, 1980, incorporate the E.E.O.C. view that sexual harassment is an unlawful employment practice and thus a violation of Title VII of the *Civil Rights Act* of 1964. The guidelines define sexual harassment as "unwelcome sexual

---

[45] 106 S.Ct. 2399 at 2406.
[46] In 1980, the E.E.O.C. published the Guidelines on Sexual Harassment as an amendment to the Guidelines on Discrimination Because of Sex, 29 C.F.R. 1604.11, 45 F.R. 25024.

advances, requests for sexual favours, and other verbal or physical conduct of a sexual nature". The guidelines set out three criteria for determining whether an action constitutes unlawful behaviour as follows:

1. when submission to the conduct is either an explicit or implicit term or condition of employment;
2. when submission to or rejection of such conduct by an individual is used as the basis for employment decisions affecting such individual; or
3. when such conduct has the purpose or effect of unreasonably interfering with an individual's work performance or creating an intimidating, hostile, or offensive working environment. (This is the so-called "quality of environment" rule.)

However, the E.E.O.C. guidelines on sexual harassment are *not* federal government regulations. They are, instead, the Commission's statement of interpretation of developing case law in the matter. It is the courts, not the E.E.O.C. that have established the principles that (a) sexual harassment is a form of sex discrimination under Title VII of the 1964 *Civil Rights Act*; (b) sexual harassment should not be a condition of employment; and (c) employers may be held liable in such cases. Further, the E.E.O.C. guidelines do not have the effect of law and they are not binding on the courts. The E.E.O.C. has no enforcement powers except through the courts. Generally the courts in the United States have found the E.E.O.C.'s Guidelines on sexual harassment quite helpful and they have gladly given them their blessing.[47]

The *Meritor Saving Bank v. Vinson*[48] case presented the first occasion on which the U.S. Supreme Court addressed the question of the use to be made of the 1980 E.E.O.C. guidelines prohibiting sexual harassment. The court noted that the guidelines are not controlling upon the courts since they are merely an administrative interpretation of Title VII by its enforcing agency. But the court recognized that the guidelines "constitute a body of experience and informed judgment to which Courts and litigants may properly resort

---

[47] See for example *Bundy v. Jackson*, 641 F. 2d 934 (D.C. Cir. 1981); *Henson v. City of Dundee*, 682 F. 2d 897, 29 E.P.D. para. 32,993 (11th Cir. 1982); *Brown v. City of Guthrie*, 30 E.P.D. para. 33,031, 22 FEP 1631 (W.D. Okla. 1980). See also *Walter v. KFGO Radio*, 518 F. Supp 1309, 28 E.P.D. para. 32,497 (D.N.D. 1981); *Morgan v. Hertz Corp.*, 27 FEP 990 (W.D. Tenn. 1981).
[48] 106 S. Ct. 2399 (1986).

for guidance".[49] The court said that the guidelines "appropriately drew from and were fully consistent with the existing case law"[50] regarding non-economic sexual harassment injury being actionable under Title VII.

2. Quality of Working Environment

The E.E.O.C. guidelines specify an employer's responsibility to maintain a workplace free of sexual harassment and intimidation. This is based on the Commission's position that sexual harassment in the workplace creates an environment that is harmful. Since 1980, the courts have begun to show a willingness to expand the scope of "sex discrimination" by relaxing the burden of proof on the plaintiff in sexual harassment cases by adopting the E.E.O.C. guidelines. *Brown v. City of Guthrie*,[51] was the first case in which the quality of the working environment[52] was the major basis for the cause of action. Although the plaintiff could not show a direct employment nexus, she was able to establish that the sexually harassing acts of her supervisor (such as lewd comments, innuendos, and gestures) substantially affected her emotional and psychological stability. This harassment, she argued, contributed to a work environment which was so unbearable that she was forced to resign.

In arriving at its decision, the court in *Brown* became the first judicial body to cite the E.E.O.C. guidelines on sexual harassment. Quoting section 1604.11(a) of the guidelines, the court noted that harassment on the basis of sex is a violation of Title VII when "such conduct has the purpose or effect of substantially interfering with an individual's work performance or creating an intimidating, hostile or offensive work environment".

However, in *Bundy v. Jackson*,[53] the case that expanded and popularized the concept of "quality of work environment", the plaintiff had suffered no tangible job-related consequences. The original court

---

[49] *Ibid.*, at 2405.
[50] *Ibid.*
[51] *Supra*, note 47.
[52] Professor Faley has used the expression of "Atmosphere of Discrimination Theory" for sexual harassment situations not leading to tangible job related consequences. See Farley, Robert H.: "Sexual Harassment: Critical Review of Legal Cases with General Principles and Preventive Measures" (1982), *Personnel Psychology* 583.
[53] 641 F. 2d 934 (D.C. Cir. 1981).

ruled that Bundy's male supervisors did not discriminate against her, even though she was able to prove that they had made sexual advances. The court noted that the sexual advances apparently were taken seriously by neither her nor her supervisors. Moreover, the court observed that her supervisors took no action against her either personally or professionally, and that Bundy apparently filed the complaint to obtain a promotion. The plaintiff's argument in the case was that it should be unnecessary for her to show that there were tangible employment consequences, in the sense that benefits were denied to her as a result of her rejection of sexual propositions. Rather, it was argued, she would only have to show that her employment circumstance were "poisoned" by the harassment.

The Court of Appeals for the District of Columbia, however, accepted that reasoning and decided that the principle in *Barnes*, should be extended:

> Thus, unless we extend the *Barnes* holding, an employer could sexually harass a female employee with impunity by carefully stopping short of firing the employee or taking other tangible actions against her in response to her resistance, thereby creating the impression... that the employer did not take the ritual of harassment and resistance "seriously".[54]

The court found that the harassment of female employees was a "standard operating practice" and a "normal condition of employment".[55] Although she did not suffer any adverse employment consequences as a result of rejecting their advances, the court found that she was subjected to sexually stereotyped insults and demeaning propositions "which caused her anxiety and debilitation ... illegally poisoned that environment."[56]

In so holding, the court referred to cases where ethnic and racial slurs had been found to constitute a violation of the *Civil Rights Act*. The court stated that an analogy could be made between those cases and sexual harassment cases:

> The relevance of these "discriminatory environment" cases to sexual harassment is beyond serious dispute. Racial or ethnic discrimination against a company's minority clients may reflect no intent to discriminate directly against the company's minority employees, but in poisoning the atmosphere of employment it violates Title VII. Sexual stereotyping through discriminatory

---

[54] *Ibid.*, at 945.
[55] *Ibid.*, at 939.
[56] *Ibid.*, at 944.

dress requirements may be benign in intent, and may offend women only in a general, atmospheric manner, yet it violates Title VII. Racial slurs, though intentional and directed at individuals, may still be just verbal insults, yet they too may create Title VII liability. *How then can sexual harassment, which injects the most demeaning sexual stereotypes into the general work environment and which always represents an intentional assault on an individual's innermost privacy, not be illegal?* [Emphasis added]

. . .

Indeed, so long as women remain inferiors in the employment hierarchy, they may have little recourse against harassment beyond the legal recourse Bundy seeks in this case. The law may allow a woman to prove that her resistance to the harassment cost her her job or some economic benefit, but this will do her no good if the employer never takes such tangible actions against her.

. . .

It may even be pointless to require the employees to prove that she "resisted" the harassment at all. So long as the employer never literally forces sexual relations on the employee "resistance" may be a meaningless alternative for her. If the employer demands no response to his verbal or physical gestures other than good-natured tolerance, the woman has no means of communicating her rejection. She neither accepts nor rejects the advances; she simply endures them. She might be able to contrive proof of rejection by objecting to the employer's advances in some very visible and dramatic way, but she would do so only at the risk of making her life on the job even more miserable. It hardly helps that the remote prospect of legal relief under *Barnes* remains available if she objects so powerfully that she provokes the employer into firing her.[57]

Thus, sexual harassment that does not otherwise adversely affect the woman's employment may nonetheless be discrimination on the basis of sex, if it simply makes the work environment unpleasant.

A year later in 1982, the Court of Appeals for the Eleventh Circuit in *Henson v. City of Dundee*,[58] confirmed and expanded on the reasoning that sexually "hostile environment", even without tangible harm, constitutes sex discrimination prohibited under Title VII of the *Civil Rights Act.* It stated:

Sexual harassment which creates a hostile or offensive environment for members of one sex is every bit the arbitrary barrier to sexual equality at the workplace

---

[57] *Ibid.*, at 945-46.
[58] 682 F. 2d. 897, 29 E.P.D. para 32,993 (11th Cir. 1982).

that racial harassment is to racial equality. Surely, a requirement that a man or woman run a gauntlet of sexual abuse in return for the privilege of being allowed to work and make a living can be as demeaning and disconcerting as the harshest of racial epithets.[59]

Since the *Brown* and *Bundy* cases, there have been additional cases[60] in which the courts have considered the concept of "atmosphere of discrimination" as ground for a Title VII suit, as well as the E.E.O.C. guidelines as supportive of that action.

In 1986, the U.S. Supreme Court, at the first available opportunity in *Meritor Savings Bank v. Vinson*,[61] confirmed in no uncertain terms that "hostile environment" sexual harassment is actionable under Title VII. However, the Court did not define the situation, which left the question, What is a "hostile environment"? unanswerable and unresolved. Subsequent decisions indicate that the lower courts differ vastly on the meaning and scope of "hostile environment".[62]

In *Rabidue v. Osceola Refining Company*,[63] the Sixth Circuit held that the plaintiff was not subject to "hostile environment". The court held when it quoted from a lower court that:

> ... indeed it cannot seriously be disputed that in some work environments, humour and language are rough hewn and vulgar. Sexual jokes, sexual conversations, and girlie magazines may abound. Title VII was not meant to, nor can, change this.[64]

The court further stated that the trier of facts must be examined in each case and "must adopt the perspective of a reasonable person's reaction to a similar environment under essentially like or similar

---

[59] *Ibid.*, at 902.
[60] See cases referred to in note 47, *supra*, especially *Walter v. KFGO Radio*, where the court held there was no sex discrimination based on a claim of sexual harassment even if the employee was correct that her supervisor patted her on the bottom, touched her in the breast area, and made an inebriated attempt to have an affair with her during a convention because there was no proof that acquiescence was a term or condition of employment. There was also no proof that the supervisor's conduct substantially interfered with the plaintiff's work performance or that it created an intimidating, hostile, or offensive working environment.
[61] 106 S. Ct. 2399, 40 E.P.D. para 36,159 (U.S. 1986).
[62] See R.K. Robinson, K. Delany and E.C. Stephens, "Hostile Environment: A Review of the Implications of *Meritor Savings Bank v. Vinson*" (1987), 38 *Labour L.J.* 179. See also William L. Woerner and Sharon L. Oswald, "Sexual Harassment in the Workplace: A View Through the Eyes of Courts" (1990), 41 *Labour L.J.* 786.
[63] 805 F. 2d 611, 41 E.P.D. para 36,643 (6th Cir. 1986).
[64] *Ibid.*, at 620.

circumstances".[65] What is reasonable to one person may be totally offensive to another.

However, just one year later, the Sixth Circuit in *Yates v. Avco Corp.*,[66] stated:

> ... [I]n a sexual harassment case involving a male supervisor's harassment of a female subordinate, it seems only reasonable that the person standing in the shoes of the employee should be the reasonable woman since the plaintiff in this type of case is required to be a member of a protected class and is by definition female.[67]

In 1988, the Fifth Circuit dealt with the issue of graffiti (cartoons that depicted both men and women in sexually demeaning postures) in *Bennett v. Corron & Black Corp.*[68] The lower court in this case held that "while sexually oriented and offensive, they were not based on the sex of the plaintiff". The Court of Appeals reversed that finding on the basis that:

> ... any reasonable person would have to regard these cartoons as highly offensive to a women who seeks to deal with her fellow employees and clients with professional dignity and without the barrier of sexual differentiation and abuse.[69]

Again in *Waltman v. International Paper Co.*,[70] the Fifth Circuit held that the presence of sexual graffiti in the plant constituted the existence of hostile environment.

However, the courts also differ on the issue of prompt remedial action by the employer. In the *Bennett* case, the court found the employer liable on the ground that it failed to take prompt and adequate action because he waited *one day* to remove offensive cartoons from the men's bathroom.[71] On the other hand, in *Steele v. Offshore Shipbuilding Inc.*,[72] despite the fact that an officer's sexual joking and innuendos created a hostile environment for two female employees, the court held that the employer was not liable because he had taken prompt and remedial action in the form of an immediate reprimand.

---

[65] *Ibid.*
[66] 819 F. 2d 630, 43 E.P.D. para 37,086 (6th Cir. 1987).
[67] *Ibid.*, at 637.
[68] 845 F. 2d 105 (5th Cir. 1988).
[69] *Ibid.*, at 106.
[70] 875 F. 2d 468, 50 E.P.D. para 39,106 (5th Cir. 1989).
[71] 845 F. 2d 105 (5th Cir. 1988).
[72] 867 F. 2d 1311, 49 E.P.D. para. 38,839 (11th Cir. 1989).

In *Nelson v. Reisher*,[73] the court found that the female supervisor and co-workers had created a "hostile environment" for the male victim with numerous criticisms and reprimands for a period of three years. The court awarded him $1,500 in damages.

This case is noteworthy because it is among the few hostile environment cases, or for that matter sexual harassment cases, involving a male victim.

In recent years, several American states[74] have specifically prohibited sexual harassment in the workplace and in education either by legislative amendments or by executive orders. Some State Civil Rights Commissions[75] as well as state courts[76] have followed the federal lead in determining that sexual harassment amounts to discrimination on the basis of sex and, thus, the conduct contravenes the state laws.

D. DEVELOPMENT OF SEXUAL HARASSMENT LAW IN CANADA

Jurisprudence on sexual harassment in Canada began in 1980 with the *Cherie Bell* case,[77] where two complainants alleged that they had been sexually harassed by their employer. The complainants claimed that they were dismissed because they refused the advances of their employer — the restaurant owner. Being the first case of this kind in Canada, Chairperson Owen Shime of the Ontario Board of Inquiry, thoroughly and lucidly discussed the purpose of the *Human Rights Code* and the general principles applicable to situations of this sort. He concluded that the purpose of human rights legislation was

---

[73] (4th Cir. 1989), 88-1133.
[74] See for example *Michigan Civil Rights Act* and *Minnesota Human Rights Act*. While Title VII sexual harassment suits are now proliferating, as yet few reported decisions interpret state legislation that directly or indirectly prohibits sexual harassment of employees. Most provisions in state legislation, regulations or guidelines that explicitly prohibit sexual harassment are of very recent origin and there appear to be only a few reported decisions concerning their interpretation. See *Continental Can Co. v. State of Minnesota*, 23 E.P.D. para. 30,997 (Minn. S. Ct. 1980).
[75] See for example Michigan Civil Rights Commission, *Annual Report*, (1979-1980), p. 7. *Hamilton v. Appleton Electric Co.*, E.R.D. Case 7301025, S. of Wisc., Department of Industry and Labour and Human Relations, October 1, 1976.
[76] See for example *Continental Can Co. v. Minnesota*, supra, note 74; *Seritis v. Lane*, 22 E.P.D. para. 30,747 (Cal. Sup. Ct. 1980).
[77] (Ont. 1980), 1 C.H.R.R. D/155 (Shime).

to establish *uniform* working conditions for employees and to remove matters such as "race, creed, colour, age, sex, marital status, nationality, or place of origin" as relevant consideration in the workplace. He pointed out that the *Human Rights Code* prohibits the commonly held values of "freedom, equality and rights" from becoming negative factors in the employment relationship.

Chairperson Shime discussed at some length whether or not "sexual harassment" constituted discrimination on the basis of sex and laid the foundation of sexual harassment law in Canada by declaring that "sexual harassment" amounts to sex discrimination prohibited under the *Human Rights Code*. He stated:

> But what about sexual harassment? Clearly a person who is disadvantaged because of her sex is being discriminated against in her employment when employer conduct denies her financial rewards because of her sex, or exacts some form of sexual compliance to improve or maintain her existing benefits. *The evil to be remedied is the utilization of economic power or authority so as to restrict a woman's guaranteed and equal access to the work place and all of its benefits, free from extraneous pressures having to do with the mere fact that she is a woman.* Where a woman's equal access is denied or when terms and conditions differ when compared to male employees, the woman is being discriminated against.
>
> *The forms of prohibited conduct that, in my view, are discriminatory run the gamut from overt gender based activity, such as coerced intercourse to unsolicited physical contact to persistent propositions to more subtle conduct such as gender based insults and taunting, which may reasonably be perceived to create a negative psychological and emotional work environment.* There is no reason why the law, which reaches into the work place so as to protect the work environment from physical or chemical pollution or extremes of temperature, ought not to protect employees as well from negative psychological and mental effects where adverse and gender directed conduct emanating from a management hierarchy may reasonably be construed to be a condition of employment.
>
> The prohibition of such conduct is not without its dangers. One must be cautious that the law not inhibit normal social contact between management and employees or normal discussion between management and employees. It is not abnormal, nor should it be prohibited, activity for a supervisor to become socially involved with an employee. *An invitation to dinner is not an invitation to a complaint. The danger or the evil that is to be avoided is coerced or compelled social contact where the employee's refusal to participate may result in a loss of employee benefits.* Such coercion or compulsion may be overt or subtle but if any feature of employment becomes reasonably dependent on reciprocating a social relationship proffered by a member of management, then the overture becomes a condition of employment and may be considered to be discriminatory.
>
> Again, The Code ought not to be seen or perceived as inhibiting free speech.

If sex cannot be discussed between supervisor and employee neither can other values such as race, colour, creed, which are contained in The Code, be discussed. Thus, differences of opinion by an employee where sexual matters are discussed may not involve a violation of The Code; *it is only when the language or words may be reasonably construed to form a condition of employment that The Code provides a remedy*. Thus, the frequent and persistent taunting by a supervisor of an employee because of his or her colour is discriminatory activity under The Code and, *similarly, the frequent and persistent taunting of an employee by a supervisor because of his or her sex is discriminatory activity under The Code..*

However, persistent and frequent conduct is not a condition for adverse finding under The Code because a single incident of an employee being denied equality of the employment because of sex is also prohibited activity.[78]

Thus, the Board, in the *Cherie Bell* case, unequivocally stated that sexual harassment came within the general prohibition against sex discrimination in relation to the terms or conditions of employment. It concluded that sexual harassment in the workplace could constitute a breach of the *Human Rights Code* and that prohibited conduct included everything from verbal solicitation to unwelcome physical contact.

However, in the result, the Board on the facts of this case did not find the respondent employer guilty of sexual harassment.[79]

Coutroubis v. Sklavos Printing[80] was the first Canadian case where the employer was found guilty of sex discrimination for causing sexual harassment to his employees in violation of the *Human Rights Code*. The Board of Inquiry, chaired by Professor E. J. Ratushny, without referring to the *Cherie Bell* decision, held that sexual harassment was prohibited under s. 4(1)(g) of the *Ontario Human Rights Code*.[81] The Board stated that where complainants choose to leave their employment rather than endure unwelcome sexual advances, the complainant may be deemed to have been dismissed. In effect, in such a situation there is a constructive termination of employment. The Board of Inquiry described the incident involving the complainant Coutroubis as follows:

> The Respondent began to "joke" with Meri Coutroubis about her being too young to have lost interest in boys. (She recently had separated from her husband.) At approximately 9:00 p.m., while she was working in the darkroom,

---

[78] *Ibid.*, at D/156 (paras. 1388-1392).
[79] The decision of Chairperson Shime in this regard has been questioned in certain circles. See C. Backhouse, "Bell v. Flaming Steer Steakhouse: Canada's First Sexual Harassment Decision" (1981), 19 *U.W.O.L. Rev.* 141.
[80] (Ont. 1981), 2 C.H.R.R. D/457 (Ratushny).
[81] R.S.O. 1980, c. 340.

he entered the room and put his arms around her and tried to kiss her. Although she resisted, he succeeded in kissing her. When she started to scream, he released her and she immediately left for home.[82]

The incident involving the complainant Kekatos was described as follows:

> Shortly after Mrs. Sklavos left for her holiday in Greece, in late July, the Respondent began to speak suggestively to Irene Kekatos with crude jokes and references to her love life. He also began touching her. She responded with angry looks and asked him to leave her alone. On the Monday in question, he approached her while she was working at the typesetter and spoke in a lewd manner. He then grabbed her with his hands on her breasts and bit her cheek. She began to scream, attracting the Respondent's brother who had been in another part of the building. However, since the door to the room had earlier been locked, he could only knock at the window. The Respondent then stopped and, after some hesitation, gave Irene Kekatos the keys, permitting her to leave.[83]

The Board found that there had been "flagrant violations of Section 4(1)(g) of the *Code* by the Respondent in relation to both complainants".[84] Professor Ratushny then went on to award the complainants special damages for lost wages and general damages for the psychological injury that they suffered.

The next case involving a complaint of sexual harassment was *Hughes v. Dollar Snack Bar*.[85] In this case, the complainants were subjected to unwelcome physical contact by the respondent to areas of their bodies that are commonly associated with sexual advances. The Board of Inquiry, chaired by Professor Robert W. Kerr, found that their refusal to submit to the employer's sexual advances had resulted in the complainants' dismissal from their employment. Chairperson Kerr adopted the reasoning of the *Cherie Bell* case and said:

> In my view, harassment based on a factor in respect of which discrimination is unlawful is inherently in violation of the Ontario Human Rights Code since it singles out the victim for treatment on the basis of that factor.[86]

---

[82] *Coutroubis v. Sklavos Printing* (Ont. 1981), 2 C.H.R.R. D/457 (para. 4128) (Ratushny).
[83] *Ibid.*, at D/458 (para. 4134).
[84] *Ibid.*, at D/458 (para. 4136).
[85] (Ont. 1982), 3 C.H.R.R. D/1014 (Kerr).
[86] *Ibid.*, at D/1015 (para. 9022).

The Board, in other words, stated that harassment itself, based upon prohibited grounds under the *Code*, is proscribed just as other forms of discrimination are. Chairperson Kerr referred to his previous decision in *Singh v. Domglas*[87] where he had adopted that reasoning in the context of racially motivated harassment.

The Board found that the complainants were subjected to sexual harassment by the respondent as a condition of their employment which constituted discrimination on account of their sex. The Board further pointed out that where the respondent was the only person with authority over the complainant in her employment, where sexual advances continued over the complainant's objections, and where these advances occurred right in the workplace during the course of employment, they should be interpreted as a condition of employment. The Board awarded the complainants compensation for past wages and general damages for the embarrassment and humiliation that they suffered.

The next case was *Cox v. Jagbritte Inc.*[88] In this case the two complainants chose to leave their employment because of the sexual harassment they suffered. The Board of Inquiry, chaired by Professor Peter A. Cumming, found that the respondent employer physically and verbally abused both complainants during their employment. Their employer persistently urged his sexual desires on the complainants and other female employees. The respondent employer was acting under the sexist impression that the female employees, despite their obvious resistance to his sexual advances, actually enjoyed such behaviour.

The Board observed that "even though he knew they objected strongly to his oral and physical sexual advances, he persisted in his attempts and made their subjection to such conduct on his part a term and condition of their employment."[89]

In this case, Professor Cumming traced the development of the jurisprudence in the United States on sexual harassment. He rejected the requirement in earlier American cases that there must be a causal connection between the harassment and adverse employment consequences. He agreed with the American decision in *Bundy v. Jackson*[90] that sexual harassment, even if it does not result in adverse employment

---

[87] (Ont. 1980), unreported (Kerr). A copy of the case can be obtained from the Ontario Human Rights Commission, 400 University Avenue, Toronto, Ontario.
[88] (Ont. 1982), 3 C.H.R.R. D/609 (Cumming).
[89] *Ibid.*, at D/616 (para. 5593).
[90] 641 F. 2d 934 (D.C. Cir. 1981).

consequences, is a discriminatory term or condition of employment simply because it poisons the work environment. He stated:

> Interestingly enough, the *Bundy* decision is very similar to the Ontario case of *Bell*, supra. there, Mr. O. B. Shime Q.C. stated that the "taunting" of female employees could amount to a violation of the *Ontario Human Rights Code*. Thus, the U.S. and Ontario position seems to be equally broad, and equally in need of specific legislation.[91]

In the *Cox* case, the Board found that the respondent employer discriminated against the complainants because of their sex within the meaning of s. 4 of the *Code*. The Board concluded:

> There is a causal connection in the instant situation between the sexual harassment and adverse employment consequences. The Complainants could only continue to be employed if they subjected themselves to sexual harassment, a condition of employment forced upon them because they were female employees. The sexual advances, in effect, were the cause of termination of the Complainants' employment. The Complainants' response to the harassment, terminating their employment, was warranted under the circumstances.[92]

Normally, sexual harassment at the workplace is alleged to have taken place after the establishment of an employer-employee relationship and during the course of employment. However, in *Mitchell v. Traveller Inn (Sudbury) Ltd.*,[93] the complainant had received an offer of employment from the respondent. When she reported for work, she spoke to the manager. He, at that time, made certain remarks (asked her to go to the backroom with him) which she interpreted as having a sexual connotation and declined. He advised her that, if she did not, she would not have a job. He also offered to drive her home, suggesting it might be fun. She insisted that he call a taxi for her and she left in the taxi.

The Board of Inquiry, chaired by Professor Kerr, found that Mr. Czaikowski's conduct constituted sexual harassment even though there was nothing explicitly sexual about his remarks. The Board observed:

> There was nothing explicitly sexual about Mr. Czaikowski's remarks, making it at least conceivable that this was simply a case of misunderstanding. On the other hand, harassment does not have to be explicit to be contrary to the Human Rights Code. Harassment can be effected by implication. Stereo-

---

[91] *Cox v. Jagbritte Inc.*, supra, note 88, at D/612 (para. 5557).
[92] *Ibid.*, at D/616 (para. 5594).
[93] (Ont. 1981), 2 C.H.R.R. D/590 (Kerr).

typing, the very thing which human rights laws are designed to combat, is actually a facilitator of insult by mere implication. It would be strange if the law allowed harassment to escape its application because, through stereotyping the harassment was implicit, rather than explicit.[94]

In *Ross v. Gendall*,[95] the Saskatchewan Board of Inquiry found that the complainant was sexually harassed *during a job interview by her prospective employer*. The Board stated that section 16 of the *Saskatchewan Human Rights Code*,[96] which prohibits sex discrimination with respect to employment, has the effect of prohibiting sexual harassment at a job interview by a prospective employer. The Board ordered the employer to pay the complainant $1,500 in compensation for the damage to her feelings and self-respect.

Thus it is evident that if an employee is refused employment, or if employment is terminated as a result of his or her refusal to participate in or to acquiesce to such gender directed conduct, then such refusal or termination is discriminatory and prohibited. If an employee's work environment or benefits are dependent upon such participation, acquiescence or endurance of such conduct, then that too is discriminatory and contrary to the human rights laws.

Olarte et al. v. Commodore Business Machines Ltd.[97] is the lengthiest[98] sex discrimination case in Ontario so far. This case is also significant because for the first time, the complaint of sexual harassment was filed against a large multinational corporation.[99] In this case, six female employees charged that their supervisor, Mr. Rafael DeFilippis, sexually harassed them, and when they refused his overtures for sexual contact, they were treated harshly and discriminated against in matters of employment. They alleged that the corporate respondent had knowledge of and acquiesced to the sexual harassment. Sexual encounters in this case ranged from verbal, lewd remarks, physical

---

[94] *Ibid.*, at D/591-92 (para. 5401).
[95] (Sask. 1989), 10 C.H.R.R. D/5836 (Piche).
[96] S.S. 1979, S-24.1.
[97] (Ont. 1983) 4 C.H.R.R. D/1705 (Cumming); affd (*sub nom. Commodore Business Machines Ltd. v. Ont. Minister of Labour*) (Ont. 1985), 6 C.H.R.R. D/2833 (Div. Ct.).
[98] The hearing in this case lasted some 36 days, including 9 days of argument, with some 56 witnesses and 117 exhibits and 37 volumes of evidence and arguments.
[99] In the earlier sexual harassment cases, it was the small employer, usually the self-employed owner of a restaurant or pizza outfit, and the owner himself was the harasser.

advances, sexual propositions and requests to the threat of sexual intercourse in the face of clear objections.

The respondent, Mr. DeFilippis, completely denied the charges of sexual harassment. Rather, Mr. DeFillipis alleged that the six complainants were lying and formed a conspiracy against him for two reasons: firstly, with the hope of pecuniary gain through this proceeding, and secondly, with the objective of getting back at him because, as a foreman, he had been too strict a disciplinarian, too demanding in terms of production, and too mean in terms of criticism towards the workers on his shift.

The Board of Inquiry, chaired by Professor Peter A. Cumming, however, rejected his defence and his testimony by observing that:

> Wherever there is a contradiction between his evidence and that of the Complainants, I accept their evidence and reject his. *He is a liar, and was prepared to say anything at all to extricate himself from the problem he confronted with the Complainants.*[100] [Emphasis added]

The Board of Inquiry found that the foreman, Mr. DeFilippis, was guilty of sexually harassing the complainants and observed:

> I have no doubt in concluding that the individual Respondent, Rafael DeFilippis was guilty of sexual harassment toward each of the six Complainants.[101]
>
> . . .
>
> It is clear from all the evidence that Mr. DeFilippis persistently sexually propositioned, used language that was overtly or implicitly sexual in connotation, made sexual advances and on occasion touched for sexual reasons, female employees working under his control, and that he persisted in this conduct, even after their initial and continuing forcefully stated rejections.[102]

The Board emphasized:

> The besieged became the besiegers, making veiled suggestions to Mr. DeFilippis that they were going to bring him to justice. This in turn caused Mr. DeFilippis to be more spiteful toward them and fearful of what they might do, so he fired Mrs. Mejia May 4, 1979, and terminated Mrs. Munoz as soon as he could manufacture an excuse (June 11, 1979), and Ms. Benel similarly when he knew

---

[100] *Olarte et al. v. Commodore Business Machines Ltd.*, *supra*, note 97 at D/1733 (para. 14787) (Cumming).
[101] *Ibid.*, at D/1732 (para. 14783).
[102] *Ibid.*, at D/1733 (para. 14787).

she had gone to a lawyer (June 13, 1979) and proceeded to ignore Mrs. Biljak's sick benefits claim after she left June 13, 1979. Similarly, Mr. DeFilippis had fired Mrs. Mejia in May because she had rejected his sexual advances and because he was fearful that she might cause difficulties for him with senior management by complaining. Mr. DeFilippis wanted Mrs. Mejia, Mrs. Munoz, and Ms. Benel fired to get back at them for rejecting his sexual advances, and so that they could not cause him difficulties by complaining.[103]

The Board concluded:

> The Complainants were exploited because they were females, and because they were dependent and vulnerable. They needed work, and had to endure continuing sexual harassment if they wished to continue to work, and had to endure increased criticism, and insults and verbal abuse because they would not subject themselves to the sexual advances of their foreman.[104]

Dealing with the issue of corporate responsibility the Board stated:

> All of the acts of sexual harassment occurred in the course of carrying on the corporation's business at its Warden Avenue plant. Once an employee, like Mr. DeFilippis, is part of the directing mind, and the contraventions come in his performing his corporate function as they did in the instant case, a corporation such as Commodore is itself also *personally* in breach of the Code.
> So far as the six Complainants were concerned, Mr. DeFilippis was, in effect, their true employer. Commodore put him in this position of management; therefore, this factor, coupled with Mr. DeFilippis' unlawful acts of sexual harassment coming within the course of carrying on the corporation's business, renders the corporation *personally* in breach of the Code.[105]

Robichaud v. Brennan[106] was the first case on sexual harassment under the *Canadian Human Rights Act.* In that case, the Chairperson

---

[103] *Ibid.*, at D/1734-35 (para. 14798).
[104] *Ibid.*, at D/1735 (para. 14801).
[105] *Ibid.*, D/1746-47 (paras. 14889-14890).
[106] *Robichaud v. Brennan* (Can. 1982), 3 C.H.R.R. D/977 (Abbott); revd (Can. 1983), 4 C.H.R.R. D/1272 (Review Tribunal — Dyer); affd in part (*sub nom. Treasury Board v. Robichaud*) (Can. 1985), 6 C.H.R.R. D/2695 (Fed. Ct.); on appeal the Federal Court of Canada unanimously upheld the Review Tribunal ruling that Bonnie Robichaud was discriminated against because of her sex when she was sexually harassed by her superior, Dennis Brennan. However, in a split decision, the court reversed the Review Tribunal on the issue of liability of the Treasury Board and found that the Treasury Board was not liable for the discrimination

of the Canadian Human Rights Tribunal, Professor Abbott, quoted the famous excerpt from Chairperson Shime's decision in the *Cherie Bell* case that sexual harassment amounts to discrimination based on sex and stated:

> I find this excerpt to be highly persuasive. With great respect I would adopt its reasoning as my own.[107]

The Tribunal pointed out:

> It will be recalled that Section 7(b) of the Act (Canadian Human Rights Act) makes no express reference to sexual harassment. But, in the light of the interpretations placed on similar terms in similar human rights legislation in other jurisdictions, I am strongly persuaded that some sexual encounters, which might be characterized as "sexual harassment", do fall within Section 7(b).[108]

The Tribunal concluded that the *Canadian Human Rights Act* was intended to prohibit the imposition of adverse employment conditions based on a person's gender. As well, the imposition of adverse employment conditions in retaliation for the rejection of an employer's or supervisor's sexual advances would likewise be contrary to the intent of s. 7(b) of the Act.[109]

The complainant in the *Robichaud* case worked as a probationary lead hand on the civilian staff at the Canadian Armed Forces Base, North Bay, Ontario. She filed a complaint alleging that her foreman made sexual advances towards her and had attempted to intimidate her once she refused his advances. The original Tribunal dismissed the complaint holding that while sexual contact had occurred, the complainant had participated voluntarily and thus there had been no harassment. The Tribunal said:

---

practised by her supervisor, Dennis Brennan. On further appeal, the Supreme Court of Canada reversed the Federal Court decision and found that the Treasury Board was liable for the discriminatory conduct of its employees (Can. 1987), 8 C.H.R.R. D/4326 (S.C.C.). For further discussion on employer's liability see Chapter 4, *infra*.

[107] *Ibid.*, at D/980 (para. 8707) (Abbott).

[108] *Ibid.*, at D/979-980 (para. 8706) (Abbott).

[109] Section 7 of the *Canadian Human Rights Act*, R.S.C. 1985, c. H-6, reads as follows:
It is a discriminatory practice, directly or indirectly,

. . .

(b) in the course of employment, to differentiate adversely in relation to an employee, on a prohibited ground of discrimination.

Section 3 of the Act designates "sex" as a prohibited ground of discrimination.

Ch. 1 - Sexual Harassment and Human Rights Legislation

> I can only conclude that Mrs. Robichaud's rejection and protests were inconsistent with her conduct, except for the protest on May 25, 1979, and were not apt to put Mr Brennan on notice that his conduct was perceived by Mrs. Robichaud as harassment.[110]

On appeal, the Review Tribunal[111] overturned the lower tribunal's decision and found that Mr. Brennan was guilty of sexual harassment. The Review Tribunal held that the complainant had established a *prima facie* case of sexual harassment and having done so the onus shifted to the defendant to show that the acts did not constitute sexual harassment. The defendant failed to discharge the reverse onus.

The Review Tribunal disagreed with the proposition contained in the original decision that the nature of the acts of fellatio, masturbation and fondling are of such a highly consensual nature that Mrs. Robichaud could not have engaged in them unless she was fully consenting to do so and it accepted her evidence that she submitted to the encounters because of fear and intimidation and threats with respect to her work. The Review Tribunal concluded:

> [T]he facts clearly showed a pattern of sexual inquiry innuendo on the part of Mr. Brennan, and his awareness of Mrs. Robichaud's vulnerability as a probationer. The cumulative effect was to create a poisoned work environment for Mrs. Robichaud. In addition, the facts showed that this pattern of harassment and abuse of authority extended not only to Mrs. Robichaud but to at least one other female on the cleaning staff.
>
> Accordingly, we have no hesitation in finding that Mr. Brennan was guilty of sexual harassment on two grounds:
>
> 1) By reason of his failure to rebut the *prima facie* case established by Mrs. Robichaud;
> 2) By reason of his creation of a poisoned work environment; both contrary to the *Canadian Human Rights Act*, Section 7(b).[112]

It may be noted that the Review Tribunal did not base its findings entirely on job related consequences but emphasized the aspect of "poisoned work environment". As stated earlier, this concept was first recognized by the American court in *Bundy v. Jackson* as a form of "sex discrimination".

---

[110] *Robichaud v. Brennan* (Can. 1982), *supra*, note 106, at D/981 (para. 8712) (Abbott).
[111] *Robichaud v. Brennan* (Can. 1983), *supra*, note 106 (Review Tribunal — Dyer).
[112] *Ibid.*, at D/1274 (paras. 11049-11050).

In *Kotyk v. Can. Employment Immigration Commn.*,[113] the Canadian Human Rights Tribunal found that the harasser's conduct went far beyond the realm of "office flirtation". It covered the entire gamut of prohibited activity: "overt gender based activity such as coerced intercourse, to unsolicited physical contact, to persistent propositions, to more subtle conduct such as gender based insults and taunting."[114] Moreover, the harasser exploited the complainant's vulnerability caused by her marital problems and knowing that she feared for her job.

The Tribunal found that the conduct of Mr. Chuba as a manager in this regard was inexcusable. It held:

> The fact that Ms. Kotyk engaged in sexual intercourse with him at Foam Lake does not weaken the conclusion that Mr. Chuba engaged in discriminatory conduct. Her consent was based on her fears for her job and was preceded by a course of conduct which had as its object to wear her down, and which succeeded in this intent. The conduct took place over a six month period, on a consistent, deliberate basis. His methods were such as to suggest that by demeaning her and constantly making sexual suggestions, he could ingratiate himself to her. There is no question but that Mr. Chuba's conduct was work-related and that it had adverse employment consequences. I refer specifically to the letter of reprimand and the circumstances surrounding the evaluation.[115]

The Tribunal concluded that the working environment in this case was such that it would have been almost impossible to carry on work in a normal way.

> Because of Mr. Chuba's pressures, Ms. Kotyk's workplace became intimidating, hostile, and offensive. It speaks well of Ms. Kotyk's stamina and strength of character that she did not quit her job or apply for a transfer. Mr. Chuba's conduct in relation to Jane Kotyk constitutes sexual harassment and as such is adverse differentiation on the grounds of sex as prohibited by section 7 of the Act.[116]

The Tribunal warned that:

> "People in Mr. Chuba's position — manager of a government office — must realize that there are great risks involved in taking this sort of advantage of their female employees. It is precisely the type of conduct that the Act is meant

---

[113] (Can., 1983), 4 C.H.R.R. D/1416 (Ashley).
[114] *Ibid.*, at D/1428 (para. 12232).
[115] *Ibid.* (para. 1225).
[116] *Ibid.* (para. 12236).

to prevent. Section 2 of the Act states that persons should be able to make the life for themselves that they wish, without being hindered in or prevented from doing so by discriminatory practices based on . . . sex."[117]

Jack Chuba, who was the Manager of the Yorkton, Saskatchewan C.E.I.C. Centre and the individual who was found by the Tribunal to have sexually harassed the complainants, appealed this decision to a three person Review Tribunal. The Review Tribunal upheld the lower Tribunal's decision and ruled that sexual harassment is prohibited by the general prohibition against sex discrimination under the Act.[118]

The Review Tribunal also rejected that appellant's argument that "sexual discrimination under the Act is only applicable where the employer or a person acting as his servant or agent differentiates adversely in relation to an employee because in the general sense that person is a male or female as the case may be and not because of sexual preferences".[119] It stated:

> [W]e do not think that it is a condition precedent to sex discrimination that the victim of the improper conduct must always be member of one gender. There are a number of theoretical permutations and combinations that could give rise to sexual harassment. For example, a male manager may commit heterosexual sexual harassment upon a female employee or homosexual sexual harassment upon a male employee. Similar combinations can be imagined if the role were reversed and the manager were female and the employee male. Indeed, the harassment may be both gender-related and based upon sexual propensity as where a homosexual employer exploits a homosexual employee.
>
> The central problem in all of these situations is that a specific employee (whether male or female and whether heterosexual or homosexual) is the subject of harassment and therefore has had on him or her, conditions of employment which were not inflicted upon employees of the opposite gender. The target of the harassment suffers disparate treatment based on sex. As was noted in *Bundy v. Jackson* (1981) 641 F. 2d at 942 (U.S. Court of Appeals):
>
> " . . . In each instance the question is one of but-for causation: would the complaining employee have suffered the harassment had he or she been of different gender? . . . Only by *reductio ad absurdum* could we imagine a case of harassment that is not sex discrimination — where a bisexual supervisor harasses men and women alike."[120]

---

[117] *Ibid.* (para. 12237).
[118] *Chuba v. Canadian Employment and Immigration Commission* (Can. 1983), 5 C.H.R.R. D/1895) (Review Tribunal — Lederman).
[119] *Ibid.*, at D/1900 (para. 16282).
[120] *Ibid.*, at D/1901 (para. 16283-84).

The Review Tribunal further rejected the argument that a manager is discriminating against a women not because of her sex, but because he finds her sexually attractive and consequently, he is not harassing all women in his employment but merely this particular woman.[121] The Review Tribunal again quoted from the famous American decision in *Bundy v. Jackson*:

> sex discrimination . . . is not limited to disparate treatment founded solely or categorically on gender. Rather discrimination is sex discrimination whenever sex is for no legitimate reason a substantial factor in the discrimination.[122]

The Review Tribunal stated that the crux of the matter is whether the basis for the specific discrimination was sex related. If so, there is discrimination by reason of sex even though other employees of the same gender are not subjected to such conduct. Applying these principles, the Review Tribunal found that the discriminatory conduct, in this case, was based upon "sex" a ground proscribed under the *Canadian Human Rights Act*.[123]

It appears that the Human Rights Tribunal in *Potapczyk v. MacBain*[124] took into consideration that wider issue of the fate of women in the workplace and gave the broadest interpretation so far to "sex discrimination". It did not confine itself to the technical meaning of "sex discrimination", rather it focussed on the disadvantageous position in which women are subjected to unhappy and unfair treatment in employment. The Tribunal, it appears, read into the *Canadian Human Rights Act*, that it prohibited not only discrimination but callous mistreatment of women in employment.

> So, although this unpleasant conduct by Mr. MacBain was only part of a more general abusive and oppressive mistreatment of these women, it was in contravention of the law. *It is now in the public interest as articulated under the Canadian Human Rights Act that women in the workplace not be subjected to this kind of discomfort merely because of their sex and they are not to be treated differentially in this fashion.*
>
> . . .
>
> It is a type of conduct by an employer who regards his female staff as sex ornaments or objects or feels at liberty to treat them as such by the nature

---

[121] *Ibid.* (para. 16285).
[122] 641 F. 2d 934, at 942 (D.C. Cir. 1981).
[123] *Ibid..* (para. 16286).
[124] (Can. 1984), 5 C.H.R.R. D/2285 (Lederman).

of his rude personal comments and unwanted physical closeness.[125] [Emphasis added]

Human Rights Tribunals in other Canadian jurisdictions have instantly followed the philosophy and reasoning of the *Cherie Bell* case, and held that sexual harassment amounts to discrimination on the basis of sex and is prohibited under their respective human rights statute. For example, in British Columbia in *Zarankin v. Johnstone c.o.b. as Wessex Inn*;[126] in Alberta in *Deisting v. Dollar Pizza 1978 Ltd.*;[127] in Saskatchewan in *Phillips v. Hermiz*;[128] in Manitoba in *Hufnagel v. Osama Enterprizes Ltd.*;[129] in Quebec in *Foisy v. Bell Canada*;[130] in New Brunswick in *Doherty v. Lodger's Int'l. Ltd.*;[131] and in Nova Scotia in *Mehta v. Mackinnon et al.*[132]

The *Cherie Bell* case, therefore, established the important precedent that sexual harassment amounts to sex discrimination under existing human rights statutes (even though those statutes do not specifically state it).

The cases discussed above clearly demonstrate that the prohibition in human rights statutes against sex discrimination in the form of sexual harassment is a far-reaching one. The statutes proscribe conduct as blatant and offensive as might constitute a trespass to the person, and as subtle as implicitly suggestive remarks. These decisions indicate that complaints have been upheld if an employer dismissed or refused to hire a complainant for her failure to comply with sexual advances, and for constructive dismissal or as an employer, by sexually harassing employees, imposed discriminatory terms or conditions of employment, or created a humiliating and poisoned working environment. There is no doubt that Human Rights Tribunals, by their creative interpretations of the human rights statutes, have made a substantial penetration into the workplace in order to eradicate sexual harassment.

It may be pointed out that the courts in various Canadian jurisdictions have also put their stamp of approval on the philosophy and reasoning of the *Cherie Bell* case. For example, the Federal Court

---

[125] *Ibid.* (paras. 19357-58).
[126] (B.C. 1984), 5 C.H.R.R. D/2274 (Smith).
[127] (Alta. 1982), 3 C.H.R.R. D/898 (Clarke).
[128] (Sask. 1984), 5 C.H.R.R. D/2450 (Katzman).
[129] (Man. 1982), 3 C.H.R.R. D/922 (Teskey).
[130] (Que. 1985), 6 C.H.R.R. D/2817 (Que. S.C.).
[131] (N.B.1982), 3 C.H.R.R. D/628 (Gross).
[132] (N.S. 1985), 6 C.H.R.R. D/2861; affd 67 N.S.R. (2d) 429 (C.A.); leave to appeal to S.C.C. dismissed Nov. 21/85, 69 N.S.R. (2d) 450.

of Canada in *Treasury Board v. Robichaud* stated that the language of s. 7 of the *Canadian Human Rights Act* is

> broad enough to cover the situation in the present case of a superior in the workplace exercising his position and authority over a subordinate of the other sex, who was in a vulnerable position, to intimidate her and secure participation in his sexual overtures and conduct. Though the harassment was by a supervisor rather than by an employer the case appears to me to be similar in principle to that referred to in *Cherie Bell and Anna Korczak v. Ernest Ladas and The Flaming Steer Steak House and Tavern Inc.*[133]

Similarly the British Columbia Supreme Court in *Johnstone c.o.b. as Wessex Inn v. Zarankin*,[134] the Supreme Court of Nova Scotia in *Mehta v. Mackinnon et al.*,[135] the Quebec Superior Court in *Foisy v. Bell Canada*,[136] and the Supreme Court of Ontario in *Commodore Business Machines Ltd. v. Ont. Minister of Labour*[137] have demonstrated their acceptance of the principle that "sexual harassment" constitutes discrimination based on the ground of "sex".

E. STATUTORY AMENDMENTS TO BAN SEXUAL HARASSMENT

Ontario was the first to amend its *Human Rights Code* to specifically ban "sexual harassment". The Ontario Legislature, by the 1981 amendments to the *Code*, had finally accepted the condemnation of "sexual harassment" as interpreted by the judiciary (Boards of Inquiry) and thereby extended support to the cause of eliminating sexual harassment from the workplace. The statutory provisions provided the much needed ammunition for human rights agencies to combat "sexual harassment"

The specific provisions of the Ontario *Human Rights Code*[138] proscribe "sexual harassment" in the workplace. Section 7(2) and (3) of the *Code* read as follows:

---

[133] *Treasury Board v. Bonnie Robichaud* (Can. 1985), 6 C.H.R.R. D/2695, at D/2701 (para. 22267) (Fed. Ct.).
[134] (B.C. 1985), 6 C.H.R.R. D/2651, 85 CLLC 17,022 (B.C. S.C.).
[135] *Supra*, note 132.
[136] (Que. 1985), 6 C.H.R.R. D/2817 (S.C.).
[137] (Ont. 1985), 6 C.H.R.R. D/2833 (Div. Ct.).
[138] R.S.O. 1990, c. H.19.

(2) Every person who is an employee has a right to freedom from harassment in the workplace because of sex by his or her employer or agent of the employer or by another employee.
(3) Every person has a right to be free from,
(a) a sexual solicitation or advance made by a person in a position to confer, grant or deny a benefit or advancement to the person where the person making the solicitation or advance knows or ought reasonably to know that it is unwelcome; or
(b) a reprisal or a threat of reprisal for the rejection of a sexual solicitation or advance where the reprisal is made or threatened by a person in a position to confer, grant or deny a benefit or advancement to the person.

Further the *Code* has defined the term "harassment" to mean "engaging in a course of vexatious comment or conduct that is known or ought reasonably to be known to be unwelcome".[139] The *Code*, however, has not defined "sexual harassment".

The amendments in the *Code* have also empowered a Board of Inquiry to make an order to prevent the continuation or repetition of harassment and to retain jurisdiction to hear complaints of continuation of violation against the party to the proceedings.[140]

41(2) Where a board makes a finding under subsection (1) that a right is infringed on the ground of harassment under subsection 2(2) or subsection 5(2) or conduct under section 7, and the board finds that a person who is a party to the proceeding,
(a) knew or was in possession of knowledge from which the person ought to have known of the infringement; and
(b) had the authority by reasonably available means to penalize or prevent the conduct and failed to use it,
the board shall remain seized of the matter and upon complaint of a continuation or repetition of the infringement of the right the Commission may investigate the complaint and, subject to subsection 36(2), request the board to re-convene and if the board finds that a person who is a party to the proceeding,
(c) knew or was in possession of knowledge from which the person ought to have known of the repetition of infringement; and
(d) had the authority by reasonably available means to penalize or prevent the continuation or repetition of the conduct and failed to use it,
the board may make an order requiring the person to take what ever sanctions or steps are reasonably available to prevent any further continuation or repetition of the infringement of the right.

---

[139] *Ibid*, s. 10(f).
[140] *Ibid.*, s. 41(2).

In 1982, Quebec amended its *Charter of Human Rights and Freedoms*[141] and provided:

> 10.1 No one may harass a person on the basis of any ground mentioned in section 10.

Section 10 designates "sex" as one of the prohibited grounds of discrimination.

In 1983, the Canadian Parliament amended the *Canadian Human Rights Act* by specifically prohibiting sexual harassment.[142] The relevant provisions read as follows:

> 14(1) It is a discriminatory practice,
> (a) in the provision of goods, services, facilities or accommodation customarily available to the general public,
> (b) in the provision of commercial premises of residential accommodation, or
> (c) in matters related to employment,
> to harass an individual on a prohibited ground of discrimination
> (2) [Sexual harassment] Without limiting the generality of subsection (1), sexual harassment shall, for the purpose of that subsection, be deemed to be harassment on a prohibited ground of discrimination.

As noted earlier s. 3 of the Act designates "sex" as one of the prohibited grounds of discrimination.

It may be noted that the amendment to the *Canadian Human Rights Act* is not as specific or clear as one finds the Ontario *Human Rights Code*. However, the amendment prohibiting sexual harassment is very encouraging as it has clearly and unmistakably spelled out federal policy on "sexual harassment" and thereby confirms the judicial philosophy and reasoning on sexual harassment as stated in the *Robichaud v. Brennan* and *Kotyk* cases.

In 1983, Newfoundland also prohibited harassment and sexual solicitation in its *Human Rights Code*:[143]

> 13 No person in an establishment shall harass another person in the establishment because of the race, religion, religious creed, sex, marital status, physical disability, mental disability, political opinion, colour or ethnic, national or social origin of that person.

---

[141] *Charter of Human Rights and Freedoms*, S. Q. 1975, c. 6, s. 10 [am. S.Q. 1982, c. 61, s. 4].
[142] *Canadian Human Rights Act*, R.S.C. 1985, c. H-6.
[143] Now S.N. 1988, c. 62, ss. 13, 14.

Ch. 1 - Sexual Harassment and Human Rights Legislation

14(1) No person who is in a position to confer, grant or deny a benefit or advancement to another person shall engage in sexual solicitation or make a sexual advance to that person where the person making the solicitation or advance knows or ought reasonably to know that it is unwelcome.

(2) No person who is in a position to confer or deny a benefit or advancement to another person shall penalize, punish or threaten reprisal against that person for the rejection of a sexual solicitation or advance.

In 1987, subsequent to the Court of Appeal decision in *Janzen v. Platy Enterprises*,[144] the Manitoba *Human Rights Act* was repealed and replaced with the *Human Rights Code*.[145] Section 19 of the new *Human Rights Code* expressly prohibits sexual harassment in the workplace.

19(1) No person who is responsible for an activity or undertaking to which this Code applies shall
(a) harass any person who is participating in the activity or undertaking; or
(b) knowingly permit, or fail to take reasonable steps to terminate, harassment of one person who is participating in the activity or undertaking by another person who is participating in the activity or undertaking.
(2) In this section "harassment" means
(a) a course of abusive and unwelcome conduct or comment undertaken or made on the basis of any characteristic referred to in subsection 9(2); or
(b) a series of objectionable and unwelcome sexual solicitations or advances; or
(c) a sexual solicitation or advance made by a person who is in a position to confer any benefit on, or deny any benefit to, the recipient of the solicitation or advance, if the person making the solicitation or advance knows or ought reasonably to know that it is unwelcome; or
(d) a reprisal or threat of reprisal for rejecting a sexual solicitation or advance.

It is worth noting, however, that in those jurisdictions (Ontario, Quebec, Newfoundland, Canada and Manitoba) the decisions given by the Human Rights Tribunals prior to those amendments unanimously came to the conclusion that sexual harassment constituted discrimination. Moreover, most jurisdictions (e.g., B.C. Alberta, Saskatchewan, Nova Scotia, etc.) have continued to rely on the prohibition against "sex discrimination" in employment as a sufficient vehicle to cope with sexual harassment. Thus, it is obvious that the explicit inclusion of harassment as a prohibited ground for discrimination was meant only to clarify the existing rights rather than to create new ones.

---

[144] (Man. 1986), 8 C.H.R.R. D/3831 (C.A.).
[145] S.M. 1987, c. 45 (C.C.S.M., H175).

The government of Canada has also prohibited sexual harassment under the *Canada Labour Code*.[146] This imposes an additional ban on sexual harassment in employment that falls under the federal jurisdiction, such as transportation, communication, banking, etc. Although sexual harassment is already prohibited in the federal jurisdiction by the *Canadian Human Rights Act*, the prohibition in the *Canada Labour Code* further reinforces this public policy and the determination on the part of the federal government to combat sexual harassment with full force. The *Canada Labour Code* provides:

Division XV.1
SEXUAL HARASSMENT

247.1 In this Division, "sexual harassment" means any conduct, comment, gesture or contract of a sexual nature
(a) that is likely to cause offence or humiliation to any employee; or
(b) that might, on reasonable grounds, be perceived by that employee as placing a condition of a sexual nature on employment or on any opportunity for training or promotion.
247.2 Every employee is entitled to employment free of sexual harassment.
247.3 Every employer shall make every reasonable effort to ensure that no employee is subjected to sexual harassment.

The *Canada Labour Code*, in fact, went a step further and made it mandatory for every employer, in the federal jurisdiction, to develop and issue a policy statement on "how it would make the working environment free from sexual harassment". The *Code* has also imposed an obligation on the employers to provide an effective redress mechanism for the victims of sexual harassment.

The provision on sexual harassment in the *Canada Labour Code* is very significant indeed. Firstly, it would provide protection against sexual harassment to a large number of women working in unorganized sectors, such as financial institutions. Secondly, it would provide an impetus to the provincial governments to prohibit sexual harassment in their respective industrial relations statutes. Thus, the issue of sexual harassment by that process would not be confined only to human rights agencies, but would also become an industrial relations concern.

It is, however, not yet clear how the ban on sexual harassment under the *Canada Labour Code* would be administered. Most likely it would be monitored and administered by the Canadian Human Rights Commission rather than by the Department of Labour. As the Canadian

---

[146] *Canada Labour Code*, R.S.C. 1985 (1st Supp.), c. 9, s. 17.

Human Rights Commission already handles complaints of sexual harassment under the *Canadian Human Rights Act*, the prohibition in the *Canada Labour Code* would provide it with extra ammunition to fight sexual harassment in the workplace.

The Human Rights Tribunals and courts in Canada have been encouraged by the judicial trends in the United States. They found a great similarity in approach to "sex discrimination" between the two countries, and willingly drew from the enriched American jurisprudence in this regard. This may be traced to the values of freedom and equity commonly shared by Americans and Canadians. However, it may be pointed out that some American courts held to their conservative views and initially were reluctant to give a broader interpretation to "sex discrimination" to include "sexual harassment". On the contrary, it is worthwhile to note that there has only been one case where a Human Rights Tribunal or a court in Canada refused to recognize that "sexual harassment" amounts to "sex discrimination".

In *Janzen v. Platy Enterprises Ltd.*[147] the adjudicator found that the complainants, Janzen and Goverea, had been sexually harassed by Tommy Grammas, an employee of Platy Enterprises. On appeal, the Court of Queen's Bench confirmed the decision of the Adjudicator and rejected the arguments of the respondent that sexual harassment does not come within the prohibition against sex discrimination in employment which is contained in the *Manitoba Human Rights Act*.[148] The court held that sexual harassment is prohibited by the general non-discrimination provision and explicit language prohibiting sexual harassment is not necessary.[149] The court stated:

> I have no difficulty in accepting Mr. Shime's reasons and find that sexual harassment is discrimination on the basis of sex as prohibited by s. 6(1) of the *Act*.

> The fact that two jurisdictions have amended their legislation to clarify the matter of sexual harassment is not sufficient for me to find that the Manitoba Act, as it now stands, is inadequate. For the sake of clarity and consistency it might be preferable if the Manitoba Legislature followed suit with the Parliament of Canada and the Legislature of Ontario but as the legislation presently stands it is not fatal to an allegation of sexual discrimination based on sexual harassment. Respondents therefore fail on this ground of appeal.[150]

---

[147] (Man. 1986), 8 C.H.R.R. D/3831 (C.A.).
[148] (Man. 1986), 6 C.H.H.R. D/2735 (Henteleff).
[149] (Man. 1986), 7 C.H.R.R. D/3309 (Q.B.).
[150] *Ibid.*, at D/3312 (paras. 26426-27).

Thus, the Queen's Bench rejected the argument that the amendments enacted by some provinces to prohibit specifically sexual harassment in their human rights legislation was to be construed as an indication that the term "sex discrimination" did not encompass sexual harassment.

However, on appeal the Manitoba Court of Appeal reversed the decision of the Court of Queen's Bench. The court held that sexual harassment of the type to which the appellants were subjected was not discrimination on the basis of sex because only some women are subjected to sexual harassment and not all. Rather, the discrimination was because of individual characteristics.[151] The Court of Appeal found that the cause of discrimination was the physical attractiveness of the complainants. Huband J.A. of the Court of Appeal began by expressing his amazement that sexual harassment had been equated with discrimination on the basis of sex and that the employer could be held vicariously responsible for the harassing conduct of the employee.[152] He stated:

> I am amazed to think that sexual harassment has been equated with discrimination on the basis of sex. I think they are entirely different concepts. But adjudicators under human rights legislation, legal scholars and writers, and jurists have said that the one is included in the other.
>
> Assuming sexual harassment to be a form of sexual discrimination, I am amazed to think that an employer could be held vicariously responsible for that form of discrimination on the part of an employee, or that a corporate employer could be found "personally responsible" for a sexually malevolent employee, except under the rarest of circumstances. Yet adjudicators, legal scholars, and judges have said otherwise.[153]

Twaddle J.A., who wrote his separate opinion, concluded that sexual harassment based on the "sex appeal" of the victim could not constitute sex discrimination. He stated:

> Where the conduct of an employer is directed at some but not all persons of one category, it must not be assumed that membership of the category is the reason for the distinction having been made. The distinction may have been based on another factor. Thus in *Bliss v. Attorney-General of Canada* (1978),

---

[151] *Supra*, note 147.
[152] *Ibid.*
[153] *Ibid.*, at D/3832 (paras. 30249-50).

92 D.L.R. (3d) 417 it was held that statutory conditions applicable only to pregnant women did not discriminate against them as women....

The gender of a woman is unquestionably a factor in most cases of sexual harassment. If she were not a woman the harassment would not have occurred. That, however, is not decisive. Only a woman can become pregnant, but that does not mean that she becomes pregnant because she is a woman. We are concerned with the effective cause of the harassment, be it a random selection, the conduct, or a particular characteristic, of the victim, a wish on the part of the aggressor to discourage women from seeking or continuing in a position of employment or a contempt for women generally. Only in the last two instances is the harassment a manifestation of discrimination.[154]

. . .

This is not a case in which an employer adopted a practice whereby women as a class were treated differently from men. Nor is it a case in which a rule of general application adversely affected the complainants because they were women. For the harassment to amount to discrimination, it must have occurred by reason of the categorical selection of the complainants because they were women.

Although not conclusive, the sex of the victims and the sexual nature of the harassment is some evidence of the basis of their selection. There is, on the other hand, no evidence that women as a class were not welcome as employees or were subject to adverse treatment. On the contrary, the evidence discloses that at the restaurant in question women were the only employees other than the cook and the corporate officer. Another female employee testified that the cook touched her a lot by putting his arm around her or touching her neck, but she interpreted that as him being friendly.... *This evidence suggests that the complainants were chosen for the harassment because of characteristics peculiar to them rather than because of their sex. That is not discrimination no matter how objectionable the conduct.*[155] [Emphasis added]

The decision of the Manitoba Court of Appeal holding that "sexual harassment" does not constitute "sex" discrimination sent shock waves throughout the country among the legal scholars and human rights advocates — not to mention the women's groups. The Manitoba Attorney General immediately announced that he would introduce an amendment to the Manitoba *Human Rights Act.*[156]

---

[154] *Ibid.*, at D/3846 (paras. 30383-84).
[155] *Ibid.*, at D/3847 (paras. 30391-82).
[156] See *Winnipeg Free Press*, November 22, 1986, p. 3.

Finally, on May 4, 1989, the Supreme Court of Canada removed the uncertainty once and for all, and overruled the Manitoba Court of Appeal by holding that sexual harassment is a form of sex discrimination.[157] Sexual harassment in the workplace is unwelcome conduct of a sexual nature that detrimentally affects the work environment or leads to adverse job-related consequences for the victims of the harassment. The court ruled that the fact that only some women and not all women are the victims of sexual harassment does not mean that the conduct is not sex discrimination. Sex discrimination does not exist only where gender is the sole ingredient in the discriminatory action and where, therefore, all members of the affected gender are mistreated identically.

The court concluded:

> The fallacy in the position advanced by the Court of Appeal is the belief that sex discrimination only exists where gender is the sole ingredient in the discriminatory action and where, therefore, all members of the affected gender are mistreated identically. While the concept of discrimination is rooted in the notion of treating an individual as part of a group rather than on the basis of the individual's personal characteristics, discrimination does not require uniform treatment of all members of a particular group. It is sufficient that ascribing to an individual a group characteristic is one factor in the treatment of that individual. If a finding of discrimination required that every individual in the affected group be treated identically, legislative protection against discrimination would be of little or no value. It is rare that a discriminatory action is so bluntly expressed as to treat all members of the relevant group identically. In nearly every instance of discrimination the discriminatory action is composed of various ingredients with the result that some members of the pertinent group are not adversely affected, at least in a direct sense, by the discriminatory action. To deny a finding of discrimination in the circumstances of this appeal is to deny the existence of discrimination in any situation where discriminatory practices are less than perfectly inclusive. It is to argue, for example, that an employer who will only hire a woman if she has twice the qualifications required as a man is not guilty of sex discrimination if, despite this policy, the employer nevertheless manages to hire some women.[158]
>
> . . .
>
> To argue that the sole factor underlying the discriminatory action was the sexual attractiveness of the appellants and to say that their gender was irrelevant strains credulity. Sexual attractiveness cannot be separated from gender. The similar gender of both appellants is not a mere coincidence, it is fundamental to

---

[157] *Janzen v. Platy Enterprises Ltd.* (Man. 1986), 10 C.H.R.R. D/6205 (S.C.C.).
[158] *Ibid.*, at D/6230-31 (para. 44457).

understanding what they experienced. All female employees were potentially subject to sexual harassment by the respondent Grammas. That his discriminatory behaviour was pinpointed against two female employees would have been small comfort to other women contemplating entering such a workplace.[159]

Judicial pronouncement that "sexual harassment" amounts to discrimination based on "sex", combined with public acknowledgement of the problem and lobbying by women's groups, has led to express prohibition of "sexual harassment" in the statutes. So far, in four Canadian jurisdictions, human rights statutes have been amended to ban "sexual harassment" and the trend indicates that many other provinces will follow this route. In the United States, however, public opinion appears to be against such a move.

All Canadian jurisdictions have prohibited "sex discrimination" in employment for some time, through respective human rights statutes. However, "sexual harassment" was not initially recognized in those statutes. Thus, in the beginning, Human Rights Commissions were unsure whether or not "sexual harassment" fell within the scope of prohibition on "sex discrimination". Therefore, they were somewhat reluctant to entertain or encourage complaints of "sexual harassment". However, this uncertainty was removed when the Ontario Board of Inquiry, chaired by Mr. Owen Shime, held, in the *Cherie Bell* case, that "sexual harassment" amounts to "sex discrimination" and therefore was prohibited under the *Human Rights Code*.

The decision of the *Cherie Bell* case paved the way for the Ontario and other Human Rights Commissions to vigorously follow "sexual harassment" complaints. The Human Rights Tribunals in other jurisdictions adopted the philosophy and reasoning of the *Cherie Bell* case without hesitation, and declared that "sexual harassment" is a prohibited conduct and falls within the scope of discrimination based on "sex".

As a matter of fact the court in various industrialized countries, including Canada, United States, Scotland and Australia, have found that "sexual harassment" indeed constitutes "sex discrimination" for the purposes of human rights statutes.[160]

---

[159] *Ibid.*, at D/6232 (para. 44460).
[160] For the Scottish case see *Porcelli v. Strathclyde Regional Council* (1985), 1 C.R. 177 (EAT-Scot.), affd (1986), 1 C.R. 564 (Ct. of Sess.).

CHAPTER 2

Characteristics of Sexual Harassment

A. SEXUAL HARASSMENT DEFINITION

It has been well established that sexual harassment is a form of discrimination based on sex. Human Rights Tribunals in all Canadian jurisdictions, without exception, have given a liberal interpretation to "sex discrimination" to include "sexual harassment" as a prohibited conduct under their respective human rights legislation.

Sexual harassment by its nature is difficult to define. The Human Rights Tribunals, however, in the absence of a statutory definition of sexual harassment (in fact, even without a dictionary definition), initially had difficulty coming to grips with the nature and scope of sexual harassment. The earlier decisions reveal that Human Rights Tribunals in search for a definition or description of sexual harassment, examined and relied on various texts and other materials.[1] Although no Canadian jurisdiction has promulgated guidelines similar to the Equal Employment Opportunity Commission (E.E.O.C.) ones, the consensus of tribunal decisions favours a definition of sexual harassment as comprehensive as the E.E.O.C. definition and inclusive of the "poisoned work environment" concept.[2] The *Cherie Bell* decision began this approach, and was followed in other Canadian tribunal decisions.[3]

---

[1] Particularly Professor Catherine MacKinnon's book: *Sexual Harassment of Working Women* (New Haven: Yale University Press, 1979); and Professor Constance Backhouse and Leah Cohen's book: *The Secret Oppression: Sexual Harassment of Working Women* (Toronto: MacMillan, 1978).

[2] *Zarankin v. Johnstone c.o.b. as Wessex Inn* (B.C. 1984), 5 C.H.R.R. D/2274 (para. 19174) (Smith); affd (B.C. 1985). 6 C.H.R.R. D/2651 (B.C.S.C.).

[3] *Robichaud v. Brennan* (Can. 1983), 4 C.H.R.R. D/1272 (Review Tribunal — Dyer); *Howard v. Lemoignan* (Alta. 1982), 3 C.H.R.R. D/1150 (Welsh); *Cox v. Jagbritte Inc.* (Ont. 1981), 3 C.H.R.R. D/609 (Cumming); *Aragona v. Elegant Lamp Co. Ltd.* (Ont. 1982), 3 C.H.R.R. D/1109 (Ratushny); *Deisting v. Dollar Pizza (1978) Ltd.* (Alta. 1982), 3 C.H.R.R. D/898 (Clarke); *Hufnagel v. Osama Enterprises Ltd.* (Man. 1982), 3 C.H.R.R. D/922 (Teskey); *Giouvanoudis v. Golden Fleece Restaurant &*

58   Ch. 2 - Characteristics of Sexual Harassment

In *Zarankin v. Johnstone c.o.b. as Wessex Inn*,[4] Chairperson Lynn Smith of a British Columbia Board of Inquiry stated:

> I conclude that the E.E.O.C. Guidelines provide a good working definition of sexual harassment, and that this definition is consistent with that used by Canadian human rights tribunals.[5]

The E.E.O.C. guidelines provide a definition of sexual harassment as follows:

> Unwelcome sexual advances, requests for sexual favours, and other verbal or physical conduct of a sexual nature constitute sexual harassment when
> (1) submission to such conduct is made either explicitly or implicitly a term or condition of an individual's employment,
> (2) submission to or rejection of such conduct by an individual is used as a basis for employment decisions affecting such individual, or
> (3) such conduct has the purpose or effect of unreasonably interfering with an individual's work performance or creating an intimidating, hostile, or offensive working environment.

A Canadian definition, similar to that of the E.E.O.C. guidelines, was prepared by York University's Presidential Advisory Committee on Sexual Harassment. That definition was first endorsed and adopted by Professor Peter Cumming,[6] and subsequently adopted by some other tribunals.[7] The definition reads as follows:

> unwanted sexual attention of a persistent or abusive nature, made by a person who knows or ought reasonably to know that such attention is unwanted;

or

Tavern Ltd. (Ont. 1983), 5 C.H.R.R. D/1967 (Cumming); *Kotyk v. Canadian Employment and Immigration Commn.* (Can. 1983), 4 C.H.R.R. D/1416 (Ashley).

[4] (B.C. 1984), 5 C.H.R.R. D/2274 (Smith).

[5] *Ibid.*, at D/2275 (para. 19175).

[6] See for example *Olarte et al. v. Commodore Business Machines Ltd.* (Ont. 1983), 4 C.H.R.R. D/1705 (Cumming); affd (*sub nom. Commodore Business Machines Ltd. v. Ont. Minister of Labour*) (Ont. 1985), 6 C.H.R.R. D/2833 (Div. Ct.); *Giouvanoudis v. Golden Fleece Restaurant and Tavern Ltd.* (Ont. 1980), 5 C.H.R.R. D/1967 (Cumming).

[7] See for example *Irving v. Medland* (Man. 1985), 6 C.H.R.R. D/2842 (para. 23216) (Leland Berg); *Makara v. Osama Enterprises Ltd.* (Man. 1985), 6 C.H.R.R. D/2935 (para. 23799) (Henteleff); *Janzen v. Platy Enterprises* (Man. 1985), 6 C.H.R.R. D/2735 (para. 22631) (Henteleff); revd in part (Man. 1986), 7 C.H.R.R. D/3309 (Q.B.); revd (Man. 1986), 8 C.H.R.R. D/3831 (C.A.), a decision quashed by the Supreme Court of Canada (Man. 1989), 10 C.H.R.R. D/6205.

implied or expressed threat or reprisal, in the form either of actual reprisal or the denial of opportunity, for refusal to comply with a sexually oriented request;

or

sexually oriented remarks and behaviour which may reasonably be perceived to create a negative psychological and emotional environment for work.[8]

The Supreme Court of Canada in *Janzen v. Platy Enterprises Ltd.*[9] thoroughly reviewed the type of conduct that constitutes sexual harassment. In attempting to define sexual harassment in the workplace, Chief Justice Dickson stated:

> Without seeking to provide an exhaustive definition of the term, I am of the view that sexual harassment in the workplace may be broadly defined as unwelcome conduct of a sexual nature that detrimentally affects the work environment or leads to adverse job-related consequences for the victims of the harassment. It is, as Adjudicator Shime observed in *Bell v. Ladas, supra*, and as has been widely accepted by other adjudicators and academic commentators, an abuse of power. When sexual harassment occurs in the workplace, it is an abuse of both economic and sexual power. Sexual harassment is a demeaning practice, one that constitutes a profound affront to the dignity of the employees forced to endure it. *By requiring an employee to contend with unwelcome sexual actions or explicit sexual demands, sexual harassment in the workplace attacks the dignity and self-respect of the victim both as an employee and as a human being.*[10] [Emphasis added]

Dealing specifically with the type of conduct that constitutes sexual harassment and is discriminatory, the Supreme Court noted the following:

> The forms of prohibited conduct that, in my view, are discriminatory run the gamut from overt gender based activity, such as coerced intercourse to unsolicited physical contact to persistent propositions to more subtle conduct such as gender based insults and taunting, which may reasonably be perceived to create a negative psychological and emotional work environment.

---

[8] Final Report of the Presidential Committee on Sexual Harassment, York University, January, 1982, at p. 2.
[9] (Man. 1989), 10 C.H.R.R. D/6205 (S.C.C.).
[10] *Ibid.*, at D/6227 (para. 44451).

Ch. 2 - Characteristics of Sexual Harassment

Sexual harassment is any sexually oriented practice that endangers an individual's continued employment, negatively affects his/her work performance, or undermines his/her sense of personal dignity. Harassment behaviour may manifest itself blatantly in forms such as leering, grabbing, and even sexual assault. More subtle forms of sexual harassment may include sexual innuendos, and propositions for dates or sexual favours. [Emphasis added]

Sexual harassment can manifest itself both physically and psychologically. In its milder forms it can involve verbal innuendo and inappropriate affectionate gestures. It can, however, escalate to extreme behaviour amounting to attempted rape and rape. Physically, the recipient may be the victim of pinching, grabbing, hugging, patting, leering, brushing against, and touching. Psychological harassment can involve a relentless proposal of physical intimacy, beginning with subtle hints which may lead to overt requests for dates and sexual favours.[11]

The court concluded that sexual harassment can take a variety of forms and commented as follows:

Sexual harassment is not limited to demands for sexual favours made under threats of adverse job consequences should the employee refuse to comply with the demands. Victims of harassment need not demonstrate that they were not hired, were denied a promotion or were dismissed from their employment as a result of their refusal to participate in sexual activity. This form of harassment, in which the victim suffers concrete economic loss for failing to submit to sexual demands, is simply one manifestation of sexual harassment, albeit a particularly blatant and ugly one. Sexual harassment also encompasses situations in which sexual demands are foisted upon unwilling employees or in which employees must endure sexual groping, propositions, and inappropriate comments, but where no tangible economic rewards are attached to involvement in the behaviour.

The main point in allegations of sexual harassment is that unwelcome sexual conduct has invaded the workplace, irrespective of whether the consequences of the harassment included a denial of concrete employment rewards for refusing to participate in sexual activity.[12] [Emphasis added]

Thus, the Supreme Court of Canada put the unqualified stamp of its approval on the principles as well as on the meaning and scope of "sexual harassment" enunciated in the first Canadian case, the

---

[11] *Ibid.*, at D/6222 (para. 44439) and D/6224 (para. 44444).
[12] *Ibid.*, at D/6226 (para. 44447) and 6227 (para. 44449).

Cherie Bell case,[13] by Owen Shime and followed by other Human Rights Tribunals throughout the country.

Thus, briefly summarized, sexual harassment is a form of discrimination based on sex. It occurs when a person is disadvantaged in the workplace as a result of differential treatment in the workplace. It is an unwarranted intrusion upon the sexual dignity of a person. It consists of acts that are unwarranted, unsolicited, and unwelcome. It can be overt or subtle. Even if the nature of the harassment is not physical, it can still be considered to be sexual harassment if it creates a poisoned environment, even if there is no economic consequence such as loss of one's job, loss of seniority, or economic consequence of a similar nature. It is also clear that even if it might be considered that what has occurred is sexual banter, common to the workplace, if a person finds it objectionable and makes it known in clear and precise terms that such actions are not acceptable to such person, then that is the standard of behaviour that is established *vis-à-vis* that person.[14]

It is difficult to imagine that by prohibiting sex discrimination, legislatures in Canada had any intention to deny supervisors and the people they supervise in the workplace *normal* social interchanges, flirtation, or even intimate sexual conduct. Interpersonal relations and sexual conduct between the supervisor and his subordinate are not prohibited conduct *per se*. Thus, if a social or sexual conduct is to be considered harassment, this of course, must go far beyond the realm of flirtation. When exactly a social contact — such as an "invitation to dinner" — amounts to "sexual harassment" remains problematic and can only be determined through a close scrutiny of the facts in each case. As the Manitoba Board in *Hufnagel v. Osama Enterprises Ltd.* stated:

> I would hasten to add a word of caution. Normal discussion or contact between management and an employee, even if it be social in nature, is not intended to be prohibited by the Act. It goes without saying that interrelationships between human beings are complex and subjective motivations may often be mixed. Each situation must be carefully considered upon its facts to determine whether the conduct complained of is sanctionable . . . .[15]

---

[13] (Ont. 1980), 1 C.H.R.R. D/155 (Shime).
[14] See for example *Makara v. Osama Enterprises Ltd.*, *supra*, note 7 at D/2936 (para. 23801).
[15] *Hufnagel v. Osama Enterprises Ltd.*, *supra*, note 3, at D/925 (para. 8222) (Teskey).

Ch. 2 - Characteristics of Sexual Harassment

In *Aragona v. Elegant Lamp Co.*, the Ontario Board stated the proposition as follows:

> Thus, sexual references which are crude or in bad taste, are not necessarily sufficient to constitute a contravention of section 4 of the [Ontario] Code on the basis of sex. The line of sexual harassment is crossed only where the conduct may be reasonably construed to create, as a condition of employment, a work environment which demands an unwarranted intrusion upon the employee's sexual dignity as a man or a woman.[16]

The basic difficulty is not to determine the principle that "sexual harassment" amounts to sex discrimination, but rather it has been to determine whether or not a particular incident (or incidents) or conduct constituted sexual harassment. The Human Rights Tribunals did not have the benefit of any predetermined criteria. They, however, over a series of cases gradually developed their own criteria, to determine whether or not an incident or a conduct of a sexual nature amounts to "sexual harassment" as a prohibited conduct.

The pertinent distinctive characteristics[17] of the sexual encounters which must be considered to be prohibited by human rights statutes are:

1. That they be unsolicited by the complainant, and unwelcome to the complainant and expressly or implicitly known to be unwelcome by the respondent. (These are the factors which remove the situation from the normal social interchange, flirtation or even intimate sexual conduct which legislatures cannot have intended to have denied to supervisors and the people they supervise in the workplace.)
2. That the conduct complained of must be persistent in the face of protests by the subject of the sexual advances, or in the alternative, though the conduct was not persistent, the rejection of the conduct had adverse employment consequences.
3. That if the complainant cooperates with the alleged harassment, sexual harassment can still be found if such compliance is shown to have been secured by employment-related threats or perhaps promises.

---

[16] *Aragona v. Elegant Lamp Co.*, *supra*, note 3, at D/1110 (para. 9725) (Ratushny).
[17] See for example *Robichaud v. Brennan* (Can. 1982), 3 C.H.R.R. D/977 (Abbott).

1. Unsolicited and Unwelcome

The primary identifying factor in sexual harassment incidents is that sexual encounters are unsolicited by the complainant and unwelcome to the complainant.

As sexual attraction often plays a role in the day-to-day social exchange between employees, "the distinction between invited, uninvited-but-welcome, offensive-but-tolerated, and flatly rejected sexual advances may well be difficult to discern.[18] But this distinction is essential because sexual conduct becomes unlawful only when it is "unwelcome".[19] The question arises, what is "unwelcome"? The court in *Henson v. City of Dundee* provided the general definition of "unwelcome" — the challenged conduct must be unwelcome "in the sense that the employee did not solicit or incite it, and in the sense that the employer regarded the conduct as undesirable."[20]

(a) "Unwelcome" versus "Voluntarily"

Recently the U.S. Supreme Court in the *Vinson* case[21] posed the question whether "voluntary" submitting to sexual demands precludes a complainant from bringing a sexual harassment claim. The court thus shifted the focus of inquiry from whether the act was "voluntary" to whether the act was "unwelcome". The District Court in that case had held that if there was an intimate relationship between Vinson and Taylor, it was a voluntary one.[22] The Circuit Court determined that "voluntary" submission by the victim of unlawful discrimination is irrelevant.[23] The Supreme Court stated that:

---

[18] *Barnes v. Costle*, 561 F. 2d 983 at 999, 14 E.P.D. para. 7755 (D.C. Cir. 1977) (Mackinn J. concurring).
[19] See E.E.O.C. Guideline, 19 C.F.R. 1604.11, 45 F.R. 25024; *Janzen v. Platy Enterprises* (Man. 1989), 10 C.H.R.R. D/6205 (S.C.C.). At D/6227 (para. 44451) the Supreme Court stated that sexual harassment "may be broadly defined as *unwelcome* conduct of a sexual nature that detrimentally affects the work environment or leads to adverse job-related consequences...".
[20] 682 F. 2d 897, 903, 29 E.P.D. para. 32,993 (11th Cir. 1982).
[21] *Meritor Savings Bank v. Vinson*, 106 S. Ct. 2399, 40 E.P.D. para. 36,159 (1986).
[22] *Ibid.*, at 2406.
[23] *Ibid.*

[The] correct inquiry is whether respondent by her conduct indicated that the alleged sexual advances were "unwelcome", not whether her actual participation in sexual intercourse was "voluntary".[24]

Therefore "voluntariness" is not a defence to a claim of sexual harassment and may not be used by the supervisor or employer to prevent the sexual harassment claim from being successful.[25] In sexual harassment cases, it is the question of welcome or unwelcome sexual advances on which the determination hinges, and not on the question of whether sexual advances were voluntarily tolerated by the victim.

There is no doubt that the area of unwelcome sexual activity presents very real problems of proof and it will turn "largely on credibility determinations committed to the trier of facts".[26] The trier of facts must determine the existence of sexual harassment in light of the "record as a whole" and the totality of circumstances, such as the nature of the sexual advances and the conduct in which the alleged incident occurred.[27]

The evidence regarding "provocative dress and publicly expressed sexual fantasies" is often relevant in determining whether the victim found particular sexual advances unwelcome.[28] There is no *per se* rule against the admissibility of such evidence on the question of whether sexual activity was unwelcome. However, the Tribunals must carefully weigh its relevance against the potential for unfair prejudices.[29]

Thus, occasional use of sexually explicit language by the victim does not necessarily negate the claim that sexual conduct was unwelcome. Although the complainant's use of sexual terms or off-colour jokes may suggest that sexual comments by others in the situation were not unwelcome, more extreme and abusive or persistent comments or physical assault will not be excused.

---

[24] *Ibid.*
[25] *Ibid.* See also Dawn D. Bennett-Alexander, "The Supreme Court Finally Speaks on the Issue of Sexual Harassment — What did it say?" (1987), 10 *Women's Rights Law Reporter* 65.
[26] *Ibid*, at 2407.
[27] *Ibid.*
[28] *Ibid.*
[29] This standard was laid by the U.S. Supreme Court in the *Vinson* case, *supra*. The standard has been the subject of severe criticism; see Wendy Pollack, "Sexual Harassment: Women's Experience vs. Legal Definition" (1990), 13 *Harvard Women's L.J.* 35; Cynthia F. Cohen, "Legal Dilemmas in Sexual Harassment Cases" (1987), 38 *Labour L.J.* 681; Kathleen Gallivan, "Sexual Harassment after *Janzen v. Platy*: The Transformative Possibilities" (1991), 49 *University of Toronto Faculty of Law Rev.* 27.

(b) Complainant's Past Conduct

The complainant's past conduct that is offered to show "welcomeness" must relate to the alleged harasser. It would be wrong to conclude that the complainant's own past conduct and use of foul language showed that "she was the kind of person who could not be offended by such comments and therefore welcomed them generally" even though she had told the harasser to leave her alone.[30] The proper inquiry in such cases should be whether the complainant welcomed the particular conduct in question from the alleged harasser. It should be noted that the complainant's use of foul language or sexual innuendo in a consensual setting does not waive her legal protection against sexual harassment.[31]

In *Re Canada Post Corp. and Canadian Union of Postal Workers (Gibson)*,[32] Arbitrator Swan, while holding that the conduct of the alleged harasser was unwelcome, stated that:

> . . . merely because an employee is prepared to engage in banter, flirtation or even sexual activity with one or more fellow employees does not mean that employee is required to accept the same conduct from everyone. As this area of law develops, it must recognize that some comments or activity may be welcome from one person, while entirely unwelcome from another, and will recognize an employee's right to choose those with whom he or she is prepared to let down some of the defences to which he or she is entitled.[33]

Thus, evidence concerning the complainant's general character and past behaviour towards others has limited, if any, probative value.

A difficult but important question arises — how to determine whether or not sexual encounters were unsolicited and unwelcome. Each case has to be determined on its merits; the facts and circumstances in each case differ, particularly when we are dealing with human behaviour and its perception by two individuals.

The test of whether the advances are unsolicited or unwelcome should be objective in the sense that it depends upon the reasonable and usual limits of social interaction in the circumstances of the case. The complainant should not need to prove an active resistance or other

---

[30] *Swentek v. U.S. Air Line Inc.* 830 F. 2d 552 at 557, 44 E.P.D. para. 37,457 (4th Cir. 1987).
[31] *Ibid.*, at 557; see also *Katz v. Dole*, 709 F. 2d 251 at 254, 32 E.P.D. para. 33,639 (4th Cir. 1983).
[32] (1987), 27 L.A.C. (3d) 27 (Swan).
[33] *Ibid.*, at 45.

explicit reaction to the activity complained of, other than a refusal or denial, unless such might reasonably be necessary to make the perpetrator aware that the activity was in fact unwelcome or exceeded the bounds of usual social interaction.

Sexually aggressive conduct and explicit conversation on the part of the complainant may bar a claim of action for (hostile environment) sexual harassment.[34] Where the plaintiff "behaved in a very flirtatious and provocative manner" around the alleged harasser, asked him to have dinner at her house on several occasions despite his repeated refusal, and continued to conduct herself in a similar manner after the alleged harassment, she could not claim that the alleged harasser was unwelcome.[35] Similarly, the complainant's allegation was found not credible because she visited her alleged harasser at the hospital, and at his brother's home, and allowed him to come into her home alone at night after the alleged harassment occurred.[36]

In one case,[37] the E.E.O.C. found that the active participation by the complainant in sexual conduct at the workplace, e.g., "using dirty remarks and telling dirty jokes", may indicate that the sexual advances complained of were not unwelcome. The Commission concluded that no harassment occurred with respect to an employee who had joined in the telling of bawdy jokes and the use of vulgar language during the first two months on the job, and failed to provide subsequent notice that the conduct was no longer welcome to her. By actively participating in the conduct, the victim had created an impression among the co-workers that she welcomed the sort of sexually oriented banter which she later asserted was objectionable. It was held that simply ceasing to participate was insufficient to show that the continuing activity was no longer welcome to her.

In *Daigle v. Hunter*,[38] the New Brunswick Board of Inquiry rejected the victim's complaint of sexual harassment on the ground that she participated in some of the alleged activities and she did not object to the conduct which she subsequently alleged constituted sexual harassment. The Board stated:

---

[34] *Ferguson v. E.I. Dupont de Nemours & Co.*, 560 F. Supp. 1172, 33 E.P.D. para. 34,141 (D. Del. 1983).
[35] *Richman v. Bureau of Affirmative Action*, 536 F. Supp. 1149 at 1172, 30 FEP 1644 (M. D. Pa. 1982).
[36] *Sardigal v. St. Louis National Stockyard Co.*, 41 E.P.D. para. 36,613 (S.D. Ill. 1986).
[37] See E.O.C.C. Decision No. 84-1 — *CCH Employment Practices*, para. 6839.
[38] (N.B. 1989), 10 C.H.R.R. D/5670 (Ruben).

Two additional factors lead me to the conclusion that Mrs. Daigle was not sexually harassed nor did she believe she was being sexually harassed. Firstly, it is inconsistent for a person such as Mrs. Daigle to find the oft described work environment offensive while at the same time willingly and actively reading aloud to at least one of the male employees, a sexually explicit article commencing with the by-line "I'm sort of embarrassed; my boyfriend's penis is so large . . ."

Secondly, Mrs. Daigle did not specifically complain about the activity until after she was dismissed. There are undoubtedly many situations where the victim of sexual harassment cannot reasonably complain until after she has left the employment, either having quit or having been fired, however, Mrs. Daigle was not in such a predicament.[39]

On the other hand, in *Dyson v. Louie Pasin Plaster & Stucco Ltd.*,[40] the B.C. Human Rights Council found that the victim neither welcomed nor voluntarily consented to sexual activities including masturbating him. The victim's evidence was to the effect that she was ultimately resigned to the fact that Pasin (alleged harasser) "wasn't going to stop until he'd ejaculated" and so she "finally gave in". She, however, emphasized that she did not consent and "did not want it to happen", but believed it was the "only way to stop it."[41]

Thus, mere acquiescence in sexual conduct at the workplace may not mean that the conduct is welcome to the individual. When welcomeness is at issue, it should be determined whether the victim's conduct is consistent or inconsistent with her assertion that the sexual conduct is unwelcome.

It is likely that a single unrepeated act is not harassment, unless it results in the denial or removal of a tangible benefit available or offered to other persons in similar circumstances, or unless it amounts to an assault, or is a proposition of such a gross or obscene nature that it could reasonably be considered to have created a negative or unpleasant emotional or psychological work environment. A "normal" proposition or suggestion would probably not have this result.

To establish that sexual conduct was unsolicited and unwelcome, the complainant is generally expected to establish that she had expressly or implicitly made it known to the harasser that his sexual advances are unwelcome. However, it remains difficult to pinpoint

---

[39] *Ibid.* (paras. 41551-52). See also *Chu v. Persichilli* (Ont. 1988), 9 C.H.R.R. D/4617 (Hovius).
[40] (B.C. 1990), 11 C.H.R.R. D/495 (Joe).
[41] *Ibid.*, at D/496 (para. 8).

precisely what conduct or action or words would be construed a clear signal to a perpetrator that his sexual advances are not welcome.

(c) "No" Does Not Mean "No"

In certain circles of our society a stereotypical belief still persists that in sexual matters "no" does not mean "no". For example, in *Kotyk v. Canadian Employment and Immigration Commission*[42] the investigation Committee which investigated the grievance (not the Human Rights Commission) of sexual harassment stated:

> "The alleged sexual harassment in this grievance was based on the fact that the manager made sexual advances on three separate occasions, when travelling together on business. The Committee was unable to conclude that the manager was guilty of sexual harassment. Although the Committee does conclude his behaviour was unbecoming of an officer of the Commission."

In Appendix "E" of the Report (page 245) the Committee dealt in more detail with the facts of the complaint. While believing her statements that the incidents took place, they felt that perhaps her refusals were not clear enough to Mr. Chuba, and in their words " . . . Mr. Chuba could have concluded that Ms. Allary's "No" was not unequivocal and he could have concluded that it was worth a second and even a third try." They say that

> "Ms. Allary's way of dealing with his advances was to simply not allow herself to be in a situation where he could pursue the matter. Thus, she used excuses designed to ensure that they did not travel together. However, he would have no way of knowing that she was making up excuses to not travel with him."[43]

The Human Rights Tribunal in *Kotyk v. Canadian Employment and Immigration Commission* rejected the argument that the harasser did not have a clear signal from the complainant that his sexual advances were not welcome to her. The Tribunal concluded:

> . . . I have accepted that she told him directly and clearly that his advances were unwelcome. It is significant that very soon after the July incident occurred Mr. Chuba tried again. Ms. Allary's reactions to these two advances was, rather

---

[42] (Can 1983), 4 C.H.R.R. D/1416 (Ashley).
[43] *Ibid.*, at D/1427 (para. 12227).

than to deal with it yet again, to remove herself from situations where Mr. Chuba would make sexual advances to her. Mr. Chuba must have known the ordinary meaning of the word "no". I disagree with the interpretation of the Administrative Investigation Committee that Mr. Chuba might not have realized that her "no" was unequivocal and that he might have felt justified in going back for a "second or even a third try."[44]

The Tribunal also made it clear that when a female employee avoids physical closeness, persistent social invitation or sexual conduct of her superior, it should be regarded as a clear signal to him that his sexual advances are not welcome.

(d) Verbal Protest Not Necessary

To establish that the sexual conduct or advances in question were unwanted or unwelcome, the complainant is not required to prove that she had "verbally protested" or expressedly said "no" to the perpetrator or conveyed to him in another way that his behaviour was unwelcome. It is sufficient for the complainant to establish that she by her conduct or body movement or body language conveyed to the perpetrator her disapproval of his advances. Where a complainant attempted to evade the harasser as much as she could, it was found that the conduct was unwelcome although no verbal protest was made. Thus, it is sufficient for the complainant to establish that she, in a non-verbal way, let the harasser know by moving quickly or just trying to avoid him that she did not like what he was doing.

In *Zarankin v. Johnstone c.o.b. as Wessex Inn*,[45] the complainant testified that the harasser frequently hit her on the "bum", and put his hand around her shoulders. One day he said "Let's go back into the backroom and I'll show you what it's all about". She added, "I did not say nothing, I just laughed". The complainant's evidence was that she did not say anything to Mr. Johnstone (the harasser) about his conduct because she was afraid of losing her job. The British Columbia Board of Inquiry held that a *reasonable person* would have known that this behaviour was unwelcome and the complainant did nothing to invite or encourage these actions.

A victim of sexual harassment need not always confront her harasser directly as long as her conduct demonstrates that the harasser's

---

[44] *Ibid.*, at D/1428 (para. 12237).
[45] (B.C. 1984), 5 C.H.R.R. D/2274 (Smith).

behaviour is unwelcome.[46] In some instances a woman may have the responsibility for telling the man directly that his comments or conduct is unwelcome. In other instances, a woman's consistent failure to respond to suggestive comments or gestures may be sufficient to communicate that the man's conduct was unwelcome. In many cases the victims do not confront their supervisor directly about his sexual remarks and gestures for fear of losing jobs. However, if the evidence shows that they demonstrated through their comments and actions that his conduct was unwelcome, it would be sufficient to support a finding of sexual harassment.[47]

An objection by the complainant, however, is a factor which comes into play in determining whether an employer should reasonably have known that his physical advances were unwelcome and exceeded the reasonable and usual limits of social interaction in the work environment.[48] Further it may be pointed out that "usual social interaction" also differs from one work environment to another, such as "office" to "bush camp" or "construction site".

(e) Constructive Knowledge — Standard of Reasonable Person

It may be pointed out that in addition to non-verbal communication of disapproval of the harasser's conduct or advances by the victim, the Boards have also introduced the element of *constructive knowledge* on the ground that a "reasonable person" should have known that the behaviour was unwelcome. This, in fact, shifts the burden of proof from the complainant to the perpetrator that his behaviour in question was, if not invited or encouraged by the complainant, at least acceptable and welcome to her.

In *Fields v. Willie's Rendezvous Inc.*,[49] a B.C. Human Rights Council found that the complainant was pinched or grabbed on various parts of her body including her breasts and bottoms and "bummed" by the respondent on several occasions. While holding that the complainant was the victim of unwanted sexual conduct amounting to sexual harassment, the council emphasized that:

---

[46] *Lipsett v. University of Puerto Rico*, 864 F. 2d 881 at 898, 48 E.P.D. para. 38,393 (1st Cir. 1988).
[47] E.O.C.C. Decision No. 84-1 — *CCH Employment Practices*, para. 6839.
[48] See for example *Potapczyk v. MacBain* (Can. 1984), 5 C.H.R.R. D/2285 at D/2297 (para. 19357) (Lederman).
[49] (B.C. 1985), 6 C.H.R.R. D/3074 (Powell).

... the complainant *did everything she thought possible to avoid the respondent's acts* while at the same time trying to maintain her employment. Ms. Fields was placed in a place where she felt compelled to tolerate the Respondent's act and limit her protests in order to keep her job.[50] [Emphasis added]

The Council used the test of constructive knowledge and stated that "Mr. Ueffing (Respondent) knew or ought to have known that overtures were at the expense of the young employee's feelings of dignity and self respect." It concluded that no person, regardless of age, should be subjected to such behaviour from a manager or employer. The so-called "effusive behaviour" must be controlled in the workplace in order that the employees may work in an environment free from sexual overtures, sexual innuendoes, touching, grabbing or pinching.

In one of the highly publicized cases, *Potapczyk v. MacBain*,[51] the complainant alleged that the respondent, Mr. MacBain, persistently subjected her and other female staff to physical closeness which was unnecessary and offensive. In this case, no apparent physical sexual conduct was involved. The Tribunal noted that unlike previous sexual harassment cases that have been heard by other tribunals to date, this case does not have the same hallmarks of overt sexual advances and propositioning. Although neither the complainant nor any other female staff had ever explicitly informed Mr. MacBain that his comments and his physical behaviour were offensive to them, the tribunal while applying the test of "constructive knowledge" noted that a reasonable person would have known that these actions were not welcome.[52] The Tribunal expanded:

> This type of crowding was not welcome by the women. They found it uncomfortable and objectionable and although they did not expressly confront him over this conduct, *their body language* was such that any reasonable person observing the scene would have concluded that the women were being subjected to physical discomfort which they did not appreciate.[53] [Emphasis added]

Thus, it is not necessary that women expressly object to their employer that they find the conduct distasteful as a precondition to their lodging a complaint under the human rights statutes.

---

[50] *Ibid.*, at D/3078 (para. 24628).
[51] (Can. 1984), 5 C.H.R.R. D/2285 (Lederman).
[52] *Ibid.*
[53] *Ibid.*, at D/2296 (para. 19355).

Ch. 2 - Characteristics of Sexual Harassment

The use of the "reasonable person" standard in sexual harassment cases has caused some concerns in certain circles. Basically there have been two concerns. First there are adjudicators who argue that an objective standard of "reasonable person" should not be applied, at least to sexual harassment discipline cases.[54] An arbitrator in the *Ottawa Board of Education* case[55] refused to apply the standard of "reasonable person" to determine whether or not the perpetrator knew that his conduct was unwelcome. The arbitrator stated:

> While this objective standard may have its place in the *Human Rights Code, 1981*, I have serious doubts as to the appropriateness of such a test in the context of employee discipline.... The employee who is disciplined for conduct which he did not realize was unwelcome but which the reasonable person would have realized was unwelcome is being blamed, in effect, for lack of sensitivity to signals from the "victim" of the harassment. I do not believe that a grievor's failure to detect subtle indications that his advances are unwelcome and offensive provides a basis for discipline. Since *I am not satisfied that the grievor had actual knowledge that his attentions to Ms. R. were unwelcome, I must conclude that the charge of sexual harassment has not been proved.*[56] [Emphasis added]

Second, there are those who feel that the use of the "reasonable person" standard in cases of sexual harassment in the stereotypical men-dominated working environment is not fair and is prejudicial to the victim.[57] Is unwelcomeness to be measured against what is presently welcomed in her workplace? It has been frequently suggested that the conduct in question be judged from the victim's perspective. One commentator has recently suggested that instead of the "reasonable person" standard or "reasonable female" standard, the "reasonable victim" standard should be used in sexual harassment cases.[58] She argues that:

> ... the "reasonable victim" standard would assess behaviour not in terms of the dominant social norms of the workplace, but by showing greater sensitivity to the fact that social norms of the so-called acceptable conduct may be oppressive to women. This standard, in fact, would attempt to emancipate women from the social norms that oppress them, rather than allowing individual

---

[54] *Re Ottawa Board of Education and Ottawa Board of Education Employees Union* (1989), 5 L.A.C. (4th) 171 (Bendel).
[55] *Ibid.*
[56] *Ibid*, at 180-81.
[57] See Kathleen Gallivan, "Sexual Harassment After Janzen v. Platy: The Transformative Possibilities" (1991), 49 *University of Toronto Faculty of Law Rev.* 27.
[58] *Ibid.*

workplaces to avoid scrutiny of the barriers to employment equity they pose to women by appealing to gender stereotype.[59]

Of course, the standard of "reasonable person" must be applied to the determination of whether the challenged conduct is of a sexual nature. Similarly, in determining whether harassment is sufficiently severe or pervasive to create a "hostile or poisonous" environment, the harasser's conduct should be evaluated from the objective standpoint of "reasonable person". However, the objective standard should not be applied in a vacuum. The adjudicators should give consideration to the context in which the alleged harassment took place. The trier of fact must "adopt the perspective of a reasonable person's reaction to a similar environment under similar or like circumstances".[60]

At the same time, the "reasonable person" standard should consider the victim's perspective and not stereotypical notions of acceptable behaviour. For example, the workplace where sexual slurs, displays of "girlie" pictures, and other offensive conduct abound can constitute a hostile work environment even if many people deem it to be harmless or insignificant.[61]

(f) Consensual Relationships

There is no doubt that consensual relationships between employer and employee which are unrelated to conditions of employment are not a violation of human rights statutes.[62] If it can be established that sexual relations or activities between the supervisor and the employee were consensual, then his sexual behaviour cannot be regarded as unwelcome or unwanted. However, it is very difficult to ascertain whether or not their sexual relations were consensual. The harasser normally in such circumstances contends that the complainant has consented and the complainant on the other hand denies it. It is very pertinent to determine whether or not their relations were consensual in order to decide whether or not the alleged conduct constituted sexual

---

[59] *Ibid.*, at 56.
[60] *Highlander v. K. F. C. National Management Co.*, 805 F. 2d 644 at 650, 41 E.P.D. para. 36,675 (6th Cir. 1986).
[61] *Rabidue v. Osceola Refining Co.*, 805 F. 2d 611 at 626, 41 E.P.D. para. 36,643 (6th Cir. 1986).
[62] See for example *Hufnagel v. Osama Enterprises, supra*, note 3 (para. 8222).

harassment. Whether or not the relationship between the parties was consensual will thus depend on the facts of each case.

The Board of Arbitration in *Re Canadian Union of Public Employees (C.U.P.E.) and Office and Professional Employees Int'l. Union (O.P.I.E.U.) Loc. 491*[63] failed to find the alleged conduct amounting to sexual harassment because the grievor gave very ambiguous signals to the alleged harasser as to whether the advances were welcome. The Board said:

> They had been frequent companions for coffee, spent a lot of time together in a small office and she made light of most of the incidents. It was not until the locked door incident that the grievor felt that she finally made it clear that she was not interested. Even here there was some ambiguity in her response — her query about how he proposed to proceed and a comment to the effect "Maybe I should sleep with you. Then I'd have some strings to pull on you in this game plan."[64]

Similarly, in *Robichaud v. Brennan*[65], the Canadian Human Rights Tribunal found that the alleged sexual encounters had, in fact, occurred but denied the complainant on the ground that the complainant had voluntarily participated in those encounters; further that "Mrs. Robichaud's rejection and protests were inconsistent with her conduct,"[66] and were not apt to put Mr. Brennan on notice that his conduct was perceived by Mrs. Robichaud as harassment. The Tribunal stated:

> Being masturbated, performing fellatio, "fondling" another's penis, and awaiting the return of someone who has failed to achieve an erection are clearly consistent only with a high degree of voluntary participation. In contrast, being hugged, kissed, slapped on the "rear end" or subjected to unwelcome and unsolicited conversations, and conduct of that sort, carry no connotation, in themselves, of voluntariness.[67]

The Tribunal concluded:

> Her protests were not such as to drive home to Mr. Brennan that his conduct was, in her view, persistent and unwelcome. Secondly, the nature of the sexual

---

[63] (1982), 4 L.A.C. (3rd) 385 (Swinton).
[64] *Ibid.*, at 401.
[65] (Can. 1982), 3 C.H.R.R. D/977 (Tribunal — Abbott), revd (Can. 1983), 4 C.H.R.R. D/1272 (Review Tribunal — Dyer); affd in part (*sub nom. Treasury Board v. Bonnie Robichaud*) (Can. 1985), 6 C.H.R.R. D/2695 (Fed. Ct.).
[66] *Ibid.*, at D/981 (para. 8712).
[67] *Ibid.* (para. 8713).

encounters about which Mrs. Robichaud testified must raise an inference that she was a voluntary participant in those encounters. Thirdly, there is insufficient evidence on which to found a conclusion that Mrs. Robichaud's participation was secured by threats or promises related to her employment.[68]

On appeal, the Review Tribunal, however, reversed the decision of Professor Abbott.[69] But it should be pointed out that the Review Tribunal did not take issue with Professor Abbott's interpretation of the elements which make up sexual harassment but disagreed with his conclusion that the respondent's behaviour was "not welcome". The divergence of opinion between the Tribunal and Review Tribunal arises because this case is one where the complainant raised objections but nevertheless complied with the demands of the alleged harasser. Especially in cases such as this, an objective test must be applied, difficult though it may be. In *Robichaud*, the complainant accepted the advances of the respondent. The Review Tribunal decided that sexual harassment had indeed occurred since the submission was "a result of the intimidation and fear that she had for [her supervisor]".[70]

Thus, consent under pressure or fear is not really consent. It must be given by free will. On this basis, in a later case, *Kotyk v. C.E.I.C.*,[71] the Canadian Human Rights Tribunal rejected the argument that sexual activities were consensual. It found that "Mr. Chuba's advances to Ms. Kotyk were unsolicited and unwelcome and that she feared that her employment would be jeopardized if she refused his advances."[72]

Thus, the position taken by Professor Abbott in *Robichaud* that rejection was the only way the respondent would have known "that his advances were unsolicited and unwelcome",[73] was rejected by the Review Tribunal and later by another Tribunal in the *Kotyk* case. For some time it appeared to have laid to rest the significant area of disagreement (between tribunals) that rejection was necessary to establish that "his advances were unwelcome".

However, in 1985, in the case of *Makara v. Osama Enterprises Ltd.*,[74] a Manitoba Human Rights Tribunal found that consensual relations existed between the complainant and her supervisor. In other

---

[68] *Ibid.* (para. 8716).
[69] *Ibid.* (Can. 1983), 4 C.H.R.R. D/1272 (Review Tribunal — Dyer).
[70] *Ibid.*, at D/1273 (para. 11040).
[71] (Can. 1983), 4 C.H.R.R. D/1416 (Ashley); affd (Can. 1983), 5 C.H.R.R. D/1895 (Review Tribunal — Lederman).
[72] *Ibid.*, at D/1425 (para. 12214) (Ashley).
[73] *Robichaud v. Brennan, supra*, note 65 at D/982 (para. 8718) (Tribunal — Abbott).
[74] (Man. 1985), 6 C.H.R.R. D/2935 (Henteleff).

words, the complainant had agreed to sexual contact with her supervisor. The Tribunal pointed out:

> I cannot help but comment on the fact that according to the complainant's evidence . . . he allegedly committed acts against her of most grievous sexual nature and yet despite that she went back to work the following day.[75]

The Tribunal concluded:

> . . .[I]t is my judgement that she [complainant] rejected his advances when she wished to do so and accepted them when she wished to do so, all of her own free will and therefore it cannot be said that they were unwanted.[76]

It is evident from this decision that where an employee accepts the sexual advances of her supervisor one time and refuses at another time without pressure, it may be difficult to establish with certainty that sexual advances were unwelcome or unwarranted. This occasional acceptance may be held against the complainant.

A complainant, however, is not required to prove an active resistance or other explicit reaction to the activity complained of, other than a refusal or denial, unless such might reasonably be necessary to make a perpetrator aware that the activity was in fact unwelcome or exceeded the bounds of usual social interaction. Nevertheless, prior consensual sexual relations with the alleged harasser may preclude a complaint of sexual harassment, because the conduct complained of may not be considered to have been unwelcome harassment.

2. Coerced and Forced

Another distinct characteristic of most sexual harassment behaviour is coercion. In situations where an unsolicited sexual advance is made by a person with the authority to hire and fire, the element of coercion is inherent.

The terms "coerced and forced" imply that the act or conduct was pressed against the will of the other. It was carried on in spite of the resistance, expressed or implied, of the employee. It was inflicted or imposed by force, or the employee was compelled to cooperate or perform an act against his/her will by a threat or promise. The

---

[75] *Ibid.*, at D/2941 (para. 23825).
[76] *Ibid.*, at D/2947 (para. 23853).

expression "coercion" invariably implies use of strength (physical or economic) or harsh measures securing compliance. In this respect the element of "coercion" goes hand in hand with the requirement of "unwelcome". Thus, if a conduct or a course of action or behaviour is not welcomed by the employee but still pursued by the supervisor it amounts to coercion. Therefore, an unwelcome and unwanted social or sexual conduct is invariably an act or behaviour forced upon an employee against the employee's free will. In this respect "coercion" may be physical, psychological, or economic (a threat of job related reprisals). Sexual harassment cases normally present one or all of these elements of coercion depending, of course, on the circumstances of each case. Physical coercion in sexual harassment cases has a trapping of criminal assault and battery, but very seldom is a criminal charge laid. Nonetheless, it is apparent that physical force is often used to obtain sexual favours. The following examples may illustrate the point:

Example 1:
The respondent entered the room and put his arms around her and tried to kiss her. Although she resisted, he succeeded in kissing her. When she started to scream, he released her and she immediately left for home.

Example 2:
The respondent began to speak suggestively to the complainant with crude jokes and references to her love life. He also began touching her. She responded with angry looks and asked him to leave her alone. He then grabbed her with his hands on her breasts and bit her cheek. She began to scream, attracting the respondent's brother. However, since the door to the room had earlier been locked, he could only knock at the window. The respondent then stopped and after some hesitation, gave the complainant the keys, permitting her to leave.[77]

Example 3:
The respondent took the complainant downstairs, where he said his office was located, to discuss the work schedule. However, once downstairs, he took her into a room and shut the door behind them. He then put his hands on her breasts and pushed her up against the wall and attempted to kiss her. The complainant became frightened.[78]

---

[77] See *Coutroubis v. Sklavos Printing* (Ont. 1981), 2 C.H.R.R. D/457 (Ratushny).
[78] See *Giouvanoudis v. Golden Fleece Restaurant & Tavern Ltd.* (Ont. 1984), 5 C.H.R.R. D/1967 (Cumming).

Example 4:
The respondent summoned the complainant to the back room and then after a brief discussion involving the bosses receiving sexual favours from their employees the complainant was grabbed by the respondent, who then forcefully put his hand under her shirt. At another occasion, she was again summoned to go to the back room where once again she was grabbed and restrained by the respondent who took this opportunity to place his hand under her shirt. While this incident was taking place the respondent enquired of the complainant if she would like full time employment.[79]

Recently in *Webb v. Cyprus Pizza*,[80] a British Columbia Board of Inquiry found that the respondent employer engaged in a series of coercive behaviour which amounted to sexual harassment. The Board concluded:

> Upon a review of the evidence as a whole, I have concluded that the Complainant was subjected to this kind of coercion based upon sex and that it had become a condition of her continuing employment. I have also concluded that Mr. Roopra sexually harassed the Complainant by:
>
> 1. Touching and combing her hair.
> 2. Putting his arms around her and holding her against her will.
> 3. Making suggestive remarks.
> 4. Leering, ogling and making suggestive gestures.
> 5. Repeatedly asking for dinner dates.
> 6. Asking her to visit a motel and view a pornographic movie.
> 7. Asking questions of a sexual nature such as personal questions about her sex life, whether she was on the birth control pills and if she had ever had an abortion.
>
> Mr. Roopra's conduct towards the Complainant was sexually oriented, whether verbal, physical, or by expression. This conduct was objectionable, offensive, intimidating and caused the Complainant discomfort on the job.[81]

The position of the employer's authority implies a possible coerced socializing, an intimidation that compliance with the employer's invitation is, in effect, a condition of employment. Clearly, if the adverse

---

[79] See *Phillips v. J. Hermiz* (Sask. 1985), 5 C.H.R.R. D/2450 (Katzman).
[80] (B.C. 1985), 6 C.H.R.R. D/2794 (Wilson).
[81] *Ibid.*, at D/2797 (paras. 22892-93).

changes in job functions are a consequence of the refusal to meet socially, there is sexual harassment.[82]

In *Kotyk v. C.E.I.C.*,[83] the tribunal found that Jack Chuba, her supervisor, made unwanted advances to Jane Kotyk, and pressed her to comply and lead her to believe that passing her employment probation depended on her positive response to his repeated demands. The tribunal emphasized the nature of coercion and stated:

> . . . Mr. Chuba exploited Ms. Kotyk's vulnerability caused by her marital problems, and knowing that she feared for her job, persisted in his conduct without informing her that she was now job-secure [she was under the impression that she was still under probation].[84]

The Tribunal concluded that Mr. Chuba's tactics in relation to Ms. Kotyk "were insensitive, bullying and persistent".

Professor Peter Cumming in *Olarte et al. v. Commodore Business Machines Ltd.*,[85] has eloquently described coercive behaviour of a supervisor, which has all the elements of coercion, threat, intimidation and job related reprisals, in the following words:

> The above described discriminatory treatment, subjecting some women workers to continuing sexual advances, sexual talk, and sexual propositions in the face of their clear objections, is in itself unlawful sexual harassment in breach of the Code.
>
> However, the circumstances of the instant case went beyond the above. It is clear that Mr. DeFilippis tried to intimidate and manipulate the female workers he desired sexually. He was in a position, as he knew, of being able to hire very dependent, immigrant female workers (very much needing work, not speaking English and being relatively inarticulate, and who perhaps appeared from their cultural backgrounds to more likely subject themselves to male authority) who he could seek to take sexual advantage of. He was careful to make sure there were no witnesses to his sexual advances. The women he chose were generally scared, and even terrified of him. They were afraid of being punished and even losing their jobs if they rejected him, they were afraid of not being believed if they reported him, afraid of losing their good reputations, and, for those who were married, were afraid of what their husbands might accuse them of, or what their husbands might do to Mr. DeFilippis if they learned what he was attempting.

---

[82] See *Potapczyk v. MacBain* (Can. 1984), 5 C.H.R.R. D/2285 at D/2292 (para. 19321) (Lederman).
[83] (Can. 1984), 4 C.H.R.R. D/1416 (Ashley).
[84] *Ibid.*, at D/1428 (para. 12232).
[85] (Ont. 1983), 4 C.H.R.R. D/1705 (Cumming).

Whenever he was rejected, Mr. DeFilippis would make life more miserable than usual for the women who had rebuffed him, criticizing constantly, being even more rude and crude than he generally was, often arbitrarily moving women from one department to another, and generally being nasty. He would try to find fault with a relatively small detail of their work, or simply make up imaginary shortcomings, and then destroy the whole position of the lady as a functioning worker. He knows how to work upon their emotions and exacerbate their fears, anxieties and nervousness. An example was his criticizing Mrs. Andrikopolous about going to the washroom and threatening to move her to a department he knew she did not want to go to. If confronted by a woman going to management, he would take the offensive, twist around what was being said, and simply try to dominate his accuser by shouting (the taped conversation of the meeting with Melanthi Tsafantakis is an example, *Exhibit* No. 40). Mr. DeFilippis is a clever individual who always has a quick answer, and will yell to beat down the opposition. He is a whimsical tyrant who will feign anger and self-righteousness to get his opponent to retreat.[86]

The employer-employee relationship embodies clear-cut power implications. The situation may be different if it occurs at a social gathering, involving a male president of one company and a female file clerk of another company. In theory, at least, the woman can freely accept or reject the invitation. The same would not be true for these two individuals in an employer-employee relationship with its inherent power implications. It is not, therefore, necessary that there be job-related reprisals attached to the sexual invitation in order for these power implications to be felt by the employee.

3. Persistent and Repeated

It is a commonly held view that sexual encounters must occur frequently before they are considered to be sexual harassment. This, however, should depend upon the type of harassment involved. More serious forms of sexual harassment, such as those involving physical assault, need not occur more than once in order to be considered as sexual harassment. Other types of subtle behaviour involving comments or propositions may occur repeatedly before the behaviour may be identified as being sexual harassment.

---

[86] *Ibid.*, at D/1734 (paras. 14791-93); (affd *sub nom. Commodore Business Machines Ltd. v. Ontario Minister of Labour*) (Ont. 1985), 6 C.H.R.R. D/2883 (Div. Ct.).

In the *Cherie Bell* case Mr. Shime expressed the view that: "persistent and frequent conduct is not a condition for an adverse finding under the *Code* because a single incident of an employee being denied equality of employment because of sex is also prohibited."[87] Professor Abbott in *Robichaud v. Brennan*,[88] on the other hand, expressed the view that persistence is a necessary characteristic of the prohibited conduct. He emphasized that if sexual encounters were not persistent, then they could only be considered to be sexual harassment in cases where a single refusal of a sexual request initiated an adverse employment consequence, such as a discharge.

The tribunals on the question of repetition are more in agreement than they may first appear. The Review Tribunal in *Robichaud* disagreed with the Tribunal's conclusion on the importance of the complainant's submission to the demands of the respondent, but did not argue with his analysis leading up to his conclusion. Professor Abbott accepted the definition of harassment found in *Cherie Bell*, but differed with the reasoning of the portion "relating to persistence". He stated that, "I think persistence is, in many circumstances, but not all, a necessary characteristic of the prohibited conduct".[89] Yet he added a significant caveat that if "the conduct was not persistent, the rejection of the conduct had adverse employment consequences".[90] Taken together, these statements coincide with the position taken in *Kotyk v. C.E.I.C.*, which also makes a link between the behaviour and the consequences which result:

> It is likely that a single unrepeated act is not harassment unless it results in the denial or removal of a tangible benefit available or offered to other persons in similar circumstances, or unless it amounts to an assault, or is a proposition of such a gross or obscene nature that it could reasonably be considered to have created a negative or unpleasant emotional or psychological work environment. A "normal" proposition or suggestion would probably not have this result. To this extent, the last quoted paragraph in *Bell* ... is adopted.[91]

In 1983, in a policy statement, the Canadian Human Rights Commission put into regulatory form much of what was said by Mr. Shime in the *Cherie Bell* case. It states, among other things:

---

[87] *Bell v. The Flaming Steer Steak House* (Ont. 1980), 1 C.H.R.R. D/155, at D/156 (para. 1392) (Shime).
[88] (Can. 1982), 3 C.H.R.R. D/977 (Tribunal — Abbott).
[89] *Ibid.*, at D/981-82 (para. 8717).
[90] *Ibid.*
[91] (Can. 1983), 4 C.H.R.R. D/1416 at D/1430 (para. 12251) (Ashley).

> ... [H]arassment may be related to any of the discriminatory grounds contained in the Canadian Human Rights Act. Such behaviour may be verbal, physical, deliberate, unsolicited or unwelcome; it may be one incident or a series of incidents. While the following is not an exhaustive list, harassment may include:
>
> ...
>
> unnecessary physical contact such as touching, patting, pinching ... physical assault,[92]

Thus, according to the Canadian Human Rights Commission a single or isolated incident of unwanted sexual behaviour may constitute sexual harassment for the purposes of the *Canadian Human Rights Act*.

This approach was also adopted by Professor Norman in the arbitration case of *Re Canada Post and Canadian Union of Postal Workers*.[93] In that case a female employee while working suddenly felt hands on her hips accompanied by bodily pressure on her buttocks. It was her immediate supervisor. The incident was over in less time than it takes to tell about it. This being a case of a single, isolated incident of unwanted sexual advances, the arbitrator posed the question:

> It remains to consider whether an isolated act of unwanted intimate physical contact on the part of an immediate supervisor constitutes sexual harassment of an employee, so as to amount to an infraction of art. 5 of the collective agreement.[94]

The arbitrator held that the incident of sexual advances in this case, though isolated, amounted to sexual harassment.

Although repetition of an action, as stated earlier, is not a necessary requirement to finding that a behaviour amounts to sexual harassment, the Human Rights Tribunals have been seriously concerned if the conduct or behaviour in question was repeated or persisted over a period of time. In *Zarankin v. Johnstone c.o.b. as Wessex Inn*,[95] a British Columbia Board of Inquiry found that the owner, Ian Johnstone, persistently made vulgar and coarse remarks which constituted sexual harassment.

---

[92] See the Policy Statement issued by the Canadian Human Rights Commission (1983), 4 C.H.R.R. ND/8.
[93] (1983), 11 L.A.C. (3d) 13 (Norman).
[94] *Ibid.*, at 18.
[95] (B.C. 1984), 5 C.H.R.R. D/2274 (Smith).

The Canadian Human Rights Tribunal in *Potapczyk v. MacBain* found that Mr. MacBain "subjected them (female staff) to physical closeness in a persistent fashion beyond that which was necessary for him to relate to his female staff in a professional way."[96] The tribunal emphasized that his conduct was illustrative of the kind of more subtle, yet persistent sexual discrimination that a multitude of women across the country have had to endure without redress.

In *Janzen v. Platy Enterprises Ltd.*,[97] a Manitoba Board of Inquiry held that "Tommy [a cook — who had supervisory powers] made a variety of sexual advances including touching the complainant for sexual reasons, and that he persisted in this conduct even though it was obvious from her evidence that she forcibly rejected his actions".[98] The Board found that both women were subjected to *persistent* and *unwelcome touching* and sexual comments amounting to physical and mental harassment of a severe nature. The Board was specifically concerned that "the harassment was *close to being constant throughout her period of employment*".

The repetition or persisting of an unsolicited socialization or sexual contact over a period of time magnifies the impact of that behaviour on the victim and the tribunals are bound to take a serious view of it.

On the other hand, if the alleged harassing conduct involves dirty jokes or remarks, the tribunals are more likely to insist on frequency before finding that the comments amounted to the commission of sexual harassment. For example, in *Watt v. Regional Municipality of Niagara*,[99] the Board of Inquiry, chaired by Professor John McCamus, stated that the incident in question would have to have a degree of frequency and offensiveness which would meet the "condition of work" threshold of s. 4 of the Ontario *Human Rights Code*. This position is further supported by s. 9(f) of the Ontario *Code*, which defines harassment in terms of "a course of vexatious comment or conduct". In interpreting the expression "a course" one author has pointed out that "one discrete action of brief duration will be insufficient to

---

[96] The *MacBain* case, *supra*, note 82, at D/2297 (para. 19355).
[97] (Man. 1985), 6 C.H.R.R. D/2735 (Henteleff); revd (Man. 1986), 8 C.H.R.R. D/3831 (C.A.) on the ground that sexual harassment is not prohibited by the Manitoba *Human Rights Act*, a decision quashed by the Supreme Court of Canada (Man. 1989), 10 C.H.R.R. D/6205.
[98] *Ibid.*, at D/2766 (para. 22632).
[99] (Ont. 1984), 5 C.H.R.R. D/2453 (para. 20349) (McCamus).

constitute harassment".[100] According to Professor McCamus "it would be very unusual indeed to find a situation in which a single insult could be reasonably construed to create"[101] an offensive condition of employment. Thus, it appears that single incidents without repercussion are unlikely to qualify as harassment, whereas repeated incidents, even where there are no tangible effects, would usually be considered an act of sexual harassment.

Thus, unless the conduct is quite severe, a single incident or isolated incidents of offensive sexual conduct or remarks generally do not create an abusive environment.[102] A "hostile environment" sexual harassment claim generally requires a showing of a pattern of offensive conduct. But a single, unusually severe incident of sexual misconduct may be sufficient to constitute sexual harassment.[103] The more severe the harassment, the less need to show a repetitive series of incidents. This is particularly true when the harassment is physical. A single unwelcome physical advance can seriously poison the victim's work environment. If a supervisor or even a co-worker sexually touches an employee, the tribunals normally would find him guilty of causing sexual harassment.[104]

---

[100] See J. Keene, *Human Rights in Ontario* (Toronto: The Carswell Company Ltd. 1983), p. 195.
[101] *Watt v. Regional Municipality of Niagara, supra,* note 99, at D/2459 (para. 20352).
[102] *Robinson v. The Company Farm Ltd.* (Ont. 1984), 5 C.H.R.R. D/2243 (Cumming). The Board of Inquiry stated at D/2246 (para. 18981): "A mere isolated invitation by an employer to an employee to have an affair is, by itself, not unlawful, but rather is simply a matter of morality." See also *Scott v. Sears Roebuck Co.,* 798 F. 2d 210 at 214, 41 E.P.D. para. 36,439 (7th Cir. 1986). The court held that offensive comments and conduct of co-workers were "too isolated and lacking the repetitive and debilitating effect necessary to maintain a hostile environment claim". See also *Moylan v. Maries County,* 792 F. 2d 746 at 749, 40 E.P.D. para. 36,228 (8th Cir. 1986) and *Downes v. Federal Aviation Administration,* 775 F. 2d 288 at 293, 38 E.P.D. para. 35,590 (D.C. Cir. 1985).
[103] *Gervais v. Agriculture Canada* (Can. 1988), 9 C.H.R.R. D/5002 (Review Tribunal — Fleck); *Purdy v. Marwick Manufacturing Co.* (Ont. 1987), 9 C.H.R.R. D/4840 (Simmons).
[104] See *Mitchell v. Traveller Inn (Sudbury) Ltd.* (Ont. 1981), 2 C.H.R.R. D/590 (Kerr); *Ross v. Gendall* (Sask. 1989), 10 C.H.R.R. D/5836 (Piche); *Elmore v. Today's Market Line (1987) Inc.* (B.C. 1989), 10 C.H.R.R. D/5861 (Hughes); see also *Barrett v. Omaha National Bank,* 584 F. Supp. 22, 35 FEP 585 (D. Neb. 1984); affd 726 F. 2d 424, 33 E.P.D. para. 34,132 (8th Cir. 1984); see also *Gilardi v. Schroeder,* 672 F. Supp. 1043, 45 FEP 283 (N.D. Ill. 1986) — the complainant who was drugged by employer's owner and raped while unconscious, then was terminated at the insistence of the owner's wife, was awarded $113,000 in damages for harassment and intentional infliction of emotional distress.

Professor Swan in *Canada Post Corp. v. C.U.P.W. (Gibson)*,[105] while dealing with the issue of whether or not one isolated or single incident of sexual teasing was unwelcome, stated:

> Moreover, the *comments about the tampons and underwear were directly related to the female employee's gender,* and could not have been made to a male employee. They were also, in my view, calculated to insult her gender, and to imply that she was unsanitary. *These are not comments that, in my view, one would ordinarily have to make more than once in order to establish that they were likely to be unwelcome.*[106] [Emphasis added]

4. Deliberate and Intentional

Whether sexual conduct constitutes sexual harassment is also dependent upon whether a person knew that his or her behaviour was offensive and unwanted. By establishing that harassment occurs only when the harasser's intentions are deliberate, this leaves a loophole for the harassers to claim that they were unaware that their behaviour was offensive.

In *Re Government of Province of Alta. and Alta. Union of Provincial Employees*,[107] the grievor was dismissed on various charges including sexual harassment of female employees. The incident of sexual harassment as described by witnesses included touching the legs of a female employee, placing hands on the waist and breasts of another and patting the buttocks of another employee. The Public Service Grievance Appeal Board held that the grievor's conduct did not constitute sexual harassment. The Board stated:

> We are of the view that the conduct as related about the grievor concerning the "sexual harassment" incidents was certainly not intended as such by the grievor. In our view, such conduct would be better classified as inappropriate behaviour.[108]

The Board's conclusion seems to be based on the finding that the behaviour in question was not "an intentional, wilful or malicious act on the part of the grievor". The Board said, "It may have been

---

[105] (1987), 27 L.A.C. (3d) 27 (Swan).
[106] *Ibid.*, at 44.
[107] (1983), 10 L.A.C. (3d) 179 (Larson).
[108] *Ibid.*, at 191.

that the grievor's actions were meant in a light vein and he did not intend them to be taken seriously . . . ."

It is difficult to predict how a Human Rights Tribunal would have decided had this case been before it. However, it is obvious that there is a basic difference in the approach taken by the Human Rights Tribunals and the Arbitrators in determining whether or not a particular sexual behaviour constitutes sexual harassment. The tribunals generally determine sexual harassment on the basis of intensity and gravity of the behaviour and its perception by the harassee rather than the motive and design of the harasser.

Human Rights Tribunals in Canada have not attached much importance to the elements of "deliberate and intentional" in human rights cases. It is the effect on the complainant and not the motive of the respondent which has been the paramount concern of the tribunals. In non-sexual harassment cases the Canadian tribunals and courts have emphasized, again and again, the importance of the adverse effect of discrimination rather than the intent of discrimination. They have held that if an effect of a conduct or practice is discrimination, it is immaterial whether or not the respondent intended to discriminate. The adverse effect principle was applied in cases such as *Sing v. Security and Investigation Services Ltd.*,[109] *Rand v. Sealy Eastern Ltd.*,[110] *Marcotte v. Rio Algom Ltd.*,[111] and *Christie v. Central Alberta Dairy Pool.*[112] In 1976, the Alberta Supreme Court in *A.G. Alta. v. Gares*,[113] a case arising out of a complaint of discrimination on the basis of sex under s. 5 of the *Individual's Rights Protection Act*,[114] (because of a lower rate of pay for female employees than for males) the court in no uncertain terms stated that "It is the discriminatory result which is prohibited and not a discriminatory intent."

In *Re Rocca Group Ltd. and Muise*,[115] MacDonald J., speaking for the Prince Edward Island Supreme Court, said in dealing with a complaint under the *Human Rights Act*:[116]

---

[109] (Ont. 1977), unreported (Cumming).
[110] (Ont. 1981), 3 C.H.R.R. D/938 (Cumming).
[111] (Can. 1983), 5 C.H.R.R. D/2010 (Review Tribunal — Hesler).
[112] (Alta. 1984), 6 C.H.R.R. D/2488 (Johanson).
[113] (1976), 67 D.L.R. (3d) 635, 76 CLLC 14,016 (Alta. S.C.).
[114] S.A. 1972, c. 2 [now R.S.A. 1980, c. 1-2].
[115] (1979), 102 D.L.R. (3d) 529 (S.C.). Leave to appeal to S.C.C. denied 102 D.L.R. (3d) 529n (S.C.C.).
[116] S.P.E.I. 1975, c. 72 [now R.S.P.E.I. 1985, c. H-12.].

I am not in absolute agreement that it was the trial Judge's finding that intention was a relevant part of his findings, however, if it were I would agree with the appellant's contention that intention plays no part in considering whether or not there has been discrimination.[117]

The matter was considered as well in *Osborne v. Inco Ltd.*,[118] where Kroft J. said:

Adjudicators in Manitoba have consistently concluded that discrimination, be it on the grounds of religion or sex, is not confined to instances where intent is shown: e.g. *Froese v. Pine Creek Sch. Div. 30*, M. Rothstein, Q.C. . . . *McDonald v. Knit-Rite Mills Ltd.* (1983), 5 C.H.R.R. D/1949 (Man. Bd. Adjud.): and *Can. Safeway Ltd. v. Steel, supra*. This is a view which I think to be totally consistent with the object of the Manitoba Act and the wording of s. 6(1) in particular.[119]

The Supreme Court of Canada in *Ont. Human Rights Commn. et al. v. Borough of Etobicoke*[120] found mandatory retirement provisions agreed upon in a collective agreement discriminatory even though "there was no evidence to indicate that the motives of the employer were other than honest and in good faith." Further, the Manitoba Court of Queen's Bench in *Re Canada Safeway Ltd. and Steel, et al.*[121] held that the object, purpose or motivation of the employer is not relevant in determining whether there is discrimination in fact.

The Supreme Court of Canada in *Ont. Human Rights Commn. v. Simpsons-Sears Ltd.*,[122] unanimously held that it is not necessary to prove that discrimination was intentional to find that a violation of human rights legislation has occurred. An employment rule, neutral on its face and honestly made, can have discriminatory effects. It is the result or the effect of an act which is important in determining whether discrimination has occurred. McIntyre J. for the court stated:

---

[117] *Supra*, note 115, at 533.
[118] (Man. 1984), 5 C.H.R.R. D/2219, [1984] 5 W.W.R. 228 (Q.B.); revd [1985] 2 W.W.R. 577 (C.A.). The Manitoba Court of Appeal, however, stated:
   that *it is not necessary to prove intent to discriminate under our Act* and that reasonable accommodation by an employer is a factor to be taken into account in determining whether there has been a contravention of the Act. [Emphasis added]
[119] *Ibid.*, at 238 (W.W.R.).
[120] (Ont. 1982), 3 C.H.R.R. D/781 (S.C.).
[121] (Man. 1984), 9 D.L.R. (4th) 330; affd 13 D.L.R. (4th) 314 (C.A.). Leave to appeal to S.C.C. dismissed B.C.S.C. Feb. 15/85.
[122] (Ont. 1985), 7 C.H.R.R. D/3102 (S.C.C.).

> A distinction must be made between what I would describe as direct discrimination and the concept already referred to as adverse effect discrimination in connection with employment. Direct discrimination occurs in this connection where an employer adopts a practice or rule which on its face discriminates on a prohibited ground. For example, "No Catholics or no women or no blacks employed here." There is, of course, no disagreement in the case at bar that direct discrimination of that nature would contravene the Act. On the other hand, there is the concept of adverse effect discrimination. . . . An employment rule honestly made for sound economic or business reasons, equally applicable to all to whom it is intended to apply, may yet be discriminatory if it affects a person or group of persons differently from others to whom it may apply. From the foregoing I therefore conclude that the appellant showed a *prima facie* case of discrimination based on creed before the board of inquiry.[123]

The Supreme Court decision in *Simpsons-Sears* leaves no doubt that the "adverse effect" rule should be a controlling factor in determining whether or not discrimination was committed. There seems to be no reason not to apply the same principle to sexual harassment cases. Thus, an employer can be found guilty of sexual harassment, even though he has no motive or intent to cause sexual harassment. For example, in the *MacBain* case, the tribunal rejected the argument that Mr. MacBain either intended or had a plan for that kind of behaviour. The Tribunal stated:

> We are not convinced on the evidence that Mr. MacBain ever had such a plan in mind either in hiring Ms. Potapczyk or in the manner in which he treated her while she was employed by him. . . . There is not sufficient evidence before us to lead us to the inference put forth by Ms. Cornish that Mr. MacBain, either consciously or subconsciously, attempted to place Ms. Potapczyk in a position of psychological dependence whereby he would ultimately be able to take sexual advantage of her.[124]

Nevertheless, the Tribunal found that Mr. MacBain was guilty of sexual harassment of his female staff.

In sexual harassment cases, even before the *Simpsons-Sears* decision, Human Rights Tribunals in sexual harassment cases had hardly given any legitimacy to the argument of motive. It is unlikely that in the light of the *Simpsons-Sears* decision, any tribunal in future will give any special weight to the lack of motive on the part of the perpetrator in sexual harassment cases.

---

[123] *Ibid.*, at D/3106 (para. 24772).
[124] The *MacBain* case (Can. 1984), 5 C.H.R.R. D/2285 at D/2295 (para. 19351) (Lederman).

5. Sexually Stereotyping Behaviour

The question is generally raised as to whether (a) crude and dirty jokes (remarks and comments, etc.) and (b) dress and grooming requirements based on sexual stereotypes (attitudes) constitute sexual harassment and thus are prohibited under the human rights statutes.

(a) Crude and Bad Jokes

Crude and bad jokes with sexual reference are not specifically forbidden by anti-discrimination laws. However, such joking behaviour may constitute sexual harassment if it creates, as a condition of employment, a work environment that undermines the employee's sexual dignity as a man or woman. Chairperson Cumming in *Torres v. Royalty Kitchenware Ltd.* expressed the following caution:

> There are some employers (and employees) who simply are very crude and who speak in bad taste in discussing in the workplace their relationships with the opposite sex, or in telling sex "jokes". It is not the intent, or effect, of the *Human Rights Code*, or the function of a Board of Inquiry, to pass judgment upon such persons. It is only "sexual harassment" that is unlawful conduct.[125]

The difficulty arises in determining what kind of humour is considered "normal" in the workplace, and what kind of humour crosses the line of social acceptance to create an offensive environment for some employees. Verbal sexual jokes and unpleasant remarks in the workplace may fall under two categories:

1. where sexual jokes and dirty remarks is the language of the floor in that particular work, business or trade; and the jokes or remarks are not directed particularly to any one individual or a group of individuals;
2. where verbal jokes, remarks and suggestions are directed expressly or by implication to a specific person, *i.e.*, where an individual or individuals alone were the recipients of those jokes.

In *Aragona v. Elegant Lamp Co.*, the Board of Inquiry pointed out that:

---

[125] (Ont. 1982), 3 C.H.R.R. D/858 at D/861 (para. 7631) (Cumming).

There is no doubt that considerable "banter" and "teasing" occurred. There is also no doubt that there were many comments with sexual connotations. However, the evidence indicates that the employees were willing participants who enjoyed the atmosphere and who "gave" as much as they "took".[126]

Where the proven conduct is freely accepted and enjoyed by other employees, it cannot "reasonably be perceived to create a negative psychological and emotional work environment." Where there is general acceptance, but where an individual employee does not care to participate, that feeling should be expressed directly and unambiguously. The objective standard could then be *applied to that individual in light of the additional fact* of expressed disapproval.

For example, a comment about one's legs might be returned with gratitude for a perceived compliment, with repartee, or with a clear statement that such comments are not acceptable to the individual involved. Subsequent comments in the face of the last response could well cross the line of harassment. Of course, much will depend on the circumstances. "A businessman who wears shorts to work or a secretary who wears a short miniskirt might well invite such comments", observed the Board of Inquiry in the *Aragona* case.

In *Howard v. Lemoignan*,[127] the complainants testified that the respondent habitually used sexual, vulgar and demeaning language, and made suggestions that the complainants were to wear tighter clothing and appear for work without bras. The Board described the atmosphere of the workplace as "one more suited to an all-male tavern or lumber camp than an office where there are staff and customers of varying backgrounds and of both sexes." The Board stated:

> The complainants have established that the Respondent behaved in a crude and rude manner . . . The complainants have also established their discomfort in the psychological environment in which their employment took place.[128]

Although the Board found the respondent's behaviour to be unacceptable, it concluded that "the discomfort that these complainants experienced does not go far enough to constitute an affront to their dignity, nor does the treatment they received go far enough to constitute sexual harassment".

---

[126] (Ont. 1982), 3 C.H.R.R. D/1109 at D/1112 (para. 9759) (Ratushny).
[127] (Alta. 1982), 3 C.H.R.R. D/1150 (Welsh).
[128] *Ibid.*, at D/1154 (para. 10170).

Sexual Harassment Definition

In *Watt v. Regional Municipality of Niagara*[129], an Ontario Board of Inquiry found that although Alex Wales (the supervisor) was admittedly biased against women working in his area and although offensive remarks were made to Ms. Watt, these remarks and jokes did not occur with sufficient frequency to create an "abusive atmosphere" contrary to the law. While commenting on the general work environment the Board stated that the language used by workers was quite crude and obscene as a general matter. There was a good deal of abuse, good natured or otherwise, meted out in conversation. The Board concluded:

> The two "jokes" in question are, of course, quite offensive but *they do appear to be isolated incidents rather than part of a continuing pattern of verbal harassment through the use of profane humour.* I have no doubt, however, that conduct of this kind could pass the threshold of the Section 4 test if it occurred with significantly greater frequency or if it were continued in the face of objections articulated by someone in the complainant's position.[130] [Emphasis added]

The Board concluded that though the language used by the supervisors was quite crude and obscene as a matter of routine, it did not constitute sexual harassment because the complainant participated in the jokes and replied back, and she never objected or complained about the use of such language. The use of profane humour was isolated.

In *Rack v. The Playgirl Cabaret*,[131] the B.C. Human Rights Council found that as a matter of fact foul and crude language was indeed used by the respondent. However, in view of the working environment of the nightclubs, it held that the language used by the respondent could not have created a "poisonous and offensive work environment" amounting to sexual harassment. The Tribunal stated:

> Bearing in mind the testimony of all witnesses that there was drinking at these staff meetings and parties, I find that Van Den Oord did use foul and profane language with his employees in the club after work, and further I find that the majority of employees reciprocated in a like fashion.[132]

Chairperson Verbrugge concluded:

---

[129] (Ont. 1984), 5 C.H.R.R. D/2453 (McCamus).
[130] *Ibid.*, at D/2467 (para. 20401).
[131] (B.C. 1985), 6 C.H.R.R. D/2857 (Verbrugge).
[132] *Ibid.*, at D/2859 (para. 23328).

> In this case, overwhelming evidence was presented to show that Van Den Oord's language was accepted and, if not exactly enjoyed, certainly reciprocated by the other employees. There was no evidence whatsoever that the Complainant expressed disapproval of the language used.... The fact that we are dealing with three nightclubs where the audience is predominantly male, of a rather rowdy nature, and that the entertainment consists of rock n'roll bands, exotic dancers and strippers, must also be borne in mind when determining what would constitute "ordinary banter". I therefore find that the language used by Van Den Oord during staff meetings and afterwards constitutes ordinary banter in the circumstances, especially in light of the fact that the employees reciprocated.[133]

Thus, according to *Rack*, the use of profane language in the working atmosphere of nightclubs (where the audience is predominantly rowdy males, rock n'roll bands, exotic dancers and strippers), where the language was reciprocated by other employees and was not expressly disapproved of by the complainant, amounts to "ordinary banter" and not sexual harassment. It follows then that in determining whether or not the use of crude and profane language in a particular case amounts to sexual harassment, the following factors should be considered:

1. the working environment of that particular business or work
2. reciprocity by the employees
3. expressed disapproval by the complainant and
4. whether or not the incidents were isolated.

On the other hand, where sexual jokes and distasteful comments were directed specifically to a particular individual employee, it was found that she was the victim of sexual harassment. In *Foisy v. Bell Canada*,[134] the complainant alleged that one day before the office party, and subsequently during the banquet, her two immediate supervisors made distasteful and uncalled for sexual comments about her before several people. In a suit for "delictual damages" the Quebec Superior Court found that the supervisors' comments and jokes amounted to sexual harassment of the complainant.

Similarly, the tribunals in other jurisdictions have found that some of the language, expression, remarks, and jokes used in the workplace are so crude, offensive and degrading that they cause humiliation and embarrassment to the victims and other female employees. The

---

[133] *Ibid.*, at D/2860 (para. 23343).
[134] (Que. 1985), 6 C.H.R.R. D/2817 (S.C.).

Sexual Harassment Definition

tribunals have held that those remarks are quite inappropriate and have no place whatsoever in the workplace. They poisoned the working environment and cause sexual harassment to the victims. The following are a few examples of the questionable verbal abuses:

"You need a good man and I am it."[135]
"You need a good lay, a good screw."[136]
"Pick up your hips and hold it."[137]
"I like the way it [her skirt] hugs your bum."[138]
"Oh baby give me a blow job."[139]
"If I did not know you so well, I would kiss your bottom lips."[140]
"He knew how to get young girls going by squeezing their bums."[141]
"I will give you my cock instead."[142]
"You have a nice body" and "you're looking good."[143]

In one case the victim had her hands on her pocket, the perpetrator approached her and put his hands in her pockets and said: "What are you playing with in there? Can I play too?"[144]

Similarly calling the female employees "baby",[145] "girlfriend",[146] "sexatary",[147] "horny",[148] "sluts"[149] and "douche bag"[150] is inappropriate and may poison the working environment, leading to sexual harassment. In the same vein, comments or inquiries about the

---

[135] *Nesvog v. Rutschmann* (B.C. 1988), 9 C.H.R.R. D/5293 (para. 39920) (Powell).
[136] *Ibid.*
[137] *Ibid.*
[138] *Humble v. K. Parsad & Co.* (B.C. 1988), 9 C.H.R.R. D/5057 (para. 38590) (Hughes).
[139] *Leith v. Community Bingo (Wetaskiwin) Ltd.* (Alta. 1988), 9 C.H.R.R. D/5165 (para. 39207) (Manning). See also *Green v. 709637 Ontario Inc.* (Ont. 1988), 9 C.H.R.R. D/4749 (Plaut).
[140] *McCaskill v. Treasury Board (Indian and Northern Affairs)* (1990), P.S.S.R.B. File No. 166-2-19524 (Chodos).
[141] *Ibid.*
[142] *Sharp v. Seasons Restaurant* (Ont. 1987), 8 C.H.R.R. D/4133 (para. 32663) (Springate).
[143] *Huhn v. Hunter's Haus of Burgers* (B.C. 1987), 8 C.H.R.R. D/4157 (para. 32897) (Wilson).
[144] *Rodin v. Herman* (Sask. 1988), 9 C.H.R.R. D/5375 (para. 40203) (Wiebe).
[145] *Morrison v. Phung* (B.C. 1988), 9 C.H.R.R. D/5282 (Hughes).
[146] *Ibid.* See also *Ostifichuk and Corrington v. C. A. M. Janitorial Ltd.* (Man. 1986), 7 C.H.R.R. D/3331 (Steel).
[147] *Voeller v. Kingfisher Sales Inc.* (B.C. 1990), 11 C.H.R.R. D/433 (Powell).
[148] *Kahlon v. Treasury Board (Solicitor General)* (1991), P.S.S.R.B. File No. 166-2-20871 (Kwavnick).
[149] *Haight v. W.W.G. Management Inc.* (B.C. 1990), 11 C.H.R.R. D/124 (Hughes).
[150] *Ibid.*

employee's (victim's) sex life, such as whether she got along with her husband,[151] "How is your sex life?"[152] and about her sexual relationship with her boyfriend[153] fall within the prohibitory domain. Discussion of women's bodies in vulgar terms, including describing the "peelers" (exotic dancers) to female employees,[154] or suggesting and asking them to go to bed with the perpetrator[155] to retain their job, falls within the prohibitory category.

It is clear from the earlier discussion that even if it might be considered that what has occurred is "sexual banter" common to the workplace, if a person found it objectionable and makes it known in clear and precise terms that such actions are not acceptable to that person, then that is the standard of behaviour that is established *vis-à-vis* that person. At the same time it is also clear that if a specific employee is a target of such sexual jokes, no protest or objection may be required. However, it may be pointed out that basically the responsibility lies with the offended person to express her disapproval of such an environment and make the perpetrators of such behaviour aware that their conduct is personally offensive.

However, basically a woman does not and should not forfeit her right to be free from sexual harassment by choosing to work in an atmosphere that has traditionally included vulgar, anti-female language. There is no justification whatsoever why an environment pre-existing the entrance of women workers should continue to set the contextual norm once women arrive. To accept as a given that a male-dominated workplace will be "rough and coarse" and that this shall be the standard against which harassment will be judged, entails accepting that existing gender stereotypes will have the weight of

---

[151] *Graham v. Sunrise Poultry Processors Ltd.* (B.C. 1988) 9 C.H.R.R. D/4771 (Barr).

[152] *Voeller v. Kingfisher Sales Inc.* (B.C. 1990), 11 C.H.R.R. D/433 (Powell); *Noffke v. McClaskin Hot House* (Ont. 1990), 11 C.H.R.R. D/407 (Zemans). See also *Button v. Westsea Construction Co.* (B.C. 1991), 13 C.H.R.R. D/1 (Powell), where the perpetrator asked questions about her ex-husband and boyfriend.

[153] *Burridge v. Katsiris* (Sask. 1989), 11 C.H.R.R. D/427 (Katzman). In *Korda v. PK and JP Enterprises Ltd.* (B.C. 1990), 12 C.H.R.R. D/201 (Barr), the council held that questions about the complainant's sexual activities and those of her mother represent some of the "more subtle forms" of sexual harassment.

[154] *Haight v. W. W. G. Management Inc.* (B.C. 1990), 11 C.H.R.R. D/124 (Hughes).

[155] *Ostifichuk and Corrington v. C. A. M. Janitorial Ltd.* (Man. 1986) 7 C.H.R.R. D/3331 (Steel); *Kahlon v. Treasury Board (Solicitor General)* (1991), P.S.S.R.B. File No. 166-2-20871 (Kwavnick). See also *Bishop v. Hardy* (Ont. 1987), 8 C.H.R.R. D/3868 (Soberman), where the perpetrator told the victim the only way that she would keep her job is if she slept with him. He had to know the person (employee) "inside and out, go to bed with them sort of thing".

law.[156] Canadian standards and expectations in this regard drastically differ from those in the United States.[157] If women are to be encouraged in the workforce, then the old standards of the male-dominated work environment must give way to the emerging new values of equity and respect for women.

The presence of pornographic magazines in the workplace and vulgar employee comments concerning them; offensive sexual comments made to and about the victim and other female employees by her supervisor or co-workers; sexually oriented pictures in a company-sponsored movie and slide presentations, and sexually oriented pictures and calendars in the workplace create a "hostile environment" in which women are viewed as men's sexual playthings rather than as their equal co-workers, and indeed are a profound affront to the dignity of women.[158] The precise purpose of the human rights law is to prevent such behaviour and attitude from poisoning the work environment, and the recent decisions support this view.

In *Haight v. W.W.G. Management Inc.*,[159] the B.C. Human Rights Council while commenting on the crude and obscene language in the workplace stated:

> Notwithstanding what the complainant said about putting up with the unpleasant environment created by Tantrum's choice of language, the fact is that employees, including those referred to by Plante as "needing their jobs" (into which category the complainant said she fell), should not have to "go along with" that kind of conduct and work in that kind of atmosphere which one could reasonably describe as detrimentally affecting the work environment. While the complain-

---

[156] See Kathleen Gallivan: "Sexual Harassment after Janzen v. Platy: The Transformative Possibilities" (1991), 49 *University of Toronto Faculty of Law Rev.* 27 at 39.

[157] See *Rabidue v. Osceola Refining Co.*, 805 F. 2d 611, 41 E.P.D. para. 36,643 (6th Cir. 1986), where the Court had rejected the plaintiff's claim of harassment on the ground of "the lexicon of obscenity that pervaded the environment of the workplace both before and after the plaintiff's introduction into its environs, coupled with the reasonable expectations of the plaintiff upon voluntarily entering the environment". Commenting further on humour and rough language, the Court stated:

> "it cannot seriously be disputed that in some work environments, humour and language are rough hewn and vulgar. Sexual jokes, sexual conversation and girlie magazines may abound. Title VII was not meant to . . . or can . . . change this".

[158] *Barbetta v. Chemlawn Services Corp.*, 669 F. Supp. 569, 45 E.P.D. para. 37,568 (W.D.N.Y. 1987). In this case the Court refused to follow the Sixth Circuit decision.

[159] (B.C. 1990), 11 C.H.R.R. D/124 (Hughes).

ant was prepared to stay on the job in this kind of environment for economic reasons, because she needed the job, the fact does not detract from the "unwelcome conduct" created by Tantrum's offensive and degrading language which I view as being totally unacceptable. By his use of crude language, he attacked the dignity and self-respect of the complainant and other female staff of the shop.

Tantrum's conduct, both verbally and physically, amounted to an abuse of both economic and sexual power in the workplace. His deportment to the complainant was indeed "a profound affront" to the dignity of the complainant. I find that Tantrum's behaviour constitutes sex discrimination as prohibited by s. 8 of the Act.[160]

In *Re Canada Post Corp. and Canadian Union of Postal Workers*,[161] Professor Swan emphasized that "if employees have a right to be protected from physical assaults by their fellow employees, they have an equivalent right to be protected from a course of verbal injury . . .". He stated:

While it may be that insults were traded generally on the dock among employees, and the female employee was only receiving her fair share of those insults for the most part, the grievor's conduct on February 26, 1986, went far beyond what one employee should be required to take from another, and was apparently calculated to be as hurtful as possible. Moreover, the comments about the tampons and underwear were directly related to the female employee's gender, and could not have been made to a male employee. They were also, in my view, calculated to insult her gender, and to imply that she was unsanitary . . .; *no employee would appreciate insult of this nature on any basis and it cannot be a term of anyone's employment to be degraded in this way.*[162] [Emphasis added]

(b) Visual Jokes, Cartoons of Sexual Nature, or Nudity

There do not seem to be many cases dealing with visual jokes, cartoons or nude pictures. However, if the anti-discrimination law is intended to protect the employees from verbal humiliation, it is safe to assume that it is equally intended to protect them from visual harassment. Thus, an exhibit of pornographic material or hanging of a nude picture or cartoon in the commonly shared workplace may

---

[160] *Ibid.*, (paras. 45 and 46).
[161] (1987), 27 L.A.C. (3d) 27 (Swan).
[162] *Ibid.*, at 44.

be degrading and humiliating to an individual or a group of individual employees. This view is shared at least by one Board of Inquiry.[163] In another recent case an employer who momentarily appeared nude before his female employee was found guilty of sexual harassment.[164] This same principle may be extended to the hanging of a nude picture in the office, where employees of the opposite sex frequently visit.

The Ontario Board of Inquiry in *Purdy v. Marwick Manufacturing Co.* found that the perpetrator dropping his pants in front of the complainant constituted sexual harassment.[165] In another case the arbitrator upheld the suspension of the perpetrator who pulled down his pants to mid-thigh and asked the complainant "if she would like to do a strip search".[166] Similarly, in a case where the perpetrator gave to the complainant a sucker in the shape of penis and an inappropriate greeting card, he was found guilty of causing sexual harassment.[167] In one case where dirty and obscene pictures and a penis carved out of soap were placed on the assembly line in full view of the victim and other employees, it was found that the victim suffered psychological disablement resulting from the stress due to sexual harassment at the workplace to the extent that she attempted to suicide.[168]

In *Sask. Human Rights Commn. v. The Engineering Students' Soc.*,[169] the Saskatchewan Board of Inquiry found that dirty jokes, sex symbols and emblems, photographs, cartoons such as a pair of unclothed female breasts, and cartoons showing women in extremely ridiculous and humiliating positions, were demeaning to women because of their sex. The Board ruled that two issues of the "Red Eye", a newspaper regularly published by the Engineering Students' Society, ridiculed, belittled, and affronted the dignity of women, contrary to s. 14 of the Saskatchewan Human Rights Code.

---

[163] See *Sask. Human Rights Commn. v. The Engineering Students' Soc.* (Sask. 1984), 5 C.H.R.R. D/2074 (Havemann).
[164] See *Irving v. Medland* (Man. 1985), 6 C.H.R.R. D/2842 (Leland Berg).
[165] (Ont. 1987), 9 C.H.R.R. D/4840 (Simmons). See also *Nesvog v. Rutschmann* (B.C. 1988), 9 C.H.R.R. D/5293 (Powell).
[166] *Lavoie v. Treasury Board (Solicitor General)* (1989), P.S.S.R.B. File No. 166-2-18953 (Galipeault).
[167] *Graham v. Sunrise Poultry Processors Ltd.* (B.C. 1988), 9 C.H.R.R. D/4771 (Barr).
[168] See Workers' Compensation Benefits in Chapter 5, *infra*.
[169] *Supra*, note 163.

(c) Dress and Grooming Requirements

The question is often asked whether or not dress and grooming requirements based on sexual stereotypes amount to sexual harassment or sex discrimination.[170] In Canada, *Doherty v. Lodger's Int'l. Ltd.*[171] was the first case of this nature. In this case, two female waitresses refused to wear uniforms on the grounds that it made them feel exploited, humiliated and degraded. They complained that they had been discriminated against on the basis of sex when they were required to wear uniforms accentuating their sexuality which brought on verbal and physical harassment from customers.

A New Brunswick Board of Inquiry held that both sexual harassment and the requirement to accent their female sexuality were discrimination on the basis of sex. It ruled that the complainants were discriminated against because of their sex when they were required to wear uniforms which they found objectionable as a condition of their continued employment as waitresses. The Board of Inquiry after citing *Cherie Bell* and an American decision in *Sage Realty*, stated:

> But the Complainants were called upon to accentuate their female sexuality and to draw attention to it by the wearing of the uniform, to a greater degree than had previously been required of them. I am satisfied that this was required of the Complainants primarily, if not exclusively, because of their sex — their gender — because they were women in circumstances which contravened the Human Rights Act.[172]

The Board found that male employees had not been required to wear uniforms accenting their sexuality.

The next significant case on this issue was *Ballantyne v. Molly "N" Me Tavern*.[173] In that case a tavern which employed both waiters and waitresses attempted to require females to go "topless". The Ontario Board of Inquiry, chaired by Professor John McCamus, held that an imposition of such a requirement was a discriminatory term or condition of employment imposed on female employees because of their sex. Professor McCamus stated:

---

[170] This issue has been eloquently discussed by Professor Peter Cumming in *Giouvanoudis v. Golden Fleece Restaurant & Tavern Ltd.* (Ont. 1984), 5 C.H.R.R. D/1967 (Cumming), and Professor Ian Hunter in *Allan v. Riverside Lodge* (Ont. 1985), 6 C.H.R.R. D/2978.
[171] (N.B. 1982), 3 C.H.R.R. D/628 (Goss).
[172] *Ibid.*, at D/634 (para. 5708).
[173] (Ont. 1983), 4 C.H.R.R. D/1191 (McCamus).

> In my view, the *Sage Realty* and *Lodger's International* cases are suggestive of one line of interpretation of the Code's provisions which may be helpful in cases of this kind. In any case, where as in Lodger's essentially similar work is done by both male and female employees, the imposition of a more burdensome dress requirement on females would constitute an infringement of the Code.[174]

He commented:

> What is objectionable under the Code, in my view, is the subjection of female employees engaging in work essentially similar to that of male employees to become, in effect, entertainers by virtue of a requirement to wear immodest dress. Such practices discriminate against female employees with respect to a term or condition of their employment.[175]

Man. Food and Commercial Workers Union v. Can. Safeway Ltd.,[176] raised an interesting question whether or not the employer's "no beards" policy for male employees was discriminatory. The Manitoba Board of Adjudication found that Safeway's "no beards" policy for male employees was discriminatory on the basis of "sex" because the policy required male employees to permanently alter their appearance while the rules for female employees did not intrude upon their personal life and individuality. The Board observed:

> This decision is not a finding that every differentiation made between men and women is discrimination on the basis of sex. Human Rights legislation is not intended to turn us into a unisexual society.

The Board, however, concluded:

> Normally speaking, it is not uncommon to formulate grooming standards taking account of basic differences in male and female physiques and common differences in customary dress of male and female employees. However, where a rule requires men to alter their personal appearance permanently for reasons unrelated to job performance and individual capability, then such a rule is questionable and should be placed under careful scrutiny. Our Act guarantees the individual the general right of equality of opportunity in employment based upon bona fide qualifications.[177]

---

[174] *Ibid.*, at D/1195 (para. 10544).
[175] *Ibid.*, at D/1196 (para. 10546).
[176] (Man. 1983), 4 C.H.R.R. D/1495 (Steel).
[177] *Ibid.*, at D/1508 (para. 12998).

On appeal the Manitoba Court of Queen's Bench, in *Re Canada Safeway Ltd. and Steel, et al.*[178] confirmed that the consequences of the "no beards" policy was to place men subject to the rule in a different employment position from women because of a characteristic unique to their sex, and this was discriminatory. However, the Court overturned the Board's decision on the ground that the "no beard" policy was a reasonable occupational qualification. (This reasoning of course is open to question. What if a male employee is Sikh, and according to his religious belief is forbidden to shave. Would the Court apply the same test? Further, what implications does the *Simpsons-Sears* decision pose for this kind of reasoning.)

Recently, in *Allan v. Riverside Lodge*,[179] two female waitresses alleged that they were discriminated against on the ground of their sex because they were required to wear "sexist and revealing" uniforms in order to retain their jobs as cocktail waitresses at Riverside Lodge. An Ontario Board of Inquiry, chaired by Professor Ian Hunter, held that the complainants were not discriminated against because of their sex because the uniforms were consistent with "*commonly accepted social norms*" both within the restaurant/tavern trade and in the wider Ontario community. The Board stated:

> True, the uniform requirement was not identical for men and women: the male employees in Greenstreets were required to wear dress slacks and a Riverside T-shirt. But I do not believe that section 4(1) of the *Ontario Human Rights Code*, either by its plain words or by what I presume to have been its legislative intention, mandates unisex dress in the work place. In fact, I regard such a suggestion as transparent nonsense and will say no more of it.[180]

The Board pointed out:

> Ms. Allan used a number of adjectives in describing the uniform in question: "degrading, embarrassing, sexist, tasteless, inappropriate." Having reviewed her evidence in detail, I conclude that her objections were primarily aesthetic; she considered the uniform unattractive, ill-fitting, and inconsistent with the otherwise "classy" atmosphere of Greenstreets. The allegedly revealing or

---

[178] *Supra*, note 121.
[179] *Supra*, note 170.
[180] *Ibid.*, at D/2986 (para. 24085).

"sexist" objection was a convenient peg on which to hang her complaint, but, I find as a fact that it was, to a large extent, an afterthought after she had been laid off.[181]

Professor Hunter concluded that "I am satisfied beyond any question, that the uniform was not so 'immodest' or 'sexist' as to transform waitresses into entertainers."

Thus, whether or not a dress and grooming requirement constitutes "sexual harassment" or "sex discrimination" may be judged by the test provided by the *Allan* case. It states:

1. that males and females perform the same or roughly similar work for the employer;
2. that the employer has imposed a requirement on employees of one sex which is clearly more burdensome or exploitative than the requirement imposed on employees of the other sex;
3. that the requirement in question lacks justification in "commonly accepted social norms"; and
4. that the requirement is not provided (by the employer) to be reasonably related to the employer's needs.

The rule of dress and grooming requirements also apply to advertising buttons. A requirement to wear an advertising button which invites sexual comments such as, "I guarantee it", may constitute sexual harassment. In one case where the female employees were required to wear a button that said, "I guarantee it", they were subjected to comments suggesting that they were guaranteeing sexual favours or sexual satisfaction. It was held that forcing the employees to wear the buttons during working hours amounted to asking them to tolerate sexual harassment as a term of condition of employment.[182]

---

[181] *Ibid.*, at D/2980 (para. 24047).
[182] See 6 *Canadian Human Rights Advocate*, No. 2, p. 9 (Feb. 1990). The case did not go to the Board of Inquiry but was mutually settled. Saskatchewan's Chief Human Rights Commissioner, Theresa Holizki, said: "When the store refused to allow Ms. Letkeman to remove the button during working hours, they were asking her to tolerate sexual harassment as a term and condition of employment". The company, Carlton Cards of Toronto, agreed to apologize to the complainant and to pay her $1400 to settle the dispute. According to the company, the button was supposed to carry a message that the card publisher guaranteed its service and its product.

6. Job-Related Consequences

(a) Reward or Punishment

Job-related consequences often result when sexual harassment is initiated by someone with power over a person with less power. This situation is termed a *"quid pro quo"*. It occurs when continued employment, advancement or other job benefits are explicitly or implicitly conditional upon the acquiescence to sexual demands. It is either stated or implied that non-compliance will lead to negative employment consequences.

In these situations an employee is forced to make a choice between submitting to sexual demands or forfeiting some employment benefits. In such cases, once it is established that the demand itself constitutes gender bias, a dismissal, or a threat of dismissal or refused promotion and things of that nature, for example, fall within the contours of prohibitions under the human rights statutes. The *Ontario Human Rights Code*,[183] as noted in the previous chapter, specifically prohibits job-related rewards or punishment in exchange for sexual favour, by a person in authority. Section 7(3) states:

> Every person has a right to be free from,
>
> (a) a sexual solicitation or advance made by a person in a position to confer, grant or deny a benefit or advancement to the person where the person making the solicitation or advance knows or ought reasonably to know that it is unwelcome; or
> (b) a reprisal or a threat of reprisal for the rejection of a sexual solicitation or advance where the reprisal is made or threatened by a person in a position to confer, grant or deny a benefit or advancement to the person.

Adverse job-related consequences may vary in form and degree of severity from employee to employee in different circumstances. They may range from assignment change, to reduction in hours, transfer, demotion, denial of promotion, or withholding confirmation (from probationary status) and finally to dismissal or threat of dismissal. A dismissal is the severest blow an employer can inflict on an employee; therefore, it is also called "capital punishment". Since a dismissal is

---

[183] R.S.O. 1990, c. H.19.

the strongest form of reprisal for non-compliance with requests of a sexual nature, this issue will be discussed first and all other job-related consequences are discussed collectively, under one heading.

The *"quid pro quo"* concept is also known as "the tangible benefits theory", under which the negative employment repercussions must be shown to have resulted directly from a refusal of the harasser's sexual demands.

(i) Dismissal

It may be stated at the outset that an employer has a common law right, or a right under the collective agreement, to dismiss an employee for just cause. A "just cause" dismissal implies that an employee will be dismissed for his/her failure to discharge job-related duties or obligations. Whenever an employee is not discharged for just cause, the question then arises of what the purpose or the motive of the employer was.

In some cases, reprisal for non-compliance to the harasser's requests results in dismissal from employment. This was the case in *Hughes v. Dollar Snack Bar*,[184] where both complainants were sexually harassed and then dismissed from their employment for rejecting the sexual advances of their employer. In reference to Ms. Hughes' dismissal, the Board stated:

> In the absence of evidence supporting some other explanation, the only reasonable conclusion is that Ms. Hughes' dismissal was because of her objections and reactions to the respondent's sexual harassment.[185]

The other complainant, Ms. White, was told that she was dismissed from her employment because she failed to report for a shift to which she had been assigned. However, she testified that she had not been notified of this shift assignment. Therefore, this leaves "the most reasonable conclusion that the real reason for dismissal was Ms. White's rejection of the respondent's sexual advances."[186]

In *Torres v. Royalty Kitchenware Ltd.*,[187] the complainant was subjected to both verbal and physical sexual harassment by her

---

[184] (Ont. 1982), 3 C.H.R.R. D/1014 (Kerr).
[185] *Ibid.*, at D/1015 (para. 9024).
[186] *Ibid.*, at D/1016 (para. 9030).
[187] (Ont. 1982), 3 C.H.R.R. D/858 (Cumming).

employer. Her continual rejection of his advances led to the termination of her employment, with the excuse that her employer "didn't need her". The Board of Inquiry found that the respondent had viewed his secretaries as his sexual objects and had believed that submitting to his sexual advances was part of the job requirement. The Board stated:

> ... [T]here was a definite connection between the sexual harassment of the Complainant and the termination of her employment.
>
> ...
>
> However, even though he knew she objected to his sexual advances, he persisted in his attempts and made her subjection to such conduct on his part a term or condition of her employment. When she continued to rebuff him, he chose to terminate her employment.[188]

There is hardly any employer in this age who will dismiss an employee openly on the ground that she refused to accept or co-operate in his sexual advances. The apparent reason for a discharge under such circumstances always appears to be justifiable such as a lack of work, inefficiency, or insubordination. The tribunals thus try to reach to the bottom of the truth to find out whether the employer had a "just and reasonable cause" for discharge or whether the apparent cause was a mere pretext, masking the employee's failure to accept sexual advances.[189]

This is not to suggest that a discharge must always be "unjust" before an employer can be found guilty of sexual harassment. There may be cases where an employer has a "just and reasonable cause" to fire an employee but at the same time he is guilty of engaging in unwelcome and unsolicited sexual advances. In other words, if an

---

[188] *Ibid.*, at D/873 (para. 7762).

[189] See for example *Foisy v. Bell Canada* (Que. 1985), 6 C.H.R.R. D/2817, where the Quebec Superior Court at D/2827 (paras. 23112-13) stated: "The court concludes that Foisy was dismissed on a pretext. Plaintiff's inability 'to function in a sales department due to emotional problems' has not been proven. Foisy's supervisors admit that her performance was satisfactory, and the evidence shows the same; how else can one explain the fact that she was dismissed 12 days after the interview of October 11, 1979, during which her results were considered satisfactory enough to give her a wage increase. No valid explanation was given." "Not only was the dismissal unjustified, Phaneuf, in recommending the dismissal, acted in a vexatious and malicious manner. He decided to take action on October 23rd because he thought he could use the six-month probationary period clause to justify dismissing the employee without giving a cause, according to the collective labour agreement. The court considers that there was bad faith and that therefore the claim for extra-contractual damages is admissible".

employee has a poor work performance, or a poor attitude, a filthy mouth or even a loose moral character[190] it does not give a licence to an employer to engage in sexual harassment.

In *Langevin v. Engineered Air Division of Air Tex Industry Ltd.*,[191] a British Columbia Human Rights Council found that the complainant's discharge was not due to sexual harassment but for "just cause", as her work performance had been admittedly poor and that "she accepted her dismissal as fair". Nevertheless, the Council held that her supervisor was guilty of sexual harassment by creating an intimidating work environment. The Council stated:

> I also find that Ms. Langevin was young, naive, inexperienced in office procedures, badly in need of a job, and also a subject of unwanted sexual advances directed toward her by Mr. Niblett. She was horrified by Mr. Niblett's sexual overtures but was unable to stop them . . .
>
> I find in the evidence given by Ms. Langevin, that the Respondent's conduct created an intimidating, hostile and offensive working environment. The conduct was based upon Ms. Langevin's gender and amounted to sexual harassment.[192]

However, there must be a clear relationship between job-related consequences and the alleged sexual advances. The complainant must establish that she was a victim of sexual harassment and her resistance was the cause of job-related consequences. Thus, in a case where the complainant was discharged for violating the employer's policy "against dating a fellow employee", it was found that her discharge constituted neither sex discrimination nor sexual harassment.[193] Thus, where an employee receives a *bona fide* punishment for violating the employer's rule or policy, the employee cannot seek protection under anti-discrimination laws.

---

[190] See for example *Robinson v. The Company Farm Ltd.* (Ont. 1984), 5 C.H.R.R. D/2243 (Cumming).

[191] (B.C. 1985), 6 C.H.R.R. D/2552 (Powell). See also *Duncan v. Afoakwah* (B.C.1991), 13 C.H.R.R. D/9 (Barr), where the B.C. Human Rights Council found that the complainant was sexually harassed by her employer but noted that her dismissal was for "just cause". It stated (at para. 17): "However . . . I am not persuaded that the complainant's failure to accede to Afoakwah's [sexual] demands was a factor in respondent's decision to terminate the complainant's employment". See also *Button v. Westsea Construction Ltd.* (B.C. 1991), 13 C.H.R.R. D/1 (Powell). In that case the B.C. Human Rights Council found that the employer sexually harassed the complainant while she was employed by him as a night security person. But it did not find that her termination was a result of the sexual harassment.

[192] *Ibid.*, at D/2555 (para. 21163-64).

[193] See for example *Rack v. The Playgirl Cabaret, supra*, note 131.

Dealing with the issue of an employee's moral character, Professor Cumming in *Robinson v. The Company Farm Ltd.*,[194] made it quite clear that an employee's morality outside his/her employment does not give an employer a licence to make sexual advances to the employee during his/her employment. He elaborated:

> Whatever a female employee's personal moral standards might be in terms of her sexual relationships, an employer is not entitled to sexually harass her. Her personal behaviour is her own business, just as his is. Moreover, if she is sexually harassed, her character and behaviour outside of the employment relationship are irrelevant. Whatever her personal behaviour outside the workplace might be, it does not excuse an employer in his sexual harassment of her.[195]

In the *Commodore* case, Professor Cumming, commenting on the morality of the respondent, stated that, "it is undisputed that Mr. DeFillipis had affairs with consenting female workers, and some might question his morals either because he was married or because females worked with him. However, Mr. DeFillipis' morality and social conduct is not, of course, in itself relevant to this issue of sexual harassment. I have also ignored this aspect of the evidence in coming to my conclusion."[196]

In *Giouvanoudis v. Golden Fleece Restaurant*,[197] the complainant was fired before she was even hired, because she resisted the sexual advances of the respondent at the interview. (It is questionable whether or not she had been actually hired before the incident. The Board held that she had been hired, and the second meeting was to arrange her schedule. Even if she was not hired, the respondent was guilty of sexual harassment by denying her the job opportunity because of her resistance to his sexual advances.) The Board of Inquiry, chaired by Professor Cumming, held:

> The Complainant was physically abused, and frightened and humiliated, but the encounter was on a single occasion and very brief. Mr. Carras retreated quickly in the face of the Complainant's resistance, and it was apparent to her that she was in no serious danger of harm. She was given the false expectation that there would be no further problems, but then humiliated by her new employer stating in the later telephone conversation that he did not want her to work

---

[194] *Supra*, note 190.
[195] *Ibid.*, at D/2246 (para. 18987).
[196] *Olarte et al. v. Commodore Business Machines* (Ont. 1983), 4 C.H.R.R. D/1705 at D/1733 (para. 14784) (Cumming).
[197] (Ont. 1984), 5 C.H.R.R. D/1967 (Cumming).

for him, it being obvious that this was because she had resisted his sexual advances.[198]

Romman v. Sea-West Holdings Ltd.[199] was the first Canadian case where a male employee was sexually harassed by his male supervisor. The complainant alleged that the skipper of a tug sexually harassed him by grabbing his genitals and patting him in the genital area. When he complained about these sexual advances to the owner, his services were terminated. A Canadian Human Rights Tribunal found that the company was guilty of sexual harassment and observed:

> It should never be part of a person's employment environment, or part of their employment situation, to have to submit to the touching of the genitals. That must be seen as unacceptable. Nobody should have to put up with that as part of having a job.[200]

(ii) Constructive Dismissal

In the case where the female employees were forced to quit their job because they could no longer tolerate the harasser's sexual advances, the employer normally took the defence that he did not discriminate by terminating their services, rather the complainants quit the employment themselves. Thus, there was no adverse differentiation on the ground of sex, and thus, no violation of the law.

However, the boards of inquiry and tribunals are unanimously of the view that where the complainants choose to leave their employment rather than endure unwelcome sexual advances, the complainants may be deemed to have been dismissed contrary to the prohibition against discriminatory dismissal of a human rights statute. Thus, where complainants are forced to quit their jobs because of sexual harassment, a complaint may be brought to a Human Rights Commission.

In *Coutroubis v. Sklavos Printing*,[201] the complainant, Meri Coutroubis, had been embraced and kissed by her employer while working alone in the employer's darkroom. She screamed, her employer released her, and she immediately left for home. The complainant, Irene

---

[198] *Ibid.*, at D/1973 (para. 16863).
[199] (Can. 1984), 5 C.H.R.R. D/2312 (Jones).
[200] *Ibid.*, at D/2314 (para. 19502).
[201] (Ont. 1982) 2 C.H.R.R. D/457 (Ratushny).

Kekatos, was subjected to a similar assault a few days after the incident involving Ms. Coutroubis. The two complainants decided to leave their employment. The Board found that there had been a constructive dismissal amounting to a violation of s. 4(1)(g) of the *Code*.

In the *McPherson v. "Mary's Donuts"* case,[202] the complainants quit their employment when the sexual harassment became unbearable. The Board of Inquiry found that their quitting amounted to constructive termination of employment. The Board observed:

> There is causal connection in the instant situation between sexual harassment and adverse employment consequences. The complainants could only continue to be employed if they subjected themselves to sexual harassment, a condition of employment forced upon each because she was a female employee. The sexual advances, in effect, were the cause of termination of the complainant's employment. Ms. Ambo was subjected to verbal abuse, insults, and embarrassment which made continued employment unbearable. She chose jail rather than continued employment under Mr. Doshoian. [She was working under a temporary absence program from jail.] Ms. McPherson finally got fed up with Mr. Doshoian's continuing conduct and decided to quit rather than continue to submit herself to his harassment.[203]

In *Cox v. Jagbritte Inc.*,[204] where two complainants chose to quit their employment because of sexual harassment, the Board of Inquiry found that a constructive dismissal had taken place. It held the employer guilty of sexual harassment and the complainants were awarded damages. Again, in *Graesser v. Porto*,[205] the Board of Inquiry found that the respondent's behaviour amounted to constructive dismissal of the complainant within the provision of the *Code*. "Ms. Graesser could not tolerate Mr. Porto's conduct and decided to quit and to face the economic insecurity of unemployment rather than to continue to submit herself to his harassment", said the Board.

In *Janzen v. Platy Enterprises*,[206] a Manitoba Board of Adjudication found that the cumulative effect of the physical and mental harassment that Ms. Janzen had been subjected to created an intolerable work environment for her. Thus, she was justified in coming to the conclusion that there was very little likelihood, if any, that the situation would

---

[202] (Ont. 1982), 3 C.H.R.R. D/961 (Cumming).
[203] *Ibid.*, at D/963 (para. 8558).
[204] (Ont. 1982), 3 C.H.R.R. D/609 (Cumming).
[205] (Ont. 1983), 4 C.H.R.R. D/1569 (Zemans).
[206] (Man. 1985), 6 C.H.R.R. D/2735 (Henteleff); revd (Man. 1986), 8 C.H.R.R. D/3831 (C.A.), a decision quashed by the Supreme Court of Canada (Man. 1989), 10 C.H.R.R. D/6205.

be rectified and that she had no other alternative but to terminate her employment. The Board concluded that her "quitting" under the circumstances amounted to "constructive dismissal" because her harassment had become a condition of her continued employment.[207]

Again in *Carignan v. Master Craft Publications*,[208] a British Columbia Board of Inquiry found that the respondent's conduct forced the complainant to resign her job; therefore, it amounted to constructive dismissal. The Board in a forthright manner stated:

> In this case, I have concluded that the complainant quit her job as a result of this kind of coercion, that it was coercion based upon her sex and that it had become a condition of her continuing employment that she endure the sort of harassment set forth above. Her failure to acquiesce to sexual harassment resulted in her quitting her job. I do not think that it was unreasonable for her to have left in the circumstances which have been recounted. I am convinced that but for the conduct of Mr. Sharma, the complainant would have remained as his employee. Put another way, I believe that the complainant had discharged her onus of establishing that compliance with Mr. Sharma's sexual advances was, in effect, a term or condition of employment.[209]

In the case of *Splett v. Sum's Family Holdings Ltd.*[210] the complainant quit her employment because of "extreme anxiety" caused by the numerous persistent sexual advances she encountered in the workplace. The Alberta Board of Inquiry found that her termination of employment amounted to constructive dismissal. It stated:

> ... we return to the question of whether the evidence also supports a claim of constructive dismissal pursuant to s. 7(1)(a) and establishes that the conduct of the respondent amounted to a refusal to continue to employ because of the sex of the complainant. We have noted the numerous persistent sexual advances which took place in the face of the clear objections of the complainant. *It was on the advice of her physician that Ms. Splett quit her job. Dr. Stroud completed a medical report stating that Ms. Splett was incapable of working by reason of "extreme anxiety".* He did not complete the query of anticipated date for return to work. A subsequent doctor, appointed by the Unemployment Insurance Commission, also saw Ms. Splett and stated in his medical report that he was of the opinion that she would not be capable of returning to work until the conclusion of the hearing into the *I.R.P. Act* complaint.[211] [Emphasis added]

---

[207] *Ibid.*, at D/2768 (paras. 22648-49).
[208] (B.C. 1984), 5 C.H.R.R. D/2282 (Rankin).
[209] *Ibid.*, at D/2284 (para. 19246).
[210] (Alta. 1991), 13 C.H.R.R. D/119 (McManus).
[211] *Ibid.*, at D/124 (para. 34).

Thus, the employer is liable for constructive dismissal when it imposes intolerable working conditions in violation of the *Human Rights Act*, when those conditions foreseeably would compel a reasonable employee to quit, whether or not the employer specifically intended to force the victim's resignation. However, if the employer has an effective internal grievance procedure (both in a union and non-union setting) and the complainant knew that effective avenue of complaint (or grieve) and redress are available, but she, without good reason, bypassed an internal complaint procedure, her quitting or resignation may not be regarded as a constructive dismissal. In one American case the court held that the plaintiff (the victim) was not constructively dismissed after an incident of harassment by a co-worker because she quit immediately, even though the employer told her she would not have to work with him again, and she did not give the employer a fair opportunity to demonstrate it could curb the harasser's conduct.[212]

(iii) Other Job-Related Consequences

In cases where the victim of sexual harassment continues in her employment position, other job-related consequences may follow. If the employee continues to refuse the employer's or supervisor's sexual advances, retaliation may result in the form of threats or denial of job-related benefits. This may include denial of raises, benefits or promotions that are available to other persons in similar circumstances. The employee may also suffer a loss of existing benefits. For example, the employee may be demoted or be denied seniority. In some cases, the victim may be transferred to an undesirable work location, be assigned to undesirable shifts, and be given poor work assignments. An employer or supervisor may also retaliate against the victim by becoming overly critical of her work, by giving her unsatisfactory job evaluations, and by giving her a poor job reference which will affect her future career. In cases where a woman is working in a non-traditional employment field, she may have her work sabotaged.

Situations may also arise where the complainant co-operates with the harasser in his sexual advances. These situations are considered to be sexual harassment as such compliance is shown to have been

---

[212] *Dornhecker v. Malibu Grand Prix Corp.*, 828 F.2d 307, 44 E.P.D. para. 37,557 (5th Cir. 1987).

secured by employment related threats or promises. For example in *Robichaud v. Brennan*,[213] the Review Tribunal, in reversing the decision of the lower tribunal, pointed out that the complainant "submitted to these encounters as a result of the intimidation and fear that she had for Mr. Brennan (the harasser)." In such cases, the complainant must have an honest and reasonable apprehension that a refusal to participate, acquiesce in, or endure such conduct may affect the existence of the employment relationship itself or any benefits or conditions arising from the employment relationship.

In *Phillips v. Hermiz*,[214] the Board of Inquiry found that although the respondent's business had increased during the period in question, yet the complainant's hours were reduced. The Board held that the respondent attempted to exact sexual favour from the complainant and her refusal to provide such was the (real) reason for reduction of hours of work and then termination of her job.

(iv) Favours for Submission

It should also be noted here that situations do occur where an employee receives job benefits for consenting to an employer's or supervisor's request for sexual favours. The job consequences may be positive for the employee, perhaps involving an advance or promotion. However, this may have a negative effect upon a co-worker who may, as a result, be denied a hard-earned promotion. Thus, where employment opportunities or benefits have been granted because of an individual's submission to the employer's sexual advances or requests for sexual favours (rather than on merits), the employer may be liable for unlawful sex discrimination against other persons who are qualified for but denied that employment opportunity or benefit. A determination of who will be entitled to relief in this situation is not very clear. Among those who are presumably disadvantaged are those females who rejected the sexual advances and those employees, male and female, who did not receive the promotion. In short, this aspect of job-related consequences opens up a new line of litigation which could be triggered when a female or male in some situations is actually promoted or otherwise advanced.

---

[213] (Can. 1983), 4 C.H.R.R. D/1272 (Review Tribunal — Dyer).
[214] (Sask. 1984), 5 C.H.R.R. D/2450 (paras. 20317-18)(Katzman).

Ch. 2 - Characteristics of Sexual Harassment

The E.E.O.C. guidelines provide that where an employment opportunity or benefit is granted because of an individual's "submission to the employer's sexual advances or requests for sexual favours" the employer may be liable for unlawful discrimination against others who were qualified for but were denied the opportunity or benefit.[215] However, the law in this regard is unsettled as to when and how a violation of human rights law, sexual harassment, can be established in these circumstances.[216]

The *Olarte v. Commodore Business Machines* case,[217] provides a typical example of adverse job-related consequences an employee could expect from resisting the sexual advances of a supervisor. The Board of Inquiry in that case found that the respondent Mr. DeFilippis engaged in a practice of sexual harassment against the complainants. In his position as foreman, Mr. DeFilippis repeatedly touched and kissed the complainants, asked them for invitations to their homes, and requested that they engage in sexual intercourse with him. When his advances were refused, DeFilippis penalized the complainants by shouting at them, finding fault with their work, and shifting them to heavier duties, with the result that some of the complainants quit and one was fired.

(b) *Poisonous and Offensive Work Environment*

Sexual harassment behaviour in the workplace creates a hostile, intimidating and discriminating environment. Various terms are used to describe this type of environment. Under this type of harassment, while submission to sexual conduct is not necessarily or explicitly made a term of employment, nevertheless the individual is given a work environment which is intimidating, hostile and offensive. This is a situation where the work environment becomes unpleasant or unbearable to the victim because of a pattern of insults and hostility. This negative work environment may result from a refusal of a sexual proposition or advance. However, it may also exist in isolation from such overt action by a supervisor or co-worker, and result from the hostility or attitude of supervisors or co-workers. No harm to benefits

---

[215] 29 C.F.R. 1604.11(g).
[216] The E.E.O.C. has recently analysed the issue in its "Policy Guidance on Employer Liability Under Title VII for Sexual Favoritism", dated January 1990.
[217] (Ont. 1983), 4 C.H.R.R. D/1705 (Cumming).

or tenure necessarily follows, although the worker's psychological health may be harmed and she may feel discomfort in the workplace.

Courts and tribunals have also used the terms "atmosphere of discrimination" and "sexually derogatory work environment" to describe a workplace which is poisoned by sexual harassment. The creation of an offensive or hostile work environment through sexual harassment can by itself constitute a violation of human rights statutes. Consequently, an employee subjected to such an environment need not prove additional tangible job detriment.

The poisoned work environment theory, as pointed out earlier in Chapter 2, was first enunciated in the American case *Bundy v. Jackson*.[218] There, the Court extended the "discriminatory environment" race cases to sex by holding that subjecting a woman to sexual stereotyping, insults and demeaning propositions "illegally poisoned the working environment". In Canada, "offensive work environment theory" was first used in relation to racial slur cases such as *Dhillon v. F. W. Woolworth Ltd.*,[219] where the Board pointed out that the employees have the right to a workplace free from harassment and that the atmosphere of the workplace is a term or condition of employment. The Board stated:

> ... [V]erbal racial harassment, through name-calling, in itself, is in my view prohibited conduct under the *Code*. The atmosphere of the workplace is a "term or condition of employment" just as much as more visible terms or conditions, such as hours of work or rate of pay. The words "terms or condition of employment" are broad enough to include the emotional and psychological circumstances in the workplace.[220]

This was extended to sexual harassment cases such as *Robichaud v. Brennan* where the Review Tribunal said that "the cumulative effect was to create a poisoned work environment for Mrs. Robichaud". While the expression "poisoned work environment" was not used in the first Canadian sexual harassment case (*Cherie Bell* case), Mr. Shime had, however, clearly stated that gender based insults and taunting may reasonably be perceived to create a negative psychological and emotional work environment.

> There is no reason why the law, which reaches into the workplace so as to protect the work environment from physical or chemical pollution or extremes

---

[218] 641 F. 2d 934 (D.C. Cir. 1981).
[219] (Ont. 1982), 3 C.H.R.R. D/743 (Cumming).
[220] *Ibid.*, at D/763 (para. 6724).

of temperature, ought not to protect employees as well from negative psychological and mental effects where adverse and gender directed conduct emanating from a management hierarchy may reasonably be construed to be a condition of employment.[221]

In *Aragona v. Elegant Lamp Co. Ltd.*,[222] Professor Ratushny considered the effect of sexual harassment on the working environment and said:

> The line of sexual harassment is crossed only where the conduct may be reasonably construed to create, as a condition of employment, a work environment which demands an unwarranted intrusion upon the employee's sexual dignity as a man or woman.[223]

In *Cox*, the Board of Inquiry stated that tangible employment consequences of refusal to comply with sexual advances need not be shown in order for a complainant to be successful.[224] A complainant need only show that the work environment was "poisoned" by the harassment. In *Kotyk v. Canadian Employment and Immigration Commission*,[225] the Canadian Human Rights Tribunal took the same approach and found that the working environment in that case was such that it would have been almost impossible to carry on work in a normal way. It held:

> Even if I were to find that there was no concrete employment consequences, there is no question but that her environment was "poisoned".[226]

Thus, where the work environment becomes unpleasant or unbearable because of sexual encounters, no harm to benefits or tenure need follow to constitute "sexual harassment".

When does a working environment become offensive? The tribunals seem to disagree on this point. Chairperson Shime in *Cherie Bell* has observed that: " . . . persistent and frequent conduct is not necessary for an adverse finding under the Code because *a single incident* of an employee being denied equality of employment because of sex is also a prohibited activity." This was interpreted to mean that

---

[221] *Bell v. The Flaming Steer Steak House* (Ont. 1980), 1 C.H.R.R. D/155 at D/156 (para. 1389) (Shime).
[222] (Ont. 1982), 3 C.H.R.R. D/1109 (Ratushny).
[223] *Ibid.*, at D/1110 (para. 9725).
[224] *Cox v. Jagbritte Inc.* (Ont. 1982), 3 C.H.R.R. D/109 (Cumming).
[225] (Can. 1983), 4 C.H.R.R. D/1416 (Ashley).
[226] *Ibid.*, at D/1428 (para. 12236).

any gender based insults may constitute a breach of the Ontario *Human Rights Code*. Dean McCamus, in *Watt v. Regional Municipality of Niagara*[227] rejected this interpretation of Chairperson Shime's above comments. He suggested that a single incident could not form sex discrimination and quoted Chairperson Shime's words that "it is only when the language or words may reasonably be construed to form a condition of employment that the *Code* provides a remedy." He explained that "it would be very unusual indeed to find a situation in which a single insult could be reasonably construed to create a condition of employment in the sense, presumably, that one must be prepared as an employee to endure such insults as a feature of the working environment."[228] However, it may constitute sexual harassment if the remarks constitute sexual solicitation or advances or some other extremely offensive situation from which an employee would reasonably conclude that continuing exposure to verbal harassment would be a feature of the working environment. Thus, it is the combination of frequency and offensiveness (gravity of offence) which warrants the inference that exposure to such conduct was a discriminatory condition of employment.

The adverse consequences of sexual harassment are not limited to the victim's job or work environment, but may also extend to the victim's health and well-being. Victims of sexual harassment often suffer psychological and physical consequences in addition to economic consequences. Stress, fear and anxiety are frequently experienced by sexual harassment victims, both on and off the job, and they may eventually feel listless, powerless, and emotionally depressed. Victims may also experience decreased ambition, a dread of going to work, and loss of self-confidence and self-esteem. Physically, victims may experience symptoms such as insomnia, headaches, neck and backaches, stomach problems and hypertension. In some cases, victims are reduced to the point of psychological and physical breakdown, to such an extent that they require hospitalization.

For example, in *Deisting v. Dollar Pizza (1978) Ltd.*,[229] the complainant had suffered emotional injury as a result of the sexual harassment she had been subjected to during her employment. The degree of emotional suffering was to such an extent that the complainant sought professional help from a psychologist. The psychologist testified that:

---

[227] (Ont. 1984), 5 C.H.R.R. D/2453 (McCamus).
[228] *Ibid.*, at D/2459 (para. 20352).
[229] (Alta. 1982), 3 C.H.R.R. D/898 (Clarke).

... [T]he Complainant was experiencing anxiety and stress which was particularly related to the incident that occurred with the complainant and the Respondents in March of 1980. She was satisfied that this anxiety and stress began with those incidents and that there was nothing in the Complainant's personality profile that would suggest that she was particularly susceptible to an injury of this type ... .[230]

The Board's decision included an award of $500 to the complainant in order that she pursue psychological counselling.

In the case of *Splett v. Sum's Family Holdings Ltd.*[231] the complainant had almost a "nervous breakdown" due to severe and persistent sexual advances. She suffered psychological disability due to "extreme anxiety". Her doctor diagnosed that she was suffering from "extreme anxiety" and advised her to quit her job. He stated, "It would seem this patient is being sexually harassed at work and this is causing intolerable stress".[232] The Alberta Board of Inquiry awarded a further sum of $1,500 to the complainant for the mental distress suffered by her.

In another case the psychological impact of the sexual harassment was so severe that the victim attempted twice to take her life.[233]

The above principles were followed and reinforced in subsequent cases such as *Commodore*,[234] *MacBain*,[235] *Robichaud v. Brennan*,[236] *Zarankin v. Johnstone*[237] and others.

7. Sex-Based Harassment

Sex-based harassment is a harassment not involving sexual activity or explicit sexual language but nevertheless causing harassment if it is "sufficiently patterned or pervasive" and directed at employees because of their sex, and is prohibited by the human right statutes. Sexual references or comments that do not amount to sexual advances or solicitations may also constitute sexual harassment. The central characteristic of a sexual harassment is that the behaviour

---

[230] *Ibid.*, at D/899 (para. 7976).
[231] (Alta. 1991), 13 C.H.R.R. D/119 (McManus).
[232] *Ibid.*, at D/123 (para. 21).
[233] See Workers' Compensation Benefits in Chapter 5, *infra*.
[234] (Ont. 1983), 4 C.H.R.R. D/1705 (Cumming).
[235] (Can. 1984), 5 C.H.R.R. D/2285 (Lederman).
[236] (Can. 1983), 4 C.H.R.R. D/1272 (Review Tribunal — Dyer).
[237] (B.C. 1984), 5 C.H.R.R. D/2274 (Smith).

should consist of "unwelcome conduct of a sexual nature". Sexual activity, whether effected, proposed or referred to, is the basis of prohibited conduct of sexual harassment. Thus, taunting, teasing and demeaning comments of a sexual nature can amount to sexual harassment.

In *Shaw v. Levac Supply Ltd.*,[238] the perpetrator, a co-worker, referred to the complainant as a "fridge sister", called her a "fat cow" and said "waddle, waddle, waddle" as she walked around the office and mimicked her expressions. At one occasion he called her a "fat cow". When the complainant was wearing nylons, the perpetrator would say "swish, swish, swish" as she walked, apparently in an attempt to imitate the sound nylons make when they rub together.

The perpetrator continued to taunt, tease and make those remarks and comments to the complainant for almost 14 years. The complainant reported the matter to the management but nothing was done. Finally, as she could not bear the harassment any more, she quit the job.

The Board held that teasing and lampooning of the complainant by the perpetrator clearly amounted to harassment. The expression and implication of sexual unattractiveness was a comment of a sexual nature. Such verbal conduct of a sexual nature constituted sexual harassment in the workplace where the harassment was repetitive and had the effect of creating an offensive work environment. The Board of Inquiry stated:

> It seems to me incontestable that to express or imply sexual unattractiveness is to make a comment of a sexual nature. Whether the harasser says "you are attractive and I want to have sex with you", or says, "you are unattractive and no one is likely to want to have sex with you," the reference is sexual. It is verbal conduct of a sexual nature, and it is sexual harassment in the workplace if it is repetitive and has the effect of creating an offensive working environment; it is sexual harassment in the form of an inappropriate comment of a sexual nature.[239]

The Board further stated:

> When a man chants "waddle, waddle" within her hearing every time an overweight woman walks about the office, or mimics the swishing sound made by her nylons rubbing together because of her weight, what purpose can he possibly have except to indicate that she is physically unattractive? Why draw attention to her bodily inelegance in such circumstances other than to indicate

---

[238] (Ont. 1991), 91 CLLC 17,007 (Hubbard).
[239] *Ibid.*

that she is sexually undesirable? What other way is the victim to take such comments?[240]

The Board concluded:

> For these reasons I must conclude that some of Mr. Robertson's harassment was of a sexual nature and that, even though many other aspects of his conduct may not have been, the course of conduct that caused Ms Shaw mental anguish and drove her from her job was sexual harassment and, therefore, harassment because of sex.[241]

Some commentators[242] are of the view that the Board of Inquiry in the *Shaw* case has gone too far in extending the scope of prohibited behaviour amounting to sexual harassment. On the first glance, it may appear to be so. But when the decision of Chairman Hubbard is analyzed in the context of legislative purpose and policy and in reference to what Chief Justice Dickson said in the *Janzen* case,[243] there cannot be much disagreement. The decision may be "out of line", as it was the first of this nature, but it was certainly not "out of time".

There is no doubt that the comments the perpetrator made in this case were unpleasant and hurt the complainant very deeply. In fact, she had migraine headaches and ultimately resigned, at least partially because of his comments. Finally, the perpetrator knew that his actions were unwanted because the complainant had told him so on a number of occasions. The question arises whether or not this type of insulting, humiliating and degrading atmosphere should be allowed to prevail in the workplace, whether or not the Legislature had intended to put an end to this kind of work environment. Chairman Hubbard is not alone in expressing the view that this sort of behaviour in the workplace is unacceptable and prohibited by the *Human Rights Code*. Professor Swan echoed similar views in *Re Canada Post Corp. and Canadian Union of Postal Workers (Gibson)*[244] when he said:

> Moreover, the comments about tampons and underwear were directly related to the female employee's gender . . . . They were also, in my view, calculated to insult her gender, and to imply that she was unsanitary . . .; no employee

---

[240] *Ibid.*
[241] *Ibid.*
[242] See 9 *Focus on Canadian Employment and Equity Rights*, No. 23, pp. 183-84.
[243] *Janzen v. Platy Enterprises Ltd.* (Man. 1989), 10 C.H.R.R. D/6205 (S.C.C.).
[244] (1987) 27 L.A.C. (3d) 27 (Swan).

would appreciate insults of this nature on any basis, and it cannot be a term of anyone's employment to be degraded in this way.[245]

He further stated that:

> ... harassment may justify discipline even where the basis for the harassment is not a prohibited ground; if employees have a right to be protected from physical assaults by their fellow employees, they have an equivalent right to be protected from a course of verbal injury.[246]

In *Re University of Manitoba and Canadian Association of Industrial, Mechanical & Allied Workers, Local 9*,[247] the grievor, a female employee, (short-order cook) was dismissed for unacceptable behaviour causing harassment and threats to fellow employees. The grievor made comments about other members of the staff, and in particular about one Joan Mandziuk, who was a supervisor. The essence of the comments were that:

— Ms. Mandziuk had gotten to be a supervisor by exchanging sexual favours of various types with male members of the supervisory staff.
— Comments were also made about the parentage of Ms. Mandziuk's children.
— Remarks were also made about the sexual habits and activities of other employees, such as "kissing management's ass" and that married women should be staying at home engaging in "sexual activities" with their husbands, rather than working.
— The grievor used offensive language and words like "whoring around".
— The grievor referred to some of the employees as "stool pigeons".

According to the university the grievor was fired because she was harassing her co-workers by virtue of the language she used in the workplace and the comments she made about their sexual activities.

The arbitrator found that the remarks the grievor made "were scurrilous in nature and to a great extent had sexual connotations. It is undisputed that the grievor made remarks about some physical attributes of some of her co-workers and about their personal lives. Many of these remarks were in sexual terms."[248]

---

[245] *Ibid.*, at 44.
[246] *Ibid.*
[247] (1989), 6 L.A.C. (4th) 182 (Chapman).
[248] *Ibid.*, at 211.

However, the arbitrator declined to find that the grievor's conduct constituted "sexual harassment". The arbitrator concluded:

> I am satisfied that the grievor's remarks did create a hostile environment. I do not, however, accept that it was the environment contemplated by definition 5 of the policy of the university. Even if it were that type of environment (and I do not believe that it was), it was not caused by the grievor's "sexually oriented behaviour".[249]
>
> . . .
>
> I hasten to add that I do not commend the grievor for her remarks. In fact I believe them to be despicable. She may well be a gossip, a rumour monger and possibly a troublemaker. She is not beloved by her co-workers. Nevertheless, I am not satisfied that her behaviour created a "severe problem" as a result off her committing any of the offences contained in art. 23.2. Accordingly, I am allowing her grievance.[250]

On appeal, the Manitoba Queen's Bench quashed the arbitrator's decision and found that the grievor's conduct did constitute "sexual harassment" as defined by the Supreme Court of Canada in the *Janzen* case and as described in the university's policy on sexual harassment.

> Here, the sexual harassment suffered by the appellants constituted sex discrimination for it was a practice or attitude which had the effect of limiting the conditions of employment or the employment opportunities available to. . . .[251]

It may be noted that in this case the sexual harassment was caused by a female employee and the victims of that harassment were also female employees. The question arises whether or not it amounts to sexual harassment when a female employee uses teasing, taunting, degrading, humiliating sexual language, remarks and comments towards other employees. It appears to be the legal consensus that it does not matter who was the perpetrator, male or female, rather what matters is the effect of the harassment on the employees, male or female. Thus, the working environment is poisoned when the employees, supervisor or non-supervisor, male or female, use taunting, teasing and demeaning comments of a sexual nature; and this interferes with the employees' right to work in an environment free of sexual harassment.

---

[249] *Ibid.*, at 219.
[250] *Ibid.*
[251] (1989), unreported (Man. Q.B.); affd. (1990), 63 Man. R. (2d) 56, 68 D.L.R. (4th) 412 (C.A.).

B. SUMMARY AND ANALYSIS

Normal discussion or contact between management and an employee, even if it be social in nature, is not intended to be prohibited by the human rights statutes. It goes without saying that relationships between human beings are complex, and subjective motivations may often be mixed. Each situation must be considered upon its facts to determine whether the conduct complained of is sanctionable. The complainant must have an honest and reasonable apprehension that a refusal to participate, acquiesce or endure such conduct may affect the employment relationship itself or any benefits or conditions arising from the relationship. It is to be noted that where the conduct is of a more subtle nature, the issue is how it "may reasonably be perceived". In other words, the conduct in question cannot be assessed only by an effect which it has upon a particular complainant (although this will be relevant to any remedy which is ordered), rather a reasonably objective standard should be applied.

Chairperson Shime in *Cherie Bell* made it clear that the *Code* does not inhibit normal discussion or social contact between management and employees:

> It is not abnormal, nor should it be prohibited, activity for a supervisor to become socially involved with an employee. An invitation to dinner is not an invitation to a complaint. The danger or the evil that is to be avoided is coerced or compelled social contact where the employee's refusal to participate may result in a loss of employment benefits.[252]

Chairperson Shime also expressed the concern that the *Code* ought not be seen as inhibiting free speech. A supervisor and an employee should feel free to discuss sex as well as race or colour or creed:

> Thus, differences of opinion by an employee where sexual matters are discussed may not involve a violation of the Code; it is only when the language or words may be reasonably construed to form a condition of employment that the Code provides a remedy.[253]

Verbal conduct is far more difficult to classify as sexual harassment, in particular discussions of sexual issues such as rape. The employees can discuss issues with a sexual connotation, whether it

---

[252] The *Cherie Bell* case, *supra*, note 221, at D/156 (para. 1390).
[253] *Ibid.* (para. 1391).

is rape laws or the problems of divorce and single parents, without risking a charge of sexual harassment because a male holds a view which a woman worker perceives as sexist. A standard of reasonableness is required in reviewing verbal exchanges, both as to its offensiveness and whether it creates a harassing and negative condition of work.

Moreover, every type of harassment in the workplace is not sexual harassment. A female employee may be harassed by her supervisor for a number of reasons — personality conflict, differences of opinion, unionism, or lack of co-operation and understanding. In *Re C.U.P.E. and O.P.I.E.U.*,[254] the Board of Arbitration pointed out that "professional harassment" cannot be characterized as "sexual harassment".

Sexual harassment behaviour must be specifically sexual in nature. Many types of harassment may be present in the workplace, but not all are sexually related. For example, if a woman employee is being criticized for work which is substandard in the view of her male boss, the subordinate is not being harassed because of her sex. Job-related difficulties between males and females in the work environment do not all result from sexual behaviour.

Whether or not the alleged sexual conduct or behaviour constitutes sexual harassment must be determined by an objective test. For an objective test, the courts and tribunals have used the standard of a "reasonable person" rather than the perception of a harassee or a harasser. Moreover, the conduct in question should be examined and tested against the norm of "socially acceptable behaviour" and the "reasonable and usual limits of social interaction" in the community.

Sexual harassment, as discussed earlier, is an unwanted, unwelcome sexual behaviour, subtle or obvious, which interferes with the sexual dignity of a person. As human rights statutes prohibit only "sex discrimination" and not "sexual harassment", Human Rights Tribunals, in initial cases, were struggling to determine how to bring "sexual harassment" within the meaning and scope of "discrimination on the basis of sex". Thus, to determine that sexual harassment amounts to "discrimination on the basis of sex" in an employment situation, they were required to establish its (sexual harassment) linkage with "adverse job differentiation". Thus, it had become almost essential to establish that resistance by the victim to sexual overtures led to specific adverse job-related consequences, such as dismissal, suspension, or shift change, etc., "*quid pro quo*". However, soon thereafter, by following

---

[254] (1982), 4 L.A.C. (3d) 385 (Swinton).

the racial harassment cases, the tribunals began to recognize that sexual harassment creates an "offensive and hostile work environment" for the victim which in itself constitutes an adverse job differentiation based on the sex of that person. Thus, offensive and hostile work environment in itself amounts to sex discrimination.

Further it should be noted that *"quid pro quo"* and "conditions of work" (offensive, humiliating or poisonous work environment) are not entirely exclusive to each other. If unwanted sexual overtures lead to adverse job-related consequences for an employee that does not mean the employee's job environment had not become offensive. In *McPherson v. "Mary's Donuts"* where the complainants were constructively dismissed because of sexual harassment, the Board of Inquiry held that they also suffered an "intimidating, hostile, offensive work environment" because of the discrimination towards them.[255] As a matter of fact, as soon as sexual harassment is committed, the working environment becomes offensive and hostile for that employee or group of employees. The offensive and hostile working environment becomes aggravated when the harasser punishes the victim who resists sexual advances with job-related reprisals.

Thus, *"quid pro quo"* and "hostile and offensive work environment" are both job-related consequences and the effects of sexual harassment (and not the type or cause of sexual harassment). Professor Cumming in *McPherson* recognized the relationship of "cause and effect", between "sexual harassment" and "job-related consequences" (*quid pro quo*), when he stated that "the sexual advances, in effect, were the cause of termination of the complainant's employment."[256] Thus, it is clear that when sexual advances amount to sexual harassment, then either one or both of the consequences *"quid pro quo"* or "hostile and offensive work environment" may follow. Thus, to briefly summarize "sexual harassment" is a cause and "hostile and offensive work environment" and "job-related consequences" are the result.

The Supreme Court of Canada in *Janzen v. Platy Enterprises Ltd.*[257] seems to have confirmed this point of view by questioning the validity of the distinction between *"quid pro quo"* and "hostile environment" harassment. Chief Justice Dickson, writing for the court, downplayed the distinction made by some Canadian courts and Human Rights

---

[255] *McPherson v. "Mary's Donuts"* (Ont. 1982), 3 C.H.R.R. D/961 (para. 8579).
[256] *Ibid.* (para. 8558).
[257] (Man. 1989) 10 C.H.R.R. D/6205 (S.C.C.).

Tribunals (borrowed from the United States) between *"quid pro quo"* and "hostile environment" sexual harassment. He stated:

> The American courts have tended to divide sexual harassment into two categories: the *"quid pro quo"* variety in which tangible employment-related benefits are made contingent upon participation in sexual activity, and conduct which creates a "hostile environment" by requiring employees to endure sexual gestures and posturing in the workplace. Both forms of sexual harassment have been recognized by the American Courts including the United States Supreme Court: *Barnes* v. *Costle*, 561 F. 2d 983 (D.C. Cir. 1977): *Bundy* v. *Jackson*, 641 F. 2d 934 (D.C. Cir. 1981); *Henson* v. *Dundee*, 682 F. 2d 897 (11th Cir. 1982); and *Meritor Savings Bank* v. *Vinson*, 106 S. Ct. 2399 (1986). Canadian human rights tribunals have also tended to rely on the *quid pro quo*/hostile work environment dichotomy. *I do not find this categorization particularly helpful. While the distinction may have been important to illustrate forcefully the range of behaviour that constitutes harassment at a time before sexual harassment was widely viewed as actionable, in my view there is no longer any need to characterize harassment as one of these forms.* The main point in allegations of sexual harassment is that unwelcome sexual conduct has invaded the workplace, irrespective of whether the consequences of the harassment included a denial of concrete employment rewards for refusing to participate in sexual activity.[258]

It is clear from the above statement that the Supreme Court of Canada gave a broad and all-inclusive definition of "sexual harassment". The court's comment that "The main point in allegations of sexual harassment is that unwelcome sexual conduct has invaded the workplace" is noteworthy. This broad interpretation is in line with the Supreme Court's other landmark decisions.[259]

Even the U.S. Supreme Court in the *Vinson* case[260] has cast doubt on the merits of the distinction between *"quid pro quo"* and "hostile environment" harassment. Although the U.S. Supreme Court has not said it as bluntly as the Supreme Court of Canada, yet the message was clear and loud. The U.S. Supreme Court upheld the concept of hostile environment harassment and further indicated that economic

---

[258] *Ibid.*, at D/6226-27 (para. 44449). See also *Noffke* v. *McClaskin Hot House* (Ont. 1990), 11 C.H.R.R. D/407 (Zemans); *Cuff* v. *Gypsy Restaurant* (Ont. 1987), 8 C.H.R.R. D/3972 (Bayefsky); and *Wilgan* v. *Wendy's Restaurants of Canada Ltd.* (B.C. 1990), 11 C.H.R.R. D/119 (Barr).

[259] *Robichaud* v. *Treasury Board* (Can. 1987), 8 C.H.R.R. D/4326 (S.C.C.): *Ontario Human Rights Commn.* v. *Simpsons-Sears Ltd.* (Ont. 1985), 7 C.H.R.R. D/3102 (S.C.C.); *C.N.R.* v. *Canadian Human Rights Commn.* (Can. 1988), 8 C.H.R.R. D/4210 (S.C.C.).

[260] *Meritor Savings Bank* v. *Vinson*, 106 S. Ct. 2399, 40 E.P.D. para 36,159 (1986).

harm is not a requirement in such cases. This indicates the acceptance of broad scope of situations which may constitute harassment in the workplace. Thus, in *Vinson* the U.S. Supreme Court contrasted hostile environment harassment to *"quid pro quo"* harassment by stating that a hostile environment may be proven whether or not the harassment is "directly linked to the grant or denial of an economic *quid pro quo*."[261] The court recognizes, though unwittingly, that *"quid pro quo"* is a consequence of a refusal to accept sexual advances and not a sexual harassment by itself. It follows then that unsolicited and unwelcome sexual behaviour constitutes sexual harassment whether or not it leads to job-related consequences called *"quid pro quo"*.

Since "sexual harassment" is specifically prohibited in certain jurisdictions, the tribunals need not take a circular route to determine that sexual harassment amounts to sex discrimination. In those jurisdictions, the complainant should not be required to establish a linkage between sexual harassment and differential treatment by proving that resistance to sexual harassment led to job-related adverse consequences. In those jurisdictions "sexual harassment" *per se* amounts to "sex discrimination" and violation of the statute, irrespective of the fact whether or not job-related consequences flowed from it. For example, the Ontario *Human Rights Code* makes it clear that harassment need not have employment consequences in order to be prohibited. Unwelcome solicitation in itself will constitute a violation of the Ontario *Code*.

---

[261] For further discussion on this point see Marlisa Vinciquerra, "The Aftermath of Meritor: A Search for Standards in the Law of Sexual Harassment" (1989), 98 *Yale L.J.* 1718-38.

CHAPTER 3

Taking Legal Action — A Predicament for the Victim

A. VICTIM'S RELUCTANCE TO COMPLAIN

A woman faced with unwanted and unsolicited sexual advances may feel confused, as well as frustrated and angry. She may not know how to react to the situation. She may think:

> Should I confront the harasser? Should I tell my husband or boyfriend? Should I discuss it with fellow employees? Should I complain to the employer (the boss of the harasser, if any)? If I tell them, how will they react? Would they believe me? Would they not say I invited it myself? Would I be labelled a troublemaker? Would they make my life hell on the job? What if I am fired? Where would I get another job? I have to have a job to make ends meet.

These fears may hound her into keeping her mouth shut. Typically, in such cases, she will suffer the humiliation and harassment silently as long as she can and then she will quietly quit. These fears are not imaginary; they are real. When harassment occurs, often the woman is unsure whether a real injustice has been committed for the aggressor may make light of it or pretend that she initiated the encounter.

Like rape, sexual harassment has been a hidden problem, treated as a joke or blamed on the victim herself. Because of a long history of silence on the subject, many women feel uncomfortable, embarrassed or ashamed when they talk about personal incidents of harassment. They are afraid that it will reflect badly on their character or that somehow they will be seen as inviting the propositions.[1] When women do speak out, they are often ignored, discredited or accused of "misunderstanding" their superior's intentions. Many women attribute their silence to practical considerations. Only 18 per cent of the

---

[1] See L. C. Pogrebin, "The Working Woman: Sex Harassment", *Ladies Home Journal* (June 1977), p. 24.

women in the Working Women United Institute survey stated that they complained about the harassment. The most common reasons given for not reporting the incidents were that they believed nothing would be done (52 per cent), that it would be treated lightly or ridiculed (43 per cent), or that they would be blamed or suffer repercussions (30 per cent).

Other reasons why women have been hesitant to file a complaint include:

1. It is difficult to protect the confidentiality of the complaint once the investigation of the charges has begun. This subjects women to embarrassment and harassment from co-workers.
2. Sexual harassment often occurs when women are economically vulnerable. Many women have to work for a living and fear that if they file a complaint they will lose their jobs.
3. Some women feel guilty about these advances. They believe that they have done something to cause them and, therefore, they are reluctant to report the incident because they think they will be incriminated.
4. The length of time it takes to process a complaint is prohibitive, considering that the complainant must continue to work with the harasser and possibly be subject to reprisals.
5. Others ignore the harassment, transfer out of their section or, in some cases, simply give in.

In addition, some women fear that the publicity a complaint may receive will not only hurt their job prospects but also their personal lives and marital relationships. They fear that they would have a difficult time explaining and convincing their husbands and children of what happened to them.

In terms of money and time, the cost of sexual harassment litigation is also a prohibitive factor. If it is convinced on the basis of its own investigation that the complainant was sexually harassed (as a matter of fact any kind of discrimination), a Human Rights Commission carries the complaint to a Board of Inquiry or a Human Rights Tribunal, as the case may be, and the Commission bears the entire cost of the litigation. In that case it does not cost a penny to the complainant. If a complainant wishes to hire her own lawyer, she can do so, but in that case she has to bear the cost of her lawyer. The Commission will not reimburse her for the cost of her own private lawyer, and the Tribunal is unlikely to award the complainant her lawyer's cost.[2]

In case the complainant pursues her complaint through the employer's internal redress mechanism, if one exists, then again the complainant has to spend her own money on legal counsel, etc. However, if the complaint is processed through the grievance procedure, under the collective agreement, the union normally bears the entire cost of arbitration. If the complainant decides to sue the employer for damages or file criminal charges against the harasser, then, of course, the complainant alone has to bear the entire cost of litigation which may be phenomenal depending on the nature of the case.

A complainant may also be afraid of a retaliatory defamation suit by the harasser. This is a genuine concern. There have been cases where the harasser had threatened to sue and actually sued the victim for a substantial amount of tort damages.[3] If the complainant somehow fails to establish her charges of sexual harassment, her vulnerability for a tort action increases drastically. Irrespective of this fact, whether the harasser wins this tort case, the complainant can hardly afford this kind of litigation. The harasser, however, achieves his basic objective of silencing the victim by frightening her through a threat of or actual tort action.

---

[2] See for example *Potapczyk v. MacBain* (Can. 1984), 5 C.H.R.R. D/2285 (Lederman). The Canadian Human Rights Tribunal while denying the complainant her lawyer's cost stated at D/2298 (para. 19367) that: "it was not necessary for Ms. Potapczyk to have engaged separate counsel.... we do not feel that two counsel were necessary to present them. The structure of the Act permits an individual who has a complaint to have it prosecuted by competent counsel for the Commission without incurring personal expense."

[3] See for example the arbitration case, *Assn. of Professors of the University of Ottawa v. University of Ottawa* (1979), unreported (O'Shea): Professor Strickler subsequently filed a civil suit against Ms. Coupel (victim) alleging defamation and seeking $250,000 in damages. See Victor Sim, "Strickler Dismissal Upheld", *CAUT Bulletin*, December 1980. At Carleton University School of Journalism in Ottawa, three women students charged members of their staff with sexual harassment. Although the women did not name specific men, three male professors threatened to sue the students for more than $100,000. At Clark University in *Peck v. Blank and Bunster*, the victims of sexual harassment were confronted with a law suit for $23.7 million. See Anne Field, "Harassment on Campus: Sex in a Tenured Position" (1981), *Ms. Magazine*, p. 68.

B. BURDEN OF PROOF IN SEXUAL HARASSMENT CASES

Generally, in human rights cases, the burden of proof lies with the complainant or the appropriate Human Rights Commission to establish that the respondent, in fact, committed discrimination against the complainant. The same principle has been extended to sexual harassment cases by requiring the complainant (or Human Rights Commission) to prove that the respondent, in fact, caused sexual harassment to the complainant.

In the first sexual harassment case, *Cherie Bell*,[4] the Board of Inquiry found that a complainant had the onus of showing that compliance with an employer's sexual advances was a term or condition of employment. Chairperson Shime suggested that it is the complainant who must establish that the balance of probabilities were in her favour and accordingly the respondent acted in a manner which is in violation of the *Code*. The matter of onus of proof was also considered in *Bhinder v. C.N.R.*[5] where the Tribunal found that the complainant must show a *prima facie* case of discrimination as a result of the respondent's employment policies or requirements; and that it is the complainant who must satisfy the onus of showing that the respondent engaged in a discriminatory practice. Furthermore, that once a *prima facie* case of discrimination has been brought against the respondent, the onus then shifts to that party. The findings in the *Cherie Bell* case were also accepted and approved by the Board of Inquiry in *Cox v. Jagbritte Inc.*[6] In that case, Professor Cumming discussed this issue further by reviewing a series of cases in the United States with respect to the question of the establishment of a *prima facie* case of sex discrimination by way of sexual harassment, and in that regard stated as follows:

> Thus, to present a prima face case of sex discrimination by way of sexual harassment, a plaintiff must plead and prove that (1) submission to sexual advances of a supervisor was a term or condition of employment, (2) this fact substantially affected the plaintiff's employment, and (3) employees of the opposite sex were not affected in the same way by these actions.[7]

---

[4] (Ont. 1980), 1 C.H.R.R. D/155 (para. 1442) (Shime).
[5] (Can. 1981), 2 C.H.R.R. D/546 (Cumming).
[6] (Ont. 1982), 3 C.H.R.R. D/609 (Cumming).
[7] *Ibid.*, at D/611 (para. 5543).

A further case that dealt with the question of burden of proof is *Currie v. China Town Restaurant.*[8] This case did not involve a matter of sexual harassment, but was a complaint by the complainant that she was discriminated against by virtue of her dismissal from her employment due to her having assisted another employee in making a complaint to the Nova Scotia Human Rights Commission. The Chairperson of the Board of Inquiry, Donald H. Oliver, discussed the question of burden of proof as follows:

> Human Rights legislation is different from many other pieces of provincial legislation in that it is designed to remedy something that may not be tangible, indeed, may be ethereal and may at times manifest itself no more clearly than being a state of mind and, like a kaleidoscope, it may change colour and complexion so very quickly and easily that it may avoid detection. Discrimination is by definition the denial of the right "to have" on the basis of wholly irrelevant human considerations. . . .
>
> Many of the subtleties of discrimination involve an analysis of something as indefinable as human soul. Accordingly, it would be wrong, in my judgment to apply a strict test or a strict burden to the interpretation of such legislation as Human Rights legislation. Even the preamble to our statute indicates that the failure to provide equality of opportunity threatens the status of all persons. The Human Rights Act is not a criminal statute and accordingly the criminal burden of proof "beyond a reasonable doubt" is not applicable.

The Chairperson concluded:

> The weight must not be greater than that required to support a finding in a civil case. In my judgment this places too heavy a burden on a complainant in a Human Rights case and if strictly followed would mean that there would be an unnecessary fetter imposed upon a Board of Inquiry in attempting to do justice in what is usually a nebulous, painfully awkward and difficult field.[9]

The matter of onus in human rights cases was further considered by the Alberta Court of Queen's Bench in *Base-Fort Patrol Ltd. v. Alta. Human Rights Commn.*[10] In that case, McDonald J. quoted from the United States Supreme Court decision in *Texas Department of Community Affairs v. Burdine*:[11]

---

[8] (N.S. 1982), 3 C.H.R.R. D/1085 (Oliver).
[9] *Ibid.*, at D/1090 (paras. 9590-93).
[10] (Alta. 1983), 4 C.H.R.R. D/1200 (Q.B.).
[11] 450 U.S. 248 (1981).

The burden of establishing a *prima facie* case of disparate treatment is not onerous. The Plaintiff must prove by a preponderance of the evidence that she was qualified, but was rejected under circumstances which give rise to an inference of unlawful discrimination. The prima facie case serves an important function in the litigation, it eliminates the most common non-discriminatory reasons for the plaintiff's rejection. . . . The prima facie case "raises an inference of discrimination only because we presume these acts, if otherwise unexplained, are more likely than not based on the consideration of impermissible factors." Establishment of the prima facie case in effect creates a presumption that the employer unlawfully discriminated against the employee. If the trier of fact believes the plaintiff's evidence and if the employer is silent in the face of the presumption, the Court must enter judgment for the plaintiff because no issue of fact remains in the case.

The burden that shifts to the defendant, therefore, is to rebut the presumption of discrimination by producing evidence that the plaintiff was rejected, or someone else was preferred, for a legitimate, non-discriminatory reason. The defendant need not persuade the court that it was actually motivated by the proferred reasons. It is sufficient if the defendant's evidence raises a genuine issue of fact as to whether it discriminated against the plaintiff. To accomplish this, the defendant must clearly set forth, through the introduction of admissible evidence, the reasons for the plaintiff's rejection. . . .

The plaintiff retains the burden of persuasion. She now must have the opportunity to demonstrate that the proferred reason was not the true reason for the employment decision. This burden now merges with the ultimate burden of persuading the court that she has been a victim of intentional discrimination. She may succeed in this either directly by persuading the court that a discriminatory reason more likely motivated the employer or indirectly by showing that the employer's proferred explanation is unworthy of credence.[12]

McDonald J. concluded that the "error of law as to the onus of proof is so fundamental" in that case that the order of the Board of Inquiry cannot stand. The court reversed the order of the board and recommended that a new Board of Inquiry be appointed to inquire into the complaint. The *Base-Fort Patrol* case in this regard has been frequently quoted with approval by other courts and Boards of Inquiry.[13] In *Makara v. Osama Enterprises Ltd.*,[14] after reviewing *Base-Fort Patrol* and other cases, the Board of Adjudication stated:

---

[12] *Base-Fort Patrol Ltd. v. Alta. Human Rights Commn.*, *supra*, note 10, at D/1201 (para. 10581).

[13] See for example *Jain v. Acadia University* (N.S. 1984), 5 C.H.R.R. D/2123 (para. 17954) (Atton); and *Makara v. Osama Enterprises Ltd.* (Man. 1985), 6 C.H.R.R. D/2935 (para. 23816) (Henteleff).

[14] *Ibid.*

It is clear from the consideration of all of the above cases that the burden of proof is satisfied by the process of balancing the probabilities as to what occurred. In order for a Complainant to establish a prima facie case, in order to shift the onus to the respondent, she must prove by a preponderance of evidence that unlawful discrimination occurred. Even if there may be an initial belief of the Complainant's evidence and the burden then shifts to the Respondent, that initial belief may be rebutted either on cross-examination and/or by the production of evidence by the Respondent that what the Complainant alleges as being discriminatory was a result of actions on the Respondent's part which were legitimate and had a non-discriminatory base. As was stated in *Jain v. Acadia University supra*, the Complainant must then show that the Respondent Employer's proferred explanation is unworthy of credence.[15]

The Supreme Court of Canada in a case involving age discrimination in *Ont. Human Rights Commn. et al. v. Borough of Etobicoke*[16] stated:

> Once a complainant has established before a board of inquiry a *prima facie* case of discrimination, in this case proof of a mandatory retirement at age sixty as a condition of employment, he is entitled to relief in the absence of justification by the employer. The only justification which can avail the employer in the case at bar, is the proof, the burden of which is upon him, that such compulsory retirement is a *bona fide* occupational qualification and requirement for the employment concerned. The proof, in my view, must be made according to the ordinary civil standard of proof, that is upon a balance of probabilities.[17]

The Supreme Court unanimously ruled that, in that case, the evidence adduced before the Board of Inquiry was inadequate to discharge the burden of proof lying upon the employer. Thus, where a claimant had established a *prima facie* case of violation of Act, the court held that the employer bore the burden of proving that the case fell within the exception.

Thus, in sexual harassment cases, like other human rights cases, the burden of proof lies on the complainant to prove that on a "balance of probabilities" or "the preponderance of evidence" there was a contravention of the appropriate human rights statute. This involves:

1. proof that the alleged conduct by the respondent occurred;
2. proof that it constituted sexual harassment in the circumstances: for example that it took place without the complainant's willing consent.

---

[15] *Ibid.*, at D/2939 (para. 23817).
[16] (Ont. 1982), 3 C.H.R.R. D/781 (S.C.C.).
[17] *Ibid.*, at D/783 (para. 6893).

If the complainant produces evidence which satisfies these requirements, then the respondent has an evidentiary burden to respond with some evidence that the acts did not occur or that they did not constitute sexual harassment and did not violate the human rights statute.[18] However, a Human Rights Act is not a criminal statute and accordingly the criminal burden of proof "beyond a reasonable doubt" is not applicable.

In terms of proof, what is required in sexual harassment cases is not yet clear. Proof of other instances, or allegations of others, or corroborating instances are helpful and would tend to persuade a Human Rights Tribunal or a court. The plaintiff faces an uphill battle in establishing her case. She must anticipate a reluctance by the court or tribunal to accept an allegation of sexual harassment. The courts in the United States, more than Human Rights Tribunals in Canada, have difficulty in conceptualizing sexual harassment as employment discrimination.[19]

The second difficulty particular to sexual harassment litigation grows out of the commonly held, but narrow, view of what conduct constitutes the wrong. Sexual harassment is most readily understood in the context of a woman fired by her male supervisor for refusing to acquiesce to his sexual demands. In actuality, sexual harassment faced by women on the job is far broader in scope. Some continue to perceive sexual advances on the job as perhaps misguided and inappropriate, but not intrinsically offensive[20] except in a minority of instances. The behaviour at issue is assigned its origin in the natural attraction between the sexes. Thus, again, there is a reluctance to hold the employer accountable for what is considered "natural" behaviour

---

[18] For further discussion on "burden of proof" in sexual harassment cases see *Zarankin v. Johnstone* (B.C. 1984), 5 C.H.R.R. D/2274 (Smith), affd (B.C. 1985), 6 C.H.R.R. D/2651 (B.C.S.C.), also *Webb v. Cyprus Pizza* (B.C. 1985), 6 C.H.R.R. D/2794 (Wilson).

[19] For an illustration see the exchange between the trial judge and plaintiff's counsel, cited in *Henson v. City of Dundee*, 682 F. 2d 897 at 900, n. 2, 29 E.P.D. para. 32, 993 (11th Cir. 1982).

[20] See for example *Re Government of Province of Alta. and Alta. Union of Provincial Employees* (1983), 10 L.A.C. (3d) 179 (Larson), where the Board stated that "she may have felt uncomfortable by the incident, but we are unable to conclude that it discloses evidence to support the allegations of sexual harassment against the grievor." Further it added that "it may have been that the grievor's actions were meant in a light vein and he did not intend them to be taken seriously . . . ."

between men and women, unless it is clearly shown that the behaviour crossed over in the area of abuse.[21]

The plaintiff may face many hurdles in trying to establish a case of sexual harassment. First of all it is very difficult to get women to come forward to testify even as witnesses because of the sensitive nature of the word "sex". The evidence comes in the form of admissions by the respondent through words and actions, statements of witnesses to the sexual advances, or statements of others subjected to the same or similar conduct as was the complainant.

During a review of sexual harassment charges by the tribunals, three elements are generally considered within each charge: (1) the type of unwelcome sexual activity alleged by the complainant, (2) the resulting harm to the complainant, and (3) the person who allegedly engaged in the activity. Then, each element is further broken down into sub-parts for analysis. It should be emphasized that an allegation of unwelcome sexual activity does not necessarily mean that a finding of sexual harassment would be made. The term "sexual advances" or "sexual activity" refers to the sexual conduct that the complainant alleged occurred. In order for sexual harassment to be found, the other requirements of the Sexual Harassment Guidelines must be met, such as the harm resulting from the sexual conduct and the liability of the respondent.

The list below describes the above three elements of sexual harassment charges with a brief description of each sub-part which the plaintiff will be required to establish.

Type of Sexual Activity

1. Physical/Touching: unwelcome physical contact of a sexual nature, such as the touching of a person's buttocks or unwelcome hugging or kissing.
2. Requests for Favours: asking or demanding that a person engage in a sexual act and promising a positive employment decision if the person does submit.
3. Other/Language: general vulgar language, calling a person sexually derogatory names, general derogatory comments about one's sex, sexually explicit pictures, photographs or cartoons.

---

[21] Joan Vermeulen, "Preparing Sexual Harassment Litigation under Title VII" (1982), 7 *Women's Rights Law Reporter* 331 at 332.

Resulting Harm

1. Promotions: failure to be promoted as a result of not submitting to sexual advances.
2. Discharge.
3. Constructive Discharge: the situation where a person had no choice but to resign when the unwelcome sexual activity became intolerable.
4. Other Terms and Conditions: less desirable work assignments, reduction in the number of work hours, transfer to a different work shift.
5. Atmosphere: the situation where a person has stayed on the job but the sexual activity interferes with work performance and/or creates an offensive working environment.

Perpetrator (person engaging in the unwelcome sexual activity)

1. Respondent: including its supervisory employees and agents.
2. Co-worker: fellow employee not in a supervisory capacity over a complainant.

In this category, by far the greater number of people allegedly engaging in unwelcome activity consisted of supervisory employees.

However, in *Janzen v. Platy Enterprises Ltd.*,[22] the Supreme Court of Canada stated that "Victims of harassment need not demonstrate that they were not hired, were denied a promotion or were dismissed from their employment as a result of their refusal to participate in sexual activity."[23]

An important matter which still remains unresolved involves the types of evidence necessary for determining the responsibility of an employer for the sexually harassing behaviour of its supervisory and other personnel. When supervisors are the source of the problem, two case law tests exist. The first requires that plaintiffs make a *prima facie* showing of sexual harassment by supervisory personnel for the employer to be liable. A second, more stringent, test places a greater burden on plaintiffs. This test requires plaintiffs to establish, in addition to a *prima facie* showing, that the employer either condoned the harassing acts by its actions, or at least acquiesced by lack of action. However, neither of these require the plaintiff to prove the defendant employer endorsed the discriminatory behaviour by its supervisory

---

[22] (Man. 1989), 10 C.H.R.R. D/6205 (S.C.C.).
[23] *Ibid.*, at D/6226 (para. 44447).

personnel, only that there had been a discriminatory effect. While the general burden of proof in a complaint under human rights statutes is on the balance of probabilities, the tribunals, however, insist that they must be persuaded on more than the balance of probabilities that one form of discrimination occurred, before they can conclude that on the balance of probabilities another rather different form of discrimination occurred.

Under most human rights statutes, the respective Human Rights Commission carries the complaint and, together with the complainant, bears the onus of establishing a *prima facie* case of discrimination or harassment, including sexual harassment. The elements to be established will, of course, vary according to what section is alleged to have been infringed.

Once a *prima facie* case has been established by the plaintiff, the onus of proof shifts to the respondent to establish that the complaint is unfounded, or that the respondent's actions were justified under one of the exceptions listed in the human rights statutes. However, it seems clear that this defence is not available in respect of a complaint of sexual harassment because the Boards have held that there is no justification whatsoever for sexual harassment in the workplace.

C. NATURE OF PROOF

Even if women have legal recourse against sexual harassment, victims have serious problems of proof. As in rape cases, women who bring complaints are often taunted with suggestions that they invited the harassment. Hearing one person's word against another may not be enough. Sometimes written evidence is barely sufficient.

Discrimination on the grounds of race, colour or sex is frequently practised in a very subtle manner. Overt discrimination on these grounds is not present in every discriminatory situation or occurrence. In a case where direct evidence of discrimination is absent, it becomes necessary for a Human Rights Tribunal to infer discrimination from the conduct of the individual or individuals whose conduct is in issue. This is not always an easy task. The conduct alleged to be discriminatory must be carefully analysed and scrutinized in the context of the situation in which it arises.[24]

---

[24] *Kennedy v. Mohawk College Board of Governors* (Ont. 1973), unreported, at pp. 4 and 5 (Borins).

It is a fact of life that, as a general rule, sexual encounters do not occur in public. One is often left with only the testimony of the accuser and the accused. How is one to determine guilt or innocence based on a quick assessment of the proponents in the witness box? It is suggested that the adversary system through the process of examination and cross-examination will lead to the truth. But quite often that is not the case. As Chairperson Shime pointed out in the *Cherie Bell* case, there is an artificiality to the process which often tends to hide the truth rather than reveal it. The proponents make brief appearances in the witness box. Very often they are examined and cross-examined by lawyers of varying skills. Some witnesses are better than others; often the most consummate liar is the better witness while the truthful person is hesitant and creates a poor impression. In those circumstances it is equally unjust to deny a remedy to an injured person as to grant a remedy against an innocent person.[25]

The Human Rights Tribunals have frequently commented on the fact that discrimination can be a subtle phenomenon and they must rely on circumstantial evidence, drawing inferences from conduct. Further, it is well recognized that nowhere are evidentiary difficulties more likely than in sexual harassment cases. According to Professor Backhouse, a renowned authority on sexual harassment in Canada, "resolution of evidentiary matters will always be critical in sexual harassment cases since corroborative witnesses are rarely available."[26] She explains:

> Furthermore, our legal system is imbued with deeprooted fears about unfounded claims of sexual abuse. In most cases of sexual harassment it is to be expected that the complainant will be the sole witness for her side and the alleged sexual harasser will deny all of the allegations. As a result, the trier of fact will be hard pressed to determine which side to believe.[27]

Moreover, the courts have confirmed that proceedings under the human rights statutes are civil proceedings; therefore, the burden of proof in sexual harassment cases is the civil standard, that is, balance of probabilities.[28] Further, these proceedings do not amount to charging

---

[25] *Bell v. The Flaming Steer Steak House* (Ont. 1980), 1 C.H.R.R. D/155 (para. 1397) (Shime).
[26] C. Backhouse, "*Bell v. The Flaming Steer Steak House*: Canada's First Sexual Harassment Decision" (1981), 19 *U.W.O.L. Rev.* 141.
[27] *Ibid.*
[28] *Herman v. Rodin* (Sask. 1989), 10 C.H.R.R. D/5798 (Q.B.).

the respondent with an offence within the meaning of s. 11 of the Charter of Rights.[29]

1. Evidentiary Problems

The first evidentiary problem in a sexual harassment case is combatting defence efforts to introduce testimony about how the complainant dressed and behaved in the workplace, her personal and possibly sexual relationships in the workplace and other evidence of her past sexual conduct.[30]

Generally, testimony about the complainant's manner of dress should be ruled inadmissible. It is irrelevant unless there is a dress code and it is prejudicial because by advancing worn-out stereotypes, the defendant creates the inference that the complainant may have encouraged the behaviour.[31] While this may be relevant in a tort suit, it has no bearing on a complaint under the Human Rights Acts. If sex discrimination is proved, it is irrelevant whether the complainant's behaviour in any way antagonized the employer or co-workers. A complainant need not be meek and submissive in order to prevail in a human rights charge. Further, the testimony about the complainant's unrelated sexual activities may put an additional burden upon the plaintiff. These testimonies are objectionable on the ground that they are not relevant to employment discrimination.[32]

The second evidentiary problem which may arise concerns the plaintiff's ability to introduce the testimony of other women who have been sexually harassed by the same man. This has been allowed in some cases where the other women worked at the same job site during approximately the same period as the plaintiff. In an American case, *Henson v. City of Dundee*,[33] the court held such evidence admissible, reasoning that due to the close questions of credibility and subjective

---

[29] *Ibid.* See also *Kodellas v. Saskatchewan (Human Rights Commn.)* (Sask. 1989), 10 C.H.R.R. D/6305 (C.A.).

[30] Joan Vermeulen, "Preparing Sexual Harassment Litigation under Title VII" (1982), 7 *Women's Rights Law Reporter* 331 at 342.

[31] *Ibid.*

[32] For example, in *Robinson v. The Company Farm Ltd.* (Ont. 1984), 5 C.H.R.R. D/2243 (Cumming), the Board of Inquiry specifically stated at D/2246 (para. 18987) that the complainant's character and behaviour outside of the employment relationship are irrelevant. "Whatever her personal behaviour outside the workplace might be, it does not excuse an employer in his harassment of her."

[33] *Supra*, note 19.

interpretation inherent in sexual harassment litigation, the existence of lack of corroborating evidence is a crucial factor. On the same basis, Human Rights Tribunals in Canada have allowed the testimony of other women who have been sexually harassed.[34]

Evidence of the defendant's treatment of other female employees is relevant and more probative than prejudicial when introduced to show a pattern of behaviour. It is admissible as proof of intent or willfulness since the courts have recognized that the recurrence of similar acts incrementally reduces the possibility that the challenged conduct was the result of mistakes or inadvertence. In *Mitchell v. Traveller Inn (Sudbury) Ltd.*,[35] the Board of Inquiry said that because of the "unlikelihood of a series of similar misunderstandings arising by pure coincidence", evidence of similar experiences of other female employees was probative and, therefore, admissible. Prior acts are also admissible on rebuttal to show that the employer's articulated reason for discharge of the complainant was actually a pretext for discrimination.

2. Credibility of Witnesses

The credibility of witnesses is more crucial in sexual harassment cases than in any other type of discrimination case because, as a general rule, sexual encounters do not occur openly in public. For example in *Phillips v. Hermiz*,[36] the counsel for the complainant and Saskatchewan Human Rights Commission stated that the complainant and the respondent were working alone at the employer's store when these incidents occurred, and therefore no witnesses to these events could be produced. Further, these events took place in the backroom where the general public would not have access. Thus, one is often left only with the testimony of the accuser and the accused. A general survey of sexual harassment cases in Canada reveals that most (almost all) of the cases were won or lost on the credibility of the witnesses, particularly that of the complainant(s) or respondent(s), rather than on any other grounds. Credibility implies that the witnesses, including the complainant and the respondent, tell the truth without any attempt

---

[34] See for example *Olarte v. Commodore Business Machines Ltd.* (Ont. 1983), 4 C.H.R.R. D/1705 (Cumming).
[35] (Ont. 1981), 2 C.H.R.R. D/590 (Kerr).
[36] (Sask. 1984), 5 C.H.R.R. D/2450 (para. 20312) (Katzman).

to hide or exaggerate the facts in a straightforward and honest manner. It is also important that they not only tell the truth but should also appear to have told the truth. It is not suggested that the witnesses for the complainant or respondent lie under oath. They most likely were not there at the time of the alleged sexual harassment, so they had not seen anything.

In the first sexual harassment case, *Bell v. The Flaming Steer Steak House*,[37] Chairperson Shime recognized the significance and difficulty of assessing the credibility of witnesses and particularly of the complainant and respondent in such cases. He stated that "Basically, the evidence and arguments turned on the question of credibility. . . . The issue of credibility was vigorously contested by the parties. As I have indicated cases involving sex rarely have a host of corroborative witnesses."[38] Thus, due to lack of credibility of the complainant's testimony, he preferred the testimony of the respondent over her and dismissed the complaint.

In *Aragona v. Elegant Lamp Co.*,[39] the Board of Inquiry, while dealing with the issue of credibility of the complainant, observed:

> Credibility is often difficult to assess, particularly when the events have occurred some three years in the past and depend upon detailed nuances for their proper interpretation. There is seldom a single factor which will establish the truth of one version of the facts. Nevertheless, in the present case, there is a cumulation of factors which indicates that the version of the Respondents is to be preferred.
>
> Discrepancies between the signed Complaint and the Complainant's testimony may be expected on occasion. However, in the present case they include the complete abandonment of perhaps the most significant allegation of harassment, since it suggested touching as well as oral comments. The Complaint states that "he would put his hands on my shoulders". The implication is that this occurred on more than one occasion. It is also significant that the phrase "without his wife" was abandoned during Mrs. Aragona's testimony. These discrepancies suggest not only some lack of credibility but perhaps, more seriously, some laxity in making allegations of this nature.
>
> Mrs. Aragona's credibility also suffers from her insistence that she normally used the address "Mr. Fillipitto" rather than "Adriano". This is contrary to all of the other evidence. Moreover, while testifying at the hearing, she freely and comfortably referred to him as "Adriano". This "colouring" of her evidence suggests an attempt to exaggerate the formality of her relationship with him. A tendency to exaggerate her evidence may also be apparent from her statement

---

[37] (Ont. 1980), 1 C.H.R.R. D/155 (Shime).
[38] *Ibid.*, at D/157 (para. 1401).
[39] (Ont. 1982), 3 C.H.R.R. D/1109 (Ratushny).

that upon quitting her job on December 17th, she did not wait until Christmas but started searching for a job before Christmas. Her husband testified that she waited until the New Year.[40]

On the other hand, in the *Commodore* case[41] the credibility of the respondent was in question. The Board of Inquiry while accepting the evidence of the complainants over the respondent left no doubt that the respondent was a totally uncredible witness. Chairperson Cumming stated:

> I accept the evidence of the six Complainants in this regard, and reject the asserted attempted defences and explanations of Mr. DeFilippis. Wherever there is contradiction between his evidence and that of the Complainants, I accept their evidence and reject his. *He is a liar, and was prepared to say anything at all to extricate himself from the problem he confronted with the Complainants.* He demonstrated a prodigious memory for the most insignificant detail when it seemed to serve his purpose. He would deny events that he thought could not be proven, or at least would simply come down to his word against that of someone else. For example, he denied the circumstances of his transfer and subsequent dismissal from his previous employment at Teledyne Stillman.
>
> The six Complainants all impressed me as truthful witnesses. Moreover, their evidence was corroborated by the similar fact evidence of five female worker witnesses . . . gave evidence that tended to confirm the allegations of sexual harassment by Mr. DeFilippis. I found them also to be truthful witnesses.[42] [Emphasis added]

Similarly in *Kotyk v. C.E.I.C. and Chuba*,[43] the Human Rights Tribunal while rejecting the evidence of the respondent stated:

> After hearing all of the evidence, and observing the demeanour of the witnesses, I find, on balance, that Ms. Kotyk's evidence is more credible and is to be believed in preference to that of Mr. Chuba where there is conflict. In particular, I find that Mr. Chuba's advances to Ms. Kotyk were unsolicited and unwelcome, and that she feared that her employment would be jeopardized if she refused his advances.[44]

In *Pachouris v. St. Vito Italian Food*,[45] the Board of Inquiry basically rejected the complainant's testimony on the basis that "there

---

[40] *Ibid.*, at D/1112 (paras. 9754-56).
[41] (Ont. 1983), 4 C.H.R.R. D/1705 (Cumming).
[42] *Ibid.*, at D/1733 (paras. 14787-88).
[43] (Can. 1983), 4 C.H.R.R. D/1416 (Ashley).
[44] *Ibid.*, at D/1425 (para. 12214).
[45] (Ont. 1984), 5 C.H.R.R. D/1944 (Dunlop).

were certain significant inconsistencies in the complainant's evidence" and "contradictions between the complainant's evidence and that of the respondent's witnesses in particular, Michelle Desjardins, a young woman who had worked in the restaurant throughout most of its brief existence." In *Watt v. Regional Municipality of Niagara*,[46] the Board of Inquiry, while rejecting the evidence of the complainant, observed:

> The complainant's evidence concerning this episode is not completely satisfactory. As noted, in her testimony, the complainant did not refer to the prefatory comment, "I have bent over backwards for Maureen and you" which places the rest of his statement in a very different light than that created by quoting the rest of his statement in isolation. The apparent willingness of the complainant to distort the facts to suit her own purposes detracts from her credibility as a witness. When confronted with this point on cross-examination, the complainant's explanation was that she did not think that Mr. Wales had, in fact, bent over backwards to be helpful to her and accordingly, she felt she was under no obligation to report the rest of his statement. A more candid witness would report the whole statement and add the qualification subsequently.[47]

In the *Janzen v. Platy Enterprises*[48] case a Manitoba Board of Adjudication evaluating the credibility of the testimony of witnesses including that of the complainants and respondents concluded:

> I accept the evidence of Ms. Govereau that no meeting of staff occurred as alleged by Phillip. Further, I find that in view of my analysis of the evidence, Phillip is not a credible witness. I reject not only his evidence that he spoke to Tommy following his meeting with Ms. Janzen and his evidence that a meeting of the staff was convened by him, but also reject his view that he did everything that could reasonably have been expected of him.
>
> I have no hesitation in concluding, as did Ms. Janzen, that not only did he appear not to take her allegations seriously at all, but in fact quite clearly blamed her for it and that if in fact acts of sexual harassment did happen, she was the one who permitted it to happen or should have taken the initiative to stop it, more so than she did. I agree with her conclusion that under the circumstances there seemed very little likelihood, if any, that the situation would be remedied and that she had no other alternative but to terminate her employment as she did.

---

[46] (Ont. 1984), 5 C.H.R.R. D/2453 (McCamus).
[47] *Ibid.*, at D/2463 (para. 20373).
[48] (Man. 1985), 6 C.H.R.R. D/2735 (Henteleff), revd (Man. 1986), 8 C.H.R.R. D/3831 (C.A.), a decision quashed by the Supreme Court of Canada (Man. 1989), 10 C.H.R.R. D/6205. See also *Ives v. Palfy* (B.C. 1990), 12 C.H.R.R. D/483 (Joe).

> I found Carol Enns to be a totally credible witness, and in all instances where her evidence differs from Phillip, I accept her evidence. She had never known the complainant before and only came to know her as a co-employee of the Corporate respondent. She gave evidence of having a good relationship with both Phillip and Tommy and therefore she had no vested interest whatsoever and no bias of any nature or kind in respect of the proceedings. She confirmed that she had in fact encouraged Ms. Govereau to speak with Phillip and that she was there at the time that the meeting took place.[49]

The credibility of the complainant (or witnesses) may be further damaged by producing in evidence a misleading exhibit or documentation. For example, in *Allan v. Riverside Lodge*,[50] a case dealing with a sexually revealing uniform to be worn by the waitresses, the complainants adduced evidence in photographs of both complainants wearing the uniform in question. In each photograph, the complainant was posed so that the slit extends sufficiently up her leg to reveal her panties, and one photograph of the top so as to reveal cleavage, a small portion of her bra, and part of her stomach. The Board of Inquiry found that these photographs were specially designed by the complainants to mislead the Human Rights Commission and the Board of Inquiry. Chairperson Hunter stated:

> I am fully satisfied that these photographs *do not* accurately reveal the uniform either as it was designed to be worn, nor as it was worn by the Riverside waitresses including the two complainants. These *photographs are in my opinion, a deliberate attempt to mislead someone, either the Human Rights Commission investigators or, conceivably, this board of inquiry.*[51] (Emphasis added]

A useful guide relating to credibility of witnesses is found in the judgement of O'Halloran J.A., of the British Columbia Court of Appeal in *Faryna v. Chorny*,[52] and adopted and quoted by a British Columbia Council of Human Rights in *Langevin v. Engineered Air Division of Air Tex Industry Ltd.*,[53] as follows:

> If a trial Judge's finding of credibility is to depend solely on which person he thinks made the better appearance of sincerity in the witness box, we are

---

[49] *Ibid.*, at D/2768 (paras. 22645, 46 and 52).
[50] (Ont. 1985), 6 C.H.R.R. D/2978 (Hunter).
[51] *Ibid.*, at D/2979 (para. 24039).
[52] [1952] 2 D.L.R. 354 at 356-58 (B.C.C.A.).
[53] (B.C. 1985), 6 C.H.R.R. D/2552 (Powell).

left with a purely arbitrary finding and justice would then depend upon the best actors in the witness box. On reflection it becomes almost axiomatic that the appearance of telling the truth is but one of the elements that enter into the credibility of the evidence of a witness. Opportunities for knowledge, powers of observation, judgment and memory, ability to describe clearly what he has seen and heard, as well as other factors, combine to produce what is called credibility. . . . A witness by his manner may create a very unfavourable impression of his truthfulness upon the trial Judge, and yet the surrounding circumstances in the case may point decisively to the conclusion that he is actually telling the truth. I am referring to the comparatively infrequent case in which a witness is caught in a clumsy lie.

The credibility of interested witnesses, particularly in cases of conflict of evidence, cannot be gauged solely by the test of whether the personal demeanour of the particular witness carried conviction of truth. The test must reasonably subject his story to an examination of its consistency with the probabilities that surround the currently existing conditions. In short, the real test of the truth of the story of a witness in such a case must be its harmony with the preponderance of the probabilities which a practical and informed person would readily recognize as reasonable in that place and in those conditions. Only thus can a Court satisfactorily appraise the testimony of those shrewd persons adept in the half-lie and of long and successful experience in combining skillful exaggeration with partial suppression of the truth.[54]

3. Hearsay Evidence

Generally, a Board of Inquiry or a Tribunal under the respective human rights statute has discretion to admit any form of evidence which it considers necessary and appropriate, whether or not it would be admissible in a court of law.[55] Thus, a Board of Inquiry or a Tribunal has a wide latitude under the respective human rights statutes to receive evidence it considers necessary and appropriate. Rather, the Boards of Inquiry should not refuse to receive any evidence which is germane, cogent and appropriate, such as evidence of an eye-witness to the alleged sexual harassment. In *Fields v. William Ueffing*,[56] the B.C. Supreme Court set aside the decision of the tribunal on the ground that its "refusal to hear cogent evidence resulted in a failure to comply with the requirements of natural justice". The court concluded:

---

[54] *Ibid.*, at D/2555 (para. 21155).
[55] See for example s. 15(1) of the Ontario *Statutory Powers Procedure Act*, R.S.O. 1990, c. S.22.
[56] (B.C. 1985), 6 C.H.R.R. D/2711 (B.C. S.C.).

Having wrongly refused to hear the offered evidence, he then ... went on to draw an inference adverse to the complainant because of its absence. A decision founded on such a breach of fundamental justice cannot be permitted to stand. The decision is therefore set aside and a new hearing ordered.[57]

However, it does not mean that a board or tribunal should simply disregard the rules of evidence as developed by the common law over the centuries. Hearsay evidence is dangerous because it is not given under oath, and it is second hand (and thus there is the risk that it is not accurately repeated). Most importantly, hearsay evidence consists of repetition in court of out-of-court statements which were not subject to cross-examination; the right to cross-examination is a crucial part of our adversary system. Thus for example, a Board of Inquiry would normally disregard the evidence by a human rights officer repeating the complainant's statements to him during his investigation, on the ground that her earlier statements to the human rights officer had not been under oath and were not subject to cross-examination. Moreover, there is no necessity to rely on the hearsay, because the complainant is there in person.[58]

Similarly, Boards of Inquiry are reluctant to admit a statement or a letter by another employee (particularly on behalf of the respondent) when the witness was seemingly available and it was within the power of the respondent, as her employer, to grant her time off to come to the hearing without a summons. Further they give very little weight, if any, to such evidence because of the circumstances in which it was written; by an employee of the respondent, who may be reluctant[59] to say anything which will injure her employer and who is not under oath or subject to cross-examination. However, the tribunals in exceptional circumstances may accept an affidavit even though the deponent was neither called as a witness nor cross-examined. For example in the *Commodore* case,[60] the Board of Inquiry admitted the affidavit of one Frank Knight tendered by the Human Rights Commission over the objection of the respondent (the affidavit was damaging to the credibility of the respondent), because Mr. Knight was 75 years of age, in ill health, and resided in Florida and had intended to attend the hearing up until a few days before the hearing

---

[57] *Ibid.*, at D/2713 (para. 22355).
[58] See for example *Zarankin v. Johnstone* (B.C. 1984), 5 C.H.R.R. D/2274 at D/2279 (para. 19214) (Smith).
[59] See for example the *Zarankin* case, *ibid.*, at D/2280 (para. 19216).
[60] *Olarte v. Commodore Business Machines* (Ont. 1983), 4 C.H.R.R. D/1705 (Cumming).

when ill health prevented him from so doing. The Board, at the time of admitting the letter, had made it clear that it would be considered only as to credibility. On appeal, the Supreme Court of Ontario held that the Board of Inquiry was entitled to admit the evidence by way of an affidavit which contained testimony regarding the character of the respondent.[61]

In *Mehta v. MacKay*,[62] the Nova Scotia Board of Inquiry, in the course of hearing, accepted into evidence the hearsay testimony that a deceased person had told a witness of incidents of sexual harassment by the perpetrator-employer. The Board allowed the hearsay evidence without any indication as to the weight to be given to the evidence. The Nova Scotia Court of Appeal quashed the Board's finding of sexual harassment because the court was unable to determine what weight, if any, had been attributed to the impugned evidence. The ruling of the Board contained nothing to indicate that the evidence against the appellant did not include the hearsay evidence of the deceased person. The court indicated that the Board had broken the rule of hearsay evidence. The court stated:

> Hearsay evidence is suspect by its very nature because the credibility of the deceased author of the statements cannot be tested and he cannot be cross-examined. It is doubly suspect from a witness whose credibility has been called into serious question. There is no exception to the exclusionary rule against hearsay evidence which might make the evidence in question admissible. The Chairman, having quoted it in his decision, made no finding as to the weight he attached to it.[63]

4. Similar Fact Evidence

The Boards of Inquiry and Tribunals in sexual harassment cases have admitted similar fact evidence practically for the same reason that circumstantial evidence is admitted, that is, because sexual encounters generally do not happen openly and in public, and the sexual behaviour in question is often ambiguous and subtle.

On the question of admissibility or non-admissibility of similar fact evidence, the courts and tribunals in Canada have followed the

---

[61] *Commodore Business Machines v. Ontario Minister of Labour* (Ont. 1985), 6 C.H.R.R. D/2833 at D/2834 (para. 23157) (Div. Ct.).
[62] (1990), 100 N.S.R. (2d) 319, 272 A.P.R. 319, 91 CLLC 17,013 (C.A.).
[63] *Ibid.*, CLLC, at pp. 16, 261-62.

148 *Ch. 3 - Taking Legal Action — A Predicament for the Victim*

principles laid down by the Australian Court almost a century ago in *Makin v. A.-G. for New South Wales*.[64] The following classic statement on the law governing similar fact evidence is frequently quoted by the courts and tribunals:

> It is undoubtedly not competent for the prosecution to adduce evidence tending to show that the accused has been guilty of criminal acts other than those covered by the indictment, for the purpose of leading to the conclusion that the accused is a person likely from his criminal conduct or character to have committed the offence for which he is being tried. On the other hand, the mere fact that the evidence adduced tends to shew the commission of other crimes does not render it inadmissible if it be relevant to an issue before the jury, and it may be so relevant if it bears upon the question whether the acts alleged to constitute the crime charged in the indictment were designed or accidental, or to rebut a defence which would otherwise be open to the accused. The statement of these general principles is easy but it is obvious that it may often be very difficult to draw the line and to decide whether a particular piece of evidence is on the one side or the other.[65]

The courts and tribunals, however, have cautioned that the danger in admitting similar fact evidence is that the accused person may be convicted not on the basis of evidence relating to the offence with which he or she is charged, but on the basis of evidence of other acts which show the accused has a disposition which makes it likely that the accused committed the offence for which he or she is being tried.[66]

The basic purpose of similar fact evidence, particularly in discrimination cases, is to compare the treatment of a person who complains of unlawful discrimination with the treatment of other employees in similar circumstances where an obvious variable is the factor which is alleged to be the basis of discrimination.[67] Further, it is necessary to compare the case in dispute with similar incidents involving the same employer to determine whether differential treatment has occurred between cases where one variable is a prohibited ground of discrimination. If such differential treatment has occurred, the incidents have to be analysed to ascertain if some variable other than a prohibited ground of discrimination explains it.[68] If the cases are sufficiently similar in other respects to provide *prima facie* basis

---

[64] [1894] A.C. 57, [1891-94] All E.R. Rep. 24 (P.C.).
[65] *Ibid.*, at 65 (A.C.).
[66] See for example the *Cherie Bell* case, *supra*, note 37.
[67] *Fuller v. Candur Plastics Ltd.* (Ont. 1981), 2 C.H.R.R. D/419 at D/420 (Kerr).
[68] *Mitchell v. Nobilium Products Ltd.* (Ont. 1981), 3 C.H.R.R. D/641 at D/643 (Kerr).

for an inference of discrimination, they call for an explanation from the respondent for the differential treatment.[69]

In *Wan v. Greygo Gardens*,[70] the Board of Inquiry, chaired by Professor Kerr, discussed whether the fact that one complainant was discriminated against could be used to corroborate another complainant's allegations of discrimination. The Board stated:

> ... [T]he correct approach to similar fact evidence is that outlined by D. K. Piragoff's *Similar Fact Evidence* (Toronto: Carswell's, 1981). As with all evidence, the primary test of admissibility is one of relevance, but similar fact evidence creates a danger of unduly prejudicing the mind of the fact-finder. In light of this, similar fact evidence should be excluded where the risk of undue prejudice outweighs the real probative value of the evidence as assessed in terms of its relevancy.
>
> Insofar as the evidence of the second incident might be used as probative in Mr. Wan's case, the main relevance of this evidence would be that it may show a proclivity on the respondent's part to engage in some form of discrimination. Where the relevance of evidence is to show proclivity to engage in certain activity, it is generally recognized that the prejudicial effect greatly outweighs the real probative value. Indeed in the courts this realization has given rise to what might be called a "rule of evidence" excluding such similar fact evidence. While I am not bound by such rules, the policy behind the rule is sound and I would decline to accept the evidence of the second incident for this purpose in relation to Mr. Wan's complaint.
>
> The main other possible relevance of this similar fact evidence would be to rebut some defence such as misunderstanding by reason of the unlikelihood that such circumstances could have happened repeatedly if it were a mere case of misunderstanding. While such a defence was raised in this case, and therefore the similar fact evidence would be relevant, care must be used in accepting similar fact evidence for this purpose to ensure that there is not some other explanation for the similarity in the facts. Particular concern is shown in cases where the parties who allege the similar facts have discussed their respective situations prior to giving evidence.[71]

The relevant facts are those which are relevant to the facts at issue only because they are similar to the facts they try to prove. These similar facts can be quite relevant. The knowledge that the defendant (harasser) had, on several occasions, sexually harassed other women, makes an allegation of sexual harassment all the more plausible. These matters, though, are considered to be collateral only and are not

---

[69] *Ibid.*
[70] (Ont. 1982), 3 C.H.R.R. D/812 (Kerr).
[71] *Ibid.*, at D/813 (paras. 7181-83).

admissible unless they fall within certain permissible categories. Evidence of similar acts cannot prove the act itself, but it can give evidence of the intention with which the act was committed. On this basis, there being a number of instances of the same conduct and not merely evidence of an isolated act, the similar fact evidence will be admitted. However, similar fact evidence can be rebutted by other similar evidence.

In the first sexual harassment case, *Bell v. The Flaming Steer Steak House*[72] the evidence was submitted on behalf of the complainants to demonstrate that the respondent, Ernest Ladas, engaged in similar conduct with other female persons in the employ of the respondent. The Board of Inquiry, after discussing the pros and cons of admitting similar fact evidence, stated:

> The general rule relating to similar fact evidence is applicable to both criminal and civil matters and thus in my view it is applicable to matters falling under the Code (Ontario Human Rights Code).[73]

However, in the instant case, the Board, after reading the testimony, decided not to admit or give weight to similar fact evidence because either it was "*completely hearsay*" or did not "*indicate a pattern*". The Board ruled:

> The only remaining aspect of this case concerns the allegations of sexual harassment during Ms. Bell's employment and the similar fact evidence called to support those allegations. In one instance the witness, Miss Carol Bassett, who testified, gave evidence that was completely hearsay and I am not prepared to accept the evidence. . . .
>
> The only other evidence that might be considered as similar fact evidence is the evidence of Anna Korczak, who is also a complainant and after considering the totality of her evidence, I am not satisfied that it should be admitted or given weight in the circumstances of this case. *I am concerned that its prejudicial value outweighs its probative value.* Based on the general admonitions against receiving similar fact evidence, I am hesitant to accept Ms. Korczak's evidence.
>
> Alternatively, I find that the acts of sexual harassment described by Ms. Korczak differ from those described by Ms. Bell and do not indicate a pattern . . . *On that basis, I am not prepared to find that the alleged sexual overtures made to the two complainants were so unusual or bore such a striking similarity, that the evidence of each of the complainants should be treated as similar fact evidence having some probative value in the other's complaint.*[74] [Emphasis added.]

---

[72] (Ont. 1980), 1 C.H.R.R. D/155 (Shime).
[73] *Ibid.*, at D/156 (para. 1396).
[74] *Ibid.*, at D/159 (paras. 1424, 27).

However, Professor Backhouse has severely criticized the exclusion of similar fact evidence in the *Cherie Bell* case as "overly conservative". Referring to the above observation of Mr. Shime, she stated:

> The degree of similarity which the Board required here was too onerous. Making sexual overtures to two subordinate female employees in the work setting and then firing each of them for failing to comply constitutes, where proved, a pattern of conduct in itself. Similarity exists in that this man chooses to make sexual advances to a female person in his employ, the approach is made on the job and both employees suffer similar ramifications for failing to comply with the advances. *Requiring a "striking similarity" in sexual approach before utilizing one complainant's testimony as probative evidence for another complaint is likely to eliminate the usefulness of this legal doctrine in sexual harassment cases.*[75]

She argued that:

> Given the obvious proof problems faced by most sexual harassment complainants, who lack witnesses or tangible evidence, testimony from other employees who have experienced sexual harassment from the same defendant will be compellingly probative. In this context, tribunals will repeatedly have to struggle to draw the difficult balance between the essential need to admit the evidence in order to enforce the legislation and the potentially prejudicial effect upon the defendant.[76] [Emphasis added]

In *Mitchell v. Traveller Inn (Sudbury) Ltd.*,[77] another sexual harassment case, the Board of Inquiry admitted into evidence the testimony of three former employees with respect to sexual advances that they alleged the employer had made to them around the time that the alleged harassment of the complainant occurred. The Board noted that there was a possibility that the allegations of harassment could have arisen from a misunderstanding by the complainant of the employer's intention. However, if it could be shown that the employer had sexually harassed other employees, it would be more probable that the employer's suggestions to the complainant were of a sexual nature. The Board said that because of the "unlikelihood of a series of similar misunderstandings arising by pure coincidence", evidence of similar experiences by other employees was probative and, therefore,

---

[75] C. Backhouse, "*Bell v. The Flaming Steer Steak House Tavern*: Canada's First Sexual Harassment Decision" (1981), 19 *U.W.O.L. Rev.* 141.
[76] *Ibid.*, at 147.
[77] (Ont. 1981), 2 C.H.R.R. D/590 (Kerr).

admissible.[78] On the facts, the Board found that the circumstances of each employee's alleged harassment were not sufficiently similar to the complainant's circumstances. The only similarity that the Board found between the situations was the employer "seemed prone to create apprehensions of harassment among the Respondent's women employees. With only one incident actually confirming those apprehensions, the probative value of this evidence seems heavily outweighed by its prejudicial effect. Therefore, I entirely disregard it."[79]

In another landmark case on sexual harassment, *Olarte et al. v. Commodore Business Machines Ltd.*,[80] a group of six female employees filed a complaint alleging sexual harassment against the corporate respondent and one of its employees. The complainants were attempting to establish corporate responsibility by proving corporate knowledge and acquiescence in the alleged harassment. The respondents were alleging as a defence that there was collusion or a conspiracy by the complainants against the respondents. The Board of Inquiry while admitting the *similar fact evidence* held that "the probative value of allowing the evidence of the referred eight persons far outweighed any possible prejudicial (in the sense of unfairness) impact."[81] The Board stated:

> All six Complainants, and the above mentioned eight persons, allege a pattern or system of conduct toward female employees on the part of the same individual within the same factory, of the same employer. The difference in time frames of employment by some witnesses is, to my mind, an irrelevant factor for the most part. *What is certainly relevant is evidence which goes to the main issue of the employment relationship between female employees, their supervisor the individual Respondent, and whether there was unlawful conduct on his part, and if this is established, then was it known and acquiesced in by the corporate Respondent.* The evidence of all these persons would relate to the same matter — the relationship of the Respondents to female employees. The evidence of each of the persons referred to, and each of the Complainants, if believed, would tend to corroborate the complaints. (However, the opposite holds true as well. If any one or more witnesses' testimony of the others is not accepted, it would tend to throw doubt upon the testimony of the others, and would tend to support the Respondent's contention that there was no discrimination, and that there is a conspiracy on the part of the Complainants.) I did not see any unfairness in the admission of evidence by these eight persons.

---

[78] *Ibid.*, at D/592.
[79] *Ibid.*, (para. 5402.)
[80] (Ont. 1983), 4 C.H.R.R. D/1705 (Cumming).
[81] *Ibid.*, at D/1708 (para. 14586).

For the same reasons, the evidence of each one of the Complainants is relevant and admissible to a determination of the other five Complainants' cases. The similar fact evidence easily met the test for admissibility set forth by the Supreme Court of Canada in a recent case, *Sweitzer v The Queen* (1982), 68 C.C.C. (2d) 193, per McIntyre, J at 196."[82]

On appeal the Supreme Court of Ontario confirmed the decision of the Board of Inquiry and stated that "the similar evidence admitted by the Board met the standards of admissibility and the Board was entitled to admit and to act on such similar fact evidence and hearsay evidence and did not err in doing either."[83] Thus, it is established that the similar fact evidence in sexual harassment cases is admissible as corroborating the complainant's story or showing what the working conditions were, where its probative value outweighs the possibility that it will create undue prejudice. However, when the complainant's story can be established on the strength of her own evidence and where there is no denial of the alleged sexual encounters, and no real attempt to say that the complainant is concocting her story, the tribunals refrain from relying on the similar fact evidence.[84]

However, recently, the Nova Scotia Court of Appeal quashed the Board of Inquiry decision for accepting the similar fact evidence.[85] The Board had accepted into evidence the testimony of a co-worker of the complainant as to similar acts of sexual harassment by the employer. The evidence was accepted by the Board over the objections of counsel for the employer and without comment as to whether its probative value overweighed its prejudicial effect. Further, the ruling of the Board contained nothing to indicate that the evidence against the employer did not include the evidence of similar facts. The court, after thorough discussion of jurisprudence on this point, described the rules for admission of similar fact evidence as follows:

> The following principles relevant to the present case may be extracted from the jurisprudence.

---

[82] *Ibid.* (para. 14587).
[83] *Commodore Business Machines v. Ontario Minister of Labour* (Ont. 1985), 6 C.H.R.R. D/2833 at D/2834 (para. 23154), 49 O.R. (2d) 17, 14 D.L.R. (4th) 118, 84 C.L.L.C. 17,028, 13 C.R.R. 338 (Div. Ct.). See also *Bishop v. Hardy* (Ont. 1986), 86 C.L.L.C. 17,022 and *Hall v. Sonap Canada* (Ont. 1989), 10 C.H.R.R. D/6126 (Plaut).
[84] See for example *Zarankin v. Johnstone c.o.b. as Wessex Inn* (B.C. 1984), 5 C.H.R.R. D/2274 (paras. 19217-20) (Smith).
[85] *Mehta v. MacKay* (1990), 100 N.S.R. (2d) 319, 272 A.P.R. 319, 91 CLLC 17,013 (C.A.).

1. The general rule is that all relevant evidence is admissible.
2. The rule excluding evidence of similar facts is an exception to the general rule.
3. Judges have a discretion to admit similar fact evidence having "regard to the general principles established by the cases."
4. Such discretion may be properly exercised after a judge has made a determination that the evidence has a clear linkage or nexus to an issue other than disposition or propensity such as intention, pattern or system, credibility, corporate knowledge or negation of denial, and its probative value to the issue outweighs its prejudice to the defendant.[86]

The court concluded:

> In the present case it is not apparent that the Chairman exercised his discretion having regard to the general principles established by the cases. The reasons given do not meet that criterion. The similar fact evidence of Shelley Ferguson was therefore improperly admitted. The danger exists that the Chairman may have inferred, consciously or unconsciously, that Dr. Mehta was "likely" to have repeated with the complainant the conduct alleged by Ms Ferguson.[87]

D. PLAINTIFF MUST PLEAD AND PROVE

In a *quid pro quo* sexual harassment complaint, when the complainant alleges harassment by management personnel which results in negative employment consequences, the complainant must establish:[88]

1. that advances or demands of a sexual nature were made upon the complainant;
2. that continued employment or advancement was conditioned on the complainant's acquiescence, thus making the demands a term or condition of employment;
3. that the demands were made on the complainant because she was a woman;

---

[86] *Ibid.*, CLLC, at p. 16,261.
[87] *Ibid.*
[88] In jurisdictions where sexual harassment is specifically prohibited by the human rights statute, a complainant may not be required to establish that acquiescence to sexual demands was the condition of employment or that she suffered job-related consequences.

4. that the sexual harassment brought about specific negative job consequences;
5. that the employer knew or should have known of the harassment.

When alleging sexual harassment by co-workers the plaintiff must plead and prove:

1. the nature of the incidents;
2. the context in which they occurred;
3. how they affected or interfered with the complainant's work;
4. allegations that the incidents were sufficient to create different terms and conditions of employment for female employees, imposed upon them because they are women;
5. facts alleged to constitute notice, either actual or constructive, to the employer;
6. that the employer failed to make a timely and appropriate response.

There is growing recognition that sexual harassment creates a hostile, intimidating, and discriminatory work environment. When sexual advances and other harassing conduct, both verbal and non-verbal, reach this level, the atmosphere created imposes more onerous terms and conditions of employment on female workers than on similarly situated male workers. Thus, when alleging a complaint on a "conditions of work theory" it is important to link the sexual harassment in the working environment to the complainant's employment, establishing its impact on her work. To prevail, the complainant must plead and prove that:

1. she was subjected to unwelcome sexual harassment which she did not solicit or incite;
2. the harassment was the result of her sex — as male employees were not treated in a similar fashion;
3. the harassment affected a "term, condition or privilege" of employment, creating an abusive working environment which affects her psychological well-being; and
4. the employer had actual and constructive notice and failed to take prompt and remedial action.

The legal recognition that a sexually derogatory work environment in and of itself violates human rights statutes is particularly helpful in constructive discharge cases where it is necessary to prove that the atmosphere or conditions were so intolerable that the complainant was forced to leave her job. Likewise, it is useful in those situations, not at all uncommon, where the complainant's work performance has indeed deteriorated as a result of the sexual harassment to which she was subjected. By acknowledging that the human rights statutes in Canada protect "the state of psychological well-being at the workplace", the tribunals have given complainants the latitude to explain poor performance in light of demoralizing emotional and psychological circumstances brought on by the harassment.

Sexual harassment cases present numerous difficulties for complainants, the Human Rights Commissions, and their lawyers that are not generally present in litigations involving more readily understood instances of employment discrimination. Some boards, tribunals, and courts still view sexual harassment as personal misbehaviour without real employment ramifications. Thus, sexual harassment cases need to be carefully developed and forcefully pleaded in order to show that such harassment has had a clear impact on the complainant's employment opportunities and conditions of work.

E. APPLICATION OF RES JUDICATA TO PROCEEDINGS BEFORE HUMAN RIGHTS TRIBUNALS

The common law doctrine of estoppel by *res judicata* is based upon two broad principles of public policy: first, that the state has an interest that there should be an end to litigation, and second, that no individual should be sued twice for the same cause.

The question frequently arises whether or not the doctrine of *res judicata* is applicable to proceedings before a human rights tribunal.

The issue of *res judicata* in employment discrimination cases is neither trivial nor theoretical. Its application may hit the basic root and frustrate the legislative goals to provide equal treatment with respect to employment without discrimination. The doctrine of estoppel by *res judicata* in employment discrimination (including sexual harassment) cases is generally invoked on the grounds: (a) that the subject matter of employment discrimination has been determined by a board of arbitration (an arbitrator) pursuant to the collective agreement; and (b) that the subject matter of employment discrimination has been dealt with in prior proceedings under the Criminal Code.

We should, therefore, discuss the legal implications of the doctrine of *res judicata* in employment discrimination (including sexual harassment) cases.

1. Decision by Board of Arbitration

The problem of employment discrimination is a mandatory subject of bargaining under the appropriate labour relations legislation. For example, the Ontario *Labour Relations Act* provides:

> 13. The Board shall not certify a trade union if any employer or any employers' organization has participated in its formation or administration or has contributed financial or other support to it or if it discriminates against any person because of any ground of discrimination prohibited by the *Human Rights Code* or the *Canadian Charter of Rights and Freedoms*.[89]

The Act further provides that:

> 49. An agreement between an employer or an employers' organization and a trade union shall be deemed not to be a collective agreement for the purposes of this Act,
>
> . . .
>
> (b) if it discriminates against any person because of any ground of discrimination prohibited by the *Human Rights Code* or the *Canadian Charter of Rights and Freedoms*.[90]

And the Ontario *Human Rights Code* prohibits discrimination in employment on the following grounds:

> 5. (1) Every person has a right to equal treatment with respect to employment without discrimination because of race, ancestry, place of origin, colour, ethnic origin, citizenship, creed, sex, sexual orientation, age, record of offences, marital status, family status or handicap.
>
> (2) Every person who is an employee has a right to freedom from harassment in the workplace by the employer or agent of the employer or by another employee because of race, ancestry, place of origin, colour, ethnic origin, citizenship, creed, age, record of offences, marital status, family status or handicap.[91]

Many collective bargaining agreements, therefore, include provisions prohibiting employment discrimination in terms similar to the

---

[89] *Labour Relations Act*, R.S.O. 1990, c. L.2, s. 13.
[90] *Ibid.*, s. 49.
[91] *Human Rights Code*, R.S.O. 1990, c. H.19, s. 5.

prohibitory provisions of the *Human Rights Act*. A typical clause prohibiting employment discrimination reads as follows:

> Article 27
> NO DISCRIMINATION
>
> 27.01(a) The parties agree that, in accordance with the provisions of the Ontario Human Rights Code, there shall be no discrimination against any employee by the Union or the Colleges, by reason of race, creed, colour, age, sex, marital status, nationality, ancestry or place of origin.
> (b) It is understood that nothing contained in (a) above limits the right of an employee to grieve in accordance with the grievance procedure as set forth in Article 11 hereof.[92]

The parties thus often incorporate no discrimination provisions of the *Human Rights Code* in the collective agreement by reference. In some instances, these contractual provisions may go beyond the minimum statutory requirements. Moreover, most collective agreements contain provisions obligating employers to refrain from discharging or otherwise disciplining employees absent just and reasonable cause. Discharge or discipline on the grounds prohibited under the *Human Rights Code* would presumably violate such a provision.

Most collective agreements contain grievance and arbitration procedures which commit the parties to informal quasi-judicial contractual remedies. In some jurisdictions, the appropriate labour relations statute requires the parties to provide in the collective agreement for the final and binding settlement by arbitration of all differences between the parties arising from the interpretation, application, administration or alleged violation of the agreement. If a collective agreement does not contain an arbitration provision, it would be deemed to contain such a provision. For example, the Ontario *Labour Relations Act* provides:

> 45(1) Every collective agreement shall provide for the final and binding settlement by arbitration, without stoppage of work, of all differences between the parties arising from the interpretation, application, administration or alleged violation of the agreement, including any question as to whether a matter is arbitrable.

---

[92] See *Re Seneca College of Applied Arts & Technology and Ontario Public Service Employees Union* (1983), 10 L.A.C. (3d) 315 (Brown).

(2) If a collective agreement does not contain a provision that is mentioned in subsection (1), it shall be deemed to contain a provision to the following effect:

> Where a difference arises between the parties relating to the interpretation, application or administration of this agreement, including any question as to whether a matter is arbitrable, or where an allegation is made that this agreement has been violated, either of the parties may, after exhausting any grievance procedure established by this agreement, notify the other party in writing of its desire to submit the difference or allegation to arbitration and the notice shall contain the name of the first party's appointee to an arbitration board. The recipient of the notice shall within five days inform the other party of the name of its appointee to the arbitration board. The two appointees so selected shall, within five days of the appointment of the second of them, appoint a third person who shall be the chair. If the recipient of the notice fails to appoint an arbitrator, or if the two appointees fail to agree upon a chair within the time limited, the appointment shall be made by the Minister of Labour for Ontario upon the request of either party. The arbitration board shall hear and determine the difference or allegation and shall issue a decision and the decision is final and binding upon the parties and upon any employee or employer affected by it. The decision of a majority is the decision of the arbitration board, but if there is no majority the decision of the chair governs.[93]

A number of Human Rights Tribunals[94] have examined and deliberated on the issue whether or not an arbitration decision constitutes a *res judicata* for the Tribunal to hear and determine an employment discrimination complaint. These cases have generally involved complaints of discrimination preceded by an arbitration decision.

In order to establish *res judicata*, it must be shown:

1. that the arbitration board was competent to consider the human rights complaint;
2. that the issue addressed by the arbitration board was the same as before the Board of Inquiry — Human Rights Tribunal; and
3. that the parties in both hearings were the same.

---

[93] *Labour Relations Act*, R.S.O. 1980, c. 228, s. 44.
[94] *Derken v. Flyer Industries* (Man. 1977), unreported (London); *Abihsira v. Arvin Automotive et al.*, (Ont. 1981), 2 C.H.R.R. D/271 (Hunter); *Erickson v. Canadian Pacific Express and Transport Ltd.* (Can. 1987), 8 C.H.R.R. D/3942 (Fetterly); *Hyman v. Southam Murray Printing and International Brotherhood of Teamsters, Local 419* (Ont. 1982), 3 C.H.R.R. D/617 (McCamus); *Dennis v. Family and Children's Services of London and Middlesex*, (Ont. 1990), 12 C.H.R.R. D/285 (Backhouse).

The issue of estoppel by *res judicata* on the ground of prior arbitration decision in employment discrimination cases was raised for the first time in *Derken v. Flyer Industries*.[95] The Human Rights Tribunal denied the application of *res judicata* in that case and concluded that:

1. The proceedings under the human rights legislation differed from a grievance arbitration. A grievance arbitration is essentially a dispute between the parties while an adjudication of a human rights complaint involves protection of public interests. A complaint under the human rights legislation might be initiated by a third party, or by the Human Rights Commission itself, as well as by the complainant.
2. The Human Rights Commission has carriage of the complaint of employment discrimination and must be a party to the proceeding before a Human Rights Tribunal. The Commission was not a party, and probably could not have joined as a party, to the proceedings before the board of arbitration. The Human Rights Commission is a necessary party to any proceedings wherein rights are determined under the human rights legislation.
3. The issues decided by the two proceedings were different. The Board of Arbitration was appointed to interpret and enforce the collective agreement while the Human Rights Tribunal was appointed to interpret and enforce the human rights legislation.
4. The remedies available to the respective tribunals were different, those available to the Human Rights Tribunal being much broader in scope.

In *Abihsira v. Arvin Automotive et al.*,[96] a grievance with respect to the event involved in the complaint had been decided against the complainant by an arbitration board. The arbitration board had based its decision on the interpretation of an anti-discrimination clause in the collective agreement which was almost identical to the comparable provision in the human rights legislation. The employer argued that the Human Rights Tribunal had no jurisdiction to hear and determine the complaint. The Human Rights Tribunal considered the two arguments: whether the arbitration provision of the Ontario *Labour Relations Act* precluded the tribunal's jurisdiction and whether the doctrine of *res judicata* applied.

---

[95] *Ibid.*
[96] *Supra*, note 94.

The Human Rights Tribunal concluded that:

1. A provision for "a final and binding settlement of arbitration . . . of all differences between the parties" in the Ontario *Labour Relations Act* can only mean final and binding for the purposes of the Act, not for all legal purposes. For example, if an employee is discharged in an offensive and insulting manner, he will not forfeit his right of access to the court for defamation simply because an arbitration board had dismissed his grievance.
2. The Human Rights Tribunal is empowered by the Act to hear and decide alleged contravention of human rights (employment discrimination). The complainant cannot be deprived of his/her right of access to the Human Rights Tribunal simply because of a pre-existing arbitration award concerning the same incident.
3. Had the legislation intended to bar an employee from having a second chance, it could easily have done so.
4. The Human Rights Tribunal has no jurisdiction to decline to hear a complaint simply because there might be another forum in which employment discrimination complaints might be heard.

Dealing with the issue of *res judicata*, the Human Rights Tribunal concluded that the test did not apply, and would not apply even if the clause in the collective agreement was identical to the wording of the *Human Rights Code*, because the question determined by the board of arbitration was not the same as the question before the Human Rights Tribunal and the parties in the two proceedings were not the same, the Ontario Human Rights Commission not having been a party to the grievance procedure.

Professor Dunlop in *Hall v. International Firefighters' Association*[97] stated that the matter of employment discrimination "is not just a private dispute between the parties to a collective agreement. It raises an issue of public importance and general concern provided for by statute, and the right of individuals to complain, and of the Commission to inquire, cannot be restricted by a collective agreement".

In *Dennis v. Family and Children's Services of London and Middlesex*,[98] the employment of the complainant, Shawna Dennis, was terminated during the probationary period while she was pregnant and had requested maternity leave. She believed that her employment was terminated for the reason of her pregnancy. She filed a grievance

---

[97] (Ont. 1977), unreported (Dunlop).
[98] (Ont. 1990), 12 C.H.R.R. D/285 (Backhouse).

pursuant to the collective agreement alleging unjust termination. The very next day she also filed a complaint with the Ontario Human Rights Commission alleging discrimination on the basis of sex.

The Board of Arbitration held that the collective agreement did not permit probationary employees to grieve discharge on the issue of just cause. Neither did it permit probationary employees to grieve under the clause prohibiting discrimination. Nevertheless, the Board of Arbitration went on to consider whether the grievor was dismissed "in an arbitrary fashion, in a discriminatory manner and for reason of bad faith". The Board concluded that the union had failed to establish any of these points. The grievance was subsequently dismissed.

On the basis of arbitration decision, the employer at the hearing before the Human Rights Tribunal raised the issue of *res judicata* on the following grounds:

1. That the issues were *res judicata* because substantially the *same issues*, between the *same parties*, had been decided at a prior proceeding (arbitration).
2. That the issue as to whether there had been a contravention of the *Human Rights Act* had already been decided in a prior proceeding (arbitration) and that the decision was binding on the parties.

The Board of Inquiry rejected the issue of *res judicata* on the grounds that there are differences between the issue that was heard by the arbitrator and the issue that is before the Board. The parties involved in the human rights complaint are not the same as those involved in the grievance because the Ontario Human Rights Commission was not involved in the arbitration. The presence of the Commission is fundamental to the proper operation of the human rights scheme because the Commission is charged with protecting the interests of the public in eliminating discriminatory behaviour.

The Tribunal stated:

> The *Code* implicitly recognizes that there may be alternate routes of proceedings which could supersede human rights litigation. Section 33 empowers the Commission to decide not to deal with a complaint if it is "one that could or should be more appropriately dealt with under an Act other than this Act". Where the Commission has concluded that a labour relations tribunal has fully canvassed the human rights issues and properly disposed of the dispute, it may indeed decide to abandon the human rights proceeding. But the Commission should be given a wide berth to make such discretionary decisions. It would only be in the most unusual of situations that a board of inquiry would decide to overrule the Commission in its exercise of this s. 33 power.

In this case, then, neither the question nor the parties were the same in the two proceedings. The prerequisite requirements for *res judicata* were not present. However, I was also persuaded by the arguments of counsel for the Commission that even if all the elements had been present, *this doctrine ought not to be utilized to stay human rights proceedings on the basis of prior arbitration rulings. The systems differ dramatically in their function, purpose, and process. A ruling in one should not preclude or bar a proceeding in the other.*

The two systems of dispute resolution were designed for different purposes. The labour relations grievance process is designed for private parties, employers, and unions, to enable them to resolve differences over interpretation of their privately bargained labour agreements. The problems of individual employees are filtered through the medium of a trade union elected by the membership. The goal is to enable the parties to develop long-term, harmonious, ongoing relationships, and labour law expertise is bent to that task.

Human rights proceedings are designed to promote the broad public interest in the elimination of discrimination. The document to be interpreted is a public statute. The complaints of individuals who have been harmed by discriminatory acts are investigated, screened, and then advocated by a publicly appointed and publicly financed Commission. As a matter of practice, human rights disputes rarely involve ongoing relationships. The goal is to compensate individuals or groups which have been treated unfairly, and the focus of human rights jurisprudence is upon developing sensitivities to the forms and manifestations of discrimination.[99] [Emphasis added]

Contractual obligations under a collective agreement are independent of statutory obligations under the human rights legislation. Pursuing a contractual remedy through the grievance arbitration does not therefore operate as an election of remedies. Nor does an arbitrator's decision have preclusive effect in a subsequent human rights complaint.

Generally speaking, the sources of statutory, common law or contractual prohibitions of employment discrimination are independent of each other. This means that an aggrieved person need not make an election of remedies, need not exhaust one remedy before pursuing another, must independently pursue each remedy in compliance with the procedural provisions of each source of prohibition and can expect a *de novo* determination of a claim under each source of prohibition to the extent that the doctrines of *res judicata* do not preclude relitigation.

In summary, the comprehensiveness and the accessibility of the enforcement mechanisms established by the human rights legislation together with the specific role assigned to the Commission by the

---

[99] *Ibid.*, at D/288 (paras. 17 to 20).

legislation strongly suggest a legislative intention which is inconsistent with the idea that boards of inquiry would be precluded from conducting an investigation, once appointed, by the result of a previous grievance arbitration. These factors, together with the absence of any explicit direction on this point in the legislation itself, lead to the conclusion that any rights which may be conferred on an individual through a collective bargaining regime to seek resolution of complaints of discrimination in the workplace must be considered to be additional to those rights conferred by the legislation and should not be considered to restrict the accessibility of the remedial scheme of the legislation to individuals covered by such schemes.

2. Prior Proceedings Under the Criminal Code

Human Rights Tribunals have determined that prior proceedings under the *Criminal Code* do not constitute *res judicata* for the Human Rights Tribunal to hear and determine employment discrimination (including sexual harassment) complaints.

In *Blair v. Progressive Products Ltd.*,[100] the complainant, Jacqueline Blair, alleged that she had been sexually harassed by Maxwell Dickoff, her immediate supervisor. The company raised the issue of *res judicata* and submitted that the human rights tribunal did not have jurisdiction to proceed with sexual harassment complaint because the issue of this complaint had been dealt with in a proceeding under the *Criminal Code* in which Dickoff was acquitted of a charge of sexual assault.

The Human Rights Tribunal examined the two basic issues which are prerequisite for the doctrine of *res judicata*: (a) whether the question to be decided by the Human Rights Tribunal is the same as was contested in the proceedings under the *Criminal Code*; and (b) whether the parties to the *Criminal Code* proceedings are the same persons as are parties to the proceeding before the Human Rights Tribunal.

The Human Rights Tribunal held that the proceedings before a Human Rights Tribunal and proceedings under the *Criminal Code* are different not only in the questions and issues to be decided but also in the standards of proof and remedies applied.

---

[100] (B.C. 1990), 11 C.H.R.R. D/130 (Barr).

(a) Were the Issues the Same?

The tribunal stated that the issues before the Criminal Court (under the *Criminal Code*) and the Human Rights Tribunal were not the same. The issue of employment discrimination was not dealt with in the proceedings under the *Criminal Code*. It concluded that:

> ...discrimination is not a matter which falls under criminal jurisdiction. In criminal proceedings, the standard of "beyond a reasonable doubt" is a stricter standard of proof than that applied under human rights legislation. The question of intent may be a necessary element in criminal proceedings, but is not a requirement for establishing discrimination under human rights legislation. Furthermore, human rights legislation is remedial rather than punitive. Clearly, the purpose and the objectives of human rights legislation are not the same as those in the *Criminal Code*.[101]

(b) Were the Parties the Same?

The tribunal stated that in the *Blair* case the parties in the two proceedings, before a Criminal Court and a Human Rights Tribunal, were not the same. The parties in the proceedings under the *Criminal Code* were the Crown and the accused. The parties before the Human Rights Tribunal were the complainant Jacqueline Blair, and Progressive Products Ltd. and not the "Crown" and the respondent was not Maxwell Dickoff. "Although Blair may be considered to have been 'privy' to the *Criminal Code* action, Progressive Products Ltd. was not."[102]

The Tribunal further stated that the difference between the respondent in the human rights proceeding and the accused in the *Criminal Code* proceeding reflects another significant distinction between human rights legislation and the *Criminal Code*. Under human rights legislation, employers have a statutory liability for the actions of their employees.[103]

---

[101] *Ibid.*, at D/131 (para. 6).
[102] *Ibid.* (para. 7).
[103] See *Robichaud v. Treasury Board* (Can. 1987), 8 C.H.R.R. D/4326 (S.C.C.).

3. Paramountcy of Human Rights Legislation

The paramountcy of human rights legislation over public and private enactments has been clearly enunciated in the legislation itself and in decisions of Human Rights Tribunals and the courts.[104]

The Supreme Court of Canada in *Winnipeg School Division No. 1 v. Craton*[105] stated the following:

> The *Human Rights Act* is legislation declaring public policy and may not be avoided by private contract.
>
> . . .
>
> Human rights legislation is of a special nature and declares public policy regarding matters of general concern. It is not constitutional in nature in the sense that it may not be altered, amended, or repealed by the Legislature. It is, however, of such a nature that it may not be altered, amended, or repealed, nor may exceptions be created to its provisions, save by clear legislative pronouncement. To adopt and apply any theory of implied repeal by later statutory enactment to legislation of this kind would be to rob it of its special nature and give scant protection to the rights it proclaims.[106]

The human rights legislation does not deal with criminal acts but with discrimination. It may well be that some elements of assault are present but those are ancillary to discrimination based on acts of sexual harassment.[107] In *Kodellas v. Saskatchewan (Human Rights Commission)*,[108] the Saskatchewan Court of Queen's Bench held that inquiry proceedings under the human rights legislation were not criminal or penal in nature and the alleged wrongdoer (harasser) was not charged with an offence within the meaning of section 11 of the *Charter of Rights and Freedoms*.

The courts in the United States have made clear for a long time that contractual remedies afforded by an applicable collective agreement need not be exhausted as a prerequisite to proceed under Title

---

[104] See also *Manitoba Food and Commercial Workers Union v. Canada Safeway Ltd.* (Man. 1983), 4 C.H.R.R. D/1495 at D/1496 (Steel); *Insurance Corp. of British Columbia v. Heerspink* (1982), 3 C.H.R.R. D/1163 (S.C.C.); *Ontario Human Rights Commn. v. Simpsons-Sears Ltd.* (Ont. 1986), 7 C.H.R.R. D/3102 at D/3105 (S.C.C.).

[105] (Man. 1985), 6 C.H.R.R. D/3014 (S.C.C.).

[106] *Ibid.*, at D/3015 (para. 24267) and D/3016 (para. 24270).

[107] *Janzen v. Platy Enterprises* (Man. 1986), 7 C.H.R.R. D/3309 at D/3313 (para. 26430) (Q.B.).

[108] (Sask. 1987), 8 C.H.R.R. D/3712 (Q.B.).

VII of the *Civil Rights Act*, 1964. In *Bowe v. Colgate-Palmolive*,[109] the court stated:

> The Court finds a fundamental difference between a claim for the violation of collective bargaining agreement and a claim for the violation of the *Civil Rights Act* of 1964. The latter is a statutory embodiment of constitutional rights that all persons are entitled to enjoy, while the former has as its primary purpose the maintenance of industrial peace between labour and management. It is the belief of the Court than an employer has the right to come before the Court and assert his claim under the *Civil Rights Act* of 1964, without regard to contractual remedies also available to him.[110]

The Ninth Circuit in *Gibson v. Longshoremen, Local 40*[111] agreed that an employer may directly pursue judicial action without exhausting arbitration, thus making clear that employee's Title VII rights are independent of contractual rights.

Further, the U.S. Supreme Court in a landmark case, *Alexander v. Gardner-Denver Co.*,[112] relying on the important social policies underlying Title VII, made it clear that (a) Title VII does not bar the arbitration of an employment discrimination claim and (b) the arbitration of a claim cognizable under Title VII will not bar a subsequent Title VII suit, even if the complainant loses in arbitration. In so holding, the Supreme Court, at least in the arbitration context, rejected not only the election of remedies and waiver arguments, but also the traditional preclusion doctrines of collateral estoppel and *res judicata*.

In *Alexander v. Gardner-Denver Co.*, a black employee alleged his discharge resulted from racial discrimination. He filed a grievance which was submitted to arbitration and was denied relief. The employer then brought suit in District Court under Title VII. The District Court held under an election of remedies theory that the employee was bound by the prior arbitral decision and had no right to sue, and the Court of Appeals affirmed. The Supreme Court, however, reversed, holding that the plaintiff had not waived his Title VII action by pursuing his grievance to final arbitration under the collective agreement.

The decision in *Gardner-Denver* reveals the following law regarding the effect of an arbitration decision on a Title VII and Section 1981 suit:

---

[109] 272 F. Supp. 322, 1 FEP 201 (S.D. Ind. 1967), affd in past revd on other grounds, 416 F. 2d 711, 2 FEP 121 (7th Cir. 1969).
[110] *Ibid.*, F. Supp. at 337-38, 1 FEP at 204.
[111] 543 F. 2d 1259, 13 FEP 997 (9th Cir. 1976).
[112] 415 U.S. 36, 7 FEP 81, 94 S. Ct. 101 (1974).

1. Contractual rights and remedies are distinct and separate from statutory Title VII and Section 1981 rights and remedies.
2. An employee does not waive his right to assert a statutory claim merely by filing and pursuing a grievance.
3. A denial of an arbitration award is not judicially conclusive of rights under Title VII and Section 1981.

The U.S. Supreme Court in *Alexander v. Gardner-Denver Co.* thus held that an arbitrator's finding of fact would not be given collateral estoppel or *res judicata* effect in a subsequent Title VII case. Further, the Ninth Circuit in *Aleem v. General Felt Industries*[113] has held that a Title VII case is not barred even if the arbitrator's decision is contested in Federal Court and the federal judge upholds the arbitration decision.

Thus, it is evident that the courts both in the United States and Canada are of the opinion that an arbitration decision on employment discrimination would not constitute *res judicata* to the proceedings under the human rights legislation.

F. DELAYS IN ADJUDICATION

A delay in adjudication of an employment discrimination claim may give an opportunity to the defendant to seek a court injunction against the Human Rights Tribunal to cease adjudicative proceedings against him. This indeed would frustrate the legislative intent on the one hand and deny the statutory remedy against discrimination on the other.

The grounds on which a stay of proceedings before the Human Rights Tribunal are generally sought are found in the *Canadian Charter of Rights and Freedoms*. Those sections state as follows:

> 7. Everyone has the right to life, liberty and security of the person and the right not to be deprived thereof except in accordance with the principles of fundamental justice.
>
> ...
>
> 11. Any person charged with an offence has the right ...
>
> > (b) to be tried within a reasonable time; ...

---

[113] 661 F. 2d 135, 27 FEP 569 (9th Cir. 1981).

(d) to be presumed innocent until proven guilty according to law in a fair and public hearing by an independent and impartial tribunal.

Whether a delay is reasonable or unreasonable depends upon the facts in each case. The courts, however, have indicated that it should not take more than a year from the date of the complaint to the beginning of the adjudication.[114] Any delay for more than two or so years is *prima facie* unreasonable.[115] In those circumstances, the courts have stayed the proceedings of the Human Rights Tribunal against the alleged harasser on the ground of unreasonable delays.[116]

In *Kodellas v. Saskatchewan Human Rights Commission*,[117] two female employees, Barbara Wahn and Elizabeth Glute, filed complaints against Gus Kodellas and Tripolis Foods Ltd. alleging that Mr. Kodellas sexually harassed them while they were employed as waitresses in the Three Star Family Restaurant owned by the respondents. The complaints were filed in 1982. A hearing before the Board of Inquiry was not scheduled until 1986. Mr. Kodellas obtained an order from the Court of Queen's Bench staying the proceedings before the Board of Inquiry. He argued successfully before the court that his section 7 right to security of the person was violated by the unreasonable delay in bringing the complaints to hearing. The Court of Queen's Bench stayed the proceedings against both Mr. Kodellas and the corporate respondent, Tripolis Foods Ltd., on the ground that if proceedings were not stayed against the corporate respondent as well as Mr. Kodellas, the stay of proceedings against Mr. Kodellas would be meaningless. The Saskatchewan Human Rights Commission filed an appeal against that decision.

The Court of Appeal was unanimous in finding that an inquiry under the *Human Rights Code* would be in accordance with the principles of fundamental justice and therefore in ordinary circumstances Mr. Kodellas would not be deprived of his security of the person unjustly by an inquiry into allegations of sexual harassment. However,

---

[114] See *Douglas v. Saskatchewan (Human Rights Commn.)* (Sask. 1990), 11 C.H.R.R. D/240 (Q.B.). The court stated at D/243 (para. 18): "There are two years and seven months between the serving of the complaint on October 17, 1985, and the hearing date of May 24, 1988. There is no indication that a process of this nature should take that long. I think less than a year should be required. I am satisfied that the delay of two years seven months is *prima facie* unreasonable".
[115] *Ibid.*.
[116] *Ibid.* See also *Kodellas v. Saskatchewan (Human Rights Commn.)* (Sask. 1989), 10 C.H.R.R. D/6305 (C.A.). In this case the delay was approximately four years.
[117] (Sask. 1989), 10 C.H.R.R. D/6305 (C.A.).

the court found that an unreasonable delay occurred in Mr. Kodellas' case, a delay that affected his ability to present a defence and which was not caused by him nor justified by the Saskatchewan Human Rights Commission. In these circumstances Mr. Kodellas' section 7 right to security of the person was violated because of the unreasonable delay in proceeding with the complaint.

The court found that the Human Rights Commission was solely responsible for the delay and it appeared that insufficient resources in the form of money for the hiring of investigative personnel had been dedicated by the provincial government to ensure that the principles and objects of the Code were vigorously pursued.

The court split on the issue of remedy. The Chief Justice found that while an order to stay proceedings might be an appropriate remedy in the circumstances, it was not just within the meaning of section 24 of the Charter because it deprived the complainants of a remedy. They were the victims of the alleged discrimination and did not cause the delay. Staying the proceeding terminated their rights.

Vancise J. and Wakeling J., forming the majority, ruled that the stay of proceedings against Mr. Kodellas was both appropriate and just. However, there was also a complaint against the corporate respondent, Tripolis Foods Ltd., and the majority found that the stay against the corporate respondent had no basis in law. The corporate respondent had no section 7 rights. The majority, therefore, upheld the stay of proceedings against Mr. Kodellas but allowed the appeal of the stay against Tripolis Foods Ltd. Barbara Wahn and Elizabeth Glute might proceed with their complaints against the corporate respondent.

1. Criteria for Determining Unreasonable Delay

The court listed a number of factors to be considered in determining "unreasonable delay" in the context of section 7 of the Charter of Rights. The five factors listed by the court are as follows:

1. Whether the delay is *prima facie* unreasonable. Here one must consider the inherent or normal time constraints of a process of the nature being considered.
2. The reason for the delay. Was the conduct of the Commission responsible for the delay? Here one must distinguish between the carriage of the proceedings and the lack of institutional resources

which could be responsible for the delay. The conduct of the wrongdoer must also be considered to determine whether or not the delay was acquiesced in, his failure to co-operate with the investigation, and the failure to find out the results.
3. Adequacy of institutional resources. Here one must examine the institutional resources required to initiate and carry out the investigative enforcement proceeding contemplated by the Act. In considering this element of institutional resources, one should distinguish it from prosecutorial or administrative bungling which results in prejudice to the wrongdoer.
4. Prejudice to the accused or wrongdoer. Here one must not only consider the impairment of the ability to make full answer and defence, but the effect of the delay on the wrongdoer, including the anxiety caused by the uncertainty and the disruption of his family and social relationships.
5. Prejudice to society. There is a social value in having trials or proceedings dealt with in an expeditious manner and without delay which assures confidence in the administration of justice. Has the process been delayed so long that to continue would denigrate the administration of justice?[118]

2. Delays Prejudicial to the Defendant

Dealing with the question of whether the defendant has been prejudiced and the delay has impaired his right to mount a full defence to the allegations, the court stated:

> *It is not necessary that there be actual prejudice to the wrongdoer as a result of the delay. Delay which causes or can cause prejudice by impairing the ability to mount a full answer and defence is a relevant consideration.* Actual prejudice is a major factor to be considered in this context. Here, by reason of the delay, Mr. Kodellas is forced to attempt to locate witnesses to testify to circumstances which took place some four years ago. The nature of the restaurant business is such that service personnel do not remain long in the employ of one employer. That mobility and the fact that service personnel frequently change their occupations compound the difficulty that one would normally encounter in locating a witness after a delay of this duration. Had these matters been proceeded with in a timely fashion, none of that additional effort or expense would have been required, nor would the potential prejudice caused by

---

[118] *Ibid.*

impairment or potential impairment of the opportunity to mount a full answer and defence caused by lack of memory or faded memory exist. In my opinion, Mr. Kodellas has demonstrated more than a potential prejudice. He has demonstrated actual prejudice to his ability to mount a fair answer and defence caused by the unexplained and unreasonable delay in proceeding with these complaints.[119] [Emphasis added]

3. Delays Prejudicial to Society (Community Interest)

Dealing with the delay in a broader context and its implications for the administration of justice, the court observed:

> The effects of the over-long delay in this case caused by the failure of the Commission to investigate and take action in a timely fashion could have a deleterious effect on the administration of justice. The public has a right to expect that complaints of this nature, indeed complaints of any kind under the *Code*, will be dealt with expeditiously in order to assure that the purposes and objects of the *Code* are attained.[120]

The court concluded that unjustified and unreasonable delay in that case had deprived the defendant of his right to security of the person as guaranteed in section 7 of the Charter. The court's reasons for this conclusion, though lengthy, are worth setting out in some details:

> To summarize, there has been an unreasonable delay which has not been satisfactorily explained by the Commission, caused either by investigative or administrative bungling or institutional delay, or a combination of both, which was not waived or contributed to in any way by Mr. Kodellas. In addition, Mr. Kodellas has suffered two forms of prejudice: first, the stigmatization, the anxiety and the disruption of family life for a period of time beyond which one would normally expect to be subjected; and, secondly, he has demonstrated actual prejudice to mount a full answer and defence. Thus, Mr. Kodellas has been deprived of his right to security of the person as guaranteed in s. 7 in a manner which is not in accordance with the principles of fundamental justice.
>
> ...
>
> Lack of action on the part of the Commission has prejudiced Mr. Kodellas' constitutional rights. He has demonstrated not only potential but *actual* prejudice in his ability to mount a fair answer and defence as a result of the unreasonable

---

[119] *Ibid.*, at D/6321 (para. 44868).
[120] *Ibid.* (para. 44869).

delay and the deprivation of his right to security of the person. Is it fair, is it just, that the proceedings should go forward against him in these circumstances? Balancing the rights of the various parties, I think not. *The delay is unexplained by the Commission. In my opinion, it would be unjust if an order were not made staying proceedings against Mr. Kodellas. To find otherwise would permit the Commission to initiate a board of inquiry, or request the Minister to appoint a board of inquiry, when there has been, as here, unreasonable delay without explanation, no matter the prejudice to the alleged wrongdoer, simply because the victims of the alleged violation have no other civil remedy.* I make that determination with considerable reluctance, and if the complainants were left with no remedy I would have used that factor as determinative in balancing the rights of the various parties. The *Charter*, which is designed to protect the rights of individuals in dealings with governments, should not be used to deprive people of their rights. It follows, therefore, that a just and appropriate remedy in these circumstances, insofar as Mr. Kodellas is concerned, is an order staying the proceedings of the Board of Inquiry as against him.

The complainants allege that they were discriminated against on the basis of sex by their employer and that discrimination resulted in the termination or constructive termination of their employment. No reason has been demonstrated why the complaints brought against the corporate employer by the complainants should not proceed and, if substantiated, an order contemplated by s. 31(7) and (8) ordering cessation of the discrimination, including an award of compensation for the termination or constructive termination of their employment, be made.

Thus, the order made staying the proceedings against the corporate employer is set aside. In this way the rights of the complainants will be preserved. The objects of the *Code* to prevent discrimination based on sex and to eradicate anti-social behaviour without regard to motive will be preserved. They will have the right to proceed against the employer to pursue the enhancement of their human rights, albeit rights that have been substantially delayed. As the Chief Justice has noted, this appeal is not concerned with the original application for the prerogative writ of *certiorari* and prohibition. Therefore, there is no reason why the proceeding cannot move forward against the corporate employer.

The inquiry can proceed to determine whether discrimination based on sex was committed by this employer by its employee, Mr. Kodellas.

One last comment is required concerning the prejudice society caused by the delay. *There is a social value in having proceedings like this dealt with in an efficient and expeditious manner. A failure by the Commission to initiate proceedings under the appropriate sections of the Code will reduce respect and confidence in the administration of justice. A failure to vigorously pursue complaints of this kind and other violations will inevitably lead to a diminution of rights sought to be provided and protected under the Code.*

174 *Ch. 3 - Taking Legal Action — A Predicament for the Victim*

> In my opinion, *it is essential that the inquiry proceed against the employer as quickly as possible in order that the objects of the Code are achieved and fundamental human rights are preserved and protected.*[121] [Emphasis added]

However, speaking for the court, Vancise J.A. recognized the fact that by staying the human rights proceedings, the complainants would be deprived of their rights to seek remedy for employment discrimination, without their fault. Vancise J.A. stated:

> Thus, a stay of the proceedings of Mr. Kodellas would deprive the complainants of an opportunity to have their complaint against him personally adjudicated and, if they were successful, deprive them of a right to compensation, in reality, damages from Mr. Kodellas. There is no other forum in which their complaint can be tried and in which they can obtain a remedy against Mr. Kodellas. They have done nothing wrong, they are the alleged victims. They are unable to do anything to advance their own cause. Section 27 of the *Code* gives the Commission the sole responsibility for the carriage of the proceedings. It is the Commission who has failed to investigate and prosecute the complaint in a timely and expeditious manner. It is that failure which has caused the delay and the diminution of their fundamental human rights, just as the delay of the Commission has caused the diminution of the constitutional rights of Mr. Kodellas. The difficulty one is faced with here is balancing the s. 7 constitutional rights of Mr. Kodellas and near or *quasi*-constitutional fundamental human rights of the complainants which are protected by the *Code*.[122]

In *Douglas v. Saskatchewan (Human Rights Commission)*,[123] John Douglas, who is alleged to have sexually harassed Brenda Marcotte while she was employed at Jonlee Holdings Ltd. during 1984 and 1985, sought an order preventing the Board of Inquiry from hearing and deciding the complaints against him. He argued that the delay was caused by the Saskatchewan Human Rights Commission, whose duty it is to investigate and settle complaints of discrimination, that the delay was unreasonable, and that it prejudiced his ability to mount a full defence. The defendant also argued that he was subjected to the uncertainty and embarrassment inherent in being the respondent in a sexual harassment case for longer than one would expect.

The court determined that the delay may have been caused by administrative bungling and by lack of resources committed to it to carry out its mandate. It stated:

---

[121] *Ibid.*, at D/6321 (para. 44870) and D/6327 (paras. 44891-94).
[122] *Ibid.*, at D/6325-26 (para. 44885).
[123] (Sask. 1990), 11 C.H.R.R. D/240 (Q.B.).

In short, was the lack of resources a result of an emergency which struck an otherwise efficiently working Commission? We have not been told that was the case and it doesn't appear to me to be so. It appears to me that the lack of resources, in this case being the lack of sufficient personnel to investigate and move these matters forward, was caused by a lack of commitment either by the government to fund the Commission to carry out its mandate or by the Commission to seek the funds and organize itself to perform its duties.[124]

Following the *Kodellas* case, the court held that a delay of 49 months between the filing of a sexual harassment complaint and a hearing before a Board of Inquiry was unreasonable delay and it violated the section 7 Charter right to security of the person of the respondent, John Douglas, (alleged harasser). Further that the delay, the concomitant impact on the ability of the respondent to defend himself and the protracted vexation constitute a violation of the respondent's section 7 Charter right not to be deprived of security of the person except in accordance with the principles of fundamental justice.

The court ordered a stay of the human rights proceedings (sexual harassment investigation), ruling that pursuant to section 24 of the Constitution this was the appropriate and just remedy.

However, an Ontario Board of Inquiry in *Dennis v. Family and Children's Services of London and Middlesex*[125] refused to stay the proceedings on the ground of unreasonable delay,[126] stating that unreasonable delay in this type of investigation does not violate the respondent's section 7 Charter right.

It may be noted that the Board of Inquiry in *Dennis* made no reference whatsoever to the Saskatchewan decisions in either *Kodellas* or *Douglas*. Further, it is not certain whether the Human Rights Tribunals and courts in other jurisdictions would follow the Saskatchewan decisions and stay human rights proceedings on the ground of unreasonable delays. It appears that until the Supreme Court of Canada decides one way or the other, this issue should be regarded as unsettled.

The question of whether an adjudication of employment discrimination should be stayed on the ground of unreasonable delay has very serious ramifications for the victims of discrimination on the one hand and for the legislative will (public policy) to eliminate discrimination

---

[124] *Ibid.*, at D/243-44 (para. 20).
[125] (Ont. 1990) 12 C.H.R.R. D/285 (Backhouse).
[126] The complaint in this case was filed on September 5, 1985 and the Board of Inquiry was appointed on January 31, 1990, approximately four years and four months later.

from society on the other. The basic questions arise, whose rights are paramount, the victim or the respondent (alleged harasser)? How do we balance the conflicting interests? What about the rights of the complainants whose human rights have been violated and who were innocent of the violation of the defendant's Charter right? A stay would block them from the forum in which they could seek compensation for their injury (employment discrimination — sexual harassment) and, in addition, a provision in the human rights legislation prevents them from suing the Human Rights Commission (whose bungling caused the delay) for negligence in the carriage of the action.

Chief Justice Bayde of the Saskatchewan Court of Appeal in *Kodellas v. Saskatchewan (Human Rights Commission)*,[127] who dissented from the majority decision, would not have allowed the stay of human rights inquiry, because, as he expressed it, not only were the rights of the complainants paramount but the purpose and public policy behind the human rights legislation were at stake.

> In considering the second factor I find that there is nothing in the material to indicate that the two complainants were in any way responsible for the delay. They appear to have done all that was required of them. Nor is there anything in the material to suggest that the alleged discriminator, Mr. Kodellas, or the other respondent was in any way responsible for the delay. Mr. Kodellas did not waive any time periods and cannot be blamed for failing to object to the length of time the matter was taking. As noted, he thought that after giving his statements and not hearing anything more, the matter had come to an end. The entire delay, it would appear, is wholly ascribable to the Commission, who had carriage of the proceeding. The Commission has not come forward to explain the delay. There is a hint in the material of inadequate institutional resources, but a hint only, not any real evidence which would enable a judge, after assessing the evidence, to come to a reasoned conclusion that inadequate institutional resources were in fact the reason for the delay.
>
> . . .
>
> It is axiomatic that a remedy which has the effect of frustrating the clear purpose of a remedial proceeding will directly affect the complainants for whose direct benefit the proceeding was initiated and maintained. The complainants are, therefore, the first class of persons who must be considered in any assessment of the justness of the remedy.
>
> Is an order preventing the inquiry a just remedy from the standpoint of the complainants in the present case? Three factors control the answer to this question. The first is that the complainants are entirely innocent of the violation

---

[127] (Sask. 1989), 10 C.H.R.R. D/6305 (C.A.).

of Mr. Kodellas' *Charter* right which created the need for remedy. *The second is that the only forum available to the complainants to compensate them for the injury caused them* (should it be found that they suffered injury) is the proposed inquiry before Mr. Kaufman, *the Board of Inquiry. To deprive them of that inquiry is to deprive them of their only access to justice.* The Supreme Court of Canada authoritatively removed any doubt that existed in this regard when it decided *Seneca College of Applied Arts and Technology v. Bhadauria,* [1981] 2 S.C.R. 181, [2 C.H.R.R. D/468]. Laskin C.J.C. speaking for the Court at p. 195 summarized the Court's finding [D/472 C.H.R.R.]:

> ... not only does the Code [*Ontario Human Rights Code*] foreclose any civil action based directly upon a breach thereof but it also excludes any common law action based on an invocation of the public policy expressed in the Code.

(See also *Saskatchewan Wheat Pool v. Government of Canada,* [1983] 1 S.C.R. 205.)

The third factor consists of the complainants' lack of legal recourse against the Commission for negligence or dereliction of obligation in the carriage of the proceedings. By virtue of s. 30(1) (a) of the *Code* the Commission was charged with the statutory obligation of "carriage of the complaint(s)". No other person or body had the power to prosecute the complaints. *The complainants did not have the power to take the carriage of the complaints out of the Commission's hands and entrust someone else with that responsibility.* And yet, the *Code* is clear that the complainants have no cause of action against the Commission for anything done or omitted to be done by it or its members. Section 34 provides:

> 34. Neither the minister, the commission, a member of the commission, the Director of Human Rights, a person designated under this Act by the commission to inquire into a complaint nor a person appointed to sit on a board of inquiry constituted under this Act is liable for any loss or damage suffered by any person by reason of any thing done or omitted to be done in good faith pursuant to or in the exercise or supposed exercise of the powers conferred by this Act.

An order preventing the inquiry leaves the complainants entirely out in the cold despite their innocence. The remedy from their standpoint creates a stark, implacable injustice.

Another class of persons likely to be affected by an order preventing the inquiry is the community at large. *Although not as direct as the complainants' interest, the community's interest is none the less real and strong. There are two aspects to it. The first pertains to the community's interest in the human family and the furtherance of public policy to discourage and eliminate discrimination.*

That aspect of the community's interest may be garnered from the *Code* and from certain pronouncements by the Supreme Court of Canada.

Section 3 of the *Code* provides as follows:

> 3. The objects of this Act are:
>
> (a) to promote recognition of the inherent dignity and the equal inalienable rights of all members of the human family; and
> (b) to further public policy in Saskatchewan that every person is free and equal in dignity and rights and to discourage and eliminate discrimination.

The Supreme Court of Canada speaking through McIntyre J. in *Ontario Human Rights Commission v. Borough of Etobicoke*, [1982] 1 S.C.R. 202, [3 C.H.R.R. D/781], in relation to the *Ontario Human Rights Code* stated (at p. 214) [D/785 C.H.R.R.]:

> The *Ontario Human Rights Code* has been enacted by the Legislature of the Province of Ontario for the benefit of the community at large and of its individual members. . . .

The strength of the community's interest may be measured by the fact that the Court went on to hold that the Ontario *Code* may not be waived or varied by private contract. In my respectful view the same may be said of the Saskatchewan *Code*.

The second aspect of the community's interest pertains to its general concern with maintaining the reputation of the administration of justice. *Of special significance in the present circumstances is the basic tenet of our system of justice that where a wrongdoer causes injury he should be the one to pay the price of any recompense to the victim. A corollary of that tenet is that an innocent person should not be made to bear the brunt of any remedy afforded the victim. It is in the community's interest that this basic tenet not be despoiled.*[128] [Emphasis added]

In spite of the fact that unreasonable delays may benefit the respondent (alleged wrongdoer) by causing suspension of human rights investigation against him/her, delays, reasonable or unreasonable, are in the interests of neither the complainants nor the victims of sexual harassment. As a matter of fact, delays in investigation by the tribunal possess at least the same difficulties, if not more, for the complainant who has the burden of proof to establish that the respondent in fact committed discrimination against the complainant. Moreover, unreasonable delays in investigation (and the possibility of suspension of

---

[128] *Ibid.*, at D/6311 (para. 44814) and D/6314 (paras. 44825-30).

the investigation altogether) will discourage further the already reluctant women from filing sexual harassment complaints. It is needless to say that unnecessary delay in the investigation of a human rights complaint does not benefit anyone: the complainant, the respondent, the Commission, the community interest or the administration of justice.

From another point of view, the Saskatchewan Court of Appeal, through its decision in *Kodellas,* has done a great service to the cause of human rights. It has indeed sent a clear, strong and unmistakable message to all governments "to put their money where their mouth is". If they do not intend to give only lip service to the cause of human rights, they must allocate sufficient funds and personnel for the implementation of legislative policies, and see that the agency of the Human Rights Commission is operating efficiently and effectively and the complaints are being processed in timely fashion without delays.

The decision in *Kodellas* is a living reminder of the fact that the governments are not doing enough for the implementation of anti-discrimination legislative policy.[129] If the wrongdoers cannot be brought to justice and the victim cannot be provided with relief because of delays caused by the administrative bungling of the Human Rights Commission, an agency responsible for the implementation of human rights legislation, then the whole exercise and efforts in this regard become futile and meaningless and the dream of a discrimination-free work environment collapses.

---

[129] The problem of delays and inefficient operation of a Human Rights Commission is not unique to Saskatchewan. The Ontario Ombudsman has found similar problems with the Ontario Human Rights Commission. In its report the Ombudsman stated: "It was my finding on March 14, 1991, that the complaints had not been adequately handled; that the commission had not taken adequate steps to implement the Case Management Plan goals set for March 31, 1991, and that the commission was not effectively carrying out its mandate." She further stated: "There was little evidence that the commission truly appreciated the extraordinary and perhaps unconscionable hardship that excessive delay in obtaining a determination from the commission could cause these individuals already burdened by the circumstances which had caused them to allege discrimination." See *Toronto Star,* Saturday, July 20, 1991, p. A6.

CHAPTER 4

Employer's Liability for Sexual Harassment of Employees

The question arises: Who is responsible for the employees' ordeal of sexual harassment in the workplace? Employees contend that their employers should be held responsible. Employers, on the other hand, argue vigorously that they should not be held responsible for sexual harassment of their employees. They put forward several arguments:

1. It is a personal affair between the two persons and the company cannot control sexual relations between two adults.
2. The employer never encourages or advocates sexual harassment or, in fact, any kind of harassment of employees.
3. The company has no way of knowing what has been going on between two employees.
4. There is no way an employer can control or interfere with the private or personal lives of its employees.

Thus, according to the employers, the perpetrators themselves should be held responsible for the conduct and not their employers. The question of corporate responsibility for sexual harassment, therefore, remains a contentious issue.

An employee in the workplace may be harassed by a supervisor (or other senior management personnel), a co-worker, a client or a customer of the employer or even by a member or members of the general public. Thus the perpetrators of sexual harassment in the workplace can be divided into two groups (a) employees and (b) non-employees. The employees can further be subdivided into two categories (1) supervisory employees and (2) non-supervisory employees or co-workers. Further, if it is a small owner-operated establishment, then the perpetrator may be the owner himself.

Human rights statutes in Canada do not directly or clearly make employers responsible for sexual harassment of their employees or in that regard for any other discriminating conduct prohibited under those statutes. Several provisions of the *Canadian Human Rights Act*[1] serve as example.

Section 4 states:

> A discriminatory practice, as described in sections 5 to 14, may be the subject of a complaint under Part III and anyone found to be engaging or to have engaged in a discriminatory practice may be made subject to an order as provided in sections 53 and 54.

The relevant portion of s. 53(2) states:

> If, at the conclusion of its inquiry, a Tribunal finds that the complaint to which the inquiry relates is substantiated, it may, subject to subsection (4) and section 54, make an order against the person found to be engaging or have engaged in the discriminatory practice....

Section 7 further states:

> It is a discriminatory practice, *directly* or *indirectly*,
>
> > (a) to refuse to employ or continue to employ any individual, or
> > (b) in the course of employment, to differentiate adversely in relation to an employee,
>
> on a prohibited ground of discrimination. [Emphasis added]

It is evident that none of these provisions makes an employer directly responsible for the sexual harassment of its employees in the workplace. This situation raises a series of questions. For example, whether the expression "directly or indirectly" in s. 7 is sufficient to apply strict liability to an employer, whether these expressions import into the statute the essence of vicarious liability, whether or not an employer can be liable if it has not actively or knowingly participated in the discriminatory practice.

Similarly, the old *Ontario Human Rights Code* authorized the Board of Inquiry to "order any party who has contravened this Act to do any act ... to make compensation thereof."[2] On that basis it has been frequently argued that the "party who has contravened the Act" in sexual harassment cases is only the harasser himself and nobody else. Thus, the Board cannot hold an employer responsible for the conduct of one of its harasser-supervisors.

---

[1] R.S.C. 1985, c. H-6.
[2] *Ontario Human Rights Code*, R.S.O 1980, c. 340, s. 19(b).

Although the Ontario *Human Rights Code* of 1981[3] made an employer responsible for the acts of its officers, agents or employees for certain discriminatory conducts, the *Code* specifically exempts, under this provision, the employer from liability in relation to sexual harassment caused by its agents or employees. Section 45(1) of the *Code* reads:

> For the purposes of this Act, except subsection 2(2), subsection 5(2), section 7 and subsection 44(1), any act or thing done or omitted to be done in the course of his or her employment by an officer, official, employee or agent of a corporation, trade union, trade or occupational association, unincorporated association or employers' organization shall be deemed to be an act or thing done or omitted to be done by the corporation, trade union, trade or occupational association, unincorporated association or employers' organization.

Sections 2(2) and 5(2) prohibit general harassment in accommodation and employment. Section 7 deals specifically with sexual harassment in accommodation and employment.

Thus, in the absence of clear statutory guidelines with regard to corporate responsibility for sexual harassment of its employees, the tribunals in Canada were forced to investigate the probabilities of employer liability under common law.

A. THE BASIS OF EMPLOYER LIABILITY FOR THE DISCRIMINATORY CONDUCT OF ITS EMPLOYEES

1. Vicarious Liability

Generally speaking, every individual is personally liable for the acts he commits. Similarly, an employee is also personally liable for the torts he commits while acting for himself or his employer. However, common law has evolved a basis for making the employer liable for harm caused by the tortious act of an employee when these acts arise in the course of employment. Accordingly, the courts have used the principle of *vicarious liability*, whereby an employer is liable to compensate persons for harm caused by an employee in the course of employment. Nevertheless, the employee remains personally liable for his torts.

---

[3] S.O. 1981, c. 53 [now R.S.O. 1990, c. H.19].

The courts and tribunals have extended the principle of vicarious liability to discrimination cases by holding the employer responsible for the discriminatory conduct of its employees. Initially, the principle of vicarious liability was applied to race, creed, religion and other discrimination cases (other than sex discrimination). In Canada, the first landmark case where an employer was held liable for the discriminatory conduct of his employee was the decision of the B.C. Board of Inquiry in *Oram v. Pho*.[4] This case involved a complaint against a restaurant owner for refusal of services because of the length of the complainant's hair. The B.C. Board of Inquiry discussed whether the owner of the bar could be held vicariously liable for the barmaid's discriminatory conduct. The Board said that if the requirement was that the owner must be found to have personally contravened the British Columbia Human Rights *Code* before the owner could be held liable, this

> ... would provide a convenient loophole through which the owners and managers of public houses and other establishments which offer services or facilities customarily available to the public could escape responsibility for violations of the Code by having an agent or servant effect the denial and enforcing the discriminatory policy without doing so personally. Fortunately, the common law of this country is not so shortsighted. The law provides that a master is responsible for the wrongful act done by his servants in the course of his employment.[5]

The Board found that the owner had delegated to the barmaid full responsibility for operating the bar and that this finding was sufficient to attach full responsibility for her discriminatory acts to the owner. The Board, however, also went on to find that the owner had, on the day in question, upheld the decision of the barmaid to refuse to serve the complainants. The owner, thereby, personally and directly committed a violation of the *Code*.

However, a few years later, in *Nelson v. Gubbins*,[6] a B.C. Board of Inquiry ruled that the respondent employer, the rental agent for the premises was "vicariously liable" for Mrs. Gubbins' contravention of the *Code*. On appeal, Taylor J. of the B.C. Supreme Court held that a master is not vicariously liable for its servant's discriminatory conduct constituting a breach of the *Human Rights Code* of British Columbia. He reversed the Board's decision, pointing out that s. 17(2)(c) of the

---

[4] (B.C. 1975). unreported (Wood).
[5] *Ibid.* at 24.
[6] *Nelson v. Gubbins* (1979), 17 B.C.L.R. 259, 106 D.L.R. (3d) 486 (S.C.)

B.C. *Code* only allows the Board to make orders for the payment of aggravated damages against the "person who contravened the Act" and cannot be read to allow orders to be made against other persons on the basis of vicarious liability. As Bryon Price did not personally contravene the *Code* he could not be held liable. The B.C. Court of Appeal[7] confirmed the decision of Taylor J. that the B.C. *Human Rights Code* did not provide for vicarious liability of an employer for the action of an employee. Justice Craig concluded:

> If the legislature had intended that an individual in the position of the Respondent should be amenable to any of the orders which may be made under s. 17, it would have been a simple matter for the legislature to have enacted words to the effect that an employer whose servant contravened the Act in the course of his employment would be deemed to have contravened the Act. The legislature has not done so either expressly or impliedly.[8]

In *Hartling v. Timmins Bd. of Police Commrs.*,[9] the Board of Police Commissioners was found liable for the Police Chief's discriminatory hiring practices. However, the *Hartling* case can be distinguished from the *Nelson* case,[10] because the Board of Police Commissioners was found not to be innocent of the Chief's practices. On the facts that the Board of Police Commissioners knew or ought to have known, the Board of Inquiry found that the Chief was discriminating against women and that the Police Commission did not try to deal effectively with the problem.

The Police Commission was held to be personally liable. It was held liable because, in authorizing the Chief to recruit on its behalf, it "did not really set up, or enforce, a rigorous system for recruitment with objective standards, but rather left hiring largely to the subjective evaluation of the Chief."[11] Also, it was held personally liable because it "knew, or most certainly should have known if it had performed its responsibilities with reasonable diligence, that Chief Schwantz was in breach of the *Code* in his recruitment practices."[12] Thus, the Board of Inquiry found that, because the Board of Police Commissioners knew the *Code* was being breached and because it did not actively do anything to ensure compliance with the *Code*, it condoned the practices

---

[7] *Nelson v. Byron Price and Associates* (B.C. 1981), 2 C.H.R.R. D/385 (B.C. C.A.).
[8] *Ibid.*, at D/387 (para. 3470).
[9] (Ont. 1981), 2 C.H.R.R. D/487 (Cumming).
[10] *Supra*, note 6.
[11] *Hartling v. Timmins Bd. of Police Commrs.*, *supra*, note 9, at D/494 (para. 4434).
[12] *Ibid.*

of the Chief. In *Nelson*, Craig J.A. had said that the master could be found personally liable if it condoned the discriminatory actions of his servant.

In *Simms v. Ford Motor Co. of Canada*,[13] the Board of Inquiry stated *obiter*, that if an employer stood by idly in the knowledge that its employees were using racially abusive language against a fellow employee in a manner that amounted to discrimination with regard to a condition of employment, the employer would be held liable for breach of the *Code*. The Board went on to say that:

> ... where an employer has adopted a policy against discriminatory treatment of, or language against, any employee and is unaware, and has no reason to believe that those instructions are being disobeyed, it is inconceivable to me that the employer automatically becomes guilty of a violation of Section 4 of the Code.[14]

The Board suggested that the mere announcement of a policy against discriminatory conduct may be insufficient. Similarly, the Board in *Hartling*,[15] had said that the passing of a "Hiring Policy" resolution was not sufficient.

These cases suggest that the employer is held liable for a breach of a human rights statute if it knows of its employee's breaches but does nothing to prevent them or remedy them. Gradually, the tribunals have extended the doctrine of vicarious liability to sex discrimination and sexual harassment cases to hold employers responsible for the conduct of their employees.

2. Organic Theory of Corporate Responsibility

The corporation is a legal entity entirely distinct and separate from its shareholders. That is, the corporate entity is a separate, legal personality, albeit an artificial person, capable of enjoying rights and duties like a natural person.

The common law has evolved a wide doctrine of both agency and vicarious liability. Just as a natural person can be bound by the acts of his or her agent, so can a corporation. A contract, if the agent has real or apparent authority, is a contract between the third party

---

[13] (Ont. 1979), unreported (Krever).
[14] *Ibid.*, at 17.
[15] *Hartling v. Timmins Bd. of Police Commrs., supra*, note 9.

and the agent's principal. In tort, as stated earlier, if the relationship between the principal and agent amounts to a master-servant relationship and the servant is tortious in the course of his employment, there is liability on the part of the master on a vicarious liability basis. However, in respect of some tortious situations the law did not allow for vicarious liability, but rather insisted upon personal fault being present on the part of the master as a prerequisite to liability. That is, the master himself had to be personally at fault to be liable.

In the famous case of *Lennard's Carrying Co. Ltd. v. Asiatic Petroleum Co. Ltd.*,[16] the issue was whether the shipowner corporation was liable for its unseaworthiness only if personal fault could be attributed to the owner. The court held that the managing director was not merely a servant for the corporation in respect of whom the corporation could be liable for torts only upon a vicarious liability basis. If so, because of the statutory exemption for vicarious liability, there would be no liability. Rather, the court held that the managing director was someone for whom the corporation was liable because the managing director's actions were the very actions of the corporation itself. This might be otherwise expressed as saying that the managing director was the "directing mind" of the corporation.

The decision extended the liability at common law of a corporation beyond that flowing from a normal master-servant relationship upon a vicarious liability basis. The corporation itself was a tortfeasor, as was the managing director, Lennard. The actions of the corporation are the actions of its directing mind. A similar problem arises when the agent commits an intentional tort.

Thus, stemming from Lord Haldane's judgment in the *Lennard's* case, the courts have elected to treat the acts of certain corporate officials as those of the corporation itself and therefore attribute personal fault to the corporation. This is sometimes known as the "organic theory". Fault is attributed to a corporation as an extension of those running the corporation's affairs. It is emphasized that this liability is not arising from agency law through a master-servant relationship with vicarious liability. Rather, the acts of the agent are treated as though they are those of the principal itself and therefore the corporation is liable on its own account for those acts. It is not liable upon a vicarious liability basis.

Professor Cumming has frequently discussed the application of organic theory of corporate responsibility in discrimination cases. In

---

[16] [1915] A.C. 705 (H.L.)

Ch. 4 - Employer's Liability for Sexual Harassment of Employees

Olarte v. Commodore Business Machines,[17] Professor Cumming, after reviewing the development of law relating to employer's liability for the breach of the human rights statute by its employees, stated that an employer may be personally in breach of the *Human Rights Code* in the following situations:

> 1. **Personal Action**: Where the employer himself, by his own personal action, directly or indirectly, intentionally infringes a protected right. . . . .
> 2. **Constructive Discrimination**: Where the employer does not intend to discriminate, but there is a constructive discrimination. . . . .
> 3. **Authorizes or Condones Discrimination**: Where the employer himself takes no direct action of discrimination, but authorizes, condones, adopts, or ratifies an employee's discrimination . . . [or] where [the employer] knew or should as [a] reasonable person have known [the commission of discriminatory conduct] and did not take reasonable steps to put an end [to] or at least minimize the discrimination, abuse or practice.
> 4. **Organic Theory of Corporate Responsibility**: Where the employer is a corporate entity, and an employee is in contravention of the . . . *Code*, and that employee is part of the "directing mind" of the corporation, then the employer corporation is itself *personally* in contravention. The act of the employee becomes the act of the corporate entity itself, in accordance with the organic theory of corporate responsibility.
> 5. [The difficulty in applying the organic theory of corporate responsibility lies in the factual determination as to whether or not the employee in question is part of the "directing mind". However, where an employee is a corporate officer, corporate director, or owner (shareholder) or sole manager, it may lead to the finding that he was a part of the directing mind of the Corporation.]
> 6. **Common Law of Agency**: Where an employee unlawfully (i.e. in contravention of the *Code*) causes the breach of contract between his employer and a complainant, then the employer is liable for a contravention of the *Code* under the common law in respect of agency, for the act of the employee-agent is the act of the employer principal so far as the third party complainant is concerned.[18]

The Board concluded:

> In my opinion, the organic theory of corporate responsibility applies in respect of breaches of the *Ontario Human Rights Code*. If an individual is in breach of the *Code* and the breach arises in the course of the individual acting as agent for the corporation in the carrying on of its business, and the individual is also the (or at least part of the) "directing mind" of the corporation, then the corporation itself is in breach of the *Code. Coxwell and Cox v. Gadhoke*,

---

[17] (Ont. 1983), 4 C.H.R.R. D/1705 (Cumming).
[18] *Ibid.*, at D/1743-44 (para. 14875).

... (See also *McPherson et al., v. Mary's Donuts and Hachik Doshoian* ... and *Torres v. Royalty Kitchenware Limited and Francesco Guercio*), ... exemplifies an application of this view of the law, in the finding that the corporate respondent was in breach of the *Code*, given the finding that the individual who was the sole shareholder, principal officer and sole or main director, was himself in breach of the *Code* because of sexual harassment in the course of carrying on the corporate respondent's business.[19]

Thus, where an employee is a part of the "directing mind" of the corporation, then the employer corporation is itself personally in contravention, so that "the act of the employee becomes the act of the corporate entity itself, in accordance with the organic theory of corporate responsibility." The question, however, remains as to when and which employee is said to be a directing mind of the corporation. Where an employee is a manager or corporate director or sole shareholder of the corporation, it is not so difficult to say that he is a "directing mind". In other situations, it requires to be determined in each case what authority, control and discretion the employee has in personnel functions to find him a "directing mind" of the corporation.

The courts and tribunals, thus, are not confined to one single legal theory in determining whether or not the employer is responsible to its employees for the sexual harassment caused by its supervisory and non-supervisory personnel. The courts and tribunals have found the employer responsible for the acts of its employees, depending upon the circumstances in each case, on the basis of *vicarious liability, law of agency, organic theory (or controlling mind)*, and doctrine of *strict liability*.

3. Statutory Liability[19a]

Prior to the Supreme Court decision in *Robichaud v. R*,[20] the Human Rights Tribunals had to go through various legal gymnastics to find that the employer is liable for the discriminatory conduct of his employees, though without any certainty that their findings would

---

[19] *Ibid.*, at D/1741 (para. 14853). These principles are generally applicable in all Canadian jurisdictions.
[19a] Portions of the following material were originally published in Arjun P. Aggarwal, "Robichaud v. R.: Confirmation of Employers' Liability for Human Rights Violations by Employees" (1987-88), *McGill L.J.*, Vol. 33, p. 194.
[20] (Can. 1987), 8 C.H.R.R. D/4326 (S.C.C.).

be upheld by the higher courts; see for example *Treasury Board v. Robichaud*.[21] The Human Rights Tribunals have basically found the employers responsible for the discriminatory conduct of their employees, depending upon the circumstances in each case, on the common law theory of "vicarious liability" (law of agency) and the "organic theory of corporate responsibility" (of controlling mind). Neither one of these bases has made it easy to establish that an employer, particularly a large corporation, a governmental ministry, department or agency, was liable for discriminatory conduct (sexual harassment) of its employees. Under the organic theory of corporate responsibility, it is required to establish that the perpetrator was the directing mind of the corporation, before the employer can be held liable for the conduct of the perpetrator. The theory of vicarious liability, on the other hand, extends only to acts of the perpetrator authorized by the employer, and the harm caused by the employee during the course of his/her employment. However, all sexual encounters causing sexual harassment to the victim do not necessarily take place during the course of the perpetrator's employment and definitely not within the scope of his authority (authorized at least expressly by his employer). Thus, under the theory of vicarious liability an employer would not be held liable for the conduct of its employees causing sexual harassment until and unless sexual encounters took place during the course of their employment and were authorized by the employer; see for example the Federal Court decision in *Treasury Board v. Robichaud*. However, the Supreme Court of Canada in *Robichaud v. R.* determined in no uncertain terms that the *Canadian Human Rights Act* (for that matter all human rights statutes) imposes a statutory duty on employers to provide safe and healthy working environments. Further, that the employer's liability is purely statutory and it is unnecessary to attach any label to this type of liability.

The Supreme Court decision thus alleviated the uncertainty and confusion regarding an employer's potential liability for the conduct of its employees, which had been created by the lower court's decision.

(a) Background to the Robichaud Case

Bonnie Robichaud began employment as a cleaner with the Department of National Defence at its Command Base in North Bay,

---

[21] (Can. 1985), 6 C.H.R.R. D/2695 (F.C.).

Ontario, in 1977. She was later promoted to the position of lead hand effective November 20, 1978, subject to a six-month probation period lasting until May 20, 1979. Throughout the period, Brennan was foreman of the cleaning department on the base and had full responsibility for the cleaning operation. He supervised two area foremen who in turn supervised the lead hands, including Robichaud.

In January 1980, Robichaud filed a complaint with the Canadian Human Rights Commission alleging that she had been sexually harassed by her supervisor, Brennan, and subsequently discriminated against and intimidated by her employer, the Department of National Defence.

A Human Rights Tribunal was appointed under section 39 of the *Canadian Human Rights Act*[22] to inquire into Robichaud's complaint. The tribunal dismissed the complaint against Brennan and against his employer, notwithstanding the fact that it found that a number of encounters of a sexual nature had occurred between Brennan and Robichaud.[23] However, an appeal was allowed to a Review Tribunal which found that Brennan had sexually harassed Robichaud and, further, that the Department of National Defence was strictly liable for the actions of its supervisory personnel.[24]

Both Brennan and the Crown (as represented by the Treasury Board, acting for the Department of National Defence) filed applications under section 28 of the *Federal Court Act*,[25] thereby requesting the Federal Court of Appeal to review and set aside the decision of the Review Tribunal. Both applications were heard at the same time. Brennan's application (which included a challenge to the concept that sexual harassment was a form of sex discrimination) was dismissed, but that of the Crown was allowed (MacGuigan J. dissenting). The Federal Court of Appeal, in setting aside the decision of the Review Tribunal, referred the matter back to it on the ground that Robichaud's complaint against the Crown was not sustainable. The latter decision was appealed to the Supreme Court of Canada.

In order to fully appreciate the Supreme Court's decision, one must examine the reasoning of the Federal Court of Appeal in reversing the Review Tribunal's finding that the employer, the Treasury Board, was liable for the sexual harassment caused by its employee. Speaking for the majority, Mr. Chief Justice Thurlow stated:

---

[22] S.C. 1976-77, c. 33 [now R.S.C. 1985, c. H-6].
[23] *Robichaud v. Brennan* (Can. 1982), 3 C.H.R.R. D/977 (Abbott).
[24] *Robichaud v. Brennan* (Can. 1983), 4 C.H.R.R. D/1272 (Review Tribunal — Dyer).
[25] R.S.C. 1970 (2nd Supp.), c. 10 [now R.S.C. 1985, c. F-7].

In my opinion, the decision of the Review Tribunal is not sustainable and should not be allowed to stand.

First, it is based on the concept that under the Canadian Human Rights legislation applicable to this case the Crown is strictly liable for the actions of its supervisor, Brennan. In my opinion there is no basis in law for applying such a concept. The applicable law is that established by the Act and there is no federal common law or federal civil law to supply such a concept in its interpretation. What the statute does is to declare certain types of discrimination to be illegal and to provide in section 4 that such discrimination may be the subject of a complaint under Part III of the Act and that "anyone found to be engaging or to have engaged in a discriminatory practice may be made subject to an order as provided in sections 41 and 42".

To be subject to the making of an order under this provision a person must be engaging or must have engaged in a prohibited discriminatory practice. In my opinion the section means that if a person has personally engaged in a discriminatory practice or if someone else does it for him on his instructions he may be subjected to an order. But nothing in the wording purports to impose on employers an obligation to prevent or to take effective measures to prevent employees from engaging in discriminatory practices for their own ends. And I see nothing in the section or elsewhere in the statute to say that a person is to be held vicariously or absolutely or strictly liable in accordance with common law tort or criminal law principles for discrimination engaged in by someone else, whether an employee or not. Compare *Re Nelson et al. and Byron Price & Associates Ltd.*

It appears to me that under the applicable legislation in the case of a corporation the authorization that will attract liability must come from the director level. In the case of the Crown, I see no basis for concluding that the conduct of public servants or officials lower than that of the public official or body under whose authority and management the public operation is carried on, in this case the Minister of National Defence or the Treasury Board, would engage the liability of the Crown. Nothing in the findings of either Tribunal or in the record suggests that Brennan had authority from such sources to harass Mrs. Robichaud. Nor is there any basis for thinking that anyone in such a position or indeed in any position senior to that of Brennan authorized or even knowingly overlooked, condoned, adopted or ratified Brennan's actions in harassing Mrs. Robichaud.[26]

(b) Implications of the Federal Court Decision

The Federal Court of Appeal dealt with the question of whether or not the Crown (Department of National Defence) should be held

---

[26] *Supra*, note 21, at D/2703 (paras. 22276-79).

vicariously responsible for Brennan's inappropriate sexual aggression. The court adopted the reasoning in *Nelson v. Byron Price & Associates Ltd.*[27] and decided that the Crown was not responsible, that there was no basis in law for imposing strict liability upon an employer for the discriminatory acts of an employee, and that it would take a clear statutory directive to create such vicarious liability.[28]

The impact of this decision was devastating in that it overruled principles of employer liability that had been accepted by most Human Rights Tribunals in earlier cases such as *Kotyk v. Canadian Employment and Immigration Commission.*[29] According to the Federal Court of Appeal, an employer, and in particular a corporate employer, could no longer be held liable for "indirectly" causing discrimination on prohibited grounds, or for "constructive discrimination". If the court's words are read literally, they suggest that only the person who actually commits discriminatory actions is liable under the Act. Although the case related more specifically to sexual harassment, the principle of liability to which the court referred would apply equally with respect

---

[27] (B.C. 1981), 2 C.H.R.R. D/385 (C.A.).

[28] It may be noted that Mr. Justice MacGuigan dissented, stating that the employer (the Treasury Board) could be found liable upon the wording of section 7 of the *Canadian Human Rights Act*, which prohibits adverse differentiation in the course of employment, either "directly or indirectly". He acknowledged that "indirect responsibility" does not necessarily entail employers' "absolute liability". The very words "directly or indirectly" connote some form of participation by those deemed responsible. An employer must, therefore, have at least an opportunity of disclaiming liability by reason of *bona fide* conduct. Further, the harasser (Brennan) was the "directing mind" of the government with respect to the cleaning operation at the Department of National Defence facilities where he and the complainant were employed. According to MacGuigan J., where there is a clear delegation of authority to a servant in a particular area of responsibility, his acts are the acts of the employer — in this case, the Treasury Board. He concluded that the employer is responsible for due care and concern, which was not shown in the instant case, and that consequently the Treasury Board is liable for the discriminatory actions of its employer, Brennan. MacGuigan J. stated the following, *supra*, note 21, at D/2709 (para. 22322):

> I also agree with the contention of the respondent Canadian Human Rights Commission that vicarious liability is a clear implication of the *Seneca College* decision. If the development of a common-law tort of discrimination, as accepted by the Ontario Court of Appeal, is pre-empted by the legislative development of a human rights code, it can only be supposed that such a development would leave those discriminated against with rights of enforcement at the very least as broad as those which they would have had at common law, and would therefore include some concept of employer liability.

[29] (Can. 1983), 4 C.H.R.R. D/1416 (Ashley), affd (Can. 1983) 5 C.H.R.R. D/1895 (Review Tribunal — Lederman).

to all kinds of discriminatory practices. Thus, any refusal of services by a government official to a person because of that person's colour or physical handicap would not attract any more liability on the part of the Crown than would an act of sexual harassment, unless vicarious liability or some other related concept of indirect employer liability was expressly spelled out in the Act.

Moreover, although a corporate employer would be held liable for the harassing conduct of any of its "directors", there would be no liability for the conduct of other supervisory personnel, unless their conduct was specifically authorized. In essence, the court decided that the common law doctrines of vicarious, absolute and strict liability do not apply to discriminatory conduct which is found to be in violation of the Act. Further, in cases where the Crown is the employer, the decision required that the act of harassment must have been committed or authorized by the minister under whose responsibility the department falls, before any liability will be imposed on the Crown.

(c) Implications of the Supreme Court Decision

In this context, the only issue before the Supreme Court was whether or not an employer could be held responsible under the Act for the unauthorized discriminatory acts committed by its employees in the course of their employment.

The high court took this opportunity to address the issues that had, until then, presented difficulties in the development of a coherent public policy and consistent judicial standards concerning sexual harassment. It reversed the Federal Court of Appeal and held that an employer could indeed be held liable under the Act for the actions of its employees, and further held that the employer in this case was so liable.

In arriving at its decision, the Supreme Court provided the following analysis of the Act, and for that matter all human rights statutes in Canada:

1. that the Act incorporates certain goals basic to our society:

— it seeks to give effect to the principle of equal opportunity for individuals by eradicating invidious discrimination;
— it is essentially concerned with the removal of discrimination, as opposed to punishment of anti-social behaviour;

The Basis of Employer Liability

— it is directed to redressing socially undesirable conditions quite apart from the reasons for their existence;

2. that the Act must be given such fair, large and liberal interpretations as will best ensure the attainment of its goals;
3. that human rights legislation does not focus on motive or intention, that its purpose is to alleviate the discriminatory effects of certain activities, and to this end, it establishes what are essentially civil remedies, rather than punitive remedies;
4. that theories of employer liability developed in the context of criminal or quasi-criminal conduct, because they are fault-oriented, are therefore of little value;
5. that "vicarious liability" in tort law, because of its restrictive limitation to acts occurring "in the course of employment", cannot meaningfully be applied to the present statutory scheme, and that the phrase "in the course of employment", as used in the Act, given a purposive interpretation of the legislation, ought to be construed as meaning "work or job-related";
6. that the remedial objectives of the statute would be stultified if the remedies enumerated therein were not available against any employer:

    — Who but an employer could order reinstatement?
    — Who but an employer could compensate for lost wages and expenses?
    — Who but an employer could provide the most important condition, a healthy work environment?

7. that a Human Rights Commission must be empowered to strike at the heart of the problem, to prevent its recurrence and to require that steps be taken to enhance the work environment;
8. that the employer's liability is purely statutory — it is unnecessary to attach any label to this type of liability.

(d) Implications for Public Policy

It is extremely significant that the Supreme Court of Canada, in determining the issue of employer liability, departed from the traditional approach, which is based on theories developed under the common law. It reviewed the *Canadian Human Rights Act* in its totality, and determined that its basic purpose is to "identify and eliminate discrimination", and that in the context of employment, these objectives cannot be achieved without attributing to the employer responsibility for its employees' conduct. The court concluded that in order for these objectives to be achieved, the remedies must be effective as well as consistent with the "almost constitutional" nature of the rights protected.

The Supreme Court of Canada has now determined that there exists a statutory obligation which requires employers to provide safe and healthy working environments, as it is the purpose and policy of human rights statutes to eradicate any socially undesirable working atmospheres. When an employee acts in violation of such statutory policy, the employer becomes statutorily liable. The court has indeed paved the way for Human Rights Tribunals, not only in sexual harassment cases, but in all cases involving violations of human rights. Thus, future Human Rights Tribunals will not be forced to undertake legal gymnastics in order to hold an employer liable for its employees' unauthorized discriminatory conduct, unless the Legislature statutorily restricts this liability. For example, the Ontario *Human Rights Code* specifically exempts employers from liability in relation to acts of sexual harassment committed by employees or agents.[30]

Moreover, the Supreme Court of Canada has recognized that sexual harassment does not necessarily occur only in the course of employment, as would normally be expected. It is suggested that the phrase "in the course of employment" should be given a broad interpretation and should be understood as meaning "work related". Thus, the court gave the statute as liberal and broad an interpretation as could have been anticipated. The court's broad interpretation of this phrase is consistent with the objectives of human rights statutes. However, such a broad interpretation could lead to very serious consequences if it were applied in cases not involving issues of human rights. For example, application of this interpretation in torts or workers' compensation cases would lead to results not intended by the court. On the other hand, this same court has often indicated that human rights statutes are special, and that the broad interpretation given to these statutes should not be extended to other types of statutes.

The *Robichaud* decision is of great importance in all cases involving human rights violations, and not only with respect to sexual harassment situations specifically. It is welcomed by women's groups

---

[30] R.S.O. 1990, c. H-19, s. 45(1) by reference to s. 5(2).

who encouraged Robichaud in her eight-year fight up to the highest court, as well as by all those interested in improving, protecting and enforcing human rights boards and commissions in the implementation of their legislative objectives and policies.

The greater significance of the decision rests in the reasoning of the court rather than in the result. The court adopted a pragmatic approach and asked itself the following question: How can the objectives of the *Canadian Human Rights Act* be achieved? It emphasized that the employer alone is in a position to enforce human rights in the workplace. For example, the employer alone can: (i) implement the policies of human rights legislation; (ii) create a healthy work environment; (iii) reinstate an employee who has been dismissed; (iv) provide benefits to the victim of the human rights violation; and (v) punish the wrongdoer, the person who violated the human rights provisions — in the present case, the harasser.

Further, the court noted that human rights statutes are remedial in nature, and are intended to create social change as well as eradicate socially undesirable behaviour (in the context of the workplace). Once again, it emphasized that protected human rights are special, "quasi-constitutional" or "fundamental" in nature. In other words, the high court has associated human rights legislation with the "equality rights" set out in the *Canadian Charter of Rights and Freedoms,* and has afforded this legislation nearly the same protection as it has to the Charter. The decision draws no distinction between individual employers, corporate employers or governments as employers. In fact, the court imposed liability without any reference whatsoever to whether the employer was a sole proprietor, a corporation or a division of municipal, provincial or federal government, nor did its analysis attribute any importance to the size of the employer. In other words, the Supreme Court implicitly stated that the employer's identity, in such cases, is totally irrelevant. The determining factor is that an employer is in a position to control its employees, and thus must share the responsibility for its employees' conduct when such conduct affects other employees' terms and conditions of employment.

In a democratic society, social change does not occur simply through the enactment of a piece of legislation. A coherent understanding and appreciation of the legislation is required, as well as support from the administration and the judiciary. If the courts fail to appreciate the social objectives of the legislation, or are in conflict therewith, they may stall the progress of social change through the interpretive process. History has not forgotten the frustration of

President Roosevelt with the United States Supreme Court in regard to his New Deal legislation. That court's decision in *Schechter Poultry Corp. v. United States*[31] held that the *National Industrial Recovery Act* was unconstitutional, notwithstanding that this legislation was intended to bring the nation out from deep economic depression.

The Supreme Court of Canada is facing a challenge during this decade similar to that faced by the United States Supreme Court during the New Deal era in terms of social change. Whereas the latter experienced difficulty in embracing Roosevelt's legislative objectives, the Canadian high court has accepted the challenge with great enthusiasm, and has exhibited a knowledgeable understanding and appreciation of Canadian social goals. This is clearly illustrated in its decision in a trilogy of human rights cases.[32]

In the instant case, the Supreme Court went directly to the root of the problem by emphasizing the basic objectives of the *Canadian Human Rights Act* and stating that it (and for that matter all human rights legislation in Canada) is social legislation which is enacted with a clear purpose and vision, that is, to eliminate socially undesirable conditions which, in this regard, amount to unhealthy working conditions.

(e) Employer Policy and Procedures

The Supreme Court of Canada has stated, in no uncertain terms, that an employer is absolutely liable for the discriminatory acts of its employees. Does this mean that an employer automatically becomes liable for his agent's actions, even when that agent is engaged in activities that are contrary to his employer's policies, that the employer and its agent are inseparable, one and the same? It would appear not, as the decision in *Robichaud* seems to recognize that the existence of a policy against sexual harassment and a mechanism to handle employee complaints could provide an employer with a good defence which could partially or totally reduce liability. The court stated:

> [An] employer who responds quickly and effectively to a complaint by instituting a scheme to remedy and prevent recurrence will *not be liable to the same extent,*

---

[31] 295 U.S. 495, 79 L. Ed. 1570 (1935).
[32] *Ontario Human Rights Commn. v. Simpson-Sears Ltd.* (Ont. 1985), 7 C.H.R.R. D/3102 (S.C.C.); *Canadian National Railway Co. v. Canadian Human Rights Commn.* (Can. 1988), 8 C.H.R.R. D/4210 (S.C.C.); and *Robichaud v. R., supra*, note 20.

if at all, as an employer who fails to adopt such steps. These matters, however, go to remedial consequences, not liability.[33] [Emphasis added]

It would appear that the court is informing employers that it is their actions, and not their words, that are the key factors in assigning liability to sexual harassment cases.

Therefore, the court has concluded that the *Canadian Human Rights Act*, by implication, intends to impose absolute liability on employers for the discriminatory conduct of their employees. It is now for the Legislature to decide whether to maintain this broad definition of liability, or to somehow limit it through recourse to the legislative process. For this reason, the court clearly distinguished between the issues of employer liability and the remedies available if liability is established. However, it is interesting to note that the United States Supreme Court recently held that an employer assumes absolute liability for acts of sexual harassment committed by its supervisory employees, regardless of whether the employer was aware, or should have been aware of the discriminatory conduct. *Meritor Savings Bank v. Vinson*[34] (cited with approval by the Supreme Court of Canada in the instant case)[35] went on to state that the mere presence of policies prohibiting the misconduct and absence of knowledge of the misconduct are not sufficient to insulate the employer from liability. Thus, an effective harassment policy does not necessarily provide total immunity for the employer, but may result in remedies being awarded which are different (lesser) than those awarded in the case of an employer who does nothing at all to protect and preserve the human rights of its employees.

(f) Conclusions

There are numerous implications for employers in the Supreme Court decision. These implications are not confined only to the employers in the federal jurisdiction; rather the employers in all jurisdictions are affected by the Supreme Court decision. They may be briefly summarized as follows:

---

[33] *Supra*, note 20, at D/4334 (para. 33946).
[34] 106 S. Ct. 2399, 89 L. Ed. (2d) 567 (1986).
[35] *Supra*, note 20, at D/4333 (para. 33944).

1. employers are responsible for the due care and protection of their employees' human rights in the workplace;
2. employers are liable for the discriminatory conduct of, and sexual harassment by, their agents and supervisory personnel;
3. sexual harassment by a supervisor is automatically imputed to the employer when such harassment results in a tangible job-related disadvantage to the employee;
4. explicit company policy forbidding sexual harassment and the presence of procedures for reporting misconduct may or may not be sufficient to offset liability;
5. employers will be pressured to take a more active role in maintaining a harassment-free work environment;
6. employers will feel a greater discomfort with intimate relationships that develop between supervisors and their subordinates because of the legal implications, and this may motivate employers to discourage such office relationships;
7. employers' intentions to have effective sexual harassment policies are insufficient. In order to avoid liability, the policies must be functional and must work as well in practice as they do in theory.

Following the Supreme Court decision in *Robichaud*, the Human Rights Tribunals, except in Ontario,[36] could find employers statutorily

---

[36] The Ontario *Human Rights Code*, section 45(1), specifically exempts employers from liability in relation to acts of sexual harassment committed by employees or agents. The Ontario Board of Inquiry in *Shaw v. Levac Supply Ltd.* (Ont. 1990), 14 C.H.R.R. D/36 (Hubbard), while refusing to find the company statutorily liable for sexual harassment committed by its employees, stated that "while the decision of the Supreme Court of Canada in *Robichaud* is of significance to certain aspects of these proceedings, it would not appear to afford the Commission and the complainant a way around section 44(1) of the *Code*". Commenting on its inability to follow *Robichaud* in view of section 44(1) [now 45(1)] of the Ontario *Code*, the Board stated (para. 232):

> However, *Robichaud* indicates that "fault" is not a true principle underlying human rights legislation. Curiously, as it turns out, not only was s. 44(1) unnecessary in order to find corporate respondents liable for employee acts done in the course of employment other than harassment, *but the only thing that its enactment may have accomplished is to shield such artificial entities from liability for an entire range of unacceptable conduct for which, but for that provision, they might now be held liable, thus relieving them from having to provide a totally "healthy work environment"*. In the context of current theory [statutory liability], s. 44(1) appears to be quite incompatible with the new generally recognized purposes of human rights law. Unfortunately, however, that does not mean that it may be ignored. [Emphasis added]

liable for sexual harassment by their employees. For example, the Canadian Human Rights Review Tribunal in *Gervais v. Agriculture Canada* reversed the original Tribunal, and held the employer, Agriculture Canada, liable for sexual harassment by its employees. The Review Tribunal stated:

> We are all of the opinion that had the Tribunal been afforded the clear and incisive language of the Supreme Court of Canada decision in the Robichaud case it would have reached a different conclusion. Both this Review Tribunal and the Tribunal in the first instance have concluded that the acts of Fetterly amounted to a discriminatory practice contrary to section 7 of the *Act*. On the authority of the *Robichaud* decision we quite clearly find that the decision of the Tribunal cannot stand as it relates to the liability of the respondent for the acts of Fetterly. We accordingly set aside the conclusion of the Tribunal dismissing the complaint of the appellant and allow the appeal holding the respondent, Agriculture Canada, liable for the conduct of Fetterly which constituted a sexual harassment of the appellant and therefore a discriminatory practice contrary to section 7 of the *Act*.[37] [Emphasis added]

B. EMPLOYER'S LIABILITY FOR SEXUAL HARASSMENT BY ITS SUPERVISORY PERSONNEL

In the first Canadian case on sexual harassment, *Bell v. The Flaming Steer Steak House*,[38] the chairperson of the Ontario Board of Inquiry, O.B. Shime, unequivocally stated, as a *dictum*, that a corporation should be liable for the actions of its foreman or supervisor:

> If a foreman or supervisor discriminates because of sex will the company be liable? *The law is quite clear that companies are liable where members of management, no matter what their rank, engage in other forms of discriminatory activity.* Thus, companies have been held liable where lower ranking members of the management team engage in anti-union activity or discriminate against employees because of race or colour, and the same general law that imposes liability in those cases ought to apply where members of the management team discriminate because of sex. *Thus, I would have no hesitation in finding the corporate respondent liable for a violation of The Code if one of its officers engaged*

However, the Board found the company liable for sexual harassment committed by its employees on the basis of "organic theory".
[37] (Can. 1988), 9 C.H.R.R. D/5002 (para. 38, 361), (Review Tribunal — Fleck).
[38] (Ont. 1980), 1 C.H.R.R. D/155 (Shime).

in prohibited conduct and, indeed, the same liability would attach if the violator had a lower rank on the management team.[39]

However, in the above case, the issue did not have to be decided as the complaint was dismissed. Further, Shime cited no cases in support of his *dictum*, thus it is not evident on what theory he would make a corporation liable for the action of its supervisor.

In *McPherson v. Mary's Donuts*,[40] the Board of Inquiry, chaired by Professor Cumming, found the corporate respondent responsible for the conduct of its supervisor. The Board stated:

> At all times material to the complaints and the inquiry, Mr. Doshoian was a Director of the corporate Respondent and supervising employee on behalf of the corporate Respondent with respect to the Complainants, and in my opinion, the corporate Respondent, in reality, was the *alter ego* of the individual Respondent. As Mr. Doshoian was the directing mind of the corporate Respondent, it is clear that as a matter of corporate law, the corporation is responsible to the complainants for the unlawful conduct of its "directing mind."[41]

Thus, the Board of Inquiry concluded that both the respondents, individual and corporate, were jointly and severally liable to pay damages to the complainants. It is not clear whether the Board based its decision on the theory of "vicarious liability" or on the "organic theory of corporate responsibility". However, in this case the individual respondent was the sole owner of the corporate respondent.

In Canada until 1983 (prior to *Robichaud v. Brennan*) in most of the cases in which employers were found liable for sexual harassment of their employees, the employers and the perpetrators of the discriminatory conduct have been one and the same person. For example, *Coutroubis v. Sklavos Printing*,[42] *Mitchell v. Traveller Inn*,[43] *Cox v. Jagbritte Inc.*,[44] *Hughes v. Dollar Snack Bar*,[45] *Torres v. Royalty Kitchenware Ltd.*,[46] and *McPherson v. Mary's Donuts*.[47]

---

[39] *Ibid.*, at D/156 (para. 1393).
[40] (Ont. 1982) 3 C.H.R.R. D/961 (Cumming).
[41] *Ibid.*, at 964 (para. 8577).
[42] (Ont. 1981), 2 C.H.R.R. D/457 (Ratushny).
[43] (Ont. 1981), 2 C.H.R.R. D/590 (Kerr).
[44] (Ont. 1982), 3 C.H.R.R. D/609 (Cumming).
[45] (Ont. 1982), 3 C.H.R.R. D/1014 (Kerr).
[46] *Torres v. Royalty Kitchenware Ltd.* (Ont. 1982), 3 C.H.R.R. D/858 (Cumming).
[47] (Ont. 1982), 3 C.H.R.R. D/961 (Cumming).

The issue of the employer's liability for the acts of its supervisors in sexual harassment cases, in the real sense, emerged for the first time in *Robichaud v. Brennan*.[48] In earlier sexual harassment cases the issue of employer liability was not seriously contested because the respondents were either owners, sole proprietors or the sole shareholder and director of the Corporation.

In *Kotyk v. Canadian Employment and Immigration Commn.*,[49] the individual respondent, a manager of a Canada Employment Office, was found guilty of sexually harassing two female employees who worked in the office he managed in contravention of the *Canadian Human Rights Act*. The Tribunal in that case also held the respondent employer, Canadian Employment and Immigration Commission, liable. The Tribunal pointed out that s. 7 of the *Canadian Human Rights Act* contains the words "directly or indirectly". It stated that "the intention of Parliament to attach employer liability for the discriminatory acts of their supervisors can be read into section 7 of the Act, without having to indulge in a tortuous interpretation process, although there are no clear precedents."[50]

The Tribunal took serious note of the fact that the respondent employer, the Commission, did not even investigate the complaint until the union threatened to go public. It observed:

> It is important that, only after the union became involved and after the phone call from Barbara Allary on February 5, wherein she threatened to go to the press, was Joe Stephan sent in. This decision was not made because of the harassment complaints (although this was one factor), but because of the grievances relating to fraud and mismanagement and the generally desperate office situation. It was only after all of this had occurred, when the whole situation was clearly out of hand, that the Administrative Investigation Committee was established to investigate all the charges.[51]

The Tribunal added:

> I am not suggesting that the employer's conduct would necessarily have been blameworthy if they had investigated the complaints and found them to have been unfounded. *However, the decision not to deal with the complaints at all*

---

[48] *Supra*, note 23.
[49] (Can. 1983), 4 C.H.R.R. D/1416 (Tribunal — Ashley).
[50] *Ibid.*, at D/1429 (para. 12245).
[51] *Ibid.*, at D/1429-30 (para. 12247).

is the point at issue. *That decision suggests that the conduct of Mr. Chuba was condoned by the Director at Regional Office.*[52] [Emphasis added]

Finally, the Tribunal concluded:

> In summary, I find that the respondent [employer] must accept both direct and indirect liability, the former by virtue of responsibility for the discriminatory conduct of a member of its management staff for the reasons stated, and the latter because of the failure to provide a workplace free from harassment or the fear of harassment.[53]

It may be pointed out that the Tribunal had not clearly stated the legal basis for holding the respondent employer liable, whether its decision was based on the theory of vicarious liability or the organic theory. The clear discussion as to whether the respondent employer is liable under the vicarious liability or organic theory was eloquently discussed by Professor Cumming in *Olarte v. Commodore Business Machines Ltd.*[54] This was the first sexual harassment case in Canada where a large multinational private sector company was charged for sexual harassment of its employees. As noted earlier, so far all sexual harassment cases have involved an employer either of a self-owned business or a department of the government. In *Commodore*, an individual respondent, Rafael DeFilippis, who was the night shift manager of the employer's plant, was found guilty of sexually harassing the complainants who worked under his control and supervision.

Professor Peter Cumming, Chairperson of the Board of Inquiry, extensively reviewed the development of the law on corporate responsibility for the conduct of its employees and the application of those principles to sexual harassment cases. The Board found that the corporate respondent, Commodore Business Machines Ltd., was liable to its employees for sexual harassment caused by its supervisor, Rafael DeFilippis. The Board stated:

> [I]t is clear that Commodore cannot be held liable for the sexual harassment of the Complainants by Mr. DeFilippis on the basis of "vicarious liability". However, in my view, and I so find, Commodore is *personally* liable to the Complainants on the basis that Commodore is personally in breach of the *Code* because of the discriminatory acts of the individual Respondent.

. . .

---

[52] *Ibid.*, at D/1430 (para. 12248).
[53] *Ibid.*, at D/1430 (para. 12250).
[54] (Ont. 1983), 4 C.H.R.R. D/1705 (Cumming).

However (as I have set forth in the previous section), where the employer is a corporate entity, and an employee is part of the "directing mind" of the corporation, then the employer is itself *personally* in contravention of the *Code*. The act of the employee becomes the act of the corporate entity itself, in accordance with the organic theory of corporate responsibility. In such a situation, the intent of the offending employee is attributed to the corporate entity, so that the corporate entity cannot be excused on the basis that it (being a legal, and not a real, personality) could not possibly intend to discriminate.

It is clear to me, and I so find, that Mr. DeFilippis provided a function of management as a foreman at the Warden Avenue plant, and therefore, he was part of Commodore's "directing mind" such that his intent and acts of sexual harassment became those of the corporation. Mr. DeFilippis had the general power to hire and fire, and discipline employees. Mr. DeFilippis was, in effect, plant manager for almost all of the second shift. . . . The point is, as far as the Complainants and other female workers on the afternoon shift were concerned, Mr. DeFilippis was *the* management. . . .

All of the acts of sexual harassment occurred in the course of carrying on the corporation's business at its Warden Avenue plant. Once an employee, like Mr. DeFilippis, is part of the directing mind, and the contraventions come in his performing his corporate function as they did in the instant case, a corporation such as Commodore is itself also *personally* in breach of the *Code*.

So far as the six complainants were concerned, Mr. DeFilippis was, in effect, their true employer. Commodore put him in this position of management; therefore, this factor, coupled with Mr. DeFilippis' unlawful acts of sexual harassment coming within the course of carrying on the corporation's business, renders the corporation *personally* in breach of the *Code*.[55]

In *Re Canada Post Corp. and Can. Union of Postal Workers*,[56] it was found that the grievor, a female employee of Canada Post in Calgary was sexually harassed by her supervisor. The arbitrator found the employer, Canada Post, liable for the sexual advances by its supervisor. The arbitrator stated:

> First, there is no evidence upon which I might conclude that the employer "exercised all due diligence to prevent the act from being committed". . . . Further, I have determined that Canada Post Corporation was remiss in not having exercised all due diligence to prevent this occurrence and in not promptly taking steps to objectively investigate the incident. . . . Accordingly, Ms. Guglich is to be paid the sum of $100 forthwith by Canada Post Corporation as damages for the emotional turmoil to which she was subjected by the violation of her

---

[55] *Ibid.*, at D/1746 (paras. 14883, 87-90).
[56] (1983), 11 L.A.C. (3d) 13 (Norman).

right to enjoy a work place free from sexual harassment as guaranteed by Art. 5 of the collective agreement.[57]

In February 1983, the Canadian Human Rights Commission issued a "Harassment Policy" which holds an employer responsible for the harassment conduct of its employees and agents. It states:

> Any act of harassment committed by an employee or an agent of any employer in the course of the employment shall be considered to be an act committed by that employer.
> An act of harassment shall not, however, be considered to be an act committed by an employer if it is established that the employer did not consent to the commission of the act and exercised all due diligence to prevent the act from being committed, and, subsequently, to mitigate or avoid its consequences.

It may be pointed out that "Harassment Policy" of the Canadian Human Rights Commission is only applicable in the federal jurisdiction. Furthermore, it is neither a guideline nor does it have the same legal standing as the E.E.O.C. guidelines in the United States. However, some tribunals have found support in the Commission's policy statement for holding the employer liable for the act of its supervisors. In *Canada Post*, the arbitrator stated:

> For the purposes of this award, I adopt the policy statement issued by the Canadian Human Rights Commission on harassment. Although it represents a regulatory interpretation of harassment under federal statute, it seems to me to properly capture the state of adjudicative analysis on the subject that we have now reached in this country.[58]

In *Janzen v. Platy Enterprises*,[59] a Manitoba Board of Adjudication reviewed the law on employer's liability in sexual harassment cases, particularly in the light of Federal Court decision in *Robichaud*. However, the Board expressly refused to follow the Federal Court decision in *Robichaud* on the ground that "the *Canadian Human Rights Act* contains no provision in any way similar to the provisions of clause 6(1)(a) of the Manitoba Act" (no employer or *person acting on behalf of an employer*). The Board stated:

---

[57] *Ibid.*, at 19-21.
[58] *Ibid.*, at 18.
[59] (Man. 1985), 6 C.H.R.R. D/2735 (Henteleff), revd (Man. 1986), 8 C.H.R.R. D/3831 (C.A.), a decision quashed by the Supreme Court of Canada (Man. 1989), 10 C.H.R.R. D/6205.

Since the *Canadian Human Rights Act* contains no provision in any way similar to the provisions of clause 6(1)(a) (specifically emphasized by me) of the Manitoba Act, I do not consider that the judgement of Thurlow, C.J.A. in *The Treasury Board v. Robichaud* is in any way binding upon me. Further, and as separate and distinct from the first point made, I do not consider *The Treasury Board v. Robichaud* binding upon me because the majority judgement deals solely with the question as to the matter of vicarious liability when the employer was the Crown. With the greatest respect, all other comments made by Thurlow, C.J.A., other than as relate to that specific situation, are obiter and not binding upon me. Therefore, since the employer Platy is a private corporation, the judgement of the Federal Court of Appeal is distinguishable upon the facts and is not binding upon me.[60]

The Board, however, accepted and adopted the principle and the reasoning for the employer's liability as stated by Professor Cumming in the *Commodore* case. Thus, on the basis of "organic theory of corporate responsibility", it found that the complainant's supervisor, Tommy Grammas, was part of the "controlling mind" of the corporate respondent because he had management responsibilities and therefore his conduct implicates the corporate respondent, Platy Enterprises Ltd.

The Board further held that the intent of s. 6(1) of the Manitoba *Human Rights Act* "is not only to make the employer liable for any acts of sexual harassment directly committed by such employer, but also makes him responsible for any such acts committed by a person in authority during the course of his employment". Further, the corporate respondent did not establish a sexual harassment policy and also failed to take any reasonable steps whatsoever to assure that the workplace would be free from fear of sexual harassment, and these facts were held against the employer.

In *Foisy v. Bell Canada*,[61] a female employee was dismissed from her employment with Bell Canada after she was sexually harassed by her immediate supervisor. The employee was subsequently reinstated with full back pay through the arbitration process provided under the collective agreement. However, the employee sued the employer, Bell Canada, for damages suffered because of "her unfair dismissal when she refused her immediate supervisor's propositions", which caused her "psychological trauma, social and professional isolation and loss of self confidence".

---

[60] *Ibid.*, at D/2753 (para. 22548); s. 6(1) [am. 1977, c. 46, s.3; now S.M. 1987, c. 45, s. 14(1)].
[61] (Que. 1985), 6 C.H.R.R. D/2817 (Que. S.C.).

The Quebec Superior Court found that the claimant was dismissed on a pretext, while the real reason of her dismissal was her rejection of the sexual advances of her supervisor. Thus, her dismissal was not only unjust but also in bad faith, therefore she was entitled to a claim for non-contractual damages. The court on the theory of *abus de droit* held that her employer, Bell Canada, was liable for the wrongful actions of its employee. In this case, the conduct of the employee was in violation of the Quebec *Charter of Human Rights and Freedoms*, which prohibits both sex discrimination and sexual harassment. Holding the employer liable, the court stated:

> Even if Bell as a company was in good faith in accepting the reasons given by the immediate supervisor in Quebec City, the *fact remains that the company is responsible for the wrongful actions of its representatives and must bear the consequences.*[62] [Emphasis added]

The court recognized that due to sexual harassment and subsequent unjust dismissal the claimant suffered psychological trauma and social and professional isolation "especially during the year of her illegal dismissal" and awarded her $3,000 in compensation.

The Quebec Superior Court in this case has joined the majority view that an employer should be held responsible for the sexual harassment caused by its supervisory personnel. The Quebec Superior Court, in *Foisy v. Bell Canada*, appears to have based its decision on the doctrine of vicarious liability when it said "the company is responsible for the wrongful actions of its representatives and must bear the consequences". The liberal interpretation in *Commodore* and *Platy Enterprises* is more in tune with the philosophy of the human rights legislation than the restrictive interpretation of the Federal Court in *Robichaud*.

This proved to be true when in 1987 the Supreme Court of Canada in *Robichaud v. R.*[63] overruled the Federal Court, holding that the employer is liable for the discriminatory conduct of his employees. The Supreme Court of Canada made it clear in no uncertain terms that an employer is statutorily liable for acts of harassment by his employees even if the employer was not aware of those actions. Further, the quantum (amount) of damages flowing from liability will depend very much upon the employer's actions, both preventive and remedial.

---

[62] *Ibid.*, at D/2827 (para. 23114).
[63] (Can. 1987) 8 C.H.R.R. D/4326, [1987] 2 S.C.R. 84. See also *Janzen v. Platy Enterprises Ltd.* (Man. 1989), 10 C.H.R.R. D/6205 (S.C.C.).

In contrast, the American courts had initially determined that sexual advances made by a supervisor do not give rise to a course of action against the employer under Title VII of the *Civil Rights Act*.[64] However, in subsequent cases,[65] the courts in the United States have determined that the victim does have a cause of action against the employer under Title VII where the supervisor conditions career enhancement on sexual submission and an employer policy and employer acquiescence is involved. Judge MacKinnon in *Barnes v. Costle*[66] listed three possible reasons for imposing vicarious liability upon the employer:

1. the employer is in a position to know of discriminatory behaviour;
2. the employer can take preventive steps; and
3. imposing vicarious liability causes the employer to be especially careful.

In *Munford v. James T. Barnes & Co.*[67] an employee alleged that she was discharged for refusing the sexual advances of her supervisor. The court concluded that an employer has an affirmative duty to investigate complaints of sexual harassment and deal appropriately with offending personnel. When an employer has knowledge that a supervisor has conditioned an employee's job status on a favourable response to sexual demands and does not take appropriate action, the employer is in violation of Title VII. In *Tomkins v. Public Service Electric Gas Co. (Tomkins II)*,[68] the Court of Appeal determined that where an employer has actual or constructive knowledge of a supervisor's sexual advances and does not take prompt and appropriate remedial action, the employer is guilty of violating Title VII.

However, the view that Title VII imposes strict liability on employers for the acts of supervisory personnel has not been uniformly accepted by the federal courts. Some decisions have rejected vicarious liability where management did not know that sexual harassment was occurring or condone it, while others have suggested that liability might be avoidable if employers corrected the situation once it was brought to their attention.

---

[64] See for example *Corne v. Bausch & Lomb Inc.*, 390 F. Supp. 161, 10 FEP 289 (D. Ariz. 1975).
[65] See for example *Williams v. Saxbe*, 413 F. Supp. 654, 12 FEP 345 (D.C.C. 1976); *Barnes v. Costle*, 561 F. 2d 983, 15 FEP 345 (D.C. Cir. 1977).
[66] 561 F. 2d 983 (D.C. Cir. 1977).
[67] 441 F. Supp. 459 (E.C. Mich. 1977).
[68] 568 F. 2d 1044, 16 FEP 22 (3rd Cir. 1977).

Thus, American case law clearly demonstrates that to hold an employer responsible for sexual harassment by its supervisory personnel, the plaintiff must establish that the sexual advances of the supervisor were a condition of employment and they were not personal, non-employment related encounters. Further, an employer can be held responsible if the employer had an actual or constructive knowledge of the supervisor's conduct, through either a direct complaint, knowledge of other supervisory personnel, or an acquiescence in the termination or job-related consequences. The following criteria are generally taken into consideration while determining the level of an employer's liability for sexual harassment caused by its supervisor:

1. When the offensive conduct contravened company policy, it occurred with the employer's knowledge and the consequences were not rectified when discovered.
2. It requires the employee to show that the employer had actual or constructive knowledge of the harassment at the time of its occurrence.
3. When the employer fails to investigate and appropriately deal with a claim of sexual harassment.

In June 1986, the U.S. Supreme Court issued its opinion in *Meritor Savings Bank v. Vinson* [69] in a landmark decision that established the principle of employer liability for sexual harassment. The Supreme Court in this case was dealing with the issue of whether or not an employer is strictly liable for an offensive working environment created by a supervisor's sexual advances when the employer does not know of, and could not reasonably have known of, the supervisor's misconduct. The Supreme Court established that both types of sexual harassment — *quid pro quo* and hostile environment — are actionable under section 703 of Title VII of the *Civil Rights Act* of 1964, as forms of sex discrimination.

The court agreed with the E.E.O.C.'s position that agency principles should be used for guidance. While declining to issue a "definite rule on employer liability", the court did reject both the Court of Appeals' rule of automatic liability for the actions of supervisors and the employer's position that notice is always required.[70] However, the court agreed with the appellate court stating that the employer

---

[69] 106 S. Ct. 2399, 40 E.P.D. para. 36, 159 (1986).
[70] *Ibid.*, at 2408-09.

would be held liable only if it knew or should have known of the alleged harassment. It further stated:

> "[Does] the mere existence of a grievance procedure and a policy against discrimination, coupled with [the victim's] failure to invoke that procedure ... insulate [the employer] from liability? ... Those facts are plainly relevant. ... The contention that [the victim's] failure should insulate [the employer] might be substantially stronger if [the employer's] procedure was ... calculated to encourage victims of harassment to come forward".[71]

Thus, the Supreme Court, while declining to issue a "definitive rule on employer liability", did make it clear that employers are not automatically liable for the acts of their supervisors. For the same reason, the court said "absence of notice to an employer does not necessarily insulate that employer from liability".[72]

1. Employer's Liability on the Principle of Agency

(a) In Quid Pro Quo Cases

The decision of the Supreme Court in the *Vinson* case makes it clear that an employer will always be held responsible for acts of *quid pro quo* harassment. A supervisor in such circumstances has made or threatened to make a decision affecting the victim's employment status, and he therefore has exercised authority delegated to him by his employer. Although the question of employer liability for *quid pro quo* harassment was not at issue in *Vinson*, the Supreme Court agreed with the E.E.O.C's position that "Congress wanted Courts to look to agency principles for guidance" in determining an employer's liability for sexual conduct by a supervisor. The court's decision noted with apparent approval the position taken by the E.E.O.C. in its brief that:

> Where a supervisor exercises the authority actually delegated to him by his employer, by making or threatening to make decisions affecting the employment status of his subordinates, such actions are properly imputed to the employer whose delegation of authority empowered the supervisor to undertake them.[73]

---

[71] *Ibid.*, at 2409.
[72] *Ibid.*, at 2408.
[73] *Ibid.*, at 2407-08.

(b) In Hostile Environment Cases

The Supreme Court clearly established that a hostile or poisonous work environment is actionable under Title VII. The employer would be liable if he knew or should have known of the alleged sexual harassment. If actual or constructive knowledge exists and if the employer failed to take immediate and appropriate corrective action, the employer would be directly liable. Most commonly, an employer acquires actual knowledge through firsthand observation, by the victim's internal complaint to others or supervisors or managers or by a charge of discrimination. Thus, an employer is liable when it "knew or upon reasonably diligent inquiry should have known" of the harassment.[74] The evidence of pervasiveness of the harassment may give rise to an inference of knowledge or establish constructive knowledge.

The Supreme Court stated that "the mere existence of a grievance procedure and a policy against discrimination, coupled with [the victim's] failure to invoke procedure" are "plainly relevant" but "not necessarily dispositive".[75] The court further stated that the employer's argument that the victim's failure to complain insulated it from liability "might be substantially stronger if its procedure were better calculated to encourage victims of harassment to come forward".[76] It means that an employer's defence would ultimately hinge on his actions and not on his intentions.

The E.E.O.C. generally will find an employer liable for hostile environment sexual harassment by a supervisor when the employer failed to establish an explicit policy against sexual harassment and did not have a reasonably available avenue by which victims of sexual harassment could complain to someone with authority to investigate and remedy the problem.[77]

---

[74] *Yates v. Avco Corp.*, 819 F. 2d 630 at 636, 43 E.P.D. para. 37, 086 (6th Cir. 1987).
[75] 106 S. Ct. 2399 at 2408-09.
[76] *Ibid.*, at 2409.
[77] See for example *E.E.O.C. v. Hacienda Hotel*, 881 F. 2d 1504, 51 E.P.D. para. 39, 250 (9th Cir. 1989).

C. SEXUAL HARASSMENT BY CO-WORKERS

The issue of whether an employer should also be held liable for acts of sexual harassment committed by non-supervisory employees has been debated both in Canada and the United States. Such harassment may not have any direct job-related consequences such as discharge or suspension, but it nevertheless could create a hostile and poisonous working environment. Further, it argued that an employer should be held liable for co-worker sexual harassment because such an employee's conduct can have a serious impact on a co-worker's ability to successfully perform his/her job. Thus, co-worker sexual harassment can lead to the same results as sexual harassment by a supervisor. Who else, other than an employer, is in a position to provide a healthy and safe working environment?

It is to be noted that a Canadian Human Rights Commission policy statement holds an employer vicariously liable even in situations where the harassment is carried out by non-supervisory personnel.[78] In the United States, the E.E.O.C. guidelines also hold an employer responsible for harassment by co-workers.[79]

Some guidance in this area may be gained by examining court decisions involving other types of discrimination (*i.e.* race). These other decisions are clear in making no distinction between supervisors and co-workers in terms of employer liability. In fact, the general rule in these decisions has been that employers are responsible for their acts and those of all their employees, whether the acts are authorized or forbidden by the employer, or whether the employer knew or should have known of their occurrence. In *Simms v. Ford Motor Co. of Canada*,[80] a case dealing with race discrimination, Professor H. Krever (now Judge Krever) had suggested that an employer had an obligation to police racial harassment by "other employees". He added that "even, I would go so far as to say by *non supervisory employees.*" This view has not been rejected by any provincial board of inquiry, although they did not have the occasion to test its applicability to sexual harassment by non-supervisory employees.

---

[78] See Canada Human Rights Commission Policy (February 1983), which states: "An act of harassment committed by an *employee* or *agent* of any employer in the course of employment shall be considered to be an act committed by that employer". (Emphasis added).

[79] See 1604.11 (d), *infra*, p. 219.

[80] (Ont. 1979), unreported (Krever), p. 12.

Ch. 4 - Employer's Liability for Sexual Harassment of Employees

However, a Canadian Review Tribunal in *Shaffer v. Treasury Board of Canada*,[81] a case involving a racial slur by a co-worker, suggested that for the purpose of finding employer liability a distinction should be made as to whether the alleged discriminatory conduct was caused by a supervisory personnel or by an ordinary fellow employee. This indicated that an employer may be held liable for the conduct of his supervisory personnel but not for the discriminatory and objectionable conduct of a "co-worker". The Review Tribunal stated:

> However, we are prepared to distinguish between the liability of the employer arising from the conduct of supervisory personnel, as opposed to that arising from the conduct between co-workers. All of the authorities provided to us involved prohibited conduct by people in authority to personnel under them as a primary factor.
> If this same conduct had been done by supervisory personnel rather than by a co-worker, we would have found a contravention of the Act by the employer and held him liable.[82]

However, the Review Tribunal pointed out that "[t]his is not to say that the employer could not be liable for discriminatory conduct between co-workers. It is merely to point out that the response required by the employer must be in proportion to the seriousness of the incident itself. By its very nature, prohibited conduct by a supervisory officer is more serious. This factor cannot be ignored in determining liability."[83] Thus, an employer may also be held liable for the sexually harassing acts of co-workers (non-supervisory employees), if the employer (or its agents or supervisory personnel) knew or should have known of the harassing conduct Therefore, employers could rebut liability under these circumstances by showing that they took immediate and corrective action upon learning of the harassment.

Where the employer has taken an action either by investigating the complaint of sexual harassment or by warning or counselling the perpetrator, he must inform the complainants that he had or was taking steps to deal with their complaint. In cases where the complainants were not informed of the management's action on their complaint and they resigned, the employer had been held liable for sexual harassment caused by its employees.[84] In *Wilgan v. Wendy's Restaurants of Canada*

---

[81] (Can. 1984), 5 C.H.R.R. D/2315 (Review Tribunal — Mullins).
[82] *Ibid.*, at D/2316 (paras. 19522-24).
[83] *Ibid.*, (para. 19524).
[84] (B.C. 1990), 11 C.H.R.R. D/119 (Barr).

Inc.,[85] the employer had taken an action on the sexual harassment complaint but he had failed to inform the complainants. The complainants, unaware of the employer's action, resigned, at least in part because of the apparent inaction on their complaints. The Human Rights Tribunal, while holding the employer liable, stated:

> I am aware that management did respond to the complaints about Glegg's conduct by telling him that his employment would be terminated if such conduct continued, and by ultimately terminating his employment. However, in the absence of a formalized complaint procedure at that time, management failed to communicate their initial actions to the complainants. This was one of the reasons for Davis' resignation.[86]

Confusion over whether the same standards of liability should apply to employers when supervisors or persons other than supervisors (co-workers) are the source of harassment will remain until more cases are heard where these issues are central.

Thus, an important question arises. Does the decision of the Supreme Court of Canada in *Robichaud v. R.*[87] extend to the actions of non-supervisory employees? Notwithstanding the fact that in *Robichaud*, the harasser (Brennan) was a supervisory employee, it is submitted that the court's observations may be interpreted to the effect that an employer will be held liable for the discriminatory conduct of all its employees, supervisory or non-supervisory. This position is supported by the following statement by Mr. Justice LaForest:

> Hence, I would conclude that the statute contemplates the imposition of liability on employers for all acts of their employees "in the course of employment", interpreted in the purposive fashion outlined earlier as being in some way related or associated with the employment. It is unnecessary to attach any label to this type of liability; it is purely statutory.[88]

In the case of *Wilgan v. Wendy's Restaurants of Canada Inc.*,[89] it was argued that the employer was not liable for the sexually harassing acts of the co-worker because, having no supervisory functions, he was not in a position to implement "reprisals for failure to submit". The B.C. Council of Human Rights rejected the arguments of the

---

[85] *Ibid.*
[86] *Ibid.*, at D/123 (para. 42).
[87] [1987] 2 S.C.R. 84.
[88] *Ibid.*, at 95.
[89] (B.C. 1990), 11 C.H.R.R. D/119 (Barr).

respondent employer and held that the employer was liable for the acts of the co-worker for poisoning the work environment by sexually harassing the other employees. The B.C. Council found support for its decision in the Supreme Court of Canada decision in *Janzen v. Platy Enterprises Ltd.*, where the court questioned the validity of the distinction between *quid pro quo* and abusive, hostile or poisoned environment harassment.[90]

The decisions of the Supreme Court of Canada in *Robichaud v. R.* and *Janzen v. Platy Enterprises* and of the Human Rights Tribunals leave no doubt whatsoever that an employer is liable for sexual harassment in the workplace, whether it was caused by supervisory or non-supervisory (co-worker) employees or whether it led to job-related reprisals. In 1991, the Saskatchewan Court of Queen's Bench in *Thessaloniki Holdings Ltd. v. Saskatchewan Human Rights Commission*[91] confirmed that employers can be held liable for work-related sexual harassment or other discrimination by their employees, including "those without supervisory powers".

In the United States, an employer is generally not liable for sexual harassment by a co-worker because a co-worker (non-supervisory employee) is not an employer for the purposes of Title VII and only an employer can violate the statute. In *Guyette v. Stauffer Chemical Co.*[92] the court held that a non-supervisory employee is not an agent of an employer and thus the employer cannot be held liable under Title VII in a sexual harassment suit. Women have also lost cases when they were harassed by co-workers who did not (or could not) promise them any change in their conditions of employment. Thus, some courts have shown substantial reluctance to hold employers liable for the conduct of non-supervisory employees.[93] This suggests that the most frequent violations of Title VII for acts of sexual harassment would have to be committed by supervisors, not by co-workers, the latter having no authority over the victim.[94] However, in some cases involving sexual harassment by co-workers, employers have been held liable because they knew or should have know of the harassment and they

---

[90] (Man. 1989), 10 C.H.R.R. D/6205 at D/6226 (para. 44449) (S.C.C.).
[91] (Sask. 1991), 91 CLLC para. 17,029 (Q.B.).
[92] 518 F. Supp 521, 27 E.P.D. para. 32,139 (1981).
[93] See for example *Fisher v. Flynn*, 598 F. 2d 663, 19 E.P.D. para. 9204 (1st Cir. 1979); *Smith v. Rust Engineering Co.*, 18 E.P.D. para. 8698 (N.D. Ala. 1978).
[94] For employer's liability in sexual harassment cases see Patricia Lindenberger and Timothy Keaveny: "Sexual Harassment: The Employer's Legal Obligations" (1981), 58 *Personnel* 60-68; and Ralph Baxter: "Judicial and Administrative Protections Against Sexual Harassment in the Workplace" (1982), *Employee Relations* 587.

failed to take timely corrective action. Examples of instances of sexual harassment by co-workers for which employers have been held liable include such "gross" behaviour as explicit derogatory sexual remarks, grabbing a woman between the legs and placing obscene cartoons at a woman's workplace.[95] In these cases, the courts ruled in favour of the women although none of the co-workers was in a position to make personnel decisions. The term "conditions of employment" was interpreted to include the quality of the workplace environment. Although the supervisory personnel did not participate in the sexual harassment, they were aware of it and permitted it to continue. As a result, the employers were found to have created conditions of employment that could harmfully affect the mental disposition and self-concept of the women. Further, the women's job performance could be affected, and this in turn would influence their future chances for promotion, raises and continued employment.[96]

The Equal Employment Opportunity Commission and the courts have held that an employer has a positive duty to maintain a workplace free from sexual harassment. Thus, if an employer knows or should have known of an action, he is in effect condoning the harassment by its non-supervisory employees. The E.E.O.C. guidelines hold the employer liable for the sexual harassment caused by a fellow worker (non-supervisory employee). Section 1604.11(d) states:

> With respect to conduct between fellow employees, an employer is responsible for acts of sexual harassment in the workplace where the employer (or its agents or supervisory employees) knows or should have known of the conduct, unless it can show that it took immediate and appropriate corrective action.

It provides that the employer is responsible for the unlawful conduct where the employer, *or* its agents, *or* its supervisory employees knew or should have known of the conduct, unless the employer can show that it took immediate and appropriate corrective action. In contrast to the provisions holding an employer strictly liable for sexual harassment committed by it, its agents or supervisory employees, this section does not impose strict liability on the employer for co-worker sexual harassment.

An employer is held liable for co-worker sexual harassment because a co-worker's conduct can have an impact on the employee's

---

[95] Lindenberger and Keaveny, "Sexual Harassment: The Employer's Legal Obligations", *supra*, note 94, at 65.
[96] *Ibid.*

ability to successfully perform his/her job. For example, although a co-worker does not have authority to make employment decisions, his/her lack of co-operation may adversely affect a fellow employee's performance and consequently result in the employer's taking action against the fellow employee.[97] Co-worker sexual harassment can lead to the same result. Clearly, such harassment can also detrimentally affect the working environment.

In *Continental Can Co. Inc. v. State of Minnesota*,[98] the Minnesota Supreme Court held that the employer's failure to take prompt and appropriate action to curtail verbal and physical sexual harassment of a female employee by her co-workers constitutes sex discrimination that violates the *Minnesota Human Rights Act*. According to the court, the employer is liable for sexual harassment by non-supervisory co-workers "when the employer knew or should have known of the employees' conduct alleged to constitute sexual harassment and fails to take timely and appropriate action".

In cases alleging sexual harassment perpetrated by co-workers, notice to the employer is a critical element. As stated earlier, the E.E.O.C. guidelines take the position that an employer is liable for co-worker's harassment only when it knows or should have known of such conduct. Furthermore, under the guidelines, the employer can avoid liability by showing that it took appropriate action to remedy the situation.

D. EMPLOYER'S LIABILITY FOR SEXUAL HARASSMENT BY NON-EMPLOYEES

As we have seen earlier, the courts and tribunals as well as human rights agencies are of the view that an employer has an obligation to maintain a workplace free from sexual harassment. If an employer is aware of sexual harassment by its supervisory or non-supervisory employees and does nothing to correct it, the employer can be found guilty of "sex discrimination" under the appropriate human rights legislation.

---

[97] See for example, Commission Decision No. 71-2725, CCH/EEOC Decision (1973), para. 6290.
[98] 22 FEP 1809, 23 E.P.D. para. 30,997, 297 N.W. 2d 241 (Minn. S. Ct. 1980). The *Minnesota Human Rights Act* is patterned after Title VII.

Liability for Sexual Harassment by Non-Employees

Typically, a supervisor makes sexual advances which are rejected by a subordinate. The refusal to submit leads to retaliation in the form of discharge, demotion or other job-related consequences. But sexual harassment is not confined to supervisory personnel or co-workers alone. Should an employer be held liable when a female employee — perhaps a waitress, lobby attendant or airline stewardess — is subjected to sexual harassment by customers, clients or the public? Thus, the issue of the employer's responsibility and the extent of its liability poses a serious but difficult question.

In the United States, according to the E.E.O.C. guidelines, an employer may be held responsible for sexual harassment caused by non-employees (such as clients and customers). Section 1604.11(e) states:

> An employer may also be held responsible for the acts of non-employees, with respect to sexual harassment of employees in the workplace, where the employer (or its agents or supervisory employees) knows or should have known of the conduct and fails to take immediate and appropriate corrective action.

Thus, an employer may be held responsible where the employer, or its agents, or its supervisory employees knew or should have known of the unlawful conduct and the employer failed to take immediate and appropriate corrective action. An employer is potentially liable for non-employee sexual harassment but the employer's actual liability depends upon the extent of the employer's control over the non-employee and any other legal responsibility which the employer may have with respect to the non-employee's conduct. Thus, the employer's liability for non-employee sexual harassment is determined on the basis of the total facts and circumstances in each case, including employer knowledge, corrective action, control, and other legal responsibility. This is illustrated through the following examples:

Example 1 — When the waitress asked if the four male customers seated at the table were ready to order, one man put his arm tightly around her waist and told her that what he wanted was not on the menu, prompting his companions to laugh and comment in the same vein. When she was finally able to finish taking their orders, the man removed his arm and patted her as she turned to leave. She went directly to the restaurant manager and reported the unwelcome sexual conduct. The employer may be responsible if, on learning of the sexual harassment, it failed to take immediate and appropriate corrective action within its control. Depending on the circumstances, such action might be as relatively simple as switching table assignments to have a waiter finish serving that table and making whatever arrangement might be necessary so that the waitress would not be financially or otherwise harmed by the substitution (for instance, by losing the amount of a tip she could have earned).

Example 2 — An employer contracted to have the office-duplicating machine serviced, which was frequently necessary. The female employee who was responsible for operating the machine dreaded service calls because the male service representative who repaired and maintained the machine made sexual advances towards her whenever he was in the office and she found his unwelcome behaviour increasingly disturbing. When he told her that he would be unable to make a rush repair unless she "co-operated" by going out with him, she complained to her supervisor. As in the preceding example, the employer may be responsible in such circumstances if it failed to take corrective measures within its control once it knew, or had reason to know, of the sexual harassment.

Whether an employer is ultimately responsible for the conduct of non-employees will depend on the relationship between the employer and the non-employee as revealed by the specific factual context in which the allegedly unlawful conduct occurred. In the limited number of circumstances in which the boards and courts have considered claims of sexual harassment by non-employees, they seem receptive to finding employers liable where the employer can be deemed responsible for creating the situation which causes or sets in motion the sexual harassment.

The first case to hold the employer liable for non-employee harassment in the United States was *E.E.O.C. v. Sage Realty Corp.*[99] In *Sage Realty*, a female lobby attendant was forced to wear a bicentennial uniform in the shape of a red, white and blue octagon, a short poncho-like uniform that left her thighs and portions of her buttocks exposed. As a result, she was subjected to sexual propositions and lewd comments and gestures by those passing through the lobby. When she complained about the harassment she was told that there were no exceptions to the uniform requirement and that she must either wear the uniform or leave the lobby floor. The employee refused to wear the uniform and was discharged.

---

[99] 507 F. Supp. 599, 25 E.P.D. para. 31, 529 (S.D.N.Y. 1981).

The court found that Sage Realty had violated Title VII by requiring the employee to wear the uniform:

> Sage ... required Hasselman (the employee) to wear, as a condition of her employment, a uniform that was revealing and sexually provocative and could reasonably be expected to subject her to sexual harassment when worn on the job and a uniform that Sage ... knew did subject her to such harassment.

The court ruled that the employer, in effect, was responsible for the sexually harassing behaviour.

In Canada, the cases of sexual harassment by non-employees have not yet surfaced with the same vengeance as sexual harassment by supervisors. In *Doherty v. Lodger's Int'l. Ltd.*[100] two female waitresses refused to wear uniforms on the grounds that the wearing of it made them feel "exploited, humiliated and degraded", that they felt they were no longer just serving drinks but had become some form of "entertainment" and that they became recipients of verbal and physical sexual harassment from customers. The New Brunswick Board of Inquiry in *Lodger's Int'l.*, following the leading U.S. decision in *Sage Realty*, held the employer liable for the sexual harassment by non-employees.

In a recent case, *Allan v. Riverside Lodge*,[101] a waitress alleged that since she was forced to wear the revealing uniform she had been the object of sexual harassment by the customers. While dismissing the complaint, the Board of Inquiry found that the uniform was not revealing, and that the complainant did not complain of customer harassment to the management. Further, the board found that when she complained of the customer's harassment, the employer took an immediate action to stop it by forcefully removing the customer and barring him from the premises for life. The Board implied that the employer did all he could do "to stop sexual harassment by non-employees" under the circumstances. (It may be noted that the complainants and the Commission, in this case, had based their case on the nature of the uniform (whether or not it was revealing) rather than on the employer's liability for the sexual harassment by customers — non-employees.)

In cases of sexual harassment by non-employees apparently it is more difficult to impute the act to the employer. After all, whether the non-employee is a customer, client, or passerby is not within the

---

[100] (N.B. 1982) 3 C.H.R.R. D/628 (Goss).
[101] (Ont. 1985), 6 C.H.R.R. D/2978 (Hunter).

employer's control. It has been frequently argued that the harassed employee seek redress from the harasser rather than the employer. Of course the employer's duty is only to take appropriate or reasonable action; what is reasonable in cases of non-employee harassment differs from what is reasonable in cases of supervisory or co-worker harassment. At times the employer's obligation is obvious. For example in *Lodger's Int'l.* the employer could not require the employees to continue wearing a sexually revealing uniform after it learned that the employees were subjected to sexual harassment. The employer had a duty to make alterations in the uniform or take other measures to stop the harassment. Sometimes the reasonable response to harassment will be less obvious. What should an employer do if an air stewardess is being harassed by a passenger or an office worker by a client?

Although the precise response may differ, the basic principle that an employer is responsible for sexual harassment both when it affirmatively engages in harassment and when it tolerates harassment by not acting to prevent and remedy it, remains the same. However, the question of an employer's responsibility and the extent of its liability will ultimately depend upon the degree of control which the employer has over those non-employees.

Thus, sexual harassment even by non-employees constitutes a violation of the human rights statutes. However, in order to establish the employer's liability the complainant must prove:

1. The employer knew (or should have known) of the harassment.
2. The employer failed to take reasonable measures to prevent or remedy the harassment.
3. The harassment affected the employee's term or condition of employment because it was sufficiently pervasive and severe to create an offensive working environment.

So far, the cases involving sexual harassment by non-employees have focused on the single issue of the provocative uniform the female employees were forced to wear. Under these circumstances, the employer was held liable for the harassment because it forced the employees to wear the revealing uniforms knowing that this subjected them to sexual harassment by non-employees. However, in view of the above, it can be assumed that the tribunals would apply the same approach to cases of sexual harassment by non-employees which may not involve sexually provocative dress.

However, recently an employer was held responsible for harassment of an employee by a customer of the employer. In *Mohammad v. Mariposa Stores Ltd.*[102] the B.C. Human Rights Council held that an employer has a legal obligation to eliminate discriminatory conditions in the workplace and to provide a healthy and respectful work environment. If an employer is not able to control the remarks of a customer, he is certainly able to control its response to discriminatory action. Thus, an employer should think seriously before disciplining an employee for rude or inappropriate behaviour towards a customer or client which is provoked by the racial remarks by the customer.

The facts in this case were as follows: The complainant, of Pakistani descent, was employed as a manager of one of the employer's women's stores. One day, a customer and his wife came into the store to return a coat purchased on sale. Due to the employer's policy, the complainant was unable to comply with the customer's request. The customer became "very upset" and, despite the complainant's explanation, repeatedly demanded a refund. During the course of the conversation, the customer called the complainant a very derogatory name. The complainant nevertheless remained calm throughout this period.

Later that day, the complainant received a telephone call from a woman inquiring about a refund on a sale purchase. While describing the respondent's credit policy, the complainant overheard a male ask, "Who is it?" and the woman reply, "It's the same lady". The complainant recognized the voices as being those of the two individuals who had been in the store earlier. The man then took the receiver and told the complainant, "You're just a fucking Hindu who should never have been hired to work in a public-related service". The complainant, provoked by this comment, swore at the customer and informed him that his business was "no longer appreciated here".

The complainant was very upset over this exchange and told her supervisor about the incident. As a result the complainant was fired for swearing at the customer.

The Human Rights Tribunal, while dealing with a question of whether or not the termination of her employment resulting from her response to a customer's disparaging remark constituted discrimination because of her race, colour, ancestry, etc., held that racial harassment is "a demeaning practice and one which constitutes a profound affront to the dignity of the employee". The Tribunal found that "there is a causal relationship between the racial harassment and the termination of the complainant's employment. Moreover, I find that, by *disciplining*

---

[102] (B.C. 1990), 14 C.H.R.R. D/215 (Barr).

an employee in such circumstances, an employer is, in effect, condoning the discriminatory conduct and allowing such conduct to invade the workplace".[103] [Emphasis added]

The Tribunal found that the complainant was discriminated against. It awarded her four months' salary with interest and $2,000 as compensation for injury to feelings of self-respect caused her by the customer's behaviour.

There is no reason to believe that this sort of reasoning would not be followed in cases of sexual harassment caused by clients and customers. While the law in this respect is still developing, it seems clear that the employer has a duty to take corrective steps when an employee complains of sexual harassment by clients, customers and other members of the general public.

In *Skelly v. Assist Realty Ltd.*[104] the Human Rights Tribunal was faced with an interesting question: whether or not an employer is liable for sexual harassment by a professional colleague employed by another employer in the same profession. The complainant was working as a real estate agent and the alleged harasser for a different real estate firm. Both of them were members of the Kamloops's B.C. Real Estate Board. According to the complainant, the respondent had sexually harassed her by grabbing her breasts on several occasions.

The tribunal concluded that it had jurisdiction to hear the complainant's allegation that the perpetrator sexually harassed her. This decision is of very far-reaching implications in expanding the scope of employment relationship. It remains to be seen whether Human Rights Tribunals in other jurisdictions follow B.C.'s lead in this direction.

E. EMPLOYER'S LIABILITY TO THE ALLEGED HARASSER

The development of guidelines and statutory provisions and the increase of sexual harassment charges have made employers painfully aware of potential liability to sexually harassed employees. There is, however, another side to the issue: employer's liability for damage to the "harasser" in the event that allegations of sexual harassment are

---

[103] *Ibid.*, at D/218 (para. 31).
[104] (B.C. 1991), unreported (Humphreys). See 11 *The Lawyers Weekly*, No. 30, p. 20 (December 6, 1991).

found false. Without adequate internal procedures and investigation methods, an employee who is unjustly terminated for alleged sexual harassment may have a legal cause for action against the employing corporation.

An employer must consider each charge of sexual harassment seriously and with caution. The charge of sexual harassment is a personal matter which has the power to jeopardize a person's professional reputation, job assignments and family relationships. A person who is wrongfully accused or punished for sexual harassment suffers the same righteous indignation felt by an innocent, yet indicted, corporate thief.

It is the employer's responsibility, therefore, to protect both the sexually harassed and the falsely accused sexual harasser. Both have a right to a fair hearing. An employer who immediately takes the complainant's side and passes judgement prematurely upon the alleged harasser may find itself faced with a court action.[105]

As discussed previously, a harasser in a workplace is normally either a supervisor or a co-worker. A supervisor generally holds a senior management position and therefore would be outside the coverage of the collective agreement[106] if there is any.

The employer has an obligation to inform the alleged harasser that there is a complaint against his questionable harassing conduct. It the alleged harasser is informed, counselled or warned at the initial stage or as soon as the complaint was lodged with the employer, it is possible that he may realize his mistake, change his behaviour and stop the harassment. The employer should not sit on the complaint and allow the alleged perpetrator to continue harassment, and then suddenly dismiss him for the offence of causing sexual harassment to the victim. The principle which must govern in such cases is that

---

[105] See Naida B. Axford: "When Women Cry Wolf: Liability for False Charges of Sexual Harassment" (1983), 10 *Employment Relations Today* 73. False accusation is a serious matter. A person making a false accusation may, in addition to a disciplinary action, be exposed to a damage suite for slandering under the civil law. For example, a British court awarded damages to a doctor falsely accused of sexual harassment by his female colleague in the amount of £150,000 plus £100,000 in costs. See 11 *The Lawyers Weekly*, No. 30, p. 20 (December 6, 1991).

[106] The situation in the federal and provincial public service may be different where the senior management personnel are also the members of the union and covered by the collective agreement. For example, in the two leading cases in federal jurisdiction in Canada, *Robichaud v. Brennan* (Can. 1983), 4 C.H.R.R. D/1272 (Dyer) and *Kotyk v. Canadian Employment and Immigration Commission* (Can. 1983), 4 C.H.R.R. D/1416 (Ashley), the harasser-supervisor and the complainant were members of the same union, the Public Service Alliance of Canada.

whenever such allegations are made and believed, the employer is duty-bound to investigate them and to give the person against whom they were made full opportunity to answer them.[107]

In *Kahlon v. Treasury Board*[108], the victim, Ms. Hein, a female employee, complained to the management in April 1989 that the perpetrator had been for some time attempting to force his attentions upon her. These efforts allegedly culminated in an assault in which the perpetrator grabbed the victim's arms and kissed her on the mouth.

The management never doubted the victim's allegation but it made no investigation when the complaint was filed in 1989 because the victim did not wish to make the matter public nor did she wish to have the perpetrator confronted. The perpetrator was subsequently discharged for sexually assaulting a female employee in the workplace.

The Adjudicator, though upholding the dismissal of the perpetrator, stated that there was something terribly wrong with the employer's handling of the victim's allegations. He stated:

> So it was that at Ms. Hein's request there was no investigation of her allegations and no confrontation with the grievor. Ms. Hein did not wish to make the matter public nor did she wish to have the grievor confronted. Warden Stonoski yielded to her views on these matters. It all seems to be so very, very reasonable. but it is all so very, very wrong.
>
> In the mind of Warden Stonoski there was not the slightest doubt that Ms. Hein was telling the truth. The grievor was thus tried and found guilty on the basis of nothing more than the untested and unsubstantiated allegations of one person. He was never confronted with those allegations and he was never given an opportunity to answer them.
>
> The fact that the grievor was not disciplined as a result of those allegations does not mean that the employer was under no obligation to give him an opportunity to answer them. The allegations were in the minds of management, they were on file and they were believed. It is inevitable that management's view of the grievor would be influenced by the allegations which it had accepted as being truthful.
>
> What would be the consequences of this influence? There are many possible consequences. The grievor might have found, for example, that his performance appraisals were no longer quite as favourable as they had been. Not actually unfavourable, but simply a shade less enthusiastic. He might have found that he was experiencing more difficulty than usual in being sent on courses leading to promotion. He might have found that his career was not advancing as it had been. He might have found that there was a subtle shift in management's

---

[107] See *Kahlon v. Treasury Board (Solicitor General)* (1991), P.S.S.R.B. File No.166-2-20871, unreported (Kwavnick).

[108] *Ibid.*

attitude toward him, nothing that he could put his finger on but certainly something that he could sense.

Suppose that at some point along the way he decided to try to get to the bottom of the matter and find out what it was that was hindering him. Suppose that he bucked up his courage, arranged for an interview with the Warden and set out his apprehensions there. What reply would he have received? I do not know what reply he would have received. However, there is not the slightest question in my mind about the reply that he would never have received. He would never have been told the truth: that as a result of certain allegations by Ms. Hein, management took a much dimmer view of him with the consequence that his prospects were no longer as bright as they once had been.

And so the poor grievor would have been left to the end of his days knowing that something had happened to change the employer's estimation of him but he would never be able to discover what that something was. The whole thing is straight out of Kafka and it is all utterly unacceptable.

I would note that if the employer is permitted to deal with such allegations in this way, the door is opened for every vengeful or vindictive woman in the public service to damage the career of any man who has gotten on the wrong side of her. Indeed, what would prevent a woman from making such allegations for the purpose of spiking the guns of a male colleague whom she regards as a serious rival for an upcoming promotion? When such a door is left open, it must be assumed that, sooner or later, someone will come through it.

In this memorandum of 24 April (Exhibit E-6) Warden Stonoski cites Ms. Hein giving it as her opinion that conducting an investigation into her allegations or confronting the grievor "would serve no useful purpose" I beg to differ.

The grievor appears to be an intelligent and responsible person. If Warden Stonoski had confronted him with Ms. Hein's allegations, even if only in a private interview, and impressed upon him the seriousness of those allegations and the possible consequences for him, I doubt very much that the attack upon Ms. Dickins would ever have occurred.[109]

Moreover, the courts insist that the alleged harasser must be given a proper opportunity to advance his side of the story before terminating his employment.[110] In *Shiels v. Saskatchewan Government Insurance*,[111] the court while awarding the damages for wrongful dismissal pointed out that they gave the plaintiff (alleged harasser) "no opportunity to prepare himself to respond. I think they should have done so. I think, too, that the plaintiff should have been given an opportunity to be heard with respect to the statements Rheault (Investigator) had

---

[109] *Ibid.*
[110] See *Shiels v. Saskatchewan Government Insurance* (1988), 51 D.L.R. (4th) 28 (Sask. Q.B.).
[111] *Ibid.*

obtained from the other employees. No doubt, these statements were considered and contributed to some degree in the decision to fire him."[112]

1. Wrongful Dismissal of Supervisory Personnel (in a Non-Union Setting)

"Wrongful dismissal litigation has become one of Canada's primary growth industries. Not only has the number of cases coming before the courts increased tenfold in the last few years, but the law applied to these cases has been undergoing rapid change", writes a lawyer.[113] Employers should realize that the "employment at will" doctrine has come under increased challenge in the courts resulting in new remedies for employees who have been disciplined "unfairly" by their employers.[114] The majority of jurisdictions now recognize a cause of action in tort for malicious or wrongful discharge. A successful suit will award the terminated employee back-pay benefits, reinstatement, damages for emotional distress and suffering,[115] even loss of reputation[116] and punitive damages.[117] The potential damages are increased when an employee has a long tenure and good employment record.

Thus, no damage resulting from wrongful dismissal should be assumed to be so removed from the act of termination as not to be deserving of the possibility of compensation by a given judge in a given court at a given time somewhere in this country.

In tort law, the test of liability is one of a general foreseeability of harm. The criterion of foreseeability, applied in torts case to determine whether there is responsibility, requires that the type of injury

---

[112] *Ibid.*, at 37.
[113] See Martin F. Hill: "Arbitration as means of Protecting Employees from Unjust Dismissal: A Statutory Proposal" (1982), 3 *Northern Illinois University L. Rev.* No. 1.
[114] B.A. Grossman, *The Executive Firing Line* (Toronto: Carswell/Methuen, 1983).
[115] See *Pilon v. Peugeot Canada Ltd.* (1980), 29 O.R. (2d) 711 (S.C.). In that case the plaintiff, Mr. Pilon, was awarded damages of $7,500 for the mental distress he had suffered. The *Pilon* case established the principle that in certain circumstances an employee who has been wrongly dismissed may be entitled to recover damages for mental distress.
[116] See for example *Abouna v. Foothills Provincial General Hospital Bd.* (1977), 77 D.L.R. (3d) 220 (S.C. Alta.); varied 83 D.L.R. (3d) 33 (C.A.).
[117] See for example *Brown v. Fidinam (Canada) Ltd.* (1980), 23 A.R. 608 (Q.B.).

be reasonably foreseeable, but is not then employed further to limit damages ensuing due to the idiosyncrasies of the victim.

Under contract law, general damages are not awarded for breach of contract. However, in some exceptional cases, general damages have been awarded in situations where an employee has been wrongfully dismissed. In these cases, the issue was whether or not it was contemplated by the parties that upon breach of contract, "vexation, frustration and distress" were likely to result. If so, then general damages for that distress were awardable.

Even in the absence of a written employment contract, an employer may be stopped from terminating an employee without adhering to company employee relations policies. Courts are recognizing that employee manuals and handbooks rise to the level of an enforceable contract such that employees may not be terminated or disciplined except in conformity with internal company policies.

If accusations of sexual harassment prove to be false and cause injury to the alleged harasser, the law of slander and libel provide the employee a remedy. The employee may sue the company or the accuser for defamation of character.[118] Court actions of this nature may escalate to hundreds of thousands of dollars. Moreover, in such cases, the courts while awarding damages for wrongful dismissal take into consideration that "dismissal for cause based on sexual harassment would likely tend to make a prospective employer wary. . . . the allegation of sexual harassment stigmatized the plaintiff, and reduced his chances of employment."[119]

The question thus arises, what should an employer do to reduce potential damages? Should or should he not fire an alleged harasser? There is no simple answer to these questions. If the employer dismissed an alleged harasser, he may face a damage suit for a wrongful dismissal. On the other hand, a failure to fire an alleged harasser might increase

---

[118] See for example *The Assn. of Professors of the University of Ottawa v. The University of Ottawa* (1979), unreported (O'Shea). Coupel (victim) alleged defamation and sought $250,000 in damages. See SIM, "Stickler Dismissal Upheld", *CAUT Bulletin*, December 1980. At Carleton University School of Journalism in Ottawa, three women students charged members of their staff with sexual harassment. Although the women did not name specific men, three male professors threatened to sue the students for more than $100,000. At Clark University in *Peck v. Blank and Bunster*, the victims of sexual harassment were confronted with a lawsuit for $23.7 million. See A. Field, "Harassment on Campus: Sex in a Tenured Position" (1981), *Ms Magazine*, p. 68.

[119] *Shiels v. Saskatchewan Government Insurance* (1988), 51 D.L.R. (4th) 28 at 38 (Sask. Q.B.).

230 *Ch. 4 - Employer's Liability for Sexual Harassment of Employees*

the employer's liability to the victim. Thus, an employer must assess all the factors very seriously before terminating the employment of the alleged harasser.

In *Shiels v. Saskatchewan Government Insurance*,[120] a company executive of 10 years' seniority was summarily dismissed for sexually harassing a fellow female employee. The cause for dismissal really came down to a complaint about the plaintiff's behaviour at a convention in Montreal. Evidence surrounding this event indicated that the plaintiff and the complainant had spent a day together shopping and that, after dinner, the plaintiff kissed the complainant in her hotel room but she gently pushed him away. He then left and the next day, his behaviour returned to normal. A consideration of the facts showed that after returning to work the complainant became very angry about the entire situation. She then complained of the plaintiff's behaviour and, after an investigation, he was fired.

The Saskatchewan Court of Queen's Bench found that the plaintiff, the company executive, was not guilty of sexual harassment and allowed his claim for wrongful dismissal. The court pointed out that the plaintiff had not been given a proper opportunity to advance his side of the story before the decision to summarily dismiss him was made.

Recently, in *Hewes v. City of Etobicoke*,[121] the Ontario Court (General Division) awarded $180,000 in damages for wrongful dismissal. In this case, Mr. Hewes, a utilities superintendent of 38 years seniority was dismissed for allegedly sexually harassing (fondling of breasts) a female radio clerk in his office (just three years prior to his retirement). It appears that the employer accepted the truthfulness of allegations of sexual harassment without thorough and proper investigation. The court had serious doubt about the credibility of at least one of the complainants, whom the court believed had animosity towards plaintiff (the alleged harasser).

The court concluded that Mr. Hewes should have been given *two years' notice* of dismissal. The court awarded him $91,698 for loss of salary and nearly $90,000 for loss of fringe benefits, including sick leave plan, medical insurance coverage and pension benefits.

This case further reinforces (1) the importance of thorough, reliable and independent investigation before terminating the employment of the alleged harasser, (2) that the employer also has a

---

[120] (1988), 51 D.L.R. (4th) 28 (Sask. Q.B.).
[121] See *The Globe and Mail*, October 4, 1991, p. 9A.

responsibility to the alleged harasser and (3) that a rash and emotional reaction may lead to serious consequences.

On the other hand, the Ontario District Court dismissed the claim of a bank manager for wrongful dismissal and found him guilty of sexually harassing a female employee.[122] In *Tellier v. Bank of Montreal*,[123] a bank manager was fired for sexually harassing a female employee by patting her on the rear and rubbing against her. The bank manager sued the bank for damages for wrongful dismissal and also sued the victim (the complainant) for damages, alleging that she induced the breach of his employment.

Dismissing the plaintiff's claim, the court stated that the bank had no alternative under the circumstances but to terminate his employment, especially in view of the senior position he held. The court also noted that the bank had a very heavy responsibility to protect its employees and, if it did not take positive action against the manager, it could leave itself open to charges under the *Canadian Human Rights Act*.

Further, in *Neigum v. Wilkie Co-operative Association Ltd.*[124], the court dismissed the plaintiff's action for wrongful dismissal on the ground that his conduct constituted sexual harassment of other employees. The court stated that the sexual harassment of employees will seriously interfere with the proper operation of an employer's business and can justify summary dismissal. Further, the company's operation manual provided that theft or sexual harassment are major offences that carry the penalty of dismissal.

In *Mackie v. Geneso Canada Ltd.*,[125] the Ontario Court (General Division) dismissed the plaintiff's action for wrongful dismissal on the ground that he had engineered the events that led to sexual harassment of a 17-year-old sales clerk. Mr. Mackie as a senior man of the company knew or should have known that his conduct with employees was expected to be exemplary. The court concluded that his behaviour towards Ms. J. constituted sexual harassment for which the company was entitled to summarily terminate his employment. The court pointed out that plaintiff was not entitled to any lesser penalty. He was no longer of value to the company. It was not a case for a second chance. The company was forced to take a strong position, which it did. The court concluded that:

---

[122] (1987), 17 C.C.E.L. 1 (Ont. Dist. Ct.).
[123] *Ibid.*
[124] (1987), 55 Sask. R. 210 (Q.B.).
[125] See 11 *The Lawyers Weekly*, No. 21, p. 15 (October 4, 1991).

> These decisions that are made by management from time to time, and these decisions made by the courts and judges from time to time, must reflect as best they can some of the community standards that we have in reference to sexual harassment in the workplace.

The court questioned:

> How in the world could this company continue to employ a man like this, believing, as they did, Ms. J.'s version of these events? How could they, in conscience, send this man into other stores where employees and perhaps customers could be open to the same kind of behaviour?

This was one of the strongest disapprovals by the court of sexually harassing behaviour by senior management in a wrongful dismissal case. The court send a very tough message to management personnel that sexual harassment in the workplace is a very serious matter which makes the accused unwanted and unemployable by an employer.

It appears that if the courts are satisfied that the plaintiff's conduct indeed constituted sexual harassment of other employees, they may allow his dismissal, even summarily, particularly if the company's policy specifically prohibits sexual harassment and makes it a serious offence, and especially if the behaviour is repeated and the perpetrator had a written warning or counselling after the first incident. The situation may be different, however, where perpetrators are members of a union and are covered by a collective agreement.

2. Discipline of a Co-Worker Harasser (in a Union Setting)

When an employer is presented with a complaint of sexual harassment by a co-worker it is required to take "immediate and appropriate corrective action" to successfully avoid liability for sexual harassment. In a union setting, a collective agreement normally contains a "just cause" clause requiring an employer to discharge or discipline an employee only for just cause. Thus, there is always a dilemma in disciplining the harassing employee sufficiently yet not too severely. Arbitrators in reviewing the merits of a disciplinary grievance will review factual evidence substantiating employee misconduct and will weigh the severity of discipline in light of the severity of the misconduct.

Some arbitrators view sexual harassment and sexual advances of a co-worker as serious misconduct in the workplace. For instance, an arbitrator upheld the discharge of an employee who pushed down a female employee, fondled her breasts and attempted to kiss her.[126] In another case the Ontario Labour Relations Board upheld the discharge of an employee, even during the union organizational campaign, for sexually harassing a female employee. In that case, the dischargee had asked a female employee if "she was excited"; when asked why, he replied "because your nipples are standing out". The O.L.R.B. in that case, found that the sexual harassment of the female employee was "an act of gross misconduct".[127]

On the other hand, some arbitrators have found discharging a harasser was too severe a discipline even though the sexual harassment of a female employee is clearly reprehensible behaviour. For instance, a Board of Arbitration ruled that the discharge of a male employee who sexually harassed a female co-worker by "sticking his hands between her legs all the way to her genitals" was too severe a discipline.[128] The disciplined employee had 17 years' seniority and had no discipline problem involving sexual misconduct in the past. The sexual misconduct was spontaneous and the harassing employee was under the influence of alcohol. The discharge was reduced to six months' suspension. In another case where a male employee was discharged for sexually harassing a female employee by "touching inside the legs, putting arms around the waist, touching the breast area, etc." the Board of Arbitration found that the sexual behaviour was not serious enough to entitle any discipline.[129] The Board said "that while we would not go so far as to call this type of behaviour 'sexual harassment', we would certainly label it as being inappropriate in the circumstances".[130] However, the Board quashed his discharge and reinstated him without loss of pay or benefits. American arbitrators have adopted a similar approach in sexual harassment cases.[131]

---

[126] The *St. Joseph's Health Centre v. C.U.P.E.* (1983), unreported (Roberts). For an American decision see *Mengel Co. and the Employees Union of Mengel Co.*, 61-2ARB #8352, where an arbitrator upheld the discharge of a male employee for making improper advances.

[127] *Hotel, Restaurant and Cafeteria Employees Union, Loc. 75 v. Constellation Hotel Corp. Ltd.* (1981), 82 CLLC para. 16,150 (O.L.R.B.).

[128] *Re Government of the Province of Alta. and Alta. Union of Provincial Employees* (1982), 5 L.A.C. (3d) 268 (Alta. Public Service Grievance Bd.).

[129] *Re Government of the Province of Alta. and Alta. Union of Provincial Employees* (1983), 10 L.A.C. (3d) 179 (Larson).

[130] *Ibid.*, at 191.

[131] See for example *Dayton Power Ltd. Co.*, 80 LA 19 (1982) where an employee was discharged for sexually harassing a female co-worker by pinching her breast

Thus, employers cannot be guaranteed that arbitrators in all cases will approve the discharge of a male employee for sexually harassing a female co-worker. The arbitrators, in determining the appropriateness of discipline for sexual harassment under the "just cause" clause, will give serious consideration to the employer's past disciplinary practices for similar misconduct, to the seriousness of the harassment, and to the past record of the harassing employee. In cases where the charges of sexual harassment against co-workers are found vexatious, in addition to an award for back wages, the employer will also be exposed to a civil action for damages. This is not suggesting that an employer should not take action against the harasser. Rather it is to emphasize that employers should have a clear and precise policy on sexual harassment, expressing their strong disapproval of sexual harassment, and making it clear that the offenders of the policy would be punished severely.

For further analysis of this topic see Chapter 6, Arbitral Review of Sexual Harassment Cases, *infra*.

---

and making kissing sounds. The Board of Arbitration found that the penalty of discharge was too severe and reduced it to a seven months' suspension. See also *Consolidated Coal Co.*, 79 LC 940 (1982), where discharge was reduced to 60 days' suspension; and *Rochester Telephone Corp. v. Communication Workers of America*, 65-2ARB #8701, where discharge was reduced to suspension for three to six months.

CHAPTER 5

Remedies Available to the Victim

In the previous chapters we examined the nature and scope of sexual harassment and its legal implications in a working environment. It was established that sexual harassment amounts to "sex discrimination" and it is prohibited in both federal and provincial jurisdictions. Further, an employer has an obligation to provide an environment free from sexually harassing behaviour by an employee, supervisor, or co-worker.

However, a mere statement of legal rights is of no comfort to a victim of sexual harassment. The victim is not interested in an empty declaration of human rights but in positive and tangible redress for his/her ordeal. Thus, the remedies and the ways and means to get them are the most relevant to a victim. In this chapter the options for redress that are available to sexually harassed employees, the type of relief they can obtain, and the pros and cons of these redress mechanisms will be discussed.

There are a number of options available to an employee to seek redress against sexual harassment. However, all options for redress are neither available nor desirable for all employees in all circumstances. Availability of a particular redress mechanism will depend upon a number of factors, including the nature and size of the employer, the nature of the bargaining relationship, the contract clause, the nature and severity of the ordeal, and the circumstances surrounding the sexual harassment.

A. EMPLOYER'S INTERNAL COMPLAINT PROCEDURE

Some public and private sector employers have developed policy and procedures on sexual harassment. If the employer has established a policy and procedure for the redress of sexual harassment, the victim may utilize the mechanism by filing a complaint in the manner prescribed in the procedure. It would be advisable to do so, unless the victim has a reason to believe that she would not get a fair hearing.

One of the major difficulties with the employer's unilateral redress mechanism is its credibility. Employees generally do not view these systems as impartial and fair. They lack confidence in these mechanisms because they fear that the procedure is designed to cover up the issue and to avoid the employer's liability. The employees are not to be blamed for the lack of confidence in the employer's hierarchy. Their suspicion is not entirely unfounded. There have been cases where senior officers, instead of investigating a complaint of sexual harassment, themselves began to make sexual advances to the complainant.[1]

The question then arises, what kind of relief should a victim expect through the employer's unilateral complaint procedure? Would a victim be able to get any tangible relief through this procedure?

It may be advantageous for the victim to use the employer's unilateral complaint procedure if it provides an independent investigation into the charges of sexual harassment. The employer's internal redress mechanism, in certain respects, is more beneficial than the other available options. It can provide the maximum privacy and confidentiality the victim may require. As noted earlier, many of the victims do not seek any redress of sexual harassment because of publicity. Further, outside agencies, like a Board of Arbitration and a Human Rights Tribunal, are limited in their powers to grant relief to the victim.

Generally speaking, a complaint by the victim to the employer puts him on notice that employees are being sexually harassed in their workplace. It provides him with an opportunity to investigate the matter and do whatever possible to stop further harassment. The employer has an absolute discretion, not restricted by any legal doctrine or precedent, to provide redress for sexual harassment. For example, the

---

[1] See for example *Janzen v. Platy Enterprises* (Man. 1985), 6 C.H.R.R. D/2735 (Henteleff). In that case, the Board of Adjudication found that when the victim complained to the superior of the harasser, he himself began to harass her. The Board stated at D/2770 (para. 22660): "I find from the evidence that Phillip [supervisor of the harasser] personally joined Tommy in acts of harassment of a persistent and abusive nature by virtue of unjustified and persistent criticism of her job performance, followed by the cessation of the actual acts of physical sexual harassment of Ms. Govereau by Tommy, and thereby created a negative psychological and emotional environment for work by Ms. Govereau in her workplace"; revd in part 24 D.L.R. (4th) 31 (Man. Q.B.); revd (Man. 1986), 8 C.H.R.R. D/3831 (C.A.), a decision quashed by the Supreme Court of Canada (Man. 1989), 10 C.H.R.R. D/6205.

See also *Bundy v. Jackson*, 641 F. 2d 934 (D.C. Cir. 1981), in which case the victim, Sandra Bundy, successively encountered sexual harassment from the very management personnel to whom she complained against her immediate supervisor.

employer can discipline or discharge the harasser, he can transfer the harasser, or force him to make an apology to the victim. Further, the employer may restore any employment benefit the victim might have been denied because of sexual harassment, such as promotion, loss of wages, etc. In many cases these steps are necessary not only to combat sexual harassment but to restore confidence in the workforce. However, it is doubtful that the employer would be willing to compensate the victim for the loss of human dignity and for psychological and emotional distress.

The employer's internal complaint procedure, however, poses some difficulties for the victim also. The entire burden falls on the single victim to prove the charges of sexual harassment. In that case, the victim may not have the support of the union or other outside agencies. The employer may not allow the victim to have legal counsel, and even if it is allowed, it is doubtful if she would be able to afford it. Further, co-workers may be reluctant to testify on her behalf in such an investigation due to fear of reprisal from their supervisors. Some of these difficulties, however, will always be there regardless of the avenue of redress.

However, it may be stated that a victim is not barred from filing a complaint with the appropriate Human Rights Commission if she fails to receive a satisfactory response from the employer.

B. REMEDIES FOR SEXUAL HARASSMENT

1. Tort Remedies

In Canada, a violation of a human rights statute neither gives rise to a common law action for tort nor to a civil cause of action. Thus, a victim of human rights violations cannot sue the employer for damages caused by infringement of his/her human rights. The aggrieved party must seek redress solely through the machinery provided under the appropriate human rights statute. The courts have held that the dismissal of a woman from her employment on grounds of sex did not give rise to a civil cause of action because the human rights statutes have established a comprehensive scheme for dealing with these matters.[2]

---

[2] See for example *MacDonald v. 283076 Ont. Inc.* (1979), 95 D.L.R. (3d) 723 (Ont. H.C.).

In *MacDonald v. 283076 Ont. Inc.*[3] the plaintiff claimed that she had been wrongfully dismissed from her job on the grounds that she was a woman and that the defendant employer wished to replace her with a man. In relief, she sought a declaration that she had been wrongfully dismissed, her reinstatement, and damages for wrongful dismissal. Griffiths J. for the Ontario High Court dismissed her claim by holding that a complaint by an employee of wrongful dismissal on the basis of sex, contrary to the Ontario *Human Rights Code*, did not give rise to any civil cause of action against the employer. Griffiths J. observed:

> In my opinion an employee did not at common law have redress for being dismissed from her employment because of discrimination against her sex *per se*, and in that respect the Act creates a new right and remedy. . . . *Thus an employee who is discharged by reason of her sex alone, would have no claim at common law if her employer had given her adequate notice.* [Emphasis added][4]

However, the Ontario Court of Appeal reversed the lower court and held that a complaint by the employee against wrongful dismissal on the basis of sex, contrary to the Ontario *Human Rights Code*, disclosed a cause of action. Whether or not a breach of the *Code* gives rise to an independent cause of action, the employee can still rely on the *Code* to show that dismissal on the basis of sex is not a dismissal for "cause".[5]

In *Bhadauria v. Seneca College of Applied Arts and Technology Bd. of Gov.*,[6] the plaintiff, instead of filing a complaint under the Ontario *Human Rights Code*, issued a writ claiming damages for discrimination for the breach of s. 4 of the *Code*. The plaintiff alleged that the respondent college was in breach of its common law duty not to discriminate against her and, secondly, that the college was also in a breach of its statutory duty under the Ontario *Human Rights Code* not to discriminate against her. The plaintiff claimed that the college, in refusing her an interview, discriminated against her on the ground of her ethnic origin. At first instance, Callaghan J. held that the plaintiff denied employment by reason of her ethnic origin had no cause of action at common law for such discrimination. That decision was reversed by the unanimous Ontario Court of Appeal, which recognized

---

[3] *Ibid.*
[4] *Ibid.*, at 726-27.
[5] *MacDonald v. 283076 Ont. Inc.* (1979), 102 D.L.R. (3d) 383 (Ont. C.A.).
[6] (1979), 105 D.L.R. (3d) 707 (Ont. C.A.).

a tort of discrimination and, therefore, found it unnecessary to decide whether a breach of the *Code* gave rise to a civil cause of action.

However, the Supreme Court of Canada unanimously rejected the judgment of the Ontario Court of Appeal by holding that a plaintiff who can establish that she was refused employment because of her ethnic origin and thereby suffered damages, does not have a right to take civil action against the person who refused her employment, either on the basis of common tort of discrimination or on the basis of an action flowing directly from a breach of the Ontario *Human Rights Code*.[7] Chief Justice Laskin concluded:

> In the present case, the enforcement scheme under the *Ontario Human Rights Code* ranges from administrative enforcement through complaint and settlement procedures to adjudicative or *quasi*-adjudicative enforcement by boards of inquiry. The boards are invested with a wide range of remedial authority including the award of compensation (damages in effect), and to full curial enforcement by wide rights of appeal, which, potentially, could bring cases under the Code to this Court. The Ontario Court of Appeal did not think that this scheme of enforcement excluded a common law remedy.
>
> . . .
>
> The view taken by the Ontario Court of Appeal is a bold one and may be commended as an attempt to advance the common law. In my opinion, however, this is foreclosed by the legislative initiative which overtook the existing common law in Ontario and established a different regime which does not exclude the Courts but rather makes them part of the enforcement machinery under the Code.
>
> For the foregoing reasons, I would hold that not only does the Code foreclose any civil action based directly upon a breach thereof but it also excludes any common law action based on an invocation of the public policy expressed in the Code. The Code itself has laid out the procedures for vindication of that public policy, procedures which the plaintiff-respondent did not see fit to use.[8]

The Supreme Court, it appears, gave preference to the old doctrine of "freedom to contract" over the newly emerging doctrine of "freedom from discrimination".[9] The decision has serious implications for the victims of human rights violations who are restricted to seek redress

---

[7] *Seneca College of Applied Arts and Technology Bd. of Gov. v. Bhadauria* (1981), 124 D.L.R. (3d) 193 (S.C.C.).

[8] *Ibid.*, at 203.

[9] For a critical review of the Supreme Court decision in the *Bhadauria* case see I.B. McKenna, a "Casenote" (1982), 10 *Can. Bar Rev.* 122-137.

only by filing a complaint to an appropriate Human Rights Commission. This may deny relief to persons who stand to suffer the discriminatory effect of certain apparently entrenched principles of common law. Availability of a common law remedy, as an alternative to the statute, would indeed be advantageous in cases where the victims are unable to seek relief through a Human Rights Commission.

However, it may be pointed out that the Supreme Court decision in *Bhadauria* was prior to the enforcement date of s. 15, the equality rights clause of the *Canadian Charter of Rights and Freedoms*. Thus it is possible that the Supreme Court, at the next opportunity, may modify its decision in *Bhadauria* by recognizing the right of civil action for the discriminatory treatment and violation of a human rights statute. Moreover, it may be pointed out that the Quebec Superior Court in *Foisy v. Bell Canada*[10] by implication recognized the complainant's right to sue for discriminatory treatment in violation of the Quebec *Charter of Rights and Freedoms*, when it awarded her damages for "psychological trauma and social and professional isolation" caused by sexual harassment and eventual dismissal. The court based its decision on the theory of *abus de droit*.

2. Civil Action For Breach of Fiduciary Duty

A question is often asked whether or not a victim of sexual harassment can sue the employer-harasser for a breach of fiduciary duty. The basic principle of fiduciary duty is based on the premises that neither party may exert influence or pressure upon the other, take selfish advantage of his trust or prejudice the other except in the exercise of the utmost good faith and full knowledge and consent of that other.

Three general characteristics typify relationships which have been held to give rise to fiduciary obligations as defined by the Supreme Court of Canada in *Frame v. Smith*:[10a]

1. The fiduciary has scope for the exercise of some discretion or power.
2. The fiduciary can unilaterally exercise that power or discretion so as to affect the beneficiary's legal or practical interests.

---

[10] (Que. 1985), 6 C.H.R.R. D/2817 (Que. S.C.).
[10a] [1987] 2 S.C.R. 99.

3. The beneficiary is peculiarly vulnerable to or at the mercy of the fiduciary holding the discretion or power.

These three elements relied on by the courts in breach of fiduciary obligation are often found in employer-employee relations and often breached in sexual harassment cases. Does not sexual harassment of the employee, particularly by her supervisor, fall into this category?[10b]

In Canada so far no employer has been found liable for breach of fiduciary duty in relation to sexual harassment, and no employer has been sued on this basis. This, however, does not mean that the civil action remedy is not available to the victims of sexual harassment. This simply means that this avenue of remedy has not yet been tapped.

In this regard a recent decision[10c] of the Ontario Court (General Division) is very significant. The court ruled that a retired minister, Harold Frid (who had sex with one of his parishioners after counselling her for marital problems) was liable to the victim, Isobel Deiwick, "for breach of fiduciary duty resulting from emotional and mental stress and anxiety" and must pay her $20,000 for mental distress damages caused by breaching his fiduciary duty.

In view of the above decision, there is a great likelihood that the courts in Canada would extend the rule of fiduciary duty to sexual harassment cases, particularly where the harasser has been the supervisor, if and when a victim sues the employer-harasser on the ground of fiduciary duty.

A fiduciary duty may not apply to all sexual harassment cases; but sexual harassment by the supervisor no doubt falls within the scope of fiduciary obligations. A civil suit on this basis may not be suitable for all cases, and many victims may not find a civil action attractive and economically viable. Nonetheless, a mere acceptance by the courts that sexual harassment, at least by the supervisor, falls within the ambit of fiduciary duty would be a very significant addition to the arsenal of remedies for the victims. A possibility of civil action on the basis of breach of fiduciary duty would provide the employers with a meaningful and economic incentive to accelerate the process of dealing with and preventing sexual harassment in the workplace. However, only time will tell whether courts would extend the rule of fiduciary

---

[10b] See for example *Olarte v. Commodore Business Machines* (Ont. 1983), 4 C.H.R.R. D/1705 (Cumming), where six female employees were sexually harassed by their supervisor. When they refused his overtures of sexual conduct, they were disciplined and even fired from the job.

[10c] *Deiwick v. Frid*, 11 *The Lawyers Weekly*, No. 28, p. 4 (Nov. 22, 1991).

duty to sexual harassment cases and whether a civil action on the ground of fiduciary duty would be practical and economically viable for the victims.

C. REMEDIES UNDER THE HUMAN RIGHTS STATUTES

Human rights statutes in Canada initially had given very limited powers to boards of inquiry. Usually, boards were empowered merely to hear complaints and, where a complaint was justified, to make recommendations to the Commission or the Minister responsible as to appropriate remedial actions to be carried out. Boards of inquiry, thus, were not allowed to fashion remedies themselves. Section 26(4) in the Prince Edward Island *Human Rights Act*[11] reads:

> Where the matter referred to the board of inquiry is not settled between the parties and the board finds a complaint is supported by a reasonable preponderance of the evidence, the board shall report its recommendation to the commission on the course that ought to be taken with respect to the complaint.

Most jurisdictions in Canada have revised their statutes to make boards of inquiry more than simply advisory bodies, by empowering them to make orders themselves. However, among these statutes, there is considerable variety and diversity of the boards' power to provide remedies. Some of the statutes leave the boards' power completely open-ended. For example, the Nova Scotia *Human Rights Act* provides:[12]

> A board of inquiry may order any party who has contravened this Act to do any act or thing that constitutes full compliance with the Act and to rectify any injury caused to any person or class of persons or to make compensation therefor.

Other statutes particularize the orders that the boards may make. For example, s. 31(1)(b) of the Alberta *Individual's Rights Protection Act* provides:[13]

---

[11] R.S.P.E.I. 1988, c. H-12.
[12] R.S.N.S. 1989, c. 214, s. 34(8). See also the Ontario *Human Rights Code*, R.S.O. 1990, c. H.19, s. 41(1)(a), which states " . . . the board may, by order, (a) direct the party *to do anything*, that in the opinion of the board, the party ought to do". [Emphasis added]
[13] R.S.A. 1980, c.-I-2. [am. S.A. 1990, c. 23, s. 12].

A board of inquiry

. . .

(b) may, if it finds that a complaint is justified in whole or in part, order the person against whom the finding was made to do any or all of the following:
   (i) to cease the contravention complained of;
   (ii) to refrain in future from committing the same or any similar contravention;
   (iii) to make available to the person discriminated against the rights, opportunities or privileges he was denied contrary to this Act;
   (iv) to compensate the person dealt with contrary to this Act for all or any part of any wages or income lost or expenses incurred by reason of the contravention of this Act;
   (v) to take any other action the board considers proper to place the person discriminated against in the position he would have been in but for the contravention of this Act.

Thus, it is evident that there is a great variety in Canadian human rights statutes as to the powers of boards of inquiry. Some boards may merely make recommendations after hearing an inquiry.[14] Other boards have open-ended powers,[15] but it appears that the wording of these statutes does not empower the boards to award anything more than compensating damages.

1. Compensatory Damages — Philosophy and Purpose

Human rights statutes in most Canadian jurisdictions have not provided specific remedies for the victims of sexual harassment. They generally authorize a board of inquiry "to rectify any injury caused to any person and to make compensation". For example, the relevant section of the Ontario *Human Rights Code*[16] reads:

41.—(1) Where the board of inquiry, after a hearing, finds that a right of the complainant under Part I has been infringed and that the infringement is a contravention of section 9 by a party to the proceeding, the board may, by order,

---

[14] See for example the human rights statutes in Prince Edward Island, Quebec, Newfoundland and New Brunswick.
[15] See for example the human rights statutes in Ontario, Nova Scotia, and Saskatchewan. See also the *Canadian Human Rights Act*, R.S.C. 1985, c. H-6.
[16] R.S.O. 1990, c. H.19.

(a) direct the party to do anything that, in the opinion of board, the party ought to do to achieve compliance with this Act, both in respect of the complaint and in respect of future practices; and
(b) direct the party to make restitution, including monetary compensation, for loss arising out of the infringement, and, where the infringement has been engaged in wilfully or recklessly, monetary compensation may include an award, not exceeding $10,000, for mental anguish.

Human rights statutes are aimed at providing relief to the complainant on the one hand and eradicating the problem of sex discrimination on the other hand by way of educating the public, particularly the employers.

One of the clearest statements on the thrust of the Ontario *Human Rights Code* is contained in the decision of Professor (now Judge) Walter Tarnopolsky in *Amber v. Leder*[17] where he stated:

> Human Rights legislation in Canada was intended to subordinate certain rights of contract and property, which existed at common law, to new rights deemed necessary for forwarding the equality, dignity and rights of all human beings. ...It follows clearly, therefore, that complaints of discrimination are not matters merely between two parties — the complainant and the respondent — but a matter concerning the public. An act of discrimination does not give rise merely to a new private claim for compensation — it amounts to a public wrong.[18]

Professor Tarnopolsky went on to discuss the matter of compensation in more detail:

> Although at common law some attempt may be made to compensate for emotional injury, I do not believe that this was contemplated by the legislature under the *Ontario Human Rights Code*. As I indicated in Part 1 of this report, the emphasis is on re-education, and on obtaining equality of access to jobs, accommodation, etc. Even (counsel for the complainant) . . . suggested that payment of monies could be a further injury to buy off complainants, and could be a further injury to dignity, rather than compensation for such injury. I would have to agree, and would not make any recommendation for such payment.[19]

Thus, it is evident that initially the tribunals were reluctant to award the complainant special damages for injury to her dignity and feelings. However, in *Shack v. London Drive-Ur-Self*[20] Professor

---

[17] (Ont. Bd. of Inquiry, 1970), unreported (Tarnopolsky).
[18] *Ibid.*, at 9.
[19] *Ibid.*, at 17.
[20] (Ont. Bd. of Inquiry, 1974), unreported (Lederman).

Lederman found that the complainant had been denied employment because of her sex, and the board did not hesitate to award damages to the complainant.

In *Hendry v. Ont. Liquor Control Board*,[21] the board awarded to the complainant back pay and a substantial amount of general damages. The Board stated:

> She has suffered emotionally as a result of the failure of L.C.B.O. to abide by the Code, and has been insulted as a woman. As the solace available in these circumstances, both to make it clear to Ms. Hendry that her unfair treatment is recognized by this Board and to the LCBO that it must take very seriously the harm done by failure to abide by the Code. I would award Ms. Hendry the additional sum of $8,000 as general compensation.[22]

It is obvious the Board implied that the award was intended to deter the respondent from further violations of the *Code*.

In *Imberto v. Coiffure*,[23] where the complainant had been refused employment because of his sex, the Board considered the possibility of awarding compensation for injuries to the complainant's psychological well-being. The Board observed:

> Although the law of contract damages has been somewhat reluctant in the past to award compensation for injuries of this kind resulting from breach of contract, there would appear to be no reason why injuries of this kind could not be the subject of compensation under the Ontario Human Rights Code. There is no reason to interpret the phrase "any injury" in Section [19(b), R.S.O. c. 340] so as to exclude injuries to an individual's psychological well-being.[24]

Thus the boards of inquiry, on the basis of a wider interpretation of the expression that a board may "rectify any injury" or "make compensation therefor", gradually began to award damages for "loss of wages", for "humiliation and injury to dignity and self-respect", as well as for "psychological sufferings". This had led to a trend away from emphasizing the purely educative aspect of human rights statutes towards the granting of compensatory awards. In most cases, compensation, both in special and general damages, is awarded as a matter of course. Further, the Review Tribunal under the *Canadian Human Rights Act*, in *Foreman et al. v. Via Rail Canada, Inc.*,[25] dispelled the

---

[21] (Ont. 1980), 1 C.H.R.R. D/160 (Soberman).
[22] *Ibid.*, at D/166 (para. 1480).
[23] (Ont. 1981), 2 C.H.R.R. D/392 (McCamus).
[24] *Ibid.*, at D/398 (para. 3578).
[25] (Can. 1980), 1 C.H.R.R. D/233 (Review Tribunal — Gibson).

notion that Human Rights Tribunals have discretion to award or not to award "compensation" by holding that the complainants should be entitled to relief as a matter of right.

The decision of the Review Tribunal in the *Foreman* case confirms the public policy that where a complaint has been made out and a loss has been established, compensation should normally be awarded, in the absence of special circumstances.

Professor Cumming in the case of *Torres v. Royalty Kitchenware Ltd.*[26] has discussed at length the scope and purpose of damages. He makes it abundantly clear that in awarding damages, the trend has shifted from awarding such damages as a punitive measure, to awarding the damages as a form of compensation to the complainant. Professor Frederick Zemans in *Graesser v. Porto*,[27] reaffirmed this fact. Thus, the principle has emerged that the complainant, in addition to damages for loss of earnings, is also entitled to further compensation, based on psychological damages, mental distress and the like. Professor Zemans concluded:

> It would appear beyond dispute that Boards of Inquiry have the power to award damages based on both monetary loss and psychological injury.[28]

(a) *Damages for Loss of Earnings*

As stated earlier, human rights statutes in Canada are neither specific nor clear about the remedies that are available to the victims of human rights violations. In relation to employment situations, however, some human rights statutes provide for an award for lost wages. For example, Alberta's *Individual's Rights Protection Act* authorizes the board of inquiry to award compensation to "the person dealt with contrary to this Act for all or any part of any wages or income lost or expenses incurred by reason of the contravention of this Act."[29] The *Saskatchewan Human Rights Code* also empowers the board to order the employer "to compensate any person injured by that contravention for any or all of the wages and other benefits of which the person so injured was deprived and any expenses incurred by the

---

[26] *Torres v. Royalty Kitchenware Ltd.* (Ont. 1982), 3 C.H.R.R. D/858 (Cumming).
[27] (Ont. 1983), 4 C.H.R.R. D/1569 (Zemans).
[28] *Ibid.*, at D/1574 (para. 13552).
[29] Alberta *Individual's Rights Protection Act*, R.S.A. 1980, c. I-2, s. 31(1)(b)(iv).

person so injured as a result of the contravention".[30] A similar provision for an award of lost wages is found under the federal[31] and Manitoba[32] human rights statutes. The Ontario *Human Rights Code*, however, does not make direct references to an award for back wages. It simply provides that a board may "direct the party to make restitution, including monetary compensation, for loss arising out of the infringement".[33] The lack of clarity and absence of specific provision for a "back pay" award in some Canadian statutes is understandable. Human rights statutes generally prohibit different types of discriminating practices over a wide range of activities, and not only in employment situations. Thus, the boards have been given very broad powers to fashion the remedy according to the circumstances, on a case-to-case basis.

Coutroubis v. Sklavos Printing[34] was the first Canadian case where two female employees were found to have been sexually harassed during their employment. The Board of Inquiry, chaired by Professor Ratushny, in that case established for the first time the principle that a victim of sexual harassment is entitled to loss of earnings due to dismissal or constructive dismissal. This principle has since been followed almost unchallenged in all Canadian jurisdictions. The obligation to establish the entitlement to wage is, of course, on the complainant.[35]

Generally, the victim is entitled to the wages that she lost only for the period of time between when she left the respondent's employment and when she acquired the next job.[36] In *Carignan v. Master Craft Publications*, the Board of Inquiry held that "the complainant should be compensated for her loss of earnings for a four-week period after she quit her job".[37] On the other hand, in *Irving v. Medland*, the Board of Adjudication, while awarding the wages for only ten days, stated: "While I am satisfied had this incident not occurred, she would have done some additional work for Medland, in light of the uncertainties involved, I am only prepared to award

---

[30] *Saskatchewan Human Rights Code*, S.S. 1979, c. S-24.1, s. 31(7)(c).
[31] *Canadian Human Rights Act*, R.S.C. 1985, c. H-6, s. 53(2)(c).
[32] Manitoba *Human Rights Code*, S.M. 1987, c. 45, s. 43(2)(b).
[33] Ontario *Human Rights Code*, R.S.O. 1990, c. H.19, s. 41(1)(b).
[34] (Ont. 1981), 2 C.H.R.R. D/457 (Ratushny).
[35] See for example *Irving v. Medland* (Man. 1985), 6 C.H.R.R. D/2842 (Leland Berg).
[36] See for example *Deisting v. Dollar Pizza (1978) Ltd.* (Alta. 1982), 3 C.H.R.R. D/898 at D/901 (para. 7988) (Clarke).
[37] (B.C. 1984), 5 C.H.R.R. D/2282 at D/2284 (para. 19250) (Rankin).

ten days salary."[38] In calculating the loss of wages, the boards of inquiry normally take into account the fringe benefits, such as tips to waitresses, and include that into a total loss of wages.[39]

However, a victim of sexual harassment would not be entitled to lost wages if her dismissal was non-discriminatory and *bona fide*.[40] In such cases, a victim would be entitled to damages only for mental anguish, humiliation, and loss of self-respect[41] caused by sexual harassment. For example in *Langevin v. Engineered Air Division of Air Tex Industry*, the Tribunal found that the respondent's conduct created an intimidating, hostile and offensive working environment for the complainant.[42] However, it found that her dismissal was not due to sexual harassment. Indeed, the complainant "agreed, under oath, that her performance as a secretary typist was poor and that she accepted the dismissal as fair".[43] The Tribunal, under these circumstances, did not make an award for lost wages but awarded her $2,000 as compensation for the humiliation and injury to feelings of self-respect.[44]

It is clear from the earlier discussion that a victim of sexual harassment is entitled to be reimbursed for the loss of earnings caused by the employer's discriminatory practices. However, in awarding "back pay", one must look to the efforts of the complainant to mitigate his or her losses. That is, after dismissal or termination of employment, a complainant has an obligation to seek other employment and thereby reduce her loss. The scope of this obligation was discussed in the *Torres* case, where Professor Cumming stated:

---

[38] (Man. 1985), 6 C.H.R.R. D/2842 at D/2847 (para. 23255 (Leland Berg).

[39] See for example *Janzen v. Platy Enterprises* (Man. 1985), 6 C.H.R.R. D/2735 (Henteleff); revd in part (Man. 1986), 7 C.H.R.R. D/3309 (Q.B.); revd (Man. 1986), 8 C.H.R.R. D/3831 (C.A.), a decision quashed by the Supreme Court of Canada (Man. 1989), 10 C.H.R.R. D/6205.

[40] See for example *Langevin v. Engineered Air Division of Air Tex Industry Ltd.* (B.C. 1985), 6 C.H.R.R. D/2552 (Powell).

[41] *Ibid.*

[42] (B.C. 1985), 6 C.H.R.R. D/2552 at D/2555 (para. 21164) (Powell).

[43] *Ibid.*, at D/2556 (para. 21165).

[44] *Ibid.* (para. 21169) See also *Ives v. Palfy* (B.C. 1990), 12 C.H.R.R. D/483 (Joe). The Tribunal, after awarding the amount of $2,000 as a compensation for humiliation, refused to award compensation for lost wages: "I am not convinced that sexual harassment was a factor in the complainant's loss of employment". See also *Button v. Westsea Construction Ltd.* (B.C. 1991), 13 C.H.R.R. D/1 (Powell) and *Duncan v. Afoakwah* (B.C. 1991), 13 C.H.R.R. D/9 (Barr).

Thus, the duty to mitigate is a duty to act reasonably. It will be a question of fact in each case as to whether a complainant made reasonable efforts to reduce his or her losses.[45]

The loss of earnings is usually to be measure by the wages the person would have earned for the period they were improperly denied to him or her, subject, however, to a recognized duty and responsibility reposed in the employee to mitigate, as far as reasonable, the amount of the loss. In *Coutroubis v. Sklavos Printing*, the Board of Inquiry, while awarding the "back pay" to the complainants recognized their efforts to mitigate the loss and stated: "Both Complainants appear to have done everything possible to mitigate their damages including the acceptance of unskilled employment at the extremely low wage of $1.50 per hour".[46] No doubt the rule of "mitigating damages" is well-established in industrial jurisprudence; however, it may not be advisable to apply it rigidly in all sexual harassment situations. Sexual harassment may often (depending upon its nature and severity) cause physical, emotional and psychological distress to such an extent that it may even impair the victim's ability to work for some time. The boards should take this into account while assessing damages in sexual harassment cases.

The complainant in addition to "back pay" may also be entitled to other employment benefits, such as wage increases, pensions, etc. In *Gadowsky v. Two Hills, No. 21 School Committee*[47] the board stated:

> In my view [the complainant] is entitled to be put in the position she would have enjoyed were it not for the actions of the school authority concerned.

The complainant in *Gadowsky* had been dismissed from her employment as a school teacher because of her age. Included in the calculation of special damages were the complainant's lost wages and *pension benefits*. The Board found that the complainant had done everything reasonable to mitigate her losses by undertaking substitute teaching. Even so, the total amount of special damages awarded to the complainant was $72,518.38.

In most cases, boards take great care in calculating the actual amount of a complainants loss. In *Rajput v. Algoma University College*,[48]

---

[45] *Torres v. Royalty Kitchenware, supra*, note 26, at D/871 (para. 7742).
[46] *Coutroubis v. Sklavos Printing, supra*, note 34, D/458 (para. 4140).
[47] (Alta. Bd. of Inquiry 1979), unreported (McLaren), affd 1 C.H.R.R. D/184 (Alta. Q.B.).
[48] (Ont. Bd. of Inquiry 1976), unreported (Tarnopolsky).

the complainant had been denied employment as a lecturer in sociology because of his national origin. The Board of Inquiry awarded the complainant damages for six months' lost wages, including pay increases over that period given to other lecturers. The board then considered the complainant's possible future losses:

> Because of the fact that it is now getting late to apply anywhere else for the following academic year, and because of the fact the Dr. Rajput has been placed in this position because of action of the respondents, *I feel he must have assurance for a further academic year of the salary he would have received for the 1976-77 year* if he had been appointed to the probationary position in July, 1975. Therefore, if he fails to get an academic appointment for next year, which would yield the same salary, after taxes, and if he can satisfy the Ontario Human Rights Commission that he made all reasonable efforts to get such an appointment, he is to be compensated for the difference.[49] [Emphasis added]

The same principle should be applied to sexual harassment cases. On this basis, a complainant should also be entitled to damages caused by a denial of promotion or a demotion to a lower paying classification. However, it is not clear if, and how, a board would calculate such losses of earnings in its award.

(b) Damages for Loss of Job Opportunity

The question often arises whether or not a complainant should also be awarded damages for the loss of an opportunity (a chance) for employment. It may be stated that under the common law a plaintiff is entitled to loss of chance damages. These common law principles have also been extended to human rights cases.

In *Dantu v. North Vancouver District Fire Department*,[50] it was held that where the parties seeking damages can show that something of real value was lost and that there was a reasonable possibility that opportunity would have produced the financial award associated with it, damages can be awarded to the complainant for loss of a chance. However, it is not necessary that the parties seeking damages must

---

[49] *Ibid.*, at 26. In *Gervais v. Agriculture Canada* (Can. 1988), 9 C.H.R.R. D/5002 (Review Tribunal — Fleck), along with the compensation for lost wages and injury to self-respect, the complainant was also awarded sick leave benefits. See also *Burridge v. Katsiris* (Sask. 1990), 11 C.H.R.R. D/427 (Katzman), where holiday pay in the amount of $227 was also awarded.

[50] (B.C. 1986), 8 C.H.R.R. D/3649 (Elliot).

show that there was a better than 50 per cent chance of producing the desired result. Damages have been awarded for lost opportunities even where the chance of success was less than 50 per cent.

However, in the *Dantu* case the B.C. Human Rights Council stated that damages for lost opportunity would only be granted provided it was satisfied that there was a reasonable possibility that Dantu would have been hired by the North Vancouver District Fire Department had he not been rejected because of his height. The Council in that case was not satisfied that there was a *reasonable possibility* and therefore no damages were awarded for lost opportunity.

A similar view was taken by the Saskatchewan Board of Inquiry in *Friesen v. Regina (City) Commissioners of Police*.[51] The Board accepted in principle the complainant's right to claim damages for lost opportunity, but denied them to the complainant in that case and stated:

> In considering the evidence as a whole, the Board is not satisfied that there was a reasonable possibility that Mr. Friesen would have been hired by the police department if it had not been for the act of discrimination. The Board cannot, therefore, order an award of damages for lost opportunity.[52]

So far, there is no sexual harassment case where damages for lost opportunity have been awarded. However, there is no reason why this principle should not be applied to sexual harassment cases. For example in cases such as *Mitchell v. Traveller Inn (Sudbury) Ltd.*,[53] *Ross v. Gendall*,[54] and *Elmore v. Today's Market Line (1987) Inc.*,[55] there was a reasonable possibility that the complainants would have been hired by the respective employers, had it not been for the acts of sexual harassment during the interviews or shortly thereafter.

2. Determination of Loss of Earnings

(a) Do Earnings Include Indirect Benefits?

Generally, an award for loss of earning includes the loss of employment benefits (fringe benefits) which an employee would have

---

[51] (Sask. 1991), 13 C.H.R.R. D/22(Sproule).
[52] *Ibid.*, at D/16 (para. 42).
[53] (Ont. 1981), 2 C.H.R.R. D/590 (Kerr).
[54] (Sask. 1989), 10 C.H.R.R. D/5836 (Piche).
[55] (B.C. 1989), 10 C.H.R.R. D/5861 (Hughes).

received, had she been in the employment during this period. An interesting question arises whether a complainant is entitled to claim unemployment insurance benefits, which she would have been entitled to, had she been employed by the respondent employer.

The complainant in *Attorney General (Canada) v. McAlpine*[56] had received an offer of employment from the respondent on May 22, 1985. The offer was, however, subject to a policy in force at the time prohibiting a person while pregnant from being engaged in employment. Predictably, when it was discovered that the complainant was pregnant, the offer of employment was withdrawn. The complainant was successful in establishing discrimination. In respect of damages, it was argued by counsel for the complainant that had there been no discriminatory policy in that the complainant would have worked for 14 weeks before taking maternity leave; that only 10 weeks were necessary to qualify for unemployment insurance benefits, and that she therefore would have received these benefits from January 27, 1986 to June 7, 1986. It was argued that since the employer's policy had caused the result, the respondent should pay the equivalent to the benefits lost to the complainant. A Canadian Human Rights Tribunal accepted this argument and awarded the complainant the sum of $4,692 in compensation.

However, the Federal Court of Appeal reversed the decision of the Canadian Human Rights Tribunal on the ground that the Act allows the Tribunal to compensate the victim of discrimination only for loss of wages, expenses incurred, and the "cost of obtaining alternative goods, services, facilities or accommodation"; and unemployment insurance benefits did not fit within any of these categories. The court further stated that "wages" are the antithesis of unemployment insurance benefits; wages are payments for services rendered, whereas unemployment insurance benefits are payment because services are not being rendered.

In other words, the court is saying that unemployment insurance benefits are neither "wages" nor "earnings", so the tribunals cannot allow the complainant unemployment insurance benefits in the claim of loss of earnings. By the same token, the question arises, if a complainant receives unemployment insurance benefits during her unemployment (now an employee who quits her job due to sexual harassment is entitled to U.I. benefits), would the tribunal order that the U.I. benefits be deducted from the amount of back-pay award?

---

[56] [1989] 3 F.C. 530 (C.A.).

Even if the tribunal does not order the employer to deduct U.I. benefits from the damage award, there is no doubt that the Unemployment Insurance Commission would demand that the amount of U.I. benefits be returned.

The tribunals and Unemployment Insurance Commission can justify the deduction of unemployment insurance benefits from the loss of earnings award on the common law principle of not compensating the injured party for more than actual loss.

(b) Deduction of Welfare Benefits

A significant question arises as to whether the welfare benefits (or social assistance payments) received by the complainant during her unemployment (caused by sexual harassment) can be deducted from the award of lost wages. In *Anthony v. B.C. (Council of Human Rights)*,[57] the B.C. Human Rights Council found that the complainant was sexually harassed by her employer. The employer was ordered to pay her $1,250 in compensation for the loss of dignity she suffered as a consequence of the sexual harassment. He was also ordered to compensate her for the wages she lost during the five and one half months period before she found another job.

The Council determined that she would have earned $4,400 had she remained employed, but that she had earned $200 from part-time work and had received $3,200 in social assistance payments. The Council characterized the social assistance payments as income received from other sources and deducted them from the amount of the award. The Council decided to compensate the complainant only for her "actual loss".

On appeal, the B.C. Supreme Court quashed the decision of the Council and held that the Legislature give no indication that it intended compensation under the Human Rights Act to be calculated otherwise than in accordance with principles which have been long accepted and acted upon when awarding damages for pecuniary loss at common law. The court stated:

> It has never been the policy of the common law, except within the narrow confines of the recognized grounds for punitive damages, *to award damages for the purpose of punishing the wrongdoer.* Nor has it been the function of

---

[57] (B.C. 1990), 11 C.H.R.R. D/58 (S.C.).

damages at common law, except again within the realm of punitive damages, *to compensate the injured party for more than his or her actual loss.*[58] [Emphasis added]

The court stated that the B.C. Human Rights Council intended to award full compensation to the complainant but it erred in applying the legal principles by which such compensation was calculated. The court concluded:

> I am bound to conclude that the member designate erred in law when she characterized the social assistance payments received by the petitioner, during the five-and-one-half months she was unemployed, as "income received from other sources" and deducted the amount of such payments from the compensation which she ordered the respondent Wolfe to pay to the petitioner under s. 17(2)(b)(ii) of the Act.[59]

IT follows then that welfare benefits or social assistance payments are not an income for the purposes of calculating lost earnings. Thus, welfare or similar kind of benefits would not be deducted from the back-pay award. The decision supports the secondary objective of the damage award, i.e., in compensating the victim, it is also a goal to deter wrongdoers from future acts of discrimination. The complainants, however, would still be required to return the unemployment insurance benefits payments, though U.I. benefits are also not an earned income.

(c) *Damages for Loss of Dignity and Humiliation*

It is clearly recognized in all jurisdictions in Canada that a sexual harassment victim is not only entitled to damages for loss of earnings but also for humiliation and loss of dignity. Section 53(3)(b) of *Canadian Human Rights Act* specifically provides that if the tribunal finds that "the victim of the discriminatory practice has suffered in respect of feelings or self-respect as a result of the practice, the Tribunal may order the person to pay such compensation to the victim, not exceeding five thousand dollars, as the Tribunal may determine". Similar provision is found in s. 31(8) of the *Saskatchewan Human Rights Code*. However, it is difficult to lay out a uniform standard for awarding general damages for sexual harassment. The nature or severity of

---

[58] *Ibid.*, at D/59 (para. 7).
[59] *Ibid.*, at D/60 (para. 10).

sexual harassment differs from case to case. Thus, the quantum of damages will ultimately depend upon the nature of the harassment, the degree of physical assault, and mental and physical health of the complainant. Thus, the determination of general damages in sexual harassment cases is not an easy task. While it is not easy to do, in fairness to the complainant, the board must estimate what appears to be fair in the circumstances.

In determining the amount, it is helpful to look at previous decisions. As Professor Cumming stated in the *Torres* case:

> Although the nature of the harassment in individual cases will be the ultimate determinant of the quantum of damages, consideration should be given to awards made in previous cases.[60]

In *Coutroubis v. Sklavos Printing*,[61] the Board, in awarding the complainants $750 each as general damages, stated:

> Once more, this Board is of the view that such an award is reasonable and, if anything, counsel for the Commission exhibited an appropriate restraint in suggesting this figure. The Complainant Coutroubis was a 17 year old girl at the time of the incident and the Respondent was old enough to be her father. While the complainant Kekatos may not have been as vulnerable, the attack upon her was more physically aggressive. The evidence indicates that the incidents have had a severe and lasting effect upon the Complainants up to the present time.[62]

A large monetary award in the form of general damages is justified in the cases of harassment because of the ongoing nature of the wrong done to the complainants through the period of harassment. In cases of sexual harassment involving physical contact, the appropriateness of sizeable awards becomes even more apparent when it is recognized that each such contact contributes a trespass to the person. The reasoning of trespass to the person emphasizes the seriousness of the wrong suffered by the complainant, even though the tribunals may not actually assess damages of such a trespass to the person.[63]

---

[60] *Torres v. Royalty Kitchenware* (Ont. 1982), 3 C.H.R.R. D/858 at D/872 (para. 7749) (Cumming).
[61] (Ont. 1981) 2 C.H.R.R. D/457 (Ratushny).
[62] *Ibid.*, at D/458 (para. 4141).
[63] See *Hughes v. Dollar Snack Bar* (Ont. 1982), 3 C.H.R.R. D/1014 (Kerr).

In *McPherson v. Mary's Donuts*,[64] Professor Cumming, while awarding $2,500 for general damages in compensation for injury to the dignity and feelings of one of the complainants, pointed out:

> This award of $2500.00 for general damages in compensation for injury to dignity and feelings is considerably higher than previous awards in sexual harassment cases, referred to above. However, the harassment of Ms. Ambo was a flagrant case of harassment and a correspondingly flagrant breach of the *Code*. Her employer, the individual Respondent, gave her the choice of submitting to his sexual advances, or being humiliated by his comments in front of customers, or returning to jail. She was under considerable mental anguish and suffering at the time because of her conviction and sentencing.[65]

In *Kotyk v. Canadian Employment and Immigration Commission*,[66] the Tribunal in assessing the damages against the perpetrator reviewed the circumstances and observed:

> It is clear from the evidence that Jane Kotyk had suffered in respect of hurt feelings and particularly in terms of self-respect. I have recounted instances in Ms. Kotyk's testimony where she described her feelings while these incidents were taking place and after they occurred. I have described the conduct as being persistent, overwhelming, deliberate and demeaning. It was conduct carried out in the face of constant refusals. It must have been known to be unwelcome.[67]

The Tribunal awarded damages in the amount of $2,500 against the perpetrator and the same amount against the Canadian Employment and Immigration Commission.

In *Janzen v. Platy Enterprises*, the Board of Inquiry while awarding damages for humiliation and loss of self-respect, pointed out that "the cumulative effect of the harassment had a substantial psychological impact upon her and she suffered damages in respect of feelings and self-respect."[68] The victim's right to obtain damages for a "poisonous work environment" and for humiliation and loss of self-respect has been recognized by now in almost all Canadian jurisdictions.[69]

---

[64] (Ont. 1982), 3 C.H.R.R. D/961 (Cumming).
[65] *Ibid.*, at D/965 (para. 8583).
[66] (Can. 1983), 4 C.H.R.R. D/1416 (Ashley).
[67] *Ibid.*, at D/1431 (para. 12258).
[68] (Man. 1985), 6 C.H.R.R. D/2735 at D/2771 (para. 22676) (Henteleff); revd (Man. 1986), 8 C.H.R.R. D/3831 (C.A.), a decision quashed by the Supreme Court of Canada (Man. 1989), 10 C.H.R.R. D/6205.
[69] See for example *Zarankin v. Johnstone* (B.C. 1984), 5 C.H.R.R. D/2274 (Smith); *Langevin v. Engineered Air Division of Air Tex Industries Ltd.* (B.C. 1985), 6 C.H.R.R.

In *Deisting v. Dollar Pizza (1978) Ltd.*,[70] in view of the severity of the sexual harassment that had occurred, the Board of Inquiry awarded the victim $1,000 in damages for injured feelings and humiliation. In addition the board awarded $500 for the treatment of psychological injury. The board stated that "a further award of $500 should be made to assist the Complainant in taking the treatment required to deal with that injury."[71] The board made the award for damages jointly and severally against the individual and corporate respondent.

However, in *Mitchell v. Traveller Inn (Sudbury) Ltd.*,[72] the Board refused to award substantial damages ($750) because the complainant did not suffer any significant physical assault. Although this case involved sexual harassment, the injury suffered by the complainant was more in the nature of that suffered by other individuals who were denied employment on discriminatory grounds. The Board held that "there is no basis for a larger award for injured feelings than $100."[73] Recently in *Piazza v. Airport Taxi Cab (Malton) Assn.*,[74] while awarding only $250 as general damages the Board of Inquiry observed:

> The incidents of harassment did not, in my opinion, have a significant effect on the Complainant; she was offended at most. The evidence does not indicated that the Complainant has been left emotionally scarred by these events.[75]

The Boards of Inquiry by now have developed a norm that a victim of sexual harassment is entitled to general damages for the intimidating, hostile and offensive work environment suffered because of the discrimination towards the victim. The quantum of damages depend upon the nature and circumstances of the sexual harassment in each particular case. Generally, in awarding general damages the Boards of Inquiry take into consideration the following factors:[76]

D/2252 (Powell); *Phillips v. Hermiz* (Sask. 1984), 5 C.H.R.R. D/2450 (Katzman); *Irving v. Medland* (Man. 1985), 6 C.H.R.R. D/2842 (Leland Berg); *Webb v. Cyprus Pizza* (B.C. 1985), 6 C.H.R.R. D/2794 (Wilson); *Fields v. Willie Rendezous Inc.* (B.C. 1985), 6 C.H.R.R. D/3074 (Powell).

[70] (Alta. 1982), 3 C.H.R.R. D/898(Clarke).
[71] *Ibid*, at D/901 (para. 7990).
[72] (Ont. 1981), 2 C.H.R.R. D/590 (Kerr).
[73] *Ibid.*, at D/592 (para. 5407).
[74] (Ont. 1986), 7 C.H.R.R. D/3196 (Zemans).
[75] *Ibid*, at D/3202 (para. 25599).
[76] These factors were first enumerated by Professor Peter Cumming in *Torres v. Royalty Kitchenware Ltd., supra*, note 60, at 873. These factors are frequently considered

1. the nature of the harassment, that is, was it simply verbal or was it physical as well?
2. the degree of aggressiveness and physical contact in the harassment;
3. the ongoing nature, that is, the time period of the harassment;
4. the frequency of the harassment;
5. the age of the victim;
6. the vulnerability of the victim; and
7. the psychological impact of the harassment upon the victim.

(d) Punitive Damages

The Manitoba *Human Rights Code* is the only Canadian human rights statute that expressly allows for an award of punitive damages. Section 43(2)(d) of the Code empowers the adjudicator to order the party to

> pay any party adversely affected by the contravention a penalty or exemplary damages in such amount, subject to subsection 3, as the adjudicator considers just and appropriate as punishment for any malice or recklessness involved in the contravention.[77]

Thus, a board in Manitoba may impose a penalty upon a wrongdoer where there has been an injury to feelings. Presumably, the phrase "or exemplary damages" in the Manitoba Act allows punitive damages in compensation for injury to feelings and self-respect.

In *Irving v. Medland*,[78] a Manitoba board adjudication specifically emphasized the significance of punitive damages and stated that "a small portion of the award [was] to be considered punitive". The Board explained that "conduct of the nature described (sexual harassment) in the workplace, cannot be tolerated, and often some form of penalty is the only way of reinforcing societal displeasure with such action. I might indicate, however, that had I thought the respondent's actions were entirely premeditated, rather than being in large part an offshoot

---

and followed by other Boards of Inquiry in different jurisdictions. See for example *Graesser v. Porto* (Ont. 1983), 4 C.H.R.R. D/1569 (Zemans); *Janzen v. Platy Enterprises, supra,* note 68; *Irving v. Medland* (Man. 1985), 6 C.H.R.R. D/2842 (Leland Berg); *Phillips v. Hermiz* (Sask. 1984), 5 C.H.R.R. D/2450 (Katzman); *Piazza v. Airport Taxi Cab (Malton) Assn.* (Ont. 1986), *supra,* note 74.

[77] The Manitoba *Human Rights Code,* S.M. 1987, c. 45.
[78] (Man. 1985), 6 C.H.R.R. D/2842 (Leland Berg).

of a serious alcohol problem, the punitive nature of the award would have been increased."[79]

In Ontario, the Board of Inquiry in *Gabbidon v. S. Golas*[80] held that punitive damages cannot be awarded under the *Code* because: (a) the empowering section refers only to "compensation"; and (b) a punishment provision is contained in Part IV of the *Code*, which accordingly implies that punishment is beyond the sphere of the board's powers. In *Torres v. Royalty Kitchenware*,[81] Professor Cumming stated that punitive damages certainly should not generally be awarded but was not "a proper interpretation of the *Code* to say that they *never* can be awarded". He stated:

> *In certain cases, it may be highly instructive for a respondent to face the paying of a penalty.* If the Board is of the opinion that no other order could be so effective as to encourage future compliance with the *Code* as a punitive order, then I believe than an order of punitive damages might be proper. Such an award would be consistent with the eductive purposes of the *Code*. It must be pointed out though, that such an award should have as its sold purpose the prevention of future breaches of the *Code*. That is, *the penalty should be made only to effect deterrence, not to denounce the act or wrongdoer, nor to exact retribution.* Any aim other than "full compliance" with the *Code*, i.e. deterrence from future breaches, would certainly be, in my opinion, beyond the powers of a Board of Inquiry.
>
> Even if this interpretation is correct, punitive awards would be very rarely made. For most respondents, the mere participation in inquiry proceedings or the awarding of compensatory damages alone will have a deterrent effect. Only where a Board is of the opinion that a greater deterrent is needed would punitive damages be necessary. One can speculate that this might be true in some sexual harassment cases. However, I find in any event the situation posed in the Inquiry presently before does not suggest that an exceptional punitive award be considered.[82] [Emphasis added]

In *Olarte v. Commodore Business Machines*,[83] Professor Cumming again refused to award punitive damages on the ground that it would amount to an act of vengeance. He concluded:

> The individual Respondent is faced with a very sizeable award against him in the form of compensation due to the six Complainants. Mr. DeFilippis

---

[79] *Ibid*, at D/2848 (para. 23260).
[80] (Ont. Bd. of Inquiry 1973), unreported (Lederman).
[81] *Torres v. Royalty Kitchenware, supra*, note 60.
[82] *Ibid.*, at D/870 (paras. 7730-31).
[83] (Ont. 1983), 4 C.H.R.R. D/1705 (Cumming).

has been made subject to the scrutiny of the community by the very close coverage in the media of these proceedings. He and his family have undoubtedly suffered a great deal of embarrassment in public at the most extraordinary revelations during the hearing. His relationship with his employer has most certainly been compromised and perhaps placed in jeopardy.

Mr. DeFilippis continues to profess his innocence. He shows no remorse for his victims, and at most feels sorry for himself in terms of the predicament he has found himself in. However, the awarding of *more* than compensatory damages would not add to the deterrent effect of the proceedings itself, my findings and the award of compensation. *A punitive award as suggested by Commission counsel would only introduce an element of retribution, an act of vengeance. A main purpose of a Board of Inquiry (or any tribunal or court adjudicating rights) is to provide a forum for the peaceful resolution of a dispute and thereby prevent or lessen the possibility of acts of private vengeance.* It would pervert the purpose of the Tribunal to seek it to become an instrument of vengeance. Moreover, to make an order to further a desire for vengeance would, quite clearly, be beyond the jurisdiction of a board of inquiry.[84] [Emphasis added]

Thus, tribunals are divided whether or not a sexual harassment victim should be entitled to punitive damages. The boards and tribunals have begun to increase the amount of "general damages" for emotional distress, humiliation and injury to self-respect. However, the maximum compensation allowed for general damages in the statute and awarded by the tribunals in Canada is still very insignificant in view of the economic hardships and ordeal (prior to and during the trial) the complainants have to go through. Moreover, the amount of the general damages is so meagre that it could hardly provide any deterrent or incentive to the employers for combatting sexual harassment.

(e) *Interest on Compensatory Damages*

There is no provision with respect to the payment of interest on compensatory awards made by a Board of Inquiry or a Tribunal either in provincial or federal human rights legislation.

However, there have been discrimination cases in which interest on the amount of compensation has been awarded. In *A-G. Alta. v. Gares*,[85] where the court found that the hospital was paying its nurses' aides lower wages for doing the same work as nursing orderlies, the hospital was ordered to pay the difference in pay retroactive to the

---

[84] *Ibid.*, at D/1748 (paras. 14901-14902).
[85] (1976), 67 D.L.R. (3d) 635 (Alta. S.C.).

date of the complaint. It was also ordered by the court to pay interest of 6 per cent on the difference in rates of pay from the time of each monthly payment of wages from the date the complaints were filed until the date of the order. Where the facts were similar, in *Civil Services Assn. of Alta. v. Foothills Provincial General Hospital*,[86] the Board of Inquiry followed *Gares*, awarding the interest on the same terms.

In Quebec, where human rights cases are heard by a Provincial Court Judge, interest is awarded from the date the writ was served. In *Larouche v. Emergency Car Rental*,[87] where there was sex discrimination in a car rental and in *Aronoff v. Hawryluk*,[88] where there was a denial of rental accommodation because of marital status, the Provincial Court judge awarded interest on compensatory damages in both the cases.

In Ontario the *Human Rights Code* provides that a board may make an order "to make compensation" for an injury to a complainant. The notion of "compensation", according to the Boards of Inquiry in Ontario, includes an interest value component for the period of time from the date of notification of the injury to the date of the order of compensation being made by the Tribunal. Further, the boards of inquiry seem to have taken a lead from the Ontario *Courts of Justice Act*[89] to award interest. The *Courts of Justice Act* sets forth the requirement and standards for the determination of interest in civil actions, and provides that a judgment bears interest at the prime rate from the date of judgment.[90] In *Olarte v. Commodore Business Machines*,[91] Professor Cumming suggested that the provisions in the *Judicature Act*, "should serve as the standard for the purpose of calculating interest in a human rights action".

Subsequently, in a non-sexual harassment case, *Mears v. Ont. Hydro*,[92] Professor Zemans followed the reasoning in *Commodore*, and allowed interest on the amount of the award. A B.C. Board of Inquiry in *Carignan v. Master Craft Publications*[93] followed the Ontario decisions in *Mears* and *Commodore* and allowed interest on the amount of compensation awarded.

---

[86] (Alta. Bd. of Inquiry 1977), unreported (Hill).
[87] (Que. 1980), 1 C.H.R.R. D/119 (Prov. Ct.).
[88] (Que. 1981), 2 C.H.R.R. D/534 (Prov. Ct.).
[89] R.S.O. 1990, c. C. 43.
[90] *Ibid.*, ss. 36 and 37.
[91] (Ont. 1983), 4 C.H.R.R. D/1705 (Cumming).
[92] (Ont. 1984), 5 C.H.R.R. D/1927 (Cumming).
[93] (B.C. 1984), 5 C.H.R.R. D/2282 (Rankin).

Interest alone in some case may constitute a significant relief for the victim.[94] *Olarte* and *Mears* have paved the way and set the pattern for allowing the interest on the amount of compensatory damages. Other boards and tribunals have followed this lead and awarded interest on the amount of damages as a matter of course.[95]

(f) Legal Costs

There is no uniform law and practice in Canada with regard to the awarding of costs in human rights cases. Statutes in most jurisdictions are silent on this issue. However, the B.C. *Human Rights Code*[96] (before it was repealed in 1983) had, and the Alberta *Individual's Rights Protection Act*[97] has provided that, "A board of inquiry may make any order as to costs that it considers appropriate."[98] Further, in Saskatchewan, Regulations made under the *Saskatchewan Human Rights Code*[99] also provide that "The board may, in its discretion, order costs."[100] Thus, the boards of inquiry in these provinces have awarded costs in appropriate cases.[101]

In the province of Quebec, where human rights cases are tried by a Provincial Court Judge, costs are generally awarded against the

---

[94] In *Gohm v. Domtar Inc. (No. 4)* (Ont. 1990), 12 C.H.R.R. D/161 (Pentney), the Board awarded the interest in the amount of over $22,000 which was approximately one third of the total damages.

[95] See for example *Hall v. Sonap Canada* (Ont. 1989), 10 C.H.R.R. D/6126 (Plaut); *Green v. 709637 Ontario Inc.* (Ont. 1988), 9 C.H.R.R. D/4749 (Plaut); *Cuff v. Gypsy Restaurant* (Ont. 1987), 8 C.H.R.R. D/3972 (Bayefsky); *Gohm v. Domtar Inc. (No. 4)* (Ont. 1990), 12 C.H.R.R. D/161 (Pentney). For the cases where interest was not awarded, see *Burridge v. Katsiris* (Sask. 1989), 11 C.H.R.R. D/427 (Katzman); *Saskatchewan Human Rights Commn. v. Saskatchewan Dept. of Social Services* (Sask. 1989), 10 C.H.R.R. D/6434 (Q.B.).

[96] R.S.B.C. 1979, c. 186, section 17(3) [Act rep. 1984; see now *Human Rights Act, 1984*, S.B.C. 1984, c. 22].

[97] R.S.A. 1980, c. I-2.

[98] *Ibid.*, s. 31(2).

[99] S.S. 1979, c. S-24.1.

[100] Saskatchewan Reg. 216/79 [am. 1979, 258/79], made pursuant to s. 46 of the Saskatchewan *Human Rights Code*, S.S. 1979, c. S-24.1.

[101] See for example *Chelsea v. Sportsman's Motel* (B.C. 1981), 2 C.H.R.R. D/424 (Flood), where the respondent was ordered to pay the costs of the Director of the Human Rights Branch; *Fazal v. Chinook Tours* (Alta. 1981), 2 C.H.R.R. D/472 (McGowan), where the Alberta Board of Inquiry, on dismissing the complaint, ordered the Commission to pay the respondent's costs.

Commission when the complain is dismissed and against the defendant when he is found to have violated the Quebec *Charter of Human Rights and Freedoms*[102] Moreover, when courts decide for judicial review or appeals from boards of inquiry decisions, in human rights cases, they generally award costs to the winning party.[103]

A Human Rights Tribunal in the federal jurisdiction also has the authority to award costs to the complainant in a suitable case. However, the structure of the Act permits an individual who has a complaint to have it prosecuted by competent counsel for the Human Rights Commission without incurring personal expenses. In *Potapczyk v. MacBain*,[104] the complainant's request for legal costs was denied because the Tribunal felt that the complainant in that case could have been adequately represented by the Human Rights Commission's counsel in its "public interest" role. The Tribunal did not feel that a separate counsel for the complainant was necessary to carry the case. In *Cashin v. Can. Broadcasting Corp.*[105] the Tribunal discussed and recognized that a complainant is entitled to legal costs, particularly where the Commission declined to prosecute the complaint of the complainant.

Prior to 1981, the *Ontario Human Rights Code* had stated the board's remedial powers in very general forms which allowed the board to order the party who contravened the Act to make compensation for "any injury caused to any person". This provision has been interpreted to allow the board to make an order that such party pay the Commission's and complainant's costs. In 1970, in *Amber v. Leder*,[106] the Board of Inquiry suggested that in some circumstances it might award a complainant's costs but that, in that case, an award of costs was not appropriate. In *Hadley v. City of Mississauga*,[107] the Board of Inquiry again suggested that costs might be awarded under

---

[102] See for example *Spears v. Antoniadis* (Que. 1980), 1 C.H.R.R. D/188 (Que. Prov. Ct.); *Leclair v. Pacquet* (Que. 1981), 2 C.H.R.R. D/444 (Que. Prov. Ct.); *Aronoff v. Hawryluk, supra*, note 88.

[103] See for example *Can. Football League v. Can. Human Rights Commn.* (Can. 1980), 1 C.H.R.R. D/45, (Fed. Ct.) and *A.-G. Can v. Can. Human Rights Commn.* (Can. 1980), 1 C.H.R.R. D/91 (Fed. Ct.), where motions for prohibition were denied with costs. See also *Ont. Human Rights Commn. et al. v. Borough of Etobicoke* (Ont. 1982), 132 D.L.R. (3d) 14 (S.C.C.), where the appeal was allowed with costs.

[104] (Can. 1984), 5 C.H.R.R. D/2284 (Tribunal — Lederman).

[105] (Can. 1986), 7 C.H.R.R. D/3203 (Tribunal — Ashley).

[106] (Ont. Bd. of Inquiry 1970) unreported, at p. 19 (Tarnopolsky).

[107] (Ont. Bd. of Inquiry 1976) unreported, at pp. 33-34 (Lederman).

s. 19(b) of the old *Code*. However, in *Wan et al. v. Greygo Gardens*,[108] the Board of Inquiry decided that costs cannot be awarded. In that case, one of the complainants had requested that she be reimbursed for the travel expenses to attend the hearing. The Board of Inquiry, while rejecting her claim, stated:

> With respect to Mrs. Chen's claim for train fare, I would observe that this item related to the conduct and not directly to the Respondent's wrongful acts. In ordinary civil litigation it would be regarded as a matter of costs, rather than as part of the claim for damages. *There is no express provision for an award of costs under the Human Rights Code.*[109] [Emphasis added]

Ontario's *Human Rights Code*, which came into force in 1982, expressly permits the board of inquiry to award the respondent costs when it dismisses the complaint. Section 41(4) of the *Code* provides:

Where, upon dismissing a complaint, the board of inquiry finds that,
(a) the complaint was trivial, frivolous, vexatious or made in bad faith; or
(b) in the particular circumstances undue hardship was caused to the person complained against,

the board of inquiry may order the Commission to pay to the person complained against such costs as are fixed by the board.[110]

Surprisingly, the new *Code* does not make any provision for the awarding of costs to the complainants. Subsection 40(1)(b) of the *Code* permits the board to award only the monetary compensation "for loss arising out of the infringement".

In Ontario, no board of inquiry has yet awarded costs to the complainant in a human rights case under the *Human Rights Code*. Some of the boards had earlier expressed the view that they do have the power to award costs to the complainants and the Commission in appropriate circumstances. However, by expressly empowering the board to award costs to the respondent but making no reference to costs to the complainant and the Commission, the new *Code* created further confusion and uncertainty in this regard.

The Ontario Board of Inquiry, however, has awarded costs to the respondents in human rights cases. For example, in *Pham v. Beach Industries Ltd.*,[111] the Ontario Board of Inquiry found that the Ontario

---

[108] (Ont. 1982), 3 C.H.R.R. D/812 (Kerr).
[109] *Ibid.*, at D/816 (para. 7213).
[110] R.S.O. 1990, c. H.19.
[111] (Ont. 1987), 8 C.H.R.R. D/4008 (Hubbard).

Human Rights Commission acted irresponsibly in pursuing this complaint, and awarded costs to the respondents. Chairman Hubbard stated that, in this case, particular undue hardship was caused to the respondents by "bad faith" and the irresponsible way in which the Commission, through its officers and agents, discharged its mandate in respect of this matter. The Board ordered the Commission to pay to the respondents their costs, including actual solicitor's costs and reasonable travel expenses of the respondents, their witnesses and their counsel.[112]

Normally, when the costs are awarded, they are meant to be the legal fees of the counsel only. It appears that the Board in this case went a little too far in awarding the travel costs, not only of the counsel, but also of the respondents and the witnesses.

In *Ouimette v. Lily Cups Ltd.*[113] (a physical disability case), the Ontario Board of Inquiry also awarded costs to the respondents (the employers). In awarding the costs the Board stated:

> This matter, in my view, fully warrants that I exercise my discretion and award costs ... there was an absence of facts necessary to prove the allegations of the complaint. And the Commission was aware of this void at the time of hearing. Further the complaint, itself, was materially deficient in law. While the complaint cannot be found to have been made in bad faith, or to have been vexatious, it was trivial and frivolous.[114]

Although the Board did not specifically mention whether it levied the costs against the Commission or the complainant or both, from its silence it would be safe to assume that the Commission alone was ordered to pay the costs of the respondents.

In *Deisting v. Dollar Pizza (1978) Ltd.*,[115] an Alberta Board of Inquiry, in a sexual harassment case, awarded the costs to both parties. In awarding the costs, the board discussed the criteria as follows:

> Lastly, the Board was asked to consider the matter of costs under the authority granted in Section 31(2) of the Individual's Rights Protection Act. ... This Board is satisfied that the initial day and a half of hearing was occasioned as a result of the failure on the part of the Human Rights Commission to properly bring the complaint. As a result, it is this Board's decision that the costs of

---

[112] *Ibid.*, at D/4024 (para. 31813).
[113] (Ont. 1990), 12 C.H.R.R. D/19 (Baum).
[114] *Ibid.*, at D/34 (para. 72).
[115] (Alta. 1982), 3 C.H.R.R. D/898 (Clarke).

the first two days of hearing should be awarded against the Human Rights Commission and in favour of the Respondents. In that regard, the Board fixes the costs of the Respondent, Dollar Pizza (1978) Ltd. and Nickolakis at the sum of $1000.00 and the Respondent Papaconstantinou at $500.00. With respect to the costs of the final two days of hearings which dealt with the merits of the complaint, this Board finds that costs should be awarded against the Respondents. The costs to be awarded would be those of counsel for the Human Rights Commission which this Board fixes in the amount of $1,500.00.[116]

The British Columbia Boards of Inquiry have also awarded costs in sexual harassment cases. In *Zarankin v. Johnstone*[117] a B.C. Board of Inquiry, while awarding the costs, observed that "the Respondent pay the costs of this hearing, in an amount to be agreed upon between the parties or, failing agreement, in an amount determined by this Board, using costs on a party and party basis under the Supreme Court Rules as an appropriate measure." A similar ruling was made by another B.C. Board of Inquiry in *Carignan v. Master Craft Publications*[118] Thus, it appears that the complainants in British Columbia, Alberta, Saskatchewan and Quebec are entitled to legal costs, whereas in Ontario and other jurisdictions the boards and tribunals still have to make a move in this direction.

(g) Costs Against the Respondent

As stated earlier, only the Ontario *Human Rights Code* specifically permits the Board of Inquiry to award the respondent costs, where the complaint is found to be trivial, frivolous or vexatious or made in bad faith, or caused undue hardship to the respondent. The Code further provides that those costs to be awarded against the Human Rights Commission and not the individual complainant.

However, the Saskatchewan Board of Inquiry in *Lamers v. Pacific Building Maintenance Ltd.*[119] ordered the complainant to pay the costs of the individual respondent (the alleged harasser). The Board found that the comments made by the individual respondent, while inap-

---

[116] *Ibid.*, at D/901 (para. 7991). See also *Splett v. Sum's Family Holdings Ltd.* (Alta. 1991), 13 C.H.R.R. D/119 (McManus), where the Alberta Board of Inquiry awarded the costs against the respondents, jointly and severally, in the sum of $1,000 with respect to the costs of the Commission.
[117] (B.C. 1984), 5 C.H.R.R. D/2274 at D/2282 (para. 19232) (Smith).
[118] (B.C. 1984), 5 C.H.R.R. D/2282 (Rankin).
[119] (Sask. 1991), 91 CLLC 17,014 (Boryski).

propriate, did not constitute sexual harassment. Thus, the complaint was dismissed. (It may be noted that the corporate respondent neither appeared nor answered the complaint). It was the individual respondent, the alleged harasser, who alone defended the complaint. Dealing with the issue of costs the Board stated:

> The final matter which I propose to address is that of costs. Regulation 30(1) of the Saskatchewan Regulations under the *Saskatchewan Human Rights Code* provides that the Board may, in its discretion, order costs. Considering the serious nature of the complaints and the grave consequences which would have followed had the complaints been established and adding to this the fact that any resulting judgment would have been enforceable jointly and severally, George David, although he was not at the time of these proceedings an employee of the Respondent, Pacific Building Maintenance Ltd., was solely burdened with the obligation of defending the action and obviously become liable for the expense of such defence. I am of the opinion that in this particular case it is only just and equitable that the complainant who initiated the proceedings and failed in her claim must bear some responsibility for her action, and I therefore order that Maureen Lamers shall forthwith pay to George David costs, which I set in the sum of $500. In addition thereto since Pacific Building Maintenance Ltd. by failing to appear or answer to the complaints of Miss Lamers effectively forced George David to adopt the responsibility of defending it, and therefore I am of the view that in this case it is equitable that it shares some of the financial burden incurred by Mr. David in defending the claims, and I therefore similarly order that Pacific Building Maintenance Ltd. forthwith pay to George David costs which I set in the sum of $500.[120]

This appears to be the first case in Canada where the complainant has been ordered to pay the costs of the respondent (the alleged harasser). There is no doubt that trivial, frivolous and vexatious complaints should neither be encouraged nor allowed to proceed to adjudication. The normal procedure in dealing with human rights complaints is to have those complaints investigated by the Human Rights Commission. Only if the complaint is found meritorious is the Commission required to proceed further to resolve it through conciliation or mediation. Only if the Commission fails to resolve the complaint to the mutual satisfaction of the parties is the complaint referred for adjudication to the Board of Inquiry.

Thus, if the complaint is in fact trivial, frivolous, vexatious or made in bad faith, it should have been denied by the Commission after its own investigation. If the complaint has reached adjudication,

---

[120] *Ibid.*, at D/243 (para. 24).

it is safe to assume that it has passed the Commission's scrutiny and is not frivolous or vexatious in the Commission's opinion. In these circumstances, if anyone should be liable for the respondent's costs, it should be the Commission and not the complainant.

Moreover, it is a well-recognized fact that the victims of sexual harassment are generally reluctant even to acknowledge their ordeal let alone file a complaint to the Human Rights Commission. The fear of costs further discourages the victims from coming forward and filing a complaint. If this decision is followed by other tribunals, it may lead to an undesirable impact, which may act against public policy and legislative purpose.

3. Reinstatement of the Victim

Reinstatement of a discharged employee amounts to a mandatory order for a specific performance of personal services, and therefore is not recognized at common law. However, under industrial relations jurisprudence, reinstatement of an employee who had been wrongfully discharged is a common remedy. Labour relations boards regularly order the reinstatement of employees who have been discharged for union activities. Similarly, the authority of an arbitrator to reinstate an employee who was unjustly discharged has never been questioned. The situation of a discriminatorily discharged employee does not seem much different.

Human rights statutes in Canada have not provided specifically for the remedy of reinstatement for the discriminatorily discharged employee. Nevertheless, a close examination of the statutory provisions dealing with the remedies leaves no doubt that the legislatures have intended to restore the discharged victim to his/her previous position as though he/she had never been discharged. For example, the Alberta *Individual's Rights Protection Act* provides that a board of inquiry may order the respondent "to place the person discriminated against in the position he/[she] would have been in but for the contravention of this Act."[121] In other jurisdictions, boards of inquiry are empowered as well as obliged to effect "full compliance" or "restitution" or "to rectify an injury". Generally speaking, in a case of discriminatory discharge, this obligation cannot be discharged without directing the respondent employer to reinstate the complainant. Professor Cumming in *Torres*

---

[121] *Individual's Rights Protection Act*, R.S.A. 1980, c. I-2, s. 3(1)(b)(v).

v. Royalty Kitchenware Ltd.[122] admitted that the boards do have the authority to order a reinstatement of a discriminatorily discharged complainant. He said:

> Another type of order that is sometimes made so as to effect "full compliance" (or to "rectify any injury") is reinstatement of an employee who had been discriminatorily dismissed. Such orders are, for obvious reasons, rarely made, yet they are appropriate in some cases where immediate, substantive compliance is desired.[123]

However, as a matter of fact, in human rights cases, the boards of inquiry and tribunals rarely order a reinstatement of an employee who has been discriminatorily dismissed. It is generally believed that a reinstatement, in the circumstances of open bitterness, may not lead to happy and cordial relations between the parties. It is no surprise that the Human Rights Commissions or the complainants have not sought the remedy of reinstatement.

In the *Commodore*[124] case, the Board of Inquiry again denied the remedy of reinstatement and stated:

> Commission counsel sought several other remedies. She asked for reinstatement but on the basis that the Complainants, if they again took positions with Commodore, not be supervised by Mr. DeFilippis. Although there was no indication by any of the Complainants that there is a desire to again work for Commodore, I think the Complainants should have the opportunity of working with Commodore again, if they wish to and if and as there are openings. *However, although I could impose an order for reinstatement I do not think, in the circumstances, that it is either necessary or appropriate. No present employee should be displaced because of any right of reinstatement being extended to the Complainants, if an order were to be made.* [Emphasis added][125]

It is not clear from the board's order whether it refused reinstatement because of bitterness and hostilities or because of fear that it might displace the present employees. If reinstatement was denied mainly for the reason that it would cause displacement of the present employees, it was certainly a serious departure from long-standing precedents in labour-management relations.

---

[122] (Ont. 1982), 3 C.H.R.R. D/858 (Cumming).
[123] *Ibid.*, at D/870 (para. 7727).
[124] (Ont. 1983), 4 C.H.R.R. D/1705 (Cumming).
[125] *Ibid.*, at D/1750 (para. 14924).

However, in a marital status discrimination case *Cashin v. Can. Broadcasting Corp.*[126] it was held that a Human Rights Tribunal under section 41(2)(b) of the *Canadian Human Rights Act* has the authority to order the respondent to rehire a complainant where discrimination has been proved in the same or a similar position. The Human Rights Tribunal ordered the respondent to *rehire the Complainant in her former position or in a similar position at the earliest possible opportunity.*

Similarly, in *Renaud v. School District No. 23 (Central Okanagan)*,[127] the B.C. Human Rights Council ordered the employer to reinstate the complainant in the next available position and ordered both respondents (the employer and the union) to accommodate his religious beliefs.

4. Apology

An apology is not a tangible remedy for the victim. It has only symbolic value. It, however, provides the victim with an emotional and psychological satisfaction. An apology is frequently granted by the courts in cases of tort of defamation.

In human rights cases, particularly in sexual harassment situations, the boards of inquiry usually order the corporate and/or the individual respondent to write a letter of apology to the complainant for the humiliation suffered due to the violation of her human rights.[128] An apology, in addition to its therapeutic value for complainants, makes respondents repent their mistakes and recognize their obligations under the Act. If an apology is taken seriously, it is a step in the right direction. However, a true apology is a voluntary recognition by the respondent of having wronged another person. The Board of Inquiry in *Mitchell*[129] expressed the view that the value of an apology is substantially diminished when it is given under compulsion. The board hoped that the respondent would see fit to give a genuine apology by correcting his behaviour towards the other female employees.

---

[126] *Supra*, note 105.
[127] (B.C. 1987), 8 C.H.R.R. D/4255 (Verbrugge).
[128] See for example *Hufnagel v. Osama Enterprises Ltd.* (Man. 1982), 3 C.H.R.R. D/922 (Teskey).
[129] *Mitchell v. Traveller Inn (Sudbury) Ltd.* (Ont. 1981), 2 C.H.R.R. D/590 (Kerr).

4. Prevention of Future Violations

Boards of inquiry and tribunals in Canada have taken the view that unlike a civil case, they have an obligation to prevent the commission of future violations of human rights, at least by the respondent employer. In *Hartling v. City of Timmins Bd. of Police Commrs.*,[130] Professor Cumming discussed the functional remedies and stated:

> In some cases, especially in Ontario and New Brunswick, Boards have required respondents to carry out certain acts in order to impress upon them the importance of compliance and the severity of violations. Such acts include the sending to the Commissions of letters expressing the respondents' willingness to comply with legislation, sending letters of apology to complainants, posting notices of compliance, etc.[131]

It is obvious that the boards of inquiry in their orders have attempted to educate the affected parties and to implement a structure that might bring about a real change in employment relations. Of course, the ultimate purpose has been to bring about future compliance with human rights statutes.

The tribunals have been concerned with not only providing redress to the complainant but also the prevention of future occurrences of sexual harassment to the complainant (if she is still employed there, although she most likely is not) or to any other female employee in that establishment by that particular harasser or by any other employee. It is possible that the tribunals may have reached the conclusion that the further continuation of the harasser in that employment would be detrimental to the work environment and to the morale of the female employees, but they seldom order the termination of his employment. In fact, it is doubtful whether the tribunals have the authority or power to order a discharge or even a demotion or transfer of the harasser. It is normally believed that the tribunals cannot interfere in the respondent's management functions.

Once the compliance with the law is ordered by the tribunal, it is for the respondent employer to decide how to comply with the tribunal's decision. If the respondent employer fails to do so, he is of course, answerable under the law. However, this does not stop the

---

[130] (Ont. 1981), 2 C.H.R.R. D/487 (Cumming).
[131] *Ibid.*, at D/499 (para. 4537). See also *Dhillon v. F. W. Woolworth Co. Ltd.* (Ont. 1982), 3 C.H.R.R. D/743 (Cumming).

employer from dismissing or disciplining the harasser for the proven misconduct of sexual harassment.[132] In fact, it is advisable for the employer to establish its credibility among its employees that the employer is committed to eradicating sexual harassment from its establishment. If a case is resolved through conciliation, Human Rights Commissions have often recommended that the employer at least remove that harasser from the immediate surroundings, by transferring him to another plant or location.

Further, the employer may be asked to change or alter the physical arrangements of the office in such a way that it discourages the harasser from committing an act of sexual harassment, such as providing glass doors on the harasser's office, so that the harasser's movement may be visible to other employees, or removing the locks from his office. These physical changes no doubt restrict the opportunities for the harasser to have private and intimate personal contact with female employees, but they appear to be more cosmetic than real and their effect in changing the work environment is questionable.

The tribunals, in fact, try to educate the affected parties on the one hand and to implement a structure that might bring about a real change in employment relations on the other. Of course, the ultimate purpose is to bring about such a change as would guarantee future compliance with the statute. Keeping this in mind, the tribunals normally issue a cease and desist order to both the individual and the corporate respondent. It may read:

1. The respondent (employer) shall do whatever is necessary to ensure that the respondent (harasser) cease and desist forthwith in the sexual harassment of its employees.[133]

---

[132] In some cases the employers, indeed, have taken the unilateral action in disciplining the harassers. See for example: *Re City of Nanticoke and C.U.P.E.* (1980), 29 L.A.C. (2d) 64 (Barton); *Re Government of Province of Alta. and Alta. Union of Provincial Employees* (1982), 5 L.A.C. (3d) 268 (Jolliffe); *Libitka v. Treasury Board* (1980), P.S.S.R.B. File No. 166-2-8128 (Ramsay); *Int'l Assn. of Machinists and Aerospace Workers, Loc. 2413 v. Wardair Canada (1975) Ltd.* (1980), unreported (O'Shea); *St. Joseph's Health Centre v. C.U.P.E., Loc. 1144* (1980), unreported (Roberts); and see also *Lewis v. Treasury Bd.* (1983), 4 C.H.R.R. D/1249 (Steward).

[133] See for example *Torres v. Royalty Kitchenware Ltd., supra,* note 122; *McPherson v. Mary's Donuts* (Ont. 1982), 3 C.H.R.R. D/961 (Cumming); *Cox v. Jagbritte Inc.* (Ont. 1982), 3 C.H.R.R. D/609 (Cumming); and *Olarte v. Commodore Business Machines, supra,* note 124.

2. The respondent (harasser) shall cease and desist forthwith in the sexual harassment of the employees who may work under his supervision in the future.[134]
3. The respondent (employer) shall post in a conspicuous place in its reception area, a placard setting out the principles of the *Human Rights Code*.[135]
4. The respondent (employer) shall undertake to establish such policies and practices to ensure that its employees are made aware of the law relating to sexual harassment.[136]

Tribunals, by these orders, intend to ensure that no sexual harassment in future takes place in that establishment.

D. WORKERS' COMPENSATION BENEFITS

It has been well recognized now that sexual harassment in the workplace may cause psychiatric disorder (stress, depression and physical symptoms), making the employee psychologically disabled and unable to perform her job functions.[137]

The question thus arises whether disablement arising from stress due to sexual harassment in the workplace is compensable under the *Workers' Compensation Act*[138]

The Quebec equivalent of the Workers' Compensation Board (hereinafter referred to as W.C.B.) was the first in Canada which, in 1986, recognized that psychological disablement caused by sexual harassment in the workplace is a "work-related injury", and the victim is entitled to compensation under the Act similar to the *Workers' Compensation Act*[139]

The Quebec Health and Safety Commission Review Board outlines four tests for the granting of compensation in matters of disability arising from sexual harassment:

---

[134] See for example *Torres v. Royalty Kitchenware, supra*, note 122; and *Graesser v. Porto* (Ont. 1983), 4 C.H.R.R. D/1569 (Zemans).
[135] See for example *Mitchell v. Traveller Inn (Sudbury) Ltd., supra*, note 129.
[136] See for example *Kotyk v. Canadian Employment and Immigration Commission* (Can. 1983), 4 C.H.R.R. D/1416 at D/1431 (Tribunal — Ashley).
[137] See for example *Deisting v. Dollar Pizza (1978) Ltd.* (Alta. 1982), 3 C.H.R.R. D/898 (Clarke).
[138] R.S.O. 1990, c. W-11.
[139] Decision of the Quebec Health & Safety Commission Review Board, Claim 8518-466 (1986).

1. the absence of any other cause to explain the nervous disorder suffered by the employee;
2. the presence in a workplace of factors capable of promoting the appearance of the said nervous disorders;
3. the medical relationship between the disability and the workplace harassment; and
4. the existence of jurisprudence confirming this relationship and thus incurring *the responsibility of the employer* [Emphasis added]

Thus, the Quebec equivalent of the W.C.B. accepted the concept of poisoned workplace environment giving rise to psychological disablement for which the worker is entitled to compensation. Implicit in the decision is the recognition that the employer is responsible for the consequences of poisoned work environment caused by sexual harassment.

In a 1990 decision, the Ontario W.C.B. for the first time awarded worker's compensation benefits for the psychological disability the victim (a female employee) suffered as a result of sexual harassment in the workplace.[140]

The applicant in this case was one of the two black employees and the only woman working in her department for the employer, Colgate-Palmolive, until she left work in April 1988. She claimed that she had been the victim of racial and sexual harassment leading to psychological disability.

She had worked as a packer, or utility person, and as an operator in a male-dominated department of the employer's plant. For a period of six years, she was subjected to demeaning, insulting and sexually provocative comments and insults by her fellow workers, culminating in one incident where a penis carved out of soap was placed on the assembly line in full view of herself and other employees.

She had, on a number of occasions, requested the management and the union to resolve the matter, but nothing was done. After complaining of the soap incident, she was again told that the matter was not going to get addressed. At this point, she ultimately broke down and had to leave the plant. She sought medical attention. The worker became very depressed and overdosed on medication. Having received psychiatric treatment for a period of time, she made an attempt to return to work six months later but the harassment continued —

---

[140] An objection by "X" Claim 15878672-2 to the Decision of the Review Branch, dated January 25, 1988 — the Decision of the Hearings Officer, J. Kot, of the Workers' Compensation Board, June 29, 1990.

dirty pictures were placed in her work area and removed when other female staff entered the department — and obscene pictures were also put in her tool kit. She ultimately left her job and placed herself under the care of a psychiatrist. She made a second attempt at suicide in April 1988.

The medical evidence disclosed the view that she had had a serious reaction to sexual harassment at the workplace and a lack of support from the union and management, and that her psychiatric difficulties were not due to any prior personality disturbance. Other medical evidence indicated "reactive depression secondary to sexual harassment". Initially her claim for workers' compensation benefits was denied. She appealed and the appeal was heard before a Hearings Officer.

It was argued for the applicant victim that she had suffered a psychological disability which was causally related to her work and she ought to be entitled to benefits under the *Workers' Compensation Act*.

The *Workers' Compensation Act* requires compensable accidents to occur in the course of the employment. Section 3(1) provides:

> Where in any employment, to which this Part applies, personal injury by accident arising out of and in the course of employment is caused to a worker, the worker and the worker's dependants are entitled to benefits in the manner and to the extent provided in the Act.

The Hearings Officer allowed the appeal. He held that the applicant was suffering from a disablement resulting from stress due to sexual harassment. It was determined that a personal injury would also encompass psychic damages disablement. The Hearings Officer concluded that persistent and vexatious harassment imposed upon the applicant led to the applicant's emotional condition. As such, there had been an accident within the meaning of the Act, the disablement was the harassment and, in particular, the penis incident culminated in the applicant's breakdown. The injury was psychological disability and fell within the "spirit and intent" of the W.C.B. guidelines pertaining to psychotraumatic disability.

The Hearings Officer, commenting on the poisoned work environment caused by persistent sexual harassment which may cause abnormal stress and psychiatric disorder, stated:

> At the workplace, the employer has an implicit and explicit responsibility for employee safety, normally enunciated by certain safety practices, and work

practices, that are conducive to a healthy and safe environment. By extension, this also includes the promotion of a work culture that does not condone discrimination or harassment. The *Human Rights Code* of Ontario provides for redress in the event of discrimination or sexual harassment. The Hearings Officer notes that the publication of such a Human Rights Code endorsement in the workplace was not produced by the employer until December 9, 1986, after Ms. X's personal experience.

Upon review of the evidence, the Hearings Officer is satisfied that the persistent and vexatious harassment endured by this worker, and exacerbated particularly by the incident of November 13, 1986, does constitute a significant event. The instances of insult were over and above that which one might expect in a factory setting; over and above what would be expected for *any* employee to endure. Unlike the normal stressors one would associate with work, these actions were intentional and at least performed with a wanton disregard for the consequences that they may have inflicted.[141]

This was a precedent-setting decision, allowing the victim the W.C.B. benefits for psychological disability caused by sexual harassment. By the same token, this decision, in some circles, has been labelled as "the saddest human rights case of the year".[142] The employer is most likely to appeal the decision of the Hearings Officer. How the Workers' Compensation Appeals Tribunal would decide is anybody's guess.

Moreover, the findings that the psychological disability caused by sexual harassment in the workplace is a compensable injury has cost implications for the employer down the road. The fear of increases in W.C.B. levies may provide an additional impetus to the employers for prevention of sexual harassment in the workplace.

In Ontario until recently psychological disabilities caused by workplace stress have been considered not compensable. However, the Workers' Compensation Appeals Tribunal since 1988 has issued a series of decisions which indicate that, in the proper case, claims for work-related stress would be allowed by the Tribunal as compensable.

In the leading case, *Decision No. 918*,[143] the Tribunal confirmed that a mental disability which resulted from stress at work could be compensable. The Panel found that such cases would be compensable as a disablement and not as an industrial disease. The Tribunal enunciated an approach that required either the showing of an unusual

---

[141] *Ibid.*
[142] See *Focus on Canadian Employment and Equity Rights*, Vol. 2, No. 24, p. 190.
[143] (1988), 9 W.C.A.T.R. 48.

stressor, or clear and convincing evidence that the usual stressors of the job predominated in producing the injury.

Decision No. 918 sets out three tests where psychological disability resulting from stress may be compensable:

1. where a psychological disability exists and disables the worker from performing the function of a job;
2. where the disability is work-related; and
3. where the workplace contributed significantly to the development of disability.

On February 23, 1989, the Tribunal issued *Decision No. 1018/87*.[144] The Panel in this case implicitly overruled *Decision No. 918* by rejecting the finding that stress cases should have a higher test than other cases. The Panel found that the appropriate test was whether or not the evidence was persuasive, on a balance of probabilities, that work was a significant contributing factor to the stress disability, as would be done with any other type of disability.

This same standard of evidence was adopted by another Panel in *Decision No. 980/89*,[145] issued on January 17, 1990. The Panel established three simple criteria for adjudicating stress cases:

1. Was there a psychological disability which disabled the worker from performing his job?
2. Was the disability work-related, based on a consideration of whether the stressors in the workplace were usual or unusual, whether other workers were affected, and whether the stressors were typical, expected or unexpected?
3. Did the workplace contribute significantly to the development of the disability, considering the personal situation of the worker and comparing it to the work situation?

On April 3, 1990, the Tribunal issued *Decision No. 145/89*.[146] This was the first stress claim allowed by the Tribunal. This case involved a long-distance truck driver who suffered from "burnout". The Panel adopted the threefold test identified in *Decision No. 980/89*. There was clear evidence of work-related stress, but the Panel's decision

---

[144] (1989), 10 W.C.A.T.R. 82.
[145] (1990), 13 W.C.A.T.R. 304.
[146] (1990), 14 W.C.A.T.R. 74.

depended to a considerable extent on the fact that in this worker's personal life there was no evidence of significant stress.

On September 24, 1990, the Tribunal issued *Decision No. 684/89*.[147] This was the second stress claim allowed by the Tribunal. This decision reviewed the Board's Options and Policy papers and previous WCAT decisions. The Panel in this case also adopted the threefold test identified in *Decision 980/89*, and was also able to come to a decision in the worker's favour because of an absence of non-work-related stress. The Panel found that the work-related stressors were predominant.

In view of these recent W.C.A.T. decisions on work-related disability, it may not be unreasonable to predict that the W.C.A.T. would uphold the Hearings Officer's decision that the victim's psychological disablement was caused by sexual harassment at the workplace and that it was a work-related injury compensable under the Act.

The approval of this decision by the W.C.A.T. is very vital for the wide recognition and development of the principle that psychological disablement caused by sexual harassment is a compensable injury. So far, only Quebec and Ontario have recognized that psychological disability caused by sexual harassment in the workplace is a compensable injury. However, in view of general influence and acceptance of the W.C.A.T. decisions in other provinces, it is not unlikely that the Workers' Compensation Boards in other jurisdictions may follow Ontario's precedent in recognizing that psychological disability caused by sexual harassment in the workplace is a compensable injury.

The victim, however, would be required to establish:

1. that her psychological disability arose "out of and in the course of employment";
2. that she did not have pre-employment psychological disability; and
3. that is was the sexual harassment in the workplace and not the non-job-related actions that were the prime cause of psychological disability.

As we have noted earlier, sexual harassment does not necessarily always take place at the workplace and not necessarily during working hours. This may, indeed, pose a serious difficulty for the victim to

---

[147] (1990), 16 W.C.A.T.R. 132.

establish her psychological disability "out of and in the course of employment".

The Supreme Court of Canada itself, in the famous *Robichaud*[148] case, had recognized that sexual harassment does not necessarily occur only in the course of employment, as would normally be expected. Thus, the Supreme Court, in dealing with vicarious liability, had suggested that the phrase "in the course of employment" should be given a broad interpretation, and should be understood as meaning "work-related". Similarly, in dealing with a victim's claim for psychological disability caused by sexual harassment in the workplace, section 3 of the *Workers' Compensation Act*, particularly the phrase "accident arising out of and in the course of employment" has to be interpreted broadly as suggested by the Supreme Court in *Robichaud v. R.* as meaning "work-related".

F. UNEMPLOYMENT INSURANCE BENEFITS

Victims of sexual harassment most often have no alternative but to quit the job. In the final analysis, most victims cannot tough it out and they succumb to the psychological and physical effects of sexual harassment which include feelings of confusion, self-blame, fear, anxiety, depression, anger, disillusionment, and low self-esteem, etc. When they could not take it any longer, they quit. In other cases, where the victims refuse to cooperate in the sexual adventures of the perpetrator, their employment is terminated on one or the other pretext.

The question thus arises whether the employees who lose their jobs and become unemployed because of sexual harassment in the workplace are eligible for unemployment insurance benefits.

In the United States many states began to allow unemployment compensation to the victims of sexual harassment (i.e., where the worker's separation from employment was caused by sexual harassment) as early as 1979. For example the Michigan Employment Security Commission (Department of Labour) of the State of Michigan, on February 23, 1979, issued a directive to the effect that separation from employment because of sexual harassment should be regarded as a separation for good reasons. It reads as follows:

---

[148] (Can. 1987), 8 C.H.R.R. D/4326 (S.C.C.).

The problem of sexual harassment in the work environment is a growing concern to many workers. Where it results in the worker's separation from employment, the implications of the problem on potential claimant eligibility and qualification for unemployment compensation must be considered. This field release is being distributed as a reminder of the problem and its impact on the claims adjudication process.

With respect to unemployment compensation, if it is found as a matter of fact that an employee (1) voluntarily left a job because of sexual harassment by the employer, supervisor, or co-worker, or (2) was discharged for not affirmatively responding to unwanted sexual advances, or (3) refuses an offer of otherwise suitable work with a former employer because of past sexual harassment, and it is found that such situation still exists, the claimant will not be disqualified or held ineligible, on that basis, from receiving unemployment benefits, if the employer either engaged in, or permitted continuation of, such sexual harassment.

Adjudication of Claims Involving Sexual Harassment

Whenever a claimant indicates some form of sexual harassment as a reason for separation, refusal of work or unavailability, the branch office should carefully question the claimant as to the details of the alleged harassment in order to make an informed (re)determination of the claimant's eligibility and qualification. Likewise, in requesting separation information from the employer, the employer should specifically be asked about the alleged act or acts of sexual harassment rather than a general question as to the reason for separation. Because complaints of sexual harassment are difficult to substantiate, it is important that as much information as is possible be obtained in order to make a proper (re)determination as to eligibility and qualification for benefits.

Although it is important to obtain as much information as possible in such a case, all the details of the sexual harassment need not be set forth in the (re)determination. It should be remembered that the (re)determination may become a public document and unnecessary verbiage concerning the details of the alleged harassment may be embarrassing to the claimant and/or the employer.

Voluntary Leaving

Section 29(1)(a) of the Michigan Employment Security (MES) Act requires the imposition of a disqualification if a claimant has "left work voluntarily without good cause attributable to the employer or employing unit." Although good cause attributable to the employer is not further defined in the MES Act, it has been consistently held in Referee decisions and in decisions of the Board of Review (formerly the Appeal Board) that sexual harassment on the part of the *employer* constitutes good cause attributable to the employer and an individual will not be disqualified for voluntarily leaving employment under such circumstances. Likewise, if an employer had *permitted other employees* to harass the claimant sexually, this too would constitute good cause attributable to the employer for the claimant's voluntary leaving. It order to avoid disqualification, the claimant must demonstrate that sexual harassment had occurred, that he or she informed the employer of such occurrence, that remedial action was requested, and that the situation was not remedied.

Misconduct
In addition, Section 29(1)(b) of the MES Act provides for a disqualification if a claimant was "discharged for misconduct connected with his work." If it is determined that the individual was discharged as a result of failure to respond to sexual advances, such individual shall be regarded under the MES Act as having been discharged for reasons other than misconduct and therefore separated under non-disqualifying circumstances.

Suitable Work
Sections 29(1)(c), (d) and (e) of the MES Act provide for disqualification from benefits in the event that a claimant has, without good cause, (1) failed to apply for available suitable work of which he or she was notified by the branch office, (2) being unemployed, failed to report to his or her former employer within a reasonable amount of time after notice from that employer for an interview concerning available suitable work, or (3) failed to accept suitable work when offered him or her when so directed by the branch office. Sections 28(1)(a) and (c) require that in order to be eligible for benefits, the claimant must seek work and be able and available to perform suitable full-time work. In determining whether work is suitable, Section 29(6) sets out specific guidelines for the Commission to consider, among which is the degree of risk involved to the claimant's health, safety, and *morals*.
An offer of employment with a former employer who has a history of sexually *harassing* that employee or *condoning* such behaviour by other employees could be deemed an offer of "unsuitable" work. As such, a refusal to accept work, apply for work, or return to work with such an employer would not be a disqualifying act. Also, failure to seek work with a former employer with a history of sexual harassment, or restrictions imposed by the claimant as to availability for employment with such employer, would not result in ineligibility for benefits. Such a position would present a risk to his or her health, safety, or *morals*. However, if the offending individual (employer or employee) or circumstance is no longer present at that place of work, such work will not continue to be deemed unsuitable on that basis.

In Canada, prior to the amendment of the *Unemployment Insurance Act* in 1990, victims of sexual harassment were disqualified from unemployment insurance benefits on the ground that they either voluntarily left their employment without "just cause" or they lost their employment by reason of their own misconduct. In any case, the victims themselves were blamed for their misfortune. Consequently, the employee was penalized for fleeing sexual harassment at work. It meant that the Unemployment Insurance Commission had difficulty in accepting that the victims of sexual harassment had a "just cause" to quit their employment to avoid harassment. The Unemployment Insurance Commission was not prepared to accept that sexual harassment fell into the category of "just cause" for voluntary quitting, unless it was provided in the Act.

To provide unemployment insurance benefits to the victims of harassment, it became essential to amend the *Unemployment Insurance Act*. In 1990, the federal government did amend the Act and defined what constitutes "just cause", including sexual harassment in that category.

Section 28 of the *Unemployment Insurance Act*[149] reads as follows:

> 28.(1) A claimant is disqualified from receiving benefits under this Part if he lost his employment by reason of his own misconduct or if he voluntarily left his employment without just cause.
>
> . . .
>
> (4) For the purposes of this section "just cause" for voluntarily leaving an employment exists where, having regard to all the circumstances, including any of the circumstances mentioned in paragraphs (a) to (e), the claimant had no reasonable alternative to immediately leaving the employment:
>
> (a) sexual or other harassment;
> (b) obligation to accompany a spouse or dependent child to another residence;
> (c) discrimination on a prohibited ground of discrimination within the meaning of the *Canadian Human Rights Act*;
> (d) working conditions that constitute a danger to health or safety; and
> (e) obligation to care for a child.

The new *Unemployment Insurance Act* goes beyond the providing of benefits to the victims of sexual harassment. It entitles benefits to all those employees who quit or lost their employment because of

---

[149] R.S.C. 1985, c. U-1 [am. 1990, c. 40, s. 21].

harassment (on any of the prohibited grounds) or other discriminatory practices in the workplace.

This is not a satisfactory solution to sexual harassment but it does provide some economic backing for the victim. This is an encouraging development and strengthens the hands of those who are committed to fighting sexual harassment in the workplace.

CHAPTER 6

*Arbitral Review of Sexual Harassment Cases**

Where a victim is covered by a collective agreement, a complaint against sexual harassment may be launched through the grievance procedure leading to arbitration. The issue of sexual harassment may surface before the arbitrators either directly or indirectly — directly, when a female employee grieves that she was sexually harassed by her supervisor or by a co-worker, and indirectly, when a male harasser files a grievance alleging that the discipline meted out for his sexual misconduct was without just cause. The basic difference between these is that in a direct complaint, the arbitrator is required to determine whether or not the victim was sexually harassed, and if so, what relief can be granted to her. In the second situation, the arbitrator is required to adjudicate whether or not the discipline imposed on the harasser was just and reasonable in the circumstances of that case.

In the second case, only the harasser who is in the bargaining unit can use the arbitration process. Thus, the case of sexual harassment by a supervisor will not surface in arbitration through the indirect process, because normally a supervisor is a part of the management team and is not covered by the collective agreement.[1] However, no matter in what shape or form a grievance may arise, the arbitrator will require an enabling clause in the collective agreement to adjudicate upon sexual harassment issues.

---

* Portions of the following material were originally published in Arjun P. Aggarwal, "Arbitral Review of Sexual Harassment in the Canadian Workplace" (1991), *Arbitration Journal*, Vol. 46, p. 4.

[1] In some cases a supervisor may be a member of the bargaining unit, such as in federal or provincial public service. In those cases, the arbitration process will be available to the supervisor-harasser to grieve his disciplinary penalty, including discharge. However, in a non-union situation or where the perpetrator is not a member of the bargaining unit, his remedies for alleged wrongful dismissal lie in the court of law; see for example the following cases: *Shiels v. Saskatchewan Government Insurance* (1988), 67 Sask. R. 220, 51 D.L.R. (4th) 20, 20 C.C.E.L. 55 (Q.B.) and *Tellier v. Bank of Montreal* (1987), 17 C.C.E.L. 1 (Ont. Dist. Ct.).

Where a male employee complains against the severity of discipline, the grievance falls under the traditional "just cause" clause in the collective agreement, and there is no doubt that it is an arbitrable grievance. However, the question arises whether a complaint by a female employee who alleges that she has been sexually harassed is arbitrable or not. If the collective agreement bans "discrimination" on the grounds prohibited in the human rights statutes or if the parties have agreed in the collective agreement to abide by the provisions of the *Human Rights Code*, the arbitrators have held that the grievance is arbitrable, even though "sexual harassment" has not been specifically prohibited in the collective agreement.[2]

There have been only a handful of cases where female victims of sexual harassment have used the arbitration procedure to remedy their ordeal. On the other hand, there have been more arbitration cases where harassers have challenged the discipline imposed by the employer for their sexual misconduct.[3]

A. GRIEVANCES BY THE VICTIMS

As stated earlier, female victims who alleged sexual harassment by male harassers generally did not use the arbitration process to seek redress. Even if the victims were willing to complain, only a few collective agreements contain an anti-discrimination clause. Moreover, remedies available to the sexual harassment victims under the collective agreement, through the arbitration process, are rather limited. Even if an anti-discrimination clause is present, it is doubtful that an arbitration board can award all the remedies that may be available from a Board of Inquiry or a Human Rights Tribunal. The arbitration board's power and authority is restricted by the provisions in the collective agreement, and legal norms established through the arbitration jurisprudence during the last 30 to 40 years.

---

[2] See for example *Re Seneca College of Applied Arts and Technology and Ontario Public Service Employees Union* (1983), 10 L.A.C. (3d) 315 (Brown).

[3] A study of American cases also supports this finding. See Marcia L. Greenbaum and Bruce Fraser, "Sexual Harassment in the Workplace" (1981), 36 *Arbitration Journal* 30-41. According to that study, only two out of 24 arbitration cases dealing with sexual harassment (between 1965-81) fall in the category of harassment by a supervisor.

In *Re C.U.P.E. and O.P.E.I.U., Loc. 491*[4] the Board of Arbitration came to the conclusion that there was no evidence of sexual harassment and that the grievor's difficulty arose from work habits and personality problems rather than sexual harassment. The board labelled it professional harassment rather than sexual harassment.

In *Richelieu Inn v. Hotel, Restaurant and Cafeteria Employees Union, Loc. 75*,[5] the union had filed a policy grievance alleging that the manager of the housekeeping department of a hotel had sexually harassed several employees of the housekeeping department. The alleged misconduct by the manager included that he "wanted to get it on in the room with (a female employee)" and asked another female employee to go out with him, firing her immediately when she refused. He called other female employees at their homes and gave another woman worker a copy of *Playgirl* magazine, saying she might learn something from it. However, the arbitrator failed to find any causal connection between their refusals and his subsequent treatment of these female employees which was unwarranted. The arbitrator held that the manager's conduct did not amount to sexual harassment. He noted that if unwelcome calls were made in off-duty hours to an employee at home, it possibly would not amount to vexatious conduct.

In *Newfoundland Assn. of Public Employees v. Treasury Board*,[6] the grievor had alleged that the management personnel sexually harassed her by kissing her and touching her breasts. The arbitrator denied the grievance on the ground that the grievor failed to discharge the burden of proof, on a balance of probabilities, that she was sexually harassed.

The Public Service Staff Relations Board, in *Broomfield v. Treasury Board*,[7] denied the grievance of a female employee that she was sexually harassed by her supervisor. The grievor had alleged that her supervisor touched the hair at the back of her neck some 50 times between 1986-87, and he "favoured" her in job assignments, etc. The grievor, however, testified that her supervisor never explicitly, directly or openly mentioned or suggested a sexual liaison. No invitation was offered, no request made, no order given. The grievor felt that the touching of her hair and the alleged comments about her dress were outward manifestations of an inner sexual interest by her supervisor. She filed her grievance (in 1988) a year after the alleged conduct took

---

[4] (1982), 4 L.A.C. (3d) 385 (Swinton).
[5] (1983), unreported (Barton).
[6] (1986), unreported (Fagon).
[7] (1989), P.S.S.R.B. File No. 166-2-18516 (Young).

place and after she had lost a chance for the monitor-trainer position she sought (for which she blamed her supervisor).

While denying the grievance, the arbitrator pointed out that the grievor did not voice her concern about the alleged sexual harassment until after she lost this opportunity. Also, she not only had a motive for launching her grievance but was motivated to do so by the loss of an opportunity to advance her career.

The arbitrator, after citing the Supreme Court decision in *Janzen v. Platy Enterprises Ltd.*,[8] stated that the test or standard of conduct which constitutes sexual harassment must be an objective one, and not simply based upon the subjective impression of the victim. The arbitrator concluded that the employer could not be said to have disregarded its obligation not to tolerate sexual harassment. The employer evidently exercised concern and was prepared to act, but found nothing to act upon. The employer's conclusions seem to have been reinforced to some extent by the fact that the grievor was known to have volunteered to work overtime assignments for her supervisor (the alleged harasser) in his new unit.

The arbitrator also pointed out that "favouritism" to a female employee alone and in itself does not constitute sexual harassment. In this case, several female witnesses (who worked with the grievor and the same supervisor) believed the grievor might have been "a favourite" of the supervisor, yet none can specifically say that they or the grievor felt sexually harassed.

The first successful grievance by a victim of sexual harassment was in *Re Canada Post Corp. and Canadian Union of Postal Workers*.[9] In this case, the grievor alleged that her male supervisor sexually harassed her by placing his hands on her hips and applying bodily pressure to her buttocks. The arbitrator found that the conduct constituted sexual harassment, though it was a single incident. He found the employer was vicariously liable. The arbitrator awarded the victim $100 in damages, but he refused to grant her an apology.

A Newfoundland arbitrator[10] found that the grievor, a female employee, had been a victim of sexual harassment by her supervisor. The foreman engaged in a course of vexatious sexual conduct and made sexual advances to the grievor which forced her to withdraw

---

[8] (Man. 1989), 10 C.H.R.R. D/6205 (S.C.C.).
[9] (1983), 11 L.A.C. (3d) 13 (Norman).
[10] *Re Newfoundland (Newfoundland Farm Products Corp.) and Newfoundland Assn. of Public Employees* (1988), 35 L.A.C. (3d) 165 (Dicks).

from employment on sick leave benefits. The arbitrator concluded that the foreman's conduct constituted sexual harassment.

The arbitrator held the employer was vicariously liable for the action of its supervisor in sexually harassing the grievor. The arbitrator ruled that sick leave benefits as taken by the grievor since November 1987, which were attributed to sexual harassment, be restored to her. The arbitrator, however, found himself without jurisdiction and legal authority to order the employer to remove the management employee from the workplace, or to require him to apologize to the victim. This appears to be a general feeling among arbitrators in Canada.

In brief, the following describes the remedies a Board of Arbitration can or cannot provide to the victim of sexual harassment.

Arbitration Boards can:

1. declare that the conduct constituted sex discrimination and violated the collective agreement and/or the *Human Rights Act* (depending on the enabling provision in the collective agreement);
2. order that the employer cease and desist from engaging in such actions;
3. order that the employer issue a sexual harassment policy and procedure and maintain the working environment free from sexual harassment;
4. order the reinstatement of the victim with full back pay and benefits;
5. order that the wrong be rectified by granting remedies such as promotion, etc.;
6. order the expiring of a negative or poor evaluation; or
7. grant compensatory damages for humiliation, loss of dignity or physical and emotional distress.

Arbitration Boards cannot:

1. award a letter of apology either from the employer or the harasser;
2. order the employer to transfer the harasser (supervisory or non-supervisory);
3. order the employer to discipline or discharge the harasser (supervisory or non-supervisory);
4. impose a fine on the harasser;
5. order the harasser to pay monetary compensation to the victim; or
6. award costs and legal fees.

A standard grievance procedure in the collective agreement is neither intended to nor does it deal with the complicated and emotionally charged problem of sexual harassment. If employees are to be encouraged to use the arbitration process to seek redress for sexual harassment, rather than the Human Rights Commission, the parties have to address this issue specifically in the collective agreement. The arbitrators may have to be empowered with a wide range of authority to provide suitable and satisfactory solutions to the problem of sexual harassment, which may extend beyond their traditional jurisdiction. For example, to transfer or discipline a supervisory or non-supervisory personnel is normally a management function and the arbitrator has no jurisdiction to interfere with that.

The parties, therefore, have begun to provide a specific provision for sexual harassment grievances in the collective agreement empowering the arbitrator to award non-traditional remedies in such cases. For example a "sexual harassment" clause in the collective agreement between the City of Victoria and C.U.P.E., Local 50 reads in part:

> In cases of sexual harassment, an Arbitration Board shall have the power to transfer or *discipline any person found guilty* of sexually harassing an employee.

The collective agreement between the Municipality of Terrace (B.C.) and C.U.P.E., Local 2012 goes a step further and provides:

> In cases of sexual harassment, an Arbitration Board shall have *the power to transfer, discipline, or levy a financial penalty against the harasser and the employer.* In cases where sexual harassment may result in the transfer of the person, it shall be the harasser who is transferred and the victim shall not be transferred against their will. [Emphasis added]

A Board of Arbitration, on the basis of provisions such as those above in a collective agreement, would be able to grant a remedy which no other court or tribunal could grant.

B. GRIEVANCES BY ALLEGED HARASSERS

Most employers respond to "sexual harassment" complaints by severe disciplinary action, including termination of employment of the alleged harasser. In a unionized situation, the alleged harasser, if he is a co-worker or a supervisor covered by the collective agreement, has the right to grieve and he normally does grieve the discipline imposed upon him.

In *Libtika v. Treasury Board*,[11] the employer imposed a penalty of five days' suspension on the grievant for grabbing a female co-worker and pulling her into his office. The Board of Arbitration found that the grievant's conduct constituted physical harassment of the female employee with sexual overtones and that the penalty imposed was not unreasonable. The Board observed that "female employees should not be put in situations where they have to submit to these unwanted advances of their co-workers. Misconduct of this type has an effect on the effectiveness of employees and creates an atmosphere which is not conducive to harmonious work relationships between the employees." The suspension of five days was upheld.

In another federal public service case,[12] a correctional officer who accosted a fellow female employee by putting his hand around her neck and saying to her, "I do strip searches after 4 [o'clock], preferably some other place than here", was suspended for three days. The board upheld the suspension.

In the *Ward Air* case,[13] the grievor persistently pestered a female co-worker for a date, showed her photos from a "girlie magazine" and invited her back for drinks, dinner and "to have a good time". When the female employee reported to the management the grievor's unwanted advances towards her, he chanted offensive words which were directed to the complainant. The grievor was suspended for 10 days for sexually harassing the victim. The arbitrator found that the grievor's conduct constituted sexual harassment and upheld the suspension.

However, in another federal public service case,[14] a 40-day suspension for causing sexual harassment was quashed because the employer failed to prove that the complainant was sexually harassed, that she was forced to consent to an affair, or agreed to it for fear of losing her job or because of hoped-for permanent employment.

1. Discharge for Sexual Harassment

Out of 27 cases of discharge for alleged harassment, the arbitrators in 13 cases have upheld the penalty of discharge imposed by the employers on the perpetrator of sexual harassment.

---

[11] (1980), P.S.S.R.B. File No. 166-2-8128 (Falardeau-Ramsay).
[12] *Yargeau v. Treasury Board* (1981), P.S.S.R.B. File No. 166-2-8614 (Galipeault).
[13] (1980), unreported (O'Shea).
[14] *Re Treasury Board (Employment and Immigration) and Gaudreau* (1988), 34 L.A.C. (3d) 419 (Wexler).

In 1977, the Board of Arbitration in *Bellemare v. Treasury Board (C.E.I.C.)*,[15] upheld the discharge of an employee of the Immigration Department who had sexual relations (including kissing, touching of the breasts and sexual intercourse) with two female applicants for landed immigrant status. The Board pointed out that the offences committed by the grievor were of a very serious nature, that these offences cause discredit on the Department and that it is inconceivable such conduct could be tolerated within the public service. (The objectionable conduct in this case was not labelled "sexual harassment" because the term was not in common use until 1978.)

Perhaps one of the earliest sexual harassment cases which came to public attention occurred in 1979 at the University of Ottawa when a professor allegedly made three separate, unwarranted and forceful sexual advances towards a female student. A Board of Arbitration, in the *University of Ottawa* case,[16] concluded that the professor's conduct "constituted unsolicited sexual harassment which was accompanied by the use of force in order to cause (the complainant) to submit to the grievor's unwarranted sexual advances" and had imperilled the credibility of the university and disrupted the complainant's learning environment. The Board upheld the professor's dismissal.

In the *Acadia University* case,[17] the university had dismissed the grievor, a professor of recreation and physical education, for subjecting female students "to sexual harassment and undue academic pressure". The Board of Arbitration found that the professor had telephoned several female students late at night to ask them out, invited them to engage in various forms of sexual activities, and, on occasions, made physical advances. The board concluded that such conduct constituted "sexual harassment of the students" and was a just and proper cause for dismissal. Moreover, the conduct of the grievor was contrary to the standards of the university and to his professional responsibilities.

In *Hotel, Restaurant and Cafeteria Employees Union, Loc. 75 v. Constellation Hotel Corp.*,[18] where a union had alleged that an employee was dismissed for union activities, the Ontario Labour Relations Board found that a union organizer was dismissed for sexually harassing a female employee. The grievor had called the complainant over and asked her "if she was excited". When she asked why, he replied "because your nipples are standing out," and pulled her close to him.

---

[15] (1977), P.S.S.R.B. File No. 166-2-2341 (Descoteaux).
[16] (1979), unreported (O'Shea).
[17] (1981), unreported (Kimball).
[18] (1981), 82 CLLC 16,510 (OLRB).

The board held that the grievor engaged in gross misconduct which was sufficient to terminate employment.

In *Re Government of the Province of Alta. and Alta. Union of Provincial Employees*,[19] the Board of Arbitration upheld the discharge of the grievor, who had engaged in sexual affairs with one or more of the female students of the residence at Westfield, a home for temporary wards of the province.

In a case where an orderly pushed a female nurse down on to her back with the weight of his upper body, fondled her breasts and attempted to kiss her, the arbitrator held that such misconduct constituted such a serious breach of trust as to warrant imposing, in all but the most extraordinary circumstances, the penalty of discharge.[20]

In *Re Government of the Province of Alta. and Alta. Union of Provincial Employees (Harding Grievance)*,[21] a meat inspector with the Alberta Ministry of Agriculture was dismissed for sexually harassing the female employees of a meat-packing plant. It was alleged that the grievor put his arm around the shoulders and waists of female employees, rubbed their upper arms and opened their shirts to examine necklines. As he moved through the close quarters of the production line, he would also rub his lower torso against them. The grievor also occasionally made sexual propositions and suggestive comments, among other examples of offensive behaviour. The Board of Arbitration rejected the grievor's argument that his conduct was unavoidable because of the close quarters on the production line, or alternatively, that he was just doing it for fun to relieve the boredom of the job. The Board found that such conduct merited discharge.

In *Re Corp. of the City of Calgary and Amalgamated Transit Union, Loc. 583*,[22] the dismissal of a bus driver for sexually harassing a female passenger on the bus was upheld, although the grievor neither was obscene nor had touched her. The grievor stopped the bus in a relatively isolated area about 6 p.m., when the victim, a 16 year-old girl, was the only passenger in the bus. After moving his mirror to make eye contact with the victim, the driver (grievor) came to the back of the bus and sat down near the victim. While upholding the discharge, the Board recognized that discipline is meant to be rehabilitative, but concluded that the trust which this employer and the public are entitled

---

[19] (1983), 8 L.A.C. (3d) 1 (Jolliffe).
[20] *St. Joseph's Health Centre v. C.U.P.E. Loc. 1144* (1983), unreported (Roberts).
[21] (1988), 34 L.A.C. (3d) 204 (McFetridge).
[22] (1988), 35 L.A.C. (3d) 279 (Jones).

to expect from bus drivers cannot be repaired in this case by substituting a lesser penalty.

In the *CNR* case,[23] the grievor was dismissed for gross physical and verbal actions. The arbitrator upheld the dismissal, observing:

> It is the most fundamental right of any employee, whether male or female, to work without fear of assault, whether sexual, physical or otherwise. The maintenance of that condition is among the first obligations of an employer and responsibilities of an employee. A sustained course of conduct that violates that condition and instills fear, humiliation or resentment among victimized employees will, absent the most extraordinary mitigating circumstances, justify the removal of the offending employee from the workplace by the termination of his or her employment.

The same arbitrator, in the *C.P. Express* case,[24] upheld the dismissal of the grievor (an employee of nine years' seniority) for sexually harassing a deaf and mute female employee by making explicit sexual gestures and for physically assaulting her. However, the arbitrator pointed out that "a *frank admission* on the part of the grievor coupled with *an apology* to his fellow employee might constitute a factor to be weighed in mitigation". This is especially true as it might bear on the acceptance of the apology by the victimized employee which, in turn, would be a significant element relating to the ability of the grievor to continue to function in the company's service without undue distress to other employees.

In Re *Toronto Hydro Electric System and C.U.P.E., Loc. 1*,[25] the employer dismissed the grievor for causing sexual harassment to a female employee by giving her flowers and inviting her to dinner. The arbitrator held that the conduct of the grievor fitted into a pattern of vexatious conduct with sexual overtones and that such conduct should have been reasonably realized by the grievor to be unwelcome. The arbitrator upheld the dismissal of the grievor and observed that there is little likelihood that the grievor would respond to any sanction less than discharge.

---

[23] (1989) 1 L.A.C. (4th) 183 (Picher).
[24] (1989), unreported (Picher).
[25] (1989) 2 L.A.C. (4th) 169 (Davis).

(a) Reduction of Discharge Penalty

Some arbitrators' refusal to uphold a discharge of the alleged perpetrator of sexual harassment does not mean that they have condoned the acts of sexual harassment by the grievant. In fact, arbitrators in most cases have disapproved, in the strongest terms, of harassment of female workers as unacceptable and intolerable behaviour in the workplace.

For example, in *Re Canada Post Corp. and C.U.P.W. (Gibson)*[26] the arbitrator stated that:

> ... harassment may justify discipline even where the basis for the harassment is not a prohibited ground; if employees have a right to be protected from physical assaults by their fellow employees, they have an equivalent right to be protected from a course of verbal injury, whether that verbal injury has a basis which is a prohibited ground of discrimination, or has some other basis, or even has no basis at all.

However, in spite of the finding by arbitrators that the conduct of the grievants did constitute sexual harassment — and as such serious misconduct and unacceptable workplace behaviour — the penalty of discharge in some cases has been reduced to a lighter penalty, "suspension ranging from three days to one year". The arbitrators in such cases have reduced the penalty on the following bases: that management failed to properly investigate the complaint made by the victim; that the employer failed to take similar action against another employee about whom the complaint of sexual harassment had also been made; and that the employer's supervision was almost totally absent: *Re City of Edmonton and Amalgamated Transit Union, Local 569.*[27]

In *Re City of Nanticoke and C.U.P.E., Loc. 246*,[28] an arbitrator reduced the penalty of discharge to a three-day suspension (in spite of the findings that the grievor's behaviour constituted serious misconduct) on the grounds that many of the activities engaged in by the male employees were condoned by the employer and that there was a lack of discipline for other male employees who engaged in similar conduct.

---

[26] (1987), 27 L.A.C. (3d) 27 (Swan).
[27] (1985), 23 L.A.C. (3d) 84 (Thomas).
[28] (1980), 29 L.A.C. (2d) 64 (Barton).

In *Re Government of the Province of Alta. and Alta. Union of Provincial Employees*,[29] the arbitrator found that the grievant engaged in serious sexual misconduct and that employees in the workplace must be protected from sexual advances by fellow employees, but nonetheless reduced the penalty of discharge to six months' suspension on the grounds that the grievant was remorseful, had no prior discipline record, and was under emotional stress and had been drinking.

In *Re Dartmouth District School Board and Nova Scotia Union of Public Employees, Unit No. 2*,[30] the Board of Arbitration held that the grievant, a school caretaker, committed a serious error in judgement and breached his position of trust by hugging and kissing a 12-year-old girl and going into the ladies' washroom, but this did not constitute sexual harassment because he had no sexual design or intent. The Board reduced the penalty of discharge to 6 1/2 months' suspension on the grounds that the grievant had 14 years of blameless employment and that it was an isolated incident. The Board, however, ordered him not to work as a school caretaker for one year.

In the *City of Edmonton* case,[31] the Board of Arbitration found that the grievant bullied and intimidated female employees over a period of time. However, it failed to find clear and cogent evidence to support the allegations of sexual harassment. Thus, it reduced the penalty of discharge to a one-year suspension on the grounds that the grievant's alleged misconduct took place two, three and even four years before the dismissal; that many of the incidents were trivial when taken in isolation from each other; and that employer supervision was almost totally absent.

In *Re Canada Cement Lafarge Ltd. and Energy & Chemical Workers Union, Loc. 219*,[32] where the grievant had attempted to invade the privacy of the female employees by using the staff shower facility, the arbitrator found that the grievant's action constituted a serious error of judgement and was analogous to sexual harassment. However, in view of the fact that the grievant admitted his guilt and apologized for his misconduct and the female victim was prepared to tolerate his return, the arbitrator replaced the penalty of discharge with a suspension of about three months followed by reinstatement without back pay and benefits.

---

[29] (1982), 5 L.A.C. (3d) 268 (Jolliffe).
[30] (1983), 12 L.A.C. (3d) 425 (Flemming).
[31] *Supra*, note 27.
[32] (1986), 24 L.A.C. (3d) 202 (Emrich).

In the *Famz Foods Ltd. (Swiss Chalet)* case,[33] where the grievor made a lewd, very offensive gesture of a sexual nature towards a female staff member causing her a great amount of personal grief, the arbitrator declined to find that the behaviour constituted sexual harassment on the ground that a single gesture falls far short of the forbidden categorization of sexual harassment. Moreover, the severity of the conduct was reduced by a remarkable degree of tolerance by management towards horseplay that could have encouraged the grievor to believe that he could get away with a wide range of behaviour that in other environments would have drawn a sharp disciplinary response. Thus, the arbitrator held that while the grievor's misconduct did not warrant imposition of the ultimate sanction of discharge, it warranted substantial disciplinary response.

In *William Neilson Ltd. v. United Food and Commercial Workers International Union*,[34] the conduct of the grievant, who was writing notes and sending small gifts but made no physical contact, was held not to constitute severe sexual harassment. The arbitrator noted that the grievant did not have mischievous sexual intent or create an intimidating, hostile, offensive work environment; nor had the victim suffered any concrete employment consequences, although she was emotionally upset. The arbitrator held that in minor cases of sexual harassment, the basic principle of progressive discipline must be applied. The penalty of discharge was reduced to a three-month suspension. Further, the grievor was forbidden to have any communication with the victim whatsoever, under a threat of immediate discharge. The arbitrator noted that this kind of behavioural problem may arise from conflicting perceptions of appropriate relations between men and women.

2. Alleged Harasser Exoneration

In only a few cases involving discharge for alleged sexual harassment were the grievants exonerated, the discharges quashed and reinstatement with full back wages ordered. In these cases, it appears that the arbitrators failed to recognize that the grievants' conduct amounted to sexual harassment or otherwise gave just cause for discharge.

---

[33] (1988), 33 L.A.C. (3d) 435 (Roberts).
[34] (1987), unreported (Deom).

In *Re Government of the Province of Alta. and Alta. Union of Provincial Employees*,[35] the Board of Arbitration found that the grievor's allegedly sexually harassing conduct was certainly not intended as such by the grievor. The Board thought such conduct was "inappropriate" rather than "sexual harassment". In *Re Ottawa Board of Education and Ottawa Board of Education Employees Union*,[36] the arbitrator held that the grievor's conduct displayed extremely poor judgement in pursuing a romantic interest but that his actions did not constitute sexual harassment.

In *Durham College v. Ontario Public Service Employees Union, Local 354*,[37] involving the discharge of a Durham College professor for allegedly sexually harassing some female students, the Board of Arbitration exonerated the grievor and reinstated him with full benefits. In that case the Board of Arbitration (by majority) found that the grievor's conduct did not constitute "sexual harassment" because he never touched the students in a sexual way; never suggested to the students that they could earn higher marks if they engaged in sexual activities with him; the students never told him that what he was saying was offensive to them, and there was no indication to the grievor by the students that he was acting in an "unwelcome" fashion.

It may be noted that out of three discharge cases involving professors in institutions of higher learning, the Boards of Arbitration in two earlier cases upheld the discharge of professors who had sexually harassed students and whose conduct was seen as being inconsistent with the overall objectives of the university.

In the *Durham College* case, a tripartite investigation committee, consisting of a departmental head, an affirmative action coordinator and a union representative, had investigated the allegations prior to the imposition of discipline. The committee had unanimously found that the allegations of sexual harassment brought against the professor (as grievor) by the three complainants were substantially true; the grievor's denial that the incidents occurred and his assertion that they were fabrications were without substance; there seemed to be no basis for the comments and actions attributed to the grievor to have been misunderstood by the students; from previous incidents, the grievor was made aware of sexual harassment as an issue; the use of sexual innuendos by the grievor and overt sexual harassment extended beyond the three complainants in the current time frame.

---

[35] (1983), 10 L.A.C. (3d) 179 (Larson).
[36] (1990), 5 L.A.C. (4th) 171 (Bendel).
[37] (1987), unreported (Samuel).

(a) Do Arbitral Standards Differ?

Arbitrators in Canada generally have no difficulty in recognizing sexual harassment as serious misconduct and unacceptable behaviour. By and large, they have found the testimony of the victims of sexual harassment to be credible. In fact, the arbitrators in most cases have preferred the testimony of the victims to that of alleged harassers. The arbitrators, however, differ on some of the key characteristics of sexual harassment, such as whether a single incident of sexual misbehaviour constitutes sexual harassment; whether repetition of the sexual misconduct is essential to constitute sexual harassment; whether the test of a "reasonable person" should be applied to determine if the conduct was "unwelcome"; whether establishment of malicious intent on the part of the perpetrator is essential in the determination of sexual harassment. Following is an examination of these points.

Arbitrators differ as to whether a single incident or conduct may constitute sexual harassment. Generally, the outcome depends on the facts and the conduct in question in any given situation. In *Re Canada Post Corp and C.U.P.W. (Gibson)* in 1987,[38] the arbitrator found that a single incident was sufficient to constitute sexual harassment. He stated:

> ... the comments about the tampons and underwear were directly related to the female employee's gender, and could not have been made to a male employee. They were also, in my view, calculated to insult her gender, and to imply that she was unsanitary. These are not comments that, in my view, one would ordinarily have to make more than once in order to establish that they were likely to be unwelcome; no employee would appreciate insults of this nature on any basis, and it cannot be a term of anyone's employment to be degraded in this way.

In *Re Canada Post Corp. and C.U.P.W* in 1983,[39] the arbitrator also found that a single incident of unwanted physical contact by the supervisor constitutes sexual harassment. However, in *Famz Foods Ltd. (Swiss Chalet)*,[40] where the grievor had made a lewd and very offensive gesture of a sexual nature towards a female staff member, the arbitrator held that a single gesture falls short of the forbidden categorization

---

[38] *Supra*, note 26, at 44.
[39] (1983), 11 L.A.C. (3d) 13 (Norman).
[40] (1988), 33 L.A.C. (3d) 435 (Roberts).

of sexual harassment. The same approach was taken by the Board of Arbitration in the *Dartmouth District School Board* case.[41]

In *Re Canada Post Corp. and C.U.P.W. (Gibson)*,[42] the arbitrator pointed out that complainant's tolerance of the perpetrator's insulting comments or conduct by the complainant for some time does not mean that the comments or conduct were welcome or not offensive, and this would not prevent the victim from later raising a complaint. That is particularly true in circumstances where there is a substantial degree of peer pressure to accept the conduct, and the victimized employee goes along with that peer pressure rather than complaining, which could have the possible unpleasant result of encouraging yet more offensive behaviour.

Second, merely because an employee is prepared to engage in banter, flirtation or even sexual activity with one or more fellow employees does not mean that employee is required to accept the same conduct from everyone. As this area of law develops, it must come to recognize that some comments or activity may be welcome from one person, while being entirely unwelcome from another. The law will recognize an employee's right to choose those with whom the employee is prepared to let down some defences to which she is otherwise entitled. However, in *Durham College* the Board of Arbitration quashed the dismissal of the alleged harasser and pointed out that "the students never told him what he was saying was offensive to them" and "there was no indication to the grievor by the students that he was acting in an 'unwelcome' fashion."

In *Re Canada Post and C.U.P.W.* (grievance of Ms. Guglich),[43] the arbitrator applied the standard of a reasonable person and stated that "a reasonable person, in Mr. Shotton's shoes, ought to have known that such behaviour was unwelcome". However, in the *Ottawa Board of Education* case,[44] the arbitrator refused to follow the reasonable person test in determining whether or not the grievor's conduct was unwelcome. The arbitrator stated that the focus for arbitrators in such cases is not the impact of the behaviour on the "victim" but the culpability of the grievor's conduct. The arbitrator concluded that the employee who is disciplined for conduct which he did not realize was unwelcome but which the reasonable person would have realized was

---

[41] *Supra*, note 30.
[42] *Supra*, note 26.
[43] *Supra*, note 39.
[44] *Supra*, note 36.

unwelcome is being blamed, in effect, for a lack of sensitivity to signals from the "victim" of harassment.

It may be noted that this kind of reasoning is contrary to the approach taken by the Human Rights Tribunal. The Supreme Court of Canada has repeatedly stressed that in human rights cases it is the impact of the discriminatory act on the victim, and not the intent of the wrongdoer, which matters.[45] However, in *Re Toronto Hydro Electric System and C.U.P.E., Loc. 1*,[46] the arbitrator stated that the conduct of the grievor fitted into a pattern of vexatious conduct with sexual overtones which should have been reasonably realized by the grievor to be unwelcome.

Arbitrators have generally refused to find that the conduct of the alleged harasser amounts to sexual harassment on the ground that sexual relations between two consenting adults, where one party does not use force or promises to obtain sexual favours from the other party, is not sexual harassment.[47] The onus in such cases in on the employer to prove that the complainant was sexually harassed. However, in *Potvin v. Treasury Board*,[48] the arbitrator held that the grievor was guilty of sexually harassing the complainant, even though she had "agreed to do whatever she did with him" (engage in sexual encounters). The arbitrator stated that the grievor's sexual harassment of the complainant consisted primarily in his taking advantage of the position he held with respect to the complainant.

3. Severe or Mild Harassment

It appears that the arbitrators, in assessing "just cause", have divided sexual harassment into two categories: severe or serious sexual harassment and mild sexual harassment.

Sexual harassment, according to those arbitrators, is "mild" when the perpetrator's behaviour does not include physical contact with the victim; malicious sexual intent; creating an intimidating or hostile work environment, and adverse employment consequences for the victim.[49] In addition, it is "mild' where "horseplay" or "locker-room conduct"

---

[45] *Ontario Human Rights Commn. v. Simpson-Sears Ltd.* (Ont. 1985), 7 C.H.R.R. D/3102 (S.C.C.).
[46] (1989), 2 L.A.C. (4th) 169 (Davis).
[47] See for example *Re C.U.P.E. and O.P.E.I.U.* (1982), 4 L.A.C. (3d) 385 (Swinton).
[48] (1985), P.S.S.R.B. File No. 166-2-14871 (Galipeault).
[49] See for example *William Neilson Ltd. v. U.F.C.W.* (1987), unreported (Deom).

among the employees is a routine event (particularly in a same-age group of young males); where the victim has frequently participated in sexual jokes; where the employer knowing of such conduct took no steps to stop it (or condoned it), or it was a single or isolated incident.[50] In such cases, the arbitrators were reluctant to uphold the discharge of the harasser.

Sexual harassment is "serious" when it involves physical contact with the victim (from sexual touching to intercourse); repeated obscene and insulting comments of a sexual nature; banter, flirtation or other sexual activity; an assault on sexual dignity;[51] where the offender held a position of responsibility or of special trust; where the victim of harassment is a client or member of the public;[52] where the harassing conduct created a hostile and poisonous work environment, or where the victim suffered job-related consequences, such as being forced to quit or go on sick leave.[53] In cases of serious or severe sexual harassment, the arbitrators have generally confirmed the discharge of the harasser.

C. THE CHOICES INVOLVED

In discharge cases, an arbitrator is basically required to determine whether or not there was a "just cause" for the discharge. If it is found that there was a "cause" for discipline but not for discharge, then the arbitrator proceeds to determine an appropriate penalty.

Unless the parties provide otherwise (that is, propose a different or special way of handling a sexual harassment discharge or grievance), the arbitrator is bound to follow the existing arbitral jurisprudence in sexual harassment discharge cases. Consequently, even if the

---

[50] See for example *Famz Foods Ltd. (Swiss Chalet)* (1988), 33 L.A.C. (3d) 435 (Roberts) and *Re City of Nanticoke and C.U.P.E., Loc. 246* (1980), 29 L.A.C. (2d) 64 (Barton).
[51] See for example *Re Canada Post Corp. and C.U.P.W. (Gibson)* (1987), 27 L.A.C. (3d) 27 (Swan).
[52] See for example *Acadia University* (1981), unreported (Kimball); *University of Ottawa* (1979), unreported (O'Shea); *Re Government of the Province of Alta. and Alta. Union of Provincial Employees* (1983), 8 L.A.C. (3d) 1 (Jolliffe); *City of Calgary* (1988), 35 L.A.C. (3d) 279 (Jones).
[53] *Re C.N.R. and Can. Brotherhood of Railway, Transport and General Workers* (1989), 1 L.A.C. (4th) 183 (Picher); *Re C.P. Express and Transportation Communications Union* (1989), unreported (Picher); *Re Toronto Hydro Electric System and C.U.P.E., Local 1*, supra, note 46.

arbitrator finds that the alleged conduct of the grievor constitutes sexual harassment, it will still be required to determine:

1. the nature and gravity of the misconduct;
2. mitigating factors such as length of the grievor's employment seniority and disciplinary record of the grievor;
3. isolated (single incident) vs. repeated misconduct;
4. procedural due process (whether or not the other employees involved in such and similar misconduct were disciplined);
5. employer's tolerance, inaction or condonation of the sexual harassment or horseplay in the workplace;
6. grievor's demeanour and attitude during the hearing (such as admission of guilt, feeling sorry, apologizing to the victim or victims);
7. principles of progressive discipline.

The arbitrator, after having considered all those factors, may reach the conclusion that the grievor's conduct constituted sexual harassment (either serious or minor misconduct), but in the circumstances the penalty of discharge was too severe and must be replaced by a lesser penalty. In such circumstances, in spite of finding that the grievor had indeed sexually harassed the victim(s), the grievor is reinstated.

D. RAMIFICATIONS OF REINSTATEMENT

If the arbitrator reaches a conclusion, based on the facts, that the grievor did not engage in sexual harassment and then reinstates him to his old position, this would not seem to be as offensive to the victim(s) or other female employees as if the arbitrator finds that the grievor had sexually harassed others but still reinstates him on the grounds of procedural technicalities, mitigating factors or progressive discipline.

Victims of sexual harassment as well as other female employees in the plant are liable to view the reinstatement of the harasser as a slap in their face as well as a slap on the wrist of the offender. Reinstatement of the harasser may offend the victim(s) and in some cases the entire female population of the plant to the extent that they may refuse to work if the harasser is allowed to return. To some degree, this consideration reinforces the value to the employer of taking preemptive measures to prevent sexual harassment in the workplace by implementing an effective sexual harassment policy and a program of educating its employees in this field.

This process raises several questions: What is an appropriate response to sexual harassment? Is discharge of the harasser an appropriate response? Who should decide what is an appropriate penalty for sexual harassment — the employer, arbitrator, or both employers and unions?

One union leader notes that:

> "Employers are making mistakes when dismissing people for sexual harassment. ... Employers have to get together to stop the victims of sexual harassment from further disadvantage by incorrectly following dismissal procedures. ... In most instances sexual harassment should be viewed as gross misconduct and the workers should be liable to instant dismissal. Unions and employers both should make it clear by their statements and their actions that sexual harassment is unacceptable. A clear message from unions and employers about the unacceptability of sexual harassment will only work if that is backed up by mediators and Labour Courts".[54]

As stated earlier, the basic issue in discharge cases before the arbitrator is to determine whether or not there was a "just cause" for the discipline and not whether the perpetrator caused sexual harassment. Does the existing jurisprudence adequately provide the solution for the disposal of sexual harassment cases? Should there be a different standard for handling discipline cases involving sexual harassment than for other industrial offences? If there should be a different, more stringent standard for sexual harassment cases, then who should create that norm — the arbitrator or the parties (employer and union) by provision in the collective agreement?

A discharge of an employee for industrial offences such as theft, drinking on the job or absenteeism, though serious in nature, normally has its impact confined to the grievor and the employer. In other words, reinstatement of an employee who has been discharged for drinking on the job or for habitual absenteeism would cause few repercussions among the co-workers. However, reinstatement of a perpetrator of sexual harassment is likely to be regarded as an assault on the victim or female population. It may create fear and resentment among women in the work force. It also sends a wrong signal to other employees, particularly bullying male workers. It is true that in reinstating a harasser without back pay the arbitrator has not condoned the grievor's

---

[54] See Martha Coleman: "A Trade Union Perspective on Sexual Harassment" (1988), 13 *New Zealand J. Industrial Relations* 295 at 297.

sexually harassing conduct; however, it is likely to be so perceived, particularly by female employees. This perception could hinder productivity as well as harmonious relations between the employer and its employees, and between the employees themselves. It raises further difficult questions, such as:

Would reinstatement of the harasser, even on technical grounds, expose the employer to further risks (financial liability, loss of reputation and creating a stigma of sexual harassment in the workplace)? What kind of signal does reinstatement send to male employees? Would that be a sufficient deterrent? Would that help an employer who wishes to eradicate sexual harassment from the workplace? Would reinstatement of the alleged harasser give him ammunition to attempt a defamation action against the complainant(s)?

If the participation of women in the workforce is to be encouraged, gender insults, horseplay and sexual harassment must be eradicated from the workplace. That responsibility rests equally with employers and unions. If they are truly committed to this objective, employers and unions must cooperate to develop stringent rules which will deter the perpetration of sexual harassment. They cannot shirk their responsibility, nor can they expect a miracle solution of their problems from the arbitrators unless they give the arbitrator a strong mandate to deal with the problem.

Following are four suggestions which may be of use in such cases:

The parties (employer and union) need to make a special provision in the collective bargaining agreement specifically for the handling of discipline in sexual harassment cases. Some parties, especially in Western Canada, do this.

Arguably, the parties could provide in the collective bargaining agreement that if sexual harassment by the grievor is established, the arbitrator shall not interfere with the penalty imposed by the employer. This, however, would appear to be a very restrictive clause which would deny the grievor the benefit of procedural due process, any mitigating circumstances and the concept of progressive discipline.

In addition, the parties may authorize an arbitrator, in case of victim's grievances, to order the transfer or removal of a supervisor.

The arbitrator may also be authorized to order an apology in appropriate cases. An apology itself is not compensation, but it has some therapeutic value in healing the victim.

CHAPTER 7

Prevention of Sexual Harassment — A Necessity

Sexual harassment in the workplace has been ignored for far too long. It is pervasive and is not an insignificant personnel issue as some people may believe it to be. Sexual harassment will clearly be a major workplace issue for years to come and must be squarely faced by both public and private sector employers.

It is already evident that sexual harassment affects the well-being and economic livelihood of women employees, while also affecting the morale, productivity and integrity of the workplace. There are additional reasons why it is essential that all employers should address the problem promptly. The majority of working age women are now in the labour force and their numbers are steadily growing.

A. ORGANIZATION'S ABILITY TO ADAPT

During the Second World War, governments and industries accommodated themselves to the influx of women that had suddenly replaced men. This ability to adapt allowed North American industry to continue, even at a time when its main workforce was unavailable to staff the organizations. Rather than flounder under the burden of change during the war, North American industries met the internal and external demands, survived, and even advanced among world powers.

Industries are now again experiencing both internal and external demands to adapt. As one writer points out: "The ability of the organization to adapt with dignity to this influx of women seems less capable now than during the war. Perhaps it is because it requires a whole new set of standards and role behaviour, although that seems a weak excuse. This ability to adapt to the re-entry of women in the workforce has resulted not only in sexual harassment but also in power struggles, individual insecurities and retaliatory behaviour, none of which promotes the longevity of the organization system."[1]

Furthermore, an increasing number of women will be employed in non-traditional occupations. They are likely to encounter resistance and harassment as they enter "a man's world". However, these women will be less likely to put up with harassment as traditional attitudes towards working women are challenged and serious open discussion of the problem spreads. An employer, whether government or industry, according to recent court and tribunal decisions, has a legal obligation to provide a working environment free from sexual harassment.[2]

Thus, it has become increasingly necessary that both private and public sector employers develop a clear and precise "Code of Conduct" regarding interaction between their male and female employees. The employer, though not a custodian of the moral values and behaviour of its employees, is required to ensure that its female employees can work with respect and dignity.

B. IMPLICATIONS OF SEXUAL HARASSMENT FOR EMPLOYERS

Unchecked sexual harassment in the workplace can be expensive for the employing organization. Sexual harassment, especially when it continues over an extended period of time, can create high levels of stress and anxiety for both the victims and the perpetrator. These psychological reactions can lead to outcomes that increase labour costs for employers. Job performance can suffer; absenteeism, sick leave and turnover may well increase. Furthermore, when sexual harassment goes unchecked it can spread throughout an organization. The survey data indicate that the incidence of sexual harassment is probably more than 40 per cent among female members of the labour force, suggesting that this has already occurred.

---

[1] M. Meyer, J. Oestriech, F. Collins and I. Berchtold, *Sexual Harassment* (New York: Petrocelli Books Inc. 1981), p. 76.
[2] See for example *Kotyk v. Canadian Employment Immigration Commn.* (Can. 1983), 4 C.H.R.R. D/1416 (Tribunal — Ashley).

C. ECONOMIC COST OF SEXUAL HARASSMENT

Losing a sexual harassment suit is the most obvious cost to employers. Over and above an award of back pay, general and consequential damages as well as an order for the legal fees of the complainant and/or the Commission may add up to a substantial monetary loss.

1. Back Pay

A woman who proves that she was discharged from her job for failing to accede to her supervisor's requests for sexual favours would be entitled to an award of back pay. An employee discharged for refusing to wear a revealing uniform would equally be entitled to an award of back pay. Similarly, if an employee is so intimidated by sexual harassment that she voluntarily quits her job, her resignation may be regarded as a "constructive dismissal", thus entitling her to back pay. In addition, a complainant is entitled to general damages for the intimidating, hostile and offensive work environment and injury to dignity and feelings suffered by her because of sexual harassment.

2. Consequential Damages

Employer liability for sexual harassment does not stop at back pay and lawyer's fees. Employers are liable for damages for causing humiliation and loss of self-respect to the victim as well as punitive damages. In some jurisdictions, employers may also be held liable for legal costs.

3. Hidden Cost of Sexual Harassment

In addition to legal liability, sexual harassment in the workplace also causes a substantial indirect loss to the employer. For example, the existence of sexual harassment in the workplace adversely affects employee morale, reduces productivity, and increases the rate of absenteeism among affected employees. Moreover, as noted above, many women who face sexual harassment choose to quit rather than fight or endure the conditions. This results in a higher rate of employee turnover with all the associated costs in training and lost production.

According to one U.S. study, in the absence of appropriate available Canadian data, sexual harassment of its employees costs the federal government an estimated $189 million during the two-year period from May 1978 to May 1980.[3] According to that study, 29,350 federal employees left their jobs over that two-year period as a result of being sexually harassed. An estimated 128,200 victims indicated that their experience of sexual harassment had a negative impact on their emotional and physical health. Approximately 50,430 federal employees' time and attendance at work suffered as a result of sexual harassment during this period, and as well, it affected the productivity of 30,680 workgroups.[4] The breakdown of the hidden cost[5] is, indeed, both alarming and revealing:

Cost of Job Turnover	=	$ 26.8 Million
Cost of Emotional and Physical Stress	=	5.0 "
Cost of Absenteeism	=	7.9 "
Cost of Decline in Individual Productivity	=	72.1 "
Cost of Decline in Workgroup Productivity	=	76.9 "
	TOTAL	$188.7 Million

Despite great public exposure and the decade-long warning that sexual harassment is unlawful, it nevertheless persists in the workplace. A more recent survey suggests that approximately 36,000 employees in the U.S. federal government quit their jobs because of sexual harassment during the two-year period between 1985 and 1987, costing the government $267 million in turnover, sick leave, and lost productivity.[6]

It is noteworthy that the number of employees who left their jobs because of sexual harassment and the economic cost of sexual harassment have risen substantially during the span of seven years. Contrary to the general expectations, it is evident that the incidence

---

[3] U.S. Merit System Protection Board, *Sexual Harassment in the Federal Workplace: Is It a Problem?* (Washington D.C.: U.S. Government Printing Office 1981), pp. 75-79.
[4] *Ibid.*
[5] *Ibid.*, at 77.
[6] U.S. Merit System Protection Board, "Report on Sexual Harassment in the Federal Government: An Update", *BNA'S Daily Reporter System*, July 1, 1988, PA1/A2.

of sexual harassment is on the rise instead of declining. These statistics speak from themselves and demand a firm, serious and unified action from both public and private sector employers to prevent this workplace cancer from spreading.

4. Prospect of Aggressive Unionism

Sexual harassment may encourage unionism in the workplace. Employers, especially those whose workforce contains a substantial proportion of females, should also be mindful that the persistence of sexual harassment in the workplace increases the likelihood of successful union-organizing campaigns. According to one union organizer, sexual harassment is "the single thing in the workplace which radicalizes women more than pay."[7]

This fact has not been lost on women's groups or on unions, especially those seeking to expand their representation of office and clerical workers. For example, in the United States, a group called "Working Women" joined forces with the 650,000 member Service Employees International Union to form a national union — District 925 — devoted to organizing the nearly 20 million female office workers.[8]

D. SHOULD EMPLOYERS PUT A COMPLETE BAN ON SEXUAL BEHAVIOUR?

Within organizations, traditionally, feelings of attraction have been looked upon with disfavour as the source of a variety of problems, because:

— personal distraction interferes with productivity;
— people may avoid working together because of fear of attraction;
— sexual relationships, when they exist, have powerful implications within organizations.

---

[7] Interview of J. DiGirolamo, Illinois Organizing Director for AFSCME, *Sexual Harassment and Labour Relations* (Washington D.C.: Bureau of National Affairs, 1981), p. 32.
[8] Jay Waks and Michael Starr: "The Sexual Shakedown in Perspective: Sexual Harassment in Its Social and Legal Contexts" (1981), 7 *Employee Relations L.J.* 567 at 571.

In the past, these conditions had generally discouraged the employment of women. Organizations treading the line between individual needs and organizational responsibility will require clear policies and programs, much sensitivity and tact, and a willingness to discuss areas previously considered taboo in business.

Currently, there are two different points of view on how far management should go to prohibit sex in the workplace. One view is that sex has no place in the workplace because it is a drain on employees' energy and causes loss of production. Therefore, the employer should have a complete ban on behaviour of a sexual nature, whether wanted or unwanted, welcome or unwelcome. Moreover, by placing a complete ban upon sexual behaviour in the workplace, an employer will protect its employees from sexual harassment and itself from legal and financial liability.

The other view argues that the corporation is well on its way to replacing the family as a source of affection, community and support. Men and women these days spend more time with their co-workers in the workplace than at home. They socialize with co-workers, confide in them, trust them with their problems and share their joys with them. So it is natural that men and women turn to the office to find prospective mates. Where men and women work together, some sort of mutual relationship and understanding is bound to develop. As the relationship is based on mutual understanding and willingness, those relationships neither harm working relationships nor affect productivity.[9] In other words, the workplace in North America is not only a place to earn a living but also a significant social institution, where men and women socialize.

It has been suggested that "Management should consider making professional resources within the organization available (i) to those who need assistance to sort out their feelings of attraction for another within the company: (ii) to those experiencing actions which they consider to be sexually harassing; and (iii) to those accused of sexual harassment by others."[10] Organizations should perhaps expand their employee counselling service to include problems of sexual attraction and harassment. Perhaps employees experiencing sexual attraction require counselling to the same extent as those experiencing sexual harassment.

---

[9] See P. Horn and J. Horn, *Sex in the Office* (Reading, Mass.: Addison-Wesley Publishing Co., 1982). See also J. B. Driscoll, "Sexual Attraction And Harassment: Management's New Problem" (1981), *Personnel Journal* 33-37.

[10] Driscoll, "Sexual Attraction and Harassment: Management's New Problem", *ibid.*

Even human rights agencies have recognized that not all sexual relationships among employees can or should be forbidden, and that an employer should not be liable for all of the offensive conduct of its employees.[11] Moreover, a complete ban on sexual behaviour is no guarantee that sexual behaviour will not occur or that sexual harassment will not be present. Women and men do not need *protection* from each other; they need *respect* for each other. This does not necessarily mean seeing everyone as non-sexual, it means seeing them as equals. Women in the workforce desire to be treated as people, not as sex objects. Like men, women wish to pursue employment goals and to have freedom in conducting their work relationships and private lives as they choose, without fear of rejection and reprisal. The employers, therefore, should concentrate on creating an atmosphere of mutual respect among employees, by not condoning sexual harassment, yet not regulating acceptable interchange between employees. Men and women should maintain freedom to pursue relationships based on mutual consent and respect. A sexual harassment policy should not be designed to restrict normal social interchange, but to control and forbid conduct which is both unwanted and offensive to an individual. In formulating a policy against sexual harassment, the employer should make clear to its employees that their private lives and their interpersonal relationships are none of the company's business — as long as they do not interfere with the productivity of the consenting employees or others at work.

E. CAN EMPLOYERS AFFORD TO BE PASSIVE?

Estimates of the incidence of sexual harassment in the workplace differ widely. Several studies of employed women have been conducted in recent years. The proportion of women reporting sexual pressures

---

[11] Suppose an employee and a supervisor engage in a mutually desired sexual relationship, but the affair turns sour. One court has held that if, as a result, the working relationship deteriorates, no sanctions against the employee can be taken without a "candid disclosure" of the nature of the problem to the actual decision-maker. In the court's view, the opportunity for abuse would otherwise be excessive, and a supervisor could take advantage of the position to use "personality conflict" as justification for removing the subordinate. The court's intent was that "accurate disclosure to the proper authorities (would) chill the willingness of the supervisor to engage in such activity". Yet the court offered no clue concerning an employer's proper conduct in such a situation. See *Williams v. Civiletti*, 23 E.P.D. para. 30,916 (D.D.C. 1980).

and intimidation on the job ranged from a low of 42 per cent to a high of 70 per cent. Even if the lower figure is the most accurate estimate, these reports suggest that this is a widespread phenomenon.

Even in the face of this evidence, some employers refuse to consider sexual harassment a serious problem and thus fail to establish a policy to deal with it. There are two common themes for justifying the lack of action. First, it can be a very sensitive undertaking for employers to establish policies pertaining to relationships between male and female employees. Second, they do not have a written policy because sexual harassment does not occur in their organization.

Public policy in Canada clearly suggests that an employer has an affirmative duty to maintain a workplace free from sexual harassment and intimidation. Further, a review of court and tribunal decisions makes it clear that employers are expected to have effective policies and practices to deal with sexual harassment in the workplace. In recent years the tribunals have awarded victims of sexual harassment back pay, benefits and compensatory damages. Companies have been required to establish policies prohibiting sexual harassment and to design a grievance procedure and mechanism for the investigation and resolution of sexual harassment complaints. Neither the guidelines nor court decisions give credence to the view that employers need do nothing to eliminate sexual harassment because the relationship between male and female employees is a sensitive topic. Nor has it been suggested that female employees who are perceived to engage in flirtatious behaviour are entitled to compensation for the consequences of this behaviour. Rather the court and tribunal decisions indicate that the employers are required to have active vigilance over the conduct of their employees, particularly that of their supervisory personnel, so that they do not cause sexual harassment to other employees.

A review of judicial decisions and public policy as expressed through human rights statutes leaves no doubt that acquiescence on the part of the employer will not be tolerated. Thus, an essential element in attempts to control sexual harassment is a strong policy statement from top management denouncing such behaviour. This, indeed, is a "sensitive" topic about which some employees might resent employers establishing a policy. However, the law is quite clear: an employer is equally liable for an active policy that encourages sexual harassment or a tacit policy that permits sexual harassment.

Implicitly the same approach has been taken by the Human Rights Commissions. Human Rights Tribunals[12] and arbitrators[13] in Canada have demanded positive and effective action by employers to prevent sexual harassment. However, none of the Human Rights Commissions in Canada has openly issued any guidelines similar to those of the E.E.O.C. in the United States. Rather, the Canadian Human Rights Commission issued a harassment policy in 1983 which makes an employer responsible for sexual harassment committed in the course of the employment. It states:

> Any act of harassment committed by an employee or an agent of any employer in the course of the employment shall be considered to be an act committed by that employer.

The policy, however, does not require the employer to either denounce or issue a policy denouncing sexual harassment. Nonetheless, almost all of the Human Rights Commissions privately (behind the scenes) encourage employers to develop and issue a policy statement on sexual harassment. They even help and assist employers in developing and planning such a policy. It is, however, not clear why the Human Rights Commissions in Canada have left the function of requiring the employers to establish an anti-sexual harassment policy to the Human Rights Tribunals. The Human Rights Commissions are

---

[12] For example in *Kotyk v. Canadian Employment Immigration Commn.* (Can. 1983), 4 C.H.R.R. D/1416 (Tribunal — Ashley), the tribunal while holding the employer (C.E.I.C.) responsible for the harassment of the complainants, emphasized the need for a strong policy against sexual harassment. It observed at D/1431 (para. 12,259): "Had a strong policy or practice on sexual harassment been in place, the incidents leading to the complaints probably would not have occurred". It added at D/1430 (para. 12,249):

> Managers and supervisors must themselves be aware that sexual harassment is prohibited conduct under the [Canadian Human Rights] Act. When a complaint is made, it must be dealt with as a serious matter, not by a gentle tap on the fingers, but as a potential breach of a statute. Employers should advise their employees that sexual interplay that has, or may reasonably appear to have, employment consequences — either direct, in the nature of firing, loss of benefits, etc. or indirect, such as an adverse effect on the work environment — is improper. The distinction between flirtation and harassment should be clarified. Complaint mechanisms should be in place, so that complaints can be made confidentially without fear of reprisals. Employers have a responsibility to advise their supervisory personnel and employees about the significance and consequences of sexual harassment.

[13] See for example *Re Canada Post Corp. and Canadian Union of Postal Workers* (1983), 11 L.A.C. (3d) 13 (Norman).

either trying to keep a low profile or higher degree of neutrality than the Equal Employment Opportunity Commission in the United States.

However, recent amendments to the *Canada Labour Code*[14] have made it mandatory for every employer in the federal jurisdiction to develop and issue a sexual harassment policy. The Code has also imposed an obligation on employers to provide an effective redress mechanism for the victims of sexual harassment. Thus, finally, the Canadian Parliament has done what the Human Rights Commissions were reluctant to do.

Many organizations believe that sexual harassment could never occur within their walls. Is this not naive? The absence of complaints does not necessarily mean that an organization has nothing to worry about. It only means that sexually abused workers do not know how to raise a complaint or they fear retaliation. Under these circumstances, if a complaint were to surface and proceed to a Human Rights Tribunal, the earlier decisions make it clear that the employer would have a difficult time in establishing a convincing defence.

First, employers should get their own houses in order by remedying existing or potentially explosive problems; and second, they should take affirmative steps to rid the workplace of sexual harassment through an effective program of prevention. Employers who do not take this opportunity to prevent problems before they arise may ultimately face more serious problems.

Preventing harassment and enforcing appropriate workplace behaviour appear to be the best, if not the only, "cure" for employer liability. Consideration, therefore, should be given to the development of programs that affirmatively meet the preventive standards outlined by the courts, Human Rights Tribunals and Human Rights Commissions. In addition to an effective policy, the employer may also be advised, as a precautionary measure, to have liability insurance to protect itself from heavy damages. However, liability insurance should not be regarded as a substitute for an effective "Sexual Harassment Policy".

There are numerous practical reasons for the employers to develop and implement a preventive program against sexual harassment.[15] Some of the benefits of such a programme may be stated as follows:

---

[14] R.S.C. 1985, c. L-2, Part III, Division XV.1, Sexual Harassment, s. 247.4.

[15] William L. Kandel, "Current Development in Employment Litigation — Sexual Harassment: Persistent, Prevalent, But Preventable," 14 *Employee Relations L.J.* 439 (1988).

1. It reduces the chances of harassment occurring when people know the rules.
2. It reduces the time for the employers to learn of the harassment and take prompt and corrective action.
3. It increases the chances for the victim to take self-help measures to prevent recurrences of offensive behaviour because they know their rights.
4. It increases the chances for successful internal resolution through early and effective intervention.
5. It increases the employer's record of good faith if the case goes to litigation, and provides a defence against liability.
6. It increases workforce productivity by reducing harassment.

F. REMEDIAL AND PREVENTIVE ACTION — A LEGAL OBLIGATION

1. Remedial Action

Review of the case law, particularly the decisions of the Supreme Court of Canada in *Robichaud*[16] and *Janzen*[17] and the U.S. Supreme Court decision in *Vinson*,[18] leave no doubt that the employer had an affirmative duty to investigate complaints of sexual harassment and to deal appropriately with the offending personnel.

When an employer receives a complaint or otherwise learns of alleged sexual harassment in the workplace, the employer should investigate promptly and thoroughly. The employer should take immediate and appropriate corrective action by doing whatever is necessary to end the harassment, make the victim whole by restoring lost benefits or opportunities, and prevent the misconduct from recurring. Appropriate disciplinary action against the perpetrator can range from reprimand to discharge. Generally, the corrective action should reflect the severity of the conduct. It is also advisable for the employer to make follow-up inquiries to ensure the harassment has

---

[16] *Robichaud v. Treasury Board*, (Can. 1987), 8 C.H.R.R. D/4326 (S.C.C.)
[17] *Janzen v. Platy Enterprises Ltd.*, (Man. 1989), 10 C.H.R.R. D/6205 (S.C.C.)
[18] *Meritor Savings Bank v. Vinson*, 106 S. Ct. 2399, 40 E.P.D. para. 36,159 (1986). The employer's affirmative duty was first enunciated in cases of harassment based on race or national origin. See also *United States v. City of Buffalo*, 457 F. Supp. 612 at 632-35, 19 FEP 776 (W.D.N.Y. 1978).

not resumed and the victim has not suffered retaliation. In a case where the employer instituted a malicious prosecution action against the victim it was found to be in retaliation for her complaining to the Human Rights Tribunal.[19] A retaliatory action against the complainant for exercising her rights under the human rights statute is illegal.

The Supreme Court of Canada in the *Robichaud* case[20] stated in no uncertain terms that "only an employer can remedy undesirable effects; only an employer can provide the most important remedy — a healthy work environment." And two years later in the *Janzen* case,[21] the Supreme Court of Canada reinforced the view that employers have a legal obligation to protect their employees from sexual harassment and provide a safe and healthy work environment.

The Human Rights Tribunal expanded it further when it stated that "where an employer or supervisor has the authority and duty to prevent wrongful conduct in the workplace, which conduct happens to constitute an infringement of the code (sexual harassment) and without lawful excuse fails to do so, thereby, indirectly infringes the right in question.... However, by facilitating, permitting, or acquiescing in (or 'authorizing, condoning, adopting or ratifying') wrongful conduct which (whether he knew it or not) constituted such an infringement, he did something indirectly that infringed" the rights of the complainant.[22]

It is important to re-emphasize, however, that no matter what the employer's policy is, the employer is always liable for any supervisory actions that affects the victim's employment states such as hiring, firing, promotion or pay. Where the employer failed to take any remedial actions as a result of the incident and took no measure to protect the complainant from further discriminatory behaviour, the employer would be held liable for causing discrimination in violation of the Human Rights Act.[23]

Thus, remedial and preventive action go hand in hand. One cannot be effective without the other in combatting sexual harassment in the workplace. It has been said beautifully that it is the action and not the intention which matters.

---

[19] *Haight v. Tantrum* (B.C. 1990), 12 C.H.R.R. D/250 (Wilson).
[20] *Supra*, note 16.
[21] *Supra*, note 17.
[22] *Shaw v. Levac Supply Ltd.* (Ont. 1991), 14 C.H.R.R. D/36 (Hubbard).
[23] *Karlenzig v. Chris' Holdings Ltd.* (Sask. 1991), 91 CLLC 17,015.

(a) Employer's Appropriate Response — An Example

In one case, the victim informed her employer that her co-worker had talked to her about sexual activities and touched her in an offensive manner. Within four days of receiving this information, the employer investigated the charges, reprimanded the guilty employee, placed him on probation, and warned him that further misconduct would result in discharge. A second co-worker who had witnessed the harassment was also reprimanded for not intervening on the victim's behalf or reporting the conduct. The court ruled that the employer's response constituted immediate and appropriate corrective action, and on this basis found the employer not liable.[24]

Like the E.E.O.C. Guidelines, the Human Rights Commissions in Canada encourage the employers to take all steps necessary to prevent sexual harassment from occurring, such as affirmatively raising the subject, expressing strong disapproval, developing appropriate sanctions, informing employees of their rights to raise and how to raise the issue of harassment and developing methods to sensitize all concerned.[25]

An effective preventive program should include an explicit policy against sexual harassment that is clearly and regularly communicated to employees and effectively implemented. The employer should affirmatively raise the subject with all supervisory and non-supervisory employees, express strong disapproval, and explain the sanctions for harassment. The employer should also have a procedure for resolving sexual harassment complaints. The procedure should be designed to "encourage victims of harassment to come forward" and should not require a victim to complain first to the offending supervisor. It should ensure confidentiality as much as possible and provide effective remedies, including protection of victims and witnesses against retaliation.

An employer should take the following initiatives:

1. Recognize and accept the fact that sexual harassment is likely to be occurring in the organization.
2. Develop a clear policy defining and prohibiting sexual harassment.
3. Establish an internal grievance system to handle complaints.
4. Communicate its policy to managers and employees alike.

---

[24] *Barrett v. Omaha National Bank*, 726 F. 2d 424, 33 E.P.D. 34,132 (8th Cir. 1984).
[25] E.E.O.C. Guidelines, 29 C.F.R. 1604.11(f).

G. WHAT CAN EMPLOYERS DO?

What measures then can employers take to prevent sexual harassment in the workplace? First and foremost, employers should have a clear, precise, and comprehensive written policy on sexual harassment, not only to avoid legal liability in a court action, but also to restore human dignity in the workplace.

Experts agree on the need for such a policy on harassment, but they differ widely on what this policy should or should not contain. Should a policy on sexual harassment be a unilateral statement by the employer or should there be consultation with a union, if any? Should a policy on sexual harassment contain a complaint procedure? If so, should it be a part of the existing grievance procedure or be independent of the grievance procedure? Many employers fear that a policy statement on sexual harassment would open a "can of worms" and that they would be in a no-win situation. Further, would a policy and procedure statement on sexual harassment protect the employer from legal liability? If such a policy is intended to prevent or eliminate sexual harassment from the workplace, these and other issues must be explored.

A policy in itself cannot prevent or protect employees from sexual harassment. It must be properly implemented and communicated in order to be effective. Even a well-implemented policy does not necessarily guarantee that harassment will never occur and that the employer will never be liable. However, the policy does provide evidence of the employer's commitment to prevent sexual harassment.

Once the employer has committed itself to the elimination of sexual harassment and has decided to draw up a policy, what should be the employer's approach?

First of all, the employer should review the existing company policy, removing any discriminatory or sex-segregating elements. The sexual harassment policy should be a separate policy, dealing specifically with the problem of sexual harassment, including a description of the programs and procedures through which the problem will be confronted. If the employer is dealing with unionized employees, it should discuss the terms of its plan with the union prior to its implementation, and to what extent the new procedures would affect unionized employees.

The company may also contact an appropriate Human Rights Commission for assistance and guidance in planning and developing a policy on sexual harassment.

H. ESSENTIAL ELEMENTS OF A SEXUAL HARASSMENT POLICY

The first and foremost element of a sexual harassment policy should be a declaration of war on sexual harassment. The employer should make a commitment to make and keep the work environment free from sexual harassment, and convey that commitment to all of its employees from top to bottom. The policy should send a clear and unequivocal message to all employees that sexual harassment is unacceptable as well as illegal and will not be tolerated by the company. The policy should set out clearly its strategy for prevention of harassment as well as procedures for handling sexual harassment complaints. A comprehensive sexual harassment policy should include:

1. A strong statement of the employer's philosophy and commitment concerning sexual harassment.
2. A clear and detailed definition of sexual harassment which includes examples of behaviours constituting verbal, non-verbal, gestures, visual, physical and psychological sexual harassment.
3. A redress mechanism, including a complaint procedure, i.e., guidelines for reporting incidents of sexual harassment, assurance of confidentiality, and protection from reprisal or retaliation and an investigation process.
4. Penalties for the harasser.
5. Remedies for the victim.
6. A provision for appeals.
7. A plan for implementation and prevention which should include ongoing communication, education and training.

1. Policy Statement

The policy should include a statement of the employer's commitment to the maintenance of a work environment that is free from sexual harassment. In committing itself to this goal, an employer is also committing itself to carry out programs and procedures that will ensure a harassment-free workplace for all employees. It must be made clear in the policy that any sexual harassment activities constitute a breach of the employer's policy and will incur punishment. For example:

> The company is proud of its tradition of maintaining a work environment in which all individuals are treated with respect and dignity. Sexual harassment in the workplace is unacceptable and will not be tolerated. It is also illegal.

This opening statement sends a clear and unmistakable message to all executive officers, managers, supervisors, and rank and file employees that the company is serious about the policy, not only because of legal and financial liability, but to enhance the working atmosphere for all employees.

In contrast, if the company's policy opens with an introduction that is either too general in substance or encased in cold legalism, it gives the impression that it is doing as little as it has to. For example:

> The company is an equal employment opportunity employer. It is the company's policy to provide equal employment opportunity to all persons consistent with employment requirements and qualifications and to comply with the *Human Rights Code* regarding discrimination because of race, colour, religion, creed, sex, national or ethnic origin, age, disability, etc.
>
> Harassment on the basis of sex is prohibited under the Ontario *Human Rights Code*.

2. Purpose

The policy should state the intent and purposes of the employer concisely and clearly. For example:

1. to maintain a working environment that is free from sexual harassment;
2. to educate and sensitize all employees to the issue of sexual harassment;
3. to provide a redress mechanism for handling and investigating sexual harassment complaints;
4. to encourage the prospective complainants to report all incidents of sexual harassment and assure them against reprisal or retaliation;
5. to assure all employees (whether complainants or alleged harassers) of fairness and objectivity at all levels of the investigation;
6. to make all employees responsible for maintaining the work environment free from sexual harassment — an employee who

believes that a co-worker has or is experiencing sexual harassment should inform the designated officer of the potential problem;
7. to provide an example of steps the company intends to take towards maintaining a work environment in which all employees can work in harmony with mutual respect and dignity.

3. Definition of Sexual Harassment

It is suggested that employers should define clearly the term "sexual harassment" in their policy because there is no universally accepted definition of sexual harassment. Although there appear to be some common elements to the various sexual harassment definitions that appear in collective agreements, policy statements, human rights legislation and commission guidelines, no two are precisely the same. Definitions vary from simple statements to extensive and explicit definitions that cover a range of behaviours.

Each definition relies heavily upon individual perception. It is difficult to determine exactly what behaviour constitutes sexual harassment because each case is different. However, if an employer decides not to include a definition of sexual harassment in the policy, the absence of any such guidelines may create confusion as to what constitutes sexual harassment.

In developing a definition of sexual harassment, language is an important consideration. The language should be concise, clear and as objective as possible. Because no definition will be complete or perfect, the definition may state "sexual harassment includes, but is not limited to". This leaves room for a broader interpretation to cover unpredictable human behaviour.

A detailed definition gives employees and the employer a clearer idea of the behaviour that constitutes sexual harassment. Elements that are common to most definitions include sexually based or oriented behaviours that may be expressed in verbal, physical or psychological terms. These behaviours must be perceived as being "unwanted" or "unwelcome" by the harassed individual. Also included should be the situational context in which these behaviours are manifested, creating sexual harassment. In the United States, the E.E.O.C. guidelines identify three circumstances in which sexual harassment may occur. These are:

1. where sexual conduct is made a condition of an individual's employment;

2. where such conduct or condition creates an employment consequence;
3. where such condition creates an offensive working environment or interferes with the job performance.

The definition should also show clearly that the victim of sexual harassment may be male or female and that the harasser may be male or female or of the same sex as the victim. In addition, it should be emphasized that sexual harassment may be caused by a person in authority, such as a supervisor, or by a co-worker, or by a non-employee, such as a customer or client of the employer.

It must be recognized that the purpose of the definition is not to constrain normal social interaction between people. However, its purpose is to make individuals aware of certain behaviours and attitudes that may be damaging and unwelcome to other employees, and thus forbid them during the course of employment.

Moreover, it is recommended that the policy should provide some examples of prohibited conduct which may constitute sexual harassment. For example:

- sexist jokes that cause awkwardness or embarrassment;
- display of sexually offensive material;
- derogatory or patronizing name calling;
- sexually suggestive or obscene comments or gestures;
- comments about a person's looks, appearance, body, etc;
- inquiries or comments about a person's sex life;
- sexual looks, such as leering and ogling with suggestive overtones;
- offensive sexual flirtations, advances and propositions;
- unwanted touching, patting or pinching;
- verbal threat or abuse;
- sexual assault.

For further detailed description of sexual behaviours that constitute sexual harassment see Chapter 1, *supra*.

Further, the policy should make it clear that this behaviour is unacceptable not only during working hours and on the employer's premises but also in other work-related settings, such as conferences, seminars and business trips as well as business-related social events.

4. Application and Scope of the Policy

It is important for an effective sexual harassment policy to identify the persons covered—male and female employees and managers. The policy should be all-inclusive.

(a) Employees at All Levels

In defining the scope or persons to be covered by the policy, it should be kept in mind that while sexual harassment most often takes place when there is an imbalance of power or a difference of status between the persons involved, it may also occur between persons of equal status and power. The object of a sexual harassment policy should be not only to insulate the company from liability, but also to ensure a positive and healthy work environment. Therefore, an effective and comprehensive sexual harassment policy should cover all employees: rank and file employees (bargaining unit employees), support staff, management (confidential and executive secretaries), supervisors, managers, senior executives, board of directors, and even vice-presidents and the president.

(b) Prospective Employees

Not only should current employees be included, but applicants, potential employees and former employees should be covered as well.

(c) Non-Employees

The policy should also cover non-employees, such as customers, clients and the employees of suppliers and service contractors, consultants, accountants and auditors.

As stated earlier, remedies may differ when the harrasser is a non-employee. The employer, however, should anticipate many sensitive issues in formulating sexual harassment policies such as ways to address non-employees who may be responsible for objectionable conduct.

The policy should emphasize that all incidents are to be reported no matter who the offender may be.

5. Consensual Relationships

The issue was discussed earlier of whether the employer should attempt to prohibit consensual relationships among the employees, and both the merits and demerits of such an approach were pointed out. A shadow of suspicion always remains of whether the subordinate in a superior/subordinate relationship is truly acting freely, and what is the possibility for retaliation if the relationship sours.

To avoid the possibility of complaints being made at the end of a relationship, employers may be advised to include in their sexual harassment policies a consensual relationship clause, cautioning against consenting romantic relationships between employees, particularly between a supervisor and an employee. For example:

> Consenting romantic and sexual relationships between employees, while not expressly forbidden, are generally considered to be very unwise. The respect and trust accorded to a person by his/her subordinate, as well as the power (authority) exercised by that person in evaluating or otherwise supervising his/her subordinates, greatly diminish the subordinate's actual freedom of choice. A supervisor who enters into a sexual relationship with another employee should realize that, if a complaint of sexual harassment is subsequently made, it will be exceedingly difficult to prove immunity on the ground of mutual consent.

It is important to remember that a relationship may begin as consensual but, after it ends, may become a harassing situation.

There are a number of decided cases when after a female employee ended and refused to resume a relationship with her supervisor, he began criticizing her work or made her life difficult and in some cases even fired her. On the other hand, she may be afraid to complain because she thought that since the relationship began consensually, her charge of retaliation would not be believed.

6. Redress Mechanism

Although a effective preventive action program may be successful in deterring many harassers, problems will still arise. Thus, the employer is required to establish a redress mechanism that will, first, provide relief for the victim, and second, impose sanctions on the harasser.

Because of the sensitive and personal nature of sexual harassment incidents, the employer should develop a separate mechanism to deal specifically with sexual harassment allegations. This must include a complaint procedure, an investigative process, a system of imposing penalties and granting remedies and an appeal procedure.

The policy should establish who will be involved in the redress mechanism. It is desirable that a specific individual or group of individuals be appointed to deal with the allegations of sexual harassment. These individuals should be neutral, unbiased, and well qualified to deal with these particular issues.

Given the fact that most sexual harassment victims are female employees, it would make eminent sense to ensure that at least one woman, if not more, be designated to hear sexual harassment complaints.

(a) Reporting of Complaints

The policy should designate a number of people, both men and women, at various levels of the company, to whom a complaint of sexual harassment could be made. It is recommended that there should be multiple entry points. This means affording more than one route to invoke the procedural process for filing a complaint. Multiple routes are important because there may be individuals whom, for various reasons, the complainant may be uncomfortable approaching about the situation. The individual about whom the complaint is being made may even be the person who would ordinarily receive the complaint. For example, the American Supreme Court in *Meritor Savings Bank v. Vinson*[26] criticized the employer for having a grievance procedure which required the employee to complain to her supervisor, who was the alleged harasser.

---

[26] 106 S. Ct. 2399, 40 E.P.D. para. 36,159 (1986).

The policy should make it clear that the complainant, in addition to the procedure provided in this policy, has the right to file a grievance under the collective agreement, if any, or file a complaint with an appropriate Human Rights Commission.

It is acceptable to encourage a prospective complainant to indicate promptly and firmly to the alleged harasser that his/her behaviour is unwelcome. This puts the perpetrator on notice that the complainant finds the behaviour offensive and considers it harassment. The policy, however, should not make such notice a prerequisite to a complaint.

For the policy to work effectively, employees should not be required to report a complaint to their immediate supervisor. The working relationship between the complainant and the supervisor could be impaired. However, the policy may suggest that if the complainant believes that the supervisor can resolve the problem informally and discreetly, the complainant has the option to report to the supervisor.

(b) *Protection Against Retaliation*

Retaliation against the complainant of sexual harassment or the persons who testify or assist the complainant is an offence under the human rights law. Thus, an absence of a policy statement on this subject will discourage the individual's willingness to report. The policy should state clearly that there will be no retaliation for reporting a complaint.

> Retaliation against any individual for reporting sexual harassment is an offence and a very serious violation of the policy, and will not be tolerated. It should be reported immediately.

The policy should also state that in cases where the harasser has also retaliated against the complainant, the disciplinary action should be harsher than would have been imposed for the sexual harassment alone.

Individuals who are not themselves complainants but who assist in the sexual harassment investigation should also be protected from retaliation under the policy.

(c) *Availability*

A key element of the redress mechanism is availability. The redress mechanism must be made available to all employees. Both men and women, employees and supervisors should be able to use this service. Also, it should be specifically mentioned that individuals who observe harassing behaviour are responsible to report this behaviour by way of the redress mechanism. However, a complainant shoud be able to bypass supervisory staff members, should the complaint involve a supervisor. The redress mechanism should be separate from the personnel department to ensure that biases will not develop among those who have power to affect employment decisions.

(d) *Confidentiality*

Confidentiality is very important when dealing with the sensitive and personal nature of sexual harassment problems. The policy should ensure that any individual who uses the redress mechanism is guaranteed maximum confidentiality. This provision of confidentiality extends to the complainant, the alleged harasser, or any other individual who reports harassing behaviour. Confidentiality should be maintained at each stage of the procedure.

Should a complaint proceed to the stage of a formal complaint requiring investigation, it will be necessary to keep a file on pertinent information. These files should be maintained separately from the employee's personnel files and be kept under lock and key. A statement of confidentiality is meant to protect the complainant and the alleged harasser. Lack of confidentiality may discourage the victim from coming forward to complain and may lead to damaged reputations.

The assurance of confidentiality can be expressed in different ways. For example, the policy may state:

> Any allegation or complaint of sexual harassment will be kept in confidence, except as is necessary to investigate and to respond to any legal and/or administrative proceedings arising out of or relating to a sexual harassment report.

(e) *Complaint Procedure*

A complaint procedure may differ from employer to employer depending on the need, size and circumstances of each employer. A complainant should make a complaint to the designated officer. In order to give all individuals an opportunity to come forward, the complaint mechanism should include both male and female officials, so that the complainants would not feel intimidated to discuss matters with a member of the opposite sex. The policy should emphasize and ensure that complainants will not be subjected to any form of reprisal. Individuals should be encouraged to report all incidents of sexual harassment.

The initial contact may involve an informal interview with the complainant in which the appointed official would advise the complainant as to his/her options. The official should also provide the complainant with emotional support, aiding the complainant in coming to an understanding of the situation.

The complainant may choose to submit a formal complaint, which is usually a written report giving a detailed account of the harassment incident(s). The company should develop a standardized complaint form that will record details such as names, dates, times, locations, incidents and other necessary information. The employer may wish to establish a time limit for the submission of complaints and this should be clearly outlined in the policy.

The official may counsel the complainant to contact the alleged harasser by letter in order to discourage him/her from further harassment. Further, the official may assign someone in authority from senior management to informally discuss the situation with the alleged harasser. If either party requests mediation and both parties are willing, a mediator may be appointed to resolve the issue. However, if these methods fail to resolve the complaint, the complaint should be dealt with through a formal investigation process.

(f) Investigation Procedure

All complaints should be taken seriously and dealt with fairly and promptly. Investigation of a complaint may involve a variety of individuals. There are different alternatives which could be pursued. For example, the employer could establish a committee for the purpose of investigating complaints. The committee should consist of both male and female officials. Persons involved in investigation procedures should have some experience in personnel or labour relations. They should also have the ability to conduct an interview and be familiar with established arbitration procedures. If it is not feasible to establish a committee of any size, the formal complaints should be investigated and decided upon by the chief executive officer of the company or its designee.

Investigative procedures should include interviews with both the complainant and the accused individual and with any possible witnesses. Existing personnel files should also be examined in order to determine whether there were previous complaints or evidence of prior friction between the two parties.

The policy should state clearly that the investigation committee will approach the investigation in an unbiased manner as both the complainant and the alleged harasser are entitled to a fair hearing. Throughout the proceedings, the investigation committee must maintain a neutral position and guard itself against any premature decision.

After investigation, the committee may draw up a draft conclusion that would be presented to and discussed with the individual in charge of discipline. This individual may also choose to consult with legal counsel prior to taking further action. The employer should take extreme care in protecting the alleged harasser against any frivolous charges, ensuring that the charges are well founded before imposing discipline or discharge measures. If there is no foundation for the charge against the alleged harasser, the case will be dismissed.

(g) Penalties for the Harasser

The employer should reinforce the idea that individuals found guilty of sexual harassment behaviours will be disciplined. The nature and type of discipline should depend upon the severity of the incident. Disciplinary measures may range from verbal reprimands and warnings for less serious offences to suspensions without pay or discharges for more serious offences. If the employer decides that a transfer will be necessary, it should be the harasser who is transferred and not the victim. However, before deciding upon the appropriate disciplinary action, factors such as the nature of the behaviour, the persistence of the behaviour, and whether or not the harasser displays co-operation and willingness to change, should be taken into consideration.

(h) Remedies to the Victim

In a case where a victim of sexual harassment has suffered a loss, such as a demotion or denial of a promotion, it is appropriate to restore such a person to his/her proper employment position. The victim should also be entitled to receive compensation for loss of benefits such as back pay. In response to damages for emotional distress and suffering, the employer should specifically state whether he plans to provide for these, and if so, it would be wise to set a monetary limit.

Other remedies may include a written or oral apology from the harasser. Where the complaint is found to be unjustified, it may be appropriate to grant similar remedies to the respondent.

(i) Appeals

The policy should provide a route by which decisions may be appealed should either party be dissatisfied with the results of the investigation. The policy should outline such a procedure, including the terms, conditions and time limits that are to be adhered to.

7. False Accusation

The policy should encourage the victims to come forward and lay charges of sexual harassment, but at the same time it should discourage false and fabricated charges against innocent persons.

False accusation is a serious matter. A person making a false accusation may, in addition to a disciplinary action, be exposed to a damage suit for slandering under the civil law. For example, a British court in 1991 awarded damages to a doctor falsely accused of sexual harassment by his female colleague in the amount of £150,000 plus £100,000 in costs.[27]

8. Implementation and Prevention

Prevention is the most effective tool an employer can use for the elimination of sexual harassment. Preventive action includes (a) communication, (b) education and (c) training.

---

[27] See 11 *The Lawyers Weekly*, No. 30, p. 20 (December 6, 1991).

(a) Communication

Merely developing a policy on sexual harassment is not sufficient. It is the dissemination of the policy among the employees that is paramount. It is the employer's responsibility to communicate its policy to all its employees. This may be done by posting it in the offices, circulating memos, or printing the policy in in-house newspapers and pamphlets. It is imperative that the employer communicate a strong disapproval of sexual harassment to all employees and supervisory personnel and maintain this strong position. The employer's personal attitude and commitment to this issue will foster awareness and disapproval of sexual harassment among employees.

(b) Education

In addition to the need for communication, the employer should provide a program by which employees and supervisors could be educated in the area of sexual harassment. All employees should receive some degree of education regarding this issue. Education could take place in the form of seminars, meetings, or workshops. If it is not possible for all employees to take part in these sessions, literature should be made available to them.

Employees should be educated in the following areas:

1. what company policy is regarding sexual harassment;
2. what sexual harassment is and what it is not;
3. the employee's right to complain;
4. how to submit a complaint.

These sessions should not become too technical or too legalistic and should be administered by an individual with proper knowledge, training, and background in handling sex discrimination and sexual harassment issues.

(c) Training

In addition to education for employees, special training sessions should be provided for supervisory and managerial staff. It is important that these individuals be trained to recognize potential problems and learn how to deal with them. Training should deal with the significance and consequences of sexual harassment within the company. Also, managers and supervisors should be informed of the role they have in the company's policy and program. In larger companies, perhaps managers and supervisors should carry out more responsibility in ensuring that the employees in their departments are aware of the policy and that they abide by it.

An ongoing training program should be provided for counsellors, grievance officers and others already involved or recruited into the redress mechanism. Training could take place through special workshops and seminars designed to increase sensitivity and awareness of sexual harassment problems. Staff members who have a responsibility to investigate sexual harassment complaints will certainly need skills in investigative questioning and research, and in responding to typical emotions and behaviours of those who file complaints and those who are accused. Although such knowledge and skill may develop with time and experience, special training will expedite an effective and efficient response and help establish the institution's credibility and reputation for dealing responsibly with complex issues like sexual harassment.

9. Conclusion

Developing a policy that emphasizes the employer's commitment to the elimination of sexual harassment and establishing the procedures by which this will be accomplished is the first step in fighting sexual harassment. However, in order to maintain a workplace free from harassment, the employer must ensure implementation of the programs and plans which have been outlined in the policy. Only then will positive changes occur in the attitudes and behaviours of all employees.

* * *

Two samples of sexual harassment policies follow, one in a unionized setting and the other in a non-union professional setting.

In drafting an effective sexual harassment policy, consideration should be given to the nature of the workplace and its characteristics, such as size, type of business and workforce, etc. It is hoped that the above discussion and the following sample policies will provide a useful starting point for employers who are interested in drafting and implementing a sexual harassment policy.

EXAMPLE OF SEXUAL HARASSMENT POLICY AND PROCEDURE IN A UNIONIZED SETTING

The City of Toronto Policy on Sexual Harassment
Reproduced with permission.

[The City of Toronto policy on sexual harassment is unique in the sense that it is jointly agreed to and signed by the mayor of the city and the presidents of three unions in the City of Toronto. The policy is in two parts. One is directed to the managers under the heading "Your Responsibilities as a Manager" and the second part is directed to the employees for their information. Further, the policy is printed in the form of a brochure and freely distributed to both the managers and the employees.]

SEXUAL HARASSMENT

A Commitment and a Responsibility

The Corporation of the City of Toronto and the unions and professional association representing its employees believe the working environment should at all times be supportive of the dignity and self-esteem of individuals.

Achieving this desired environment greatly depends upon mutual respect, co-operation and understanding among fellow workers. Attitudes and behaviour that undermine this goal are detrimental to all and should not be tolerated.

High on the list of unacceptable behaviour is sexual harassment — a serious and offensive problem.

Victims of sexual harassment need little explanation of this degrading and humiliating experience. It is important, however, that we all have a clear understanding of what constitutes sexual harassment and what steps can and will be taken to put an end to this practice.

This brochure provides some observations and practical solutions with this goal in mind.

SIGNED

Art Eggleton
Mayor, City of Toronto

Jeff Rose
President, Local 79
Canadian Union of
Public Employees

Leslie Kovacsi
President, Local 43
Canadian Union of
Public Employees

Ralph Berger
President, COTAPSAI

PART I — SEXUAL HARASSMENT

Your Responsibilities as a Manager

Sexual harassment can be expressed in a number of ways which may include:

— Unnecessary touching or patting
— Suggestive or other sexually aggressive remarks
— Leering (suggestive staring) at a person's body
— Demands for sexual favours
— Compromising invitations
— Physical assault

Repetition and irritation characterize these actions when initiated by a co-worker or supervisor.

According to the Human Rights Code they need occur only once when initiated by a supervisor.

A reprisal or a threat of reprisal by a supervisor for the rejection of such behaviour is also a form of sexual harassment.

For the most part, the victims of sexual harassment are women. However, sexual harassment can also occur between homosexuals and by women towards men. It is a phenomenon present in every job level and occupation.

Common Reactions to the Problem

As with many people first discussing the subject, your reaction is probably one of disbelief. "It couldn't happen to her"; "Oh well, her, she asks for it" are common responses.

Effects and Consequences: On the Victim

Victims of sexual harassment suffer tension, anger, fear and frustration. These psychological effects often manifest themselves in such physical ailments as headaches, ulcers, and other nervous disorders. In some cases these ailments are so serious they require medical attention.

Although sexual harassment can occur between peers, most incidents take place between supervisors and employees. If the victims report the incident or refuse to comply, the harasser often attempts to affect their working conditions, training, promotional opportunities and job security. Even after victims leave the job, which they often feel is their only recourse, the harasser may jeopardize the victims' future job opportunities by giving poor references.

Effects and Consequences: On You, the Manager

The psychological and physical effects of sexual harassment can have a negative impact on job performance and ultimately on you. Work may suffer to such an extent that you may begin to question the employees' abilities. You may even take disciplinary actions without seeking the real cause of the deteriorating performance.

If a sexual harassment complaint is filed with the Human Rights Commission you as a supervisor can be ordered to take action to prevent the continuation or repetition of the harassment.

Be advised the problem of sexual harassment does not end when a worker leaves the job. Harassers are often repeaters.

The next person hired to fill the victim's position may also become a victim as may other employees in the same workplace.

What You, as a Manager, can do about the Problem

As a manager you have the responsibility to: Assist in upholding the related clauses of COTAPSAI Local 43 and Local 79 Collective Agreements.

The Local 43 and Local 79 Collective Agreements contain a clear prohibition against sexual harassment which can form the basis of a very strong grievance.

The relevant clauses of the Collective Agreements read as follows:

> Every employee has a right to be free from sexual harassment and from any reprisal or threat of reprisal for the rejection of such behaviour.
>
> Where an allegation is made by an employee that the "Sexual Harassment" clause has been violated, a grievance shall be initiated at step two within five (5) days after such violation is alleged to have occurred.

If you're approached by a union steward or an association representative assist them in the investigation of the complaint.

You can also act as a mediator by approaching the harasser on behalf of the victim.

Protect employees from sexual harassment.

See that sexual harassment by supervisors or peers is terminated.

THE FOLLOWING PREVENTIVE MEASURES WILL HELP YOU IN FULFILLING YOUR RESPONSIBILITIES

1. Let your staff know that you take the issue of sexual harassment seriously. Distribute a memo to all employees defining sexual harassment and reiterate the clause of the Collective Agreements which address the issue. Post a copy of the clause on a bulletin board in the department.
2. Discuss sexual harassment in management and supervisory training sessions. Make sure supervisory personnel are aware of the repercussions that can result from sexual harassment.

3. See to it that the theory and practice of deterring and terminating sexual harassment coincide. For example, remove all nude or sexually explicit photographs displayed in the office.
4. Evidence is always a major factor in sexual harassment complaints. You could be called upon to act as a witness. Be on the look out for the possible harasser. Since most harassment occurs behind closed doors, this can be an extremely difficult task. However, if you suspect someone, be particularly aware of her/his actions.
5. Question sudden changes in evaluations of employees submitted by supervisors.
6. Follow up employee complaints concerning performance appraisals or the behaviour of supervisors. They may be unaware that their behaviour is offensive. Treat this discussion as a warning and record any further complaints from either the initial victim or any others.
7. Arrange exit interviews with employees who are resigning or have resigned to discover their reasons for leaving. If sexual harassment is the cause, encourage those who haven't yet resigned to stay. Provide them with information to process a formal complaint.
8. In orientation sessions with new employees deal with the issue of sexual harassment and make it known that the department will not tolerate it and that all complaints will be followed up.
9. Explore the possibility of holding labour/management seminars in order to gain the co-operation of union/association representatives in dealing effectively with sexual harassment.
10. Watch out for the symptoms of the sexually harassed person, e.g. reduced productivity, psychological effects such as anger, fear, frustration, increased sick leave and sudden changes in work performance evaluation.
11. Approach employees if you suspect something. They may be reluctant to approach you, but by letting them know you're aware of negative changes, they may welcome the opportunity to share their concerns with you.
12. Instruct the victims of their rights, of how to corroborate evidence and what process to follow to file a formal complaint.
13. Parties to complaints of sexual harassment should be protected from reprisals from each other, or co-workers, during and after the investigation process.

HELP STOP SEXUAL HARASSMENT IN THE WORKPLACE

Although sexual harassment in the workplace is not a new issue, it is only recently that effective solutions to the problem are being sought. By following the steps stated here, you can improve the working conditions of your employees, which in turn will affect the overall working environment and productivity of the area for which you, as a manager, are responsible.

PART II — SEXUAL HARASSMENT

Information for Employees

Effects and Consequences

Victims of sexual harassment suffer two distinct kinds of consequences: physical/psychological distress and career blockage.

Psychological effects suffered, such as tension, anger, fear and frustration, will often manifest themselves in such physical ailments as headaches, ulcers, and other nervous disorders. In some cases these ailments are serious enough to require medical attention.

Career Blockage

The psychological and physical effects of sexual harassment may have a further negative consequence particularly as they affect job performance. Although sexual harassment can occur between peers, most incidents take place between supervisors and employees. Work may suffer to such an extent that a supervisor may question victims' work abilities and take disciplinary action without seeking the real cause of their deteriorating performance.

If victims report the incident or refuse to comply, the harasser often attempts to affect their working conditions, training, promotion opportunities and job security. Even after victims leave the job, which they often feel is their only recourse, the harasser may jeopardize their future job opportunities by giving poor references.

The problem of sexual harassment does not end when an employee leaves the job. Harassers are often repeaters. The next person hired to fill the position may also become a victim, as may other employees in the same workplace.

Solutions

If you know or suspect sexual harassment is happening to a co-worker: Support the victim. As a co-worker and union/association member, you owe it to yourself and the victim to give the needed understanding and support. With the consent of the victim . . . Speak to your steward, or if a non-union employee, to your association representative. The union/association wants to help solve this kind of problem.

The COTAPSAI memorandum of understanding includes a mechanism for filing employees' complaints which are referred to the association's Staff Relations Committee. The Local 43 and Local 79 Collective Agreements contain a clear prohibition against sexual harassment which can form the basis of a very strong grievance. The union steward or association representative can act as a mediator by approaching the harasser on behalf of the victim and can assist in filing a grievance.

The relevant clauses of the Collective Agreements read as follows:

> Every employee has a right to be free from sexual harassment and from any reprisal or threat of reprisal for the rejection of such behaviour.
> Where an allegation is made by an employee that the "Sexual Harassment" clause has been violated, a grievance shall be initiated at step two within five (5) days after such violation is alleged to have occurred.

Contact the harasser's supervisor and ask that the harasser be spoken to and/or report the problem to the staff of the Equal Opportunity Division and/or the Employee Advisory Service of the Personnel Services Division. Staff there are concerned about the issue and are prepared to support victims. They are also committed to implementing educational programs on the subject for all City employees including management.

Solutions: If You are a Victim

1. **Don't feel guilty**. Sexual harassment is an expression of power. Studies have shown that it is usually practised with little regard for age, appearance or marital status. Harassers or their supporters may accuse you of wearing enticing clothing or using enticing actions, in order to justify their aggressive behaviour. But remember, in sexual harassment situations it is the harasser who is in the wrong, not the victim.
2. **Take action**. If you don't, your non-action may be interpreted as consent. You will continue to suffer the consequences or be forced to leave your job. Your harasser will continue harassing you and probably your replacement.
3. **Ask the harasser to stop the offensive actions**. You can do this verbally in the presence of a witness and/or by a warning letter written by yourself or with the help of your union or association. (Keep a copy of the letter.)
4. If these steps don't stop the harasser's behaviour, you can **speak to your union steward, or** if a non-union employee, **to your association representative**. Your steward/association representative can act as a mediator by approaching the harasser on your behalf and will assist in filing a grievance/complaint. You can also approach management staff from the Equal Opportunity Division and/or Employee Advisory Service of the Personnel Services Division and Rehabilitation staff from the Office of Labour Relations. Any of these services can act as a mediator and approach the harasser on your behalf.
5. **Keep track of each incident of harassment**, where and when it occurred and what was said and done. Remember, evidence is often your only recourse. Your records will support you when you need them the most. If you file a grievance that goes to arbitration, this kind of documentation is vital to your case.
6. **Find witnesses and other victims**. Discuss the problem with colleagues. They may have witnessed your experience or been harassed themselves, but have been reluctant to take any action. Also, contact previous employees and find out if their leaving was the result of sexual harassment. If your inquiries indicate that other and/or former employees were also harassed, seek their co-operation. Confronting the harasser or filing a grievance is much less threatening when you have the support of colleagues. The more evidence you compile the stronger the case for disciplinary action and/or prevention of future abuse.

7. **Be prepared**. Keep a record of compliments and accomplishments achieved relating to your work. If your harasser gives you a poor job performance appraisal you'll have a rebuttal ready.
8. If none of the above suggestions seem appropriate, you may wish to consult a lawyer, the police or the Human Rights Commission.

HELP STOP SEXUAL HARASSMENT IN THE WORKPLACE

Many people have suffered in silence as a result of sexual harassment in the workplace. Although not a new issue it is only recently that effective solutions to the problems are being sought. By following the steps outlined here, you can educate people about the issue, familiarize yourself with your rights, and protect yourself should you become a victim.

EXAMPLE OF SEXUAL HARASSMENT POLICY AND PROCEDURE IN A NON-UNION PROFESSIONAL SETTING

The Law Society of Upper Canada Sexual Harassment Policy Recommended for Member Law Firms

Reproduced with permission of the Law Society of Upper Canada (footnotes omitted).

POLICY STATEMENT

1. [Name of firm] is committed to providing a collegial working environment in which all individuals are treated with respect and dignity. Each individual has the right to work in a professional atmosphere which promotes equal opportunities and prohibits discriminatory practices.

Sexual harassment is a form of discrimination based on sex. It is prohibited in Ontario by the *Human Rights Code* (R.S.O. 1990, c. H.19) and is illegal: . . . .

Sexual harassment is offensive, degrading and threatening. [Name of firm] has adopted this personnel policy to make clear that sexual harassment will not be tolerated in our firm. Individuals, regardless of seniority, found to have engaged in conduct constituting sexual harassment may be severely disciplined.

2. This policy applies to all those working for [name of firm] including secretarial, support, professional and administrative staff, articling and summer students, associates and partners. [Name of firm] will not tolerate sexual harassment whether engaged in by fellow employees, supervisors, associates or partners.

The firm recognizes that its members and employees may be subjected to sexual harassment by clients or others who conduct business with the firm, by opposing counsel, court personnel or judges. In these circumstances the firm acknowledges its responsibility to do all in its power to support and assist the person subjected to such harassment.

The firm encourages reporting of all incidents of sexual harassment, regardless of who the offender may be.

3. Notwithstanding the existence of this policy, every person continues to have the right to seek assistance from the Ontario Human Rights Commission, even when steps are being taken under this policy.

4. The purposes of this policy are:

    (a) to maintain a working environment that is free from sexual harassment;
    (b) to alert all members and employees of the firm to the fact that sexual harassment in the workplace is an offence under the law;
    (c) to set out the types of behaviour that may be considered offensive;
    (d) to establish a mechanism for receiving complaints of sexual harassment and to provide a procedure by which [name of firm] will deal with these complaints; and
    (e) to provide an example of the steps a responsible employer can take towards maintaining a working environment in which members and employees treat each other with mutual respect.

5. This policy is not intended to constrain social interaction between people in the firm.

DEFINITIONS

6. (a) For the purposes of this policy "**sexual harassment**" is defined as:

    One or a series of incidents involving unwelcome sexual advances, requests for sexual favours, or other verbal or physical conduct of a sexual nature

    (i) when such conduct might reasonably be expected to cause insecurity, discomfort, offence or humiliation to another person or group; or
    (ii) when submission to such conduct is made either implicitly or explicitly a condition of employment; or
    (iii) when submission to or rejection of such conduct is used as a basis for any employment decision (including, but not limited to, matters of promotion, raise in salary, job security and benefits affecting the employee); or
    (iv) when such conduct has the purpose or the effect of interfering with a person's work performance or creating an intimidating, hostile or offensive work environment.

    (b) Types of behaviour which constitute sexual harassment include, but are not limited to:

    - sexist jokes causing embarrassment or offence, told or carried out after the joker has been advised that they are embarrassing or offensive, or that are by their nature clearly embarrassing or offensive
    - leering
    - the display of sexually offensive material
    - sexually degrading words used to describe a person
    - derogatory or degrading remarks directed towards members of one sex or one sexual orientation
    - sexually suggestive or obscene comments or gestures
    - unwelcome inquiries or comments about a person's sex life
    - unwelcome sexual flirtations, advances, propositions
    - persistent unwanted contact or attention after the end of a consensual relationship
    - requests for sexual favours
    - unwanted touching
    - verbal abuse or threats
    - sexual assault.

(c) Sexual harassment most commonly occurs in the form of behaviour by men towards women; however, sexual harassment can also occur between men, between women, or as behaviour by women towards men.

7. For the purposes of this policy, retaliation against an individual

   (a) for having invoked this policy (whether on behalf of oneself or another individual); or
   (b) for having participated or cooperated in any investigation under this policy; or
   (c) for having been associated with a person who has invoked this policy or participated in these procedures.

   will be treated as sexual harassment.

8. For the purposes of this policy "**employment-related sexual harassment**" means sexual harassment by a member or employee of the firm which occurs

   (i) in the working environment, or
   (ii) anywhere else as a result of employment responsibilities or employment relationships.

   It includes, but is not limited to, sexual harassment

   - at the office
   - outside the office
   - at office-related social functions
   - in the course of work assignments outside the office
   - in the courtroom
   - at work-related conferences or training sessions
   - during work-related travel
   - over the telephone.

RESPONSIBILITIES

9. [The managing body of the firm] is responsible for:

   (a) discouraging and preventing employment-related sexual harassment; this is a continuing responsibility, whether or not formal written complaints of sexual harassment have been brought to the attention of [the managing body of the firm];

Essential Elements of a Sexual Harassment Policy

    (b) investigating every formal written complaint of sexual harassment;
    (c) imposing strict disciplinary measures, when a complaint of employment-related sexual harassment is found to have been substantiated, regardless of the seniority of the offender;
    (d) doing all in its power to support and assist any member or employee of the firm who complains of sexual harassment by a person who is not a member or employee of the firm (e.g. client, opposing counsel, judge, member of court staff, messenger);
    (e) providing advice and support to persons who are subjected to sexual harassment;
    (f) formally acknowledging to a person who has been found to have been sexually harassed that sexual harassment has taken place;
    (g) regularly reviewing the procedures of this policy to ensure that they adequately meet the policy objectives;
    (h) maintaining records as required by this policy;
    (i) making all members and employees of the firm aware of the problem of sexual harassment and the existence of the procedures available under this policy; and
    (j) appointing Advisors, and providing the training and resources for them to fulfil their responsibilities under this policy.

10. Every member and employee of the firm has a responsibility to play a part in ensuring that the working environment is free from sexual harassment. This responsibility is to be discharged by avoidance of any conduct which might constitute sexual harassment. In addition, any member or employee of the firm who believes that a colleague has experienced or is experiencing sexual harassment, or retaliation for having brought forward a complaint of sexual harassment, is encouraged to notify one of the Advisors appointed under this policy.

DISCIPLINARY ACTION

11. Members and employees of the firm against whom a complaint of employment-related sexual harassment is substantiated may be severely disciplined, up to and including dismissal or removal from partnership. This policy will be applied irrespective of seniority.

CONFIDENTIALITY

12. [Name of firm] understands that it is difficult to come forward with a complaint of sexual harassment and recognizes a complainant's interest in keeping the matter confidential.

13. To protect the interests of the complainant, the person complained against and any others who may report incidents of sexual harassment, confidentiality will be maintained throughout the investigatory process to the extent practicable and appropriate under the circumstances.

14. All records of complaints, including contents of meetings, interviews, results of investigations and other relevant material will be kept confidential by [name of firm], except where disclosure is required by a disciplinary or other remedial process.

ADVISORS

15. The firm will appoint at least two persons who are themselves members or employees of the firm to serve as Advisors under this policy.

16. Each Advisor shall have access to notes and records kept by any other Advisor.

17. In carrying out their duties under this policy, Advisors will be directly responsible to [the managing body of the firm].

18. The firm will arrange for the Advisors to receive appropriate initial and continuing training as well as other institutional support and assistance for carrying out their responsibilities under this policy.

PROCEDURE

19. (a) A person who considers that she or he has been subjected to sexual harassment (or retaliation for having brought forward a complaint of sexual harassment) is encouraged to bring the matter to the attention of the person responsible for the conduct.

For convenience, a person who considers that she or he has been subjected to sexual harassment (or retaliation for having brought forward a complaint of sexual harassment) is hereinafter referred to as the "complainant" even though that individual may not lay a formal written complaint.

(b) Where the complainant does not wish to bring the matter directly to the attention of the person responsible, or where such an approach is attempted and does not produce a satisfactory result, the complainant should seek the advice of an Advisor.

(c) The Advisor will advise the complainant of:

  (i) the right to lay a formal written complaint under this policy when the alleged harasser is a member or employee of the firm;
  (ii) the availability of counselling and other support services provided by the firm;
  (iii) the right to be represented by legal counsel or other person of choice during at any stage of the process when the complainant is required or entitled to be present;
  (iv) the right to withdraw from any further action in connection with the complaint at any stage (even though the firm may continue to investigate the complaint);
  (v) other avenues of recourse such as the right to file a complaint with the Ontario Human Rights Commission or, where appropriate, the right to lay an information under the *Criminal Code*; and
  (vi) any time limits which may apply to such other avenues of recourse.

(d) Where the alleged harasser is a member or employee of the firm, there are three possible outcomes to a meeting between a complainant and an Advisor:

  (i) **Where complainant and Advisor agree that the conduct does not constitute sexual harassment.**

  If the complainant and the Advisor, after discussing the matter, agree that the conduct in question does not constitute sexual harassment as defined in this policy, the Advisor will take no further action and will make no record in any file.

  (ii) **Where complainant brings evidence of sexual harassment but does not wish to lay a formal written complaint.**

  It may happen that a complainant (or a third party) brings to the attention of the Advisor facts which constitute *prima facie* evidence of sexual harassment but, after discussion with the Advisor, the complainant decides not to lay a formal written complaint.

In some such cases, the complainant may not wish any further action whatsoever to be taken. In other such cases, the complainant may wish the Advisor to speak to the person whose conduct has caused offence.

In all such cases, the Advisor, having received *prima facie* evidence of sexual harassment, must decide whether or not to lay a formal written complaint (even if the decision is contrary to the wishes of the complainant).

Where the Advisor decides that the laying of a formal written complaint would not be appropriate, the Advisor will make no record in any file unless the Advisor decides to speak to the person whose conduct has caused the offence, in which case the Advisor will keep a written record of what the Advisor said to that person.

Where the Advisor decides that the evidence and the surrounding circumstances are such as to require the laying of a formal written complaint, the Advisor will

(A) issue a formal written complaint signed by the Advisor;
(B) provide copies of the complaint, without delay, to the person against whom the complaint is laid and to the person who was the subject of the alleged harassment; and
(C) without delay, file the complaint with [the managing body of the firm].

(iii) **Where complainant decides to lay formal written complaint.**

If the complainant, after meeting with the Advisor, decides to lay a formal complaint, including the situation where the Advisor is of the opinion the conduct in question does not constitute sexual harassment as defined in this policy, the Advisor will

(A) assist the complainant to draft a formal written complaint which must be signed by the complainant;
(B) give copies of the complaint, without delay, to the person against whom the complaint is laid and to the complainant; and

(C) without delay, file the complaint with [the managing body of the firm].

(e) Where the Advisor gives a copy of the complaint to the person against whom the complaint is laid, the Advisor will include with the complaint a copy of this policy and a notice that the person has the right to be represented by legal counsel or other person of choice at any stage of the process when the person against whom the claim is laid is required or entitled to be present.

(f) (i) Where the complainant decides to lay a formal written complaint, the Advisor may, if the complainant consents, seek a meeting with the person against whom the complaint is laid with a view to obtaining an apology or such other resolution as will satisfy the complainant.

(ii) Where, in accordance with (i) above, the Advisor meets with the person against whom the complaint is laid, the Advisor will advise both parties that, even if the matter is resolved to the satisfaction of the complainant, [the managing body of the firm] is nonetheless obliged under this policy to pursue the investigation and to take whatever disciplinary action is appropriate.

(g) When a formal written complaint (whether issued by an Advisor or by a complainant) is filed with [the managing body of the firm], a copy will be filed in the personnel file of the person against whom the complaint is laid.

(h) (i) [The managing body of the firm] will investigate every formal written complaint and where appropriate take disciplinary action.

(ii) The investigation will be undertaken by a person, or persons, appointed by [the managing body of the firm].

(iii) Advisors will not undertake such investigations.

(i) Where the investigation results in a finding that the complaint of sexual harassment is substantiated, the outcome of the investigation, and any disciplinary action, will be recorded in the personnel file of the person against whom the complaint was laid. These written records will be maintained for [ten years] unless new circumstances dictate that the file should be kept for a longer period of time.

(j) Where the investigation results in a finding that the complaint of sexual harassment is not proved, all record of the complaint shall be removed from the personnel file of the person against whom the complaint was laid.

(k) The complainant will be informed of the outcome of the investigation and any disciplinary action taken by [the managing body of the firm]. If the complainant is not satisfied with the outcome of the investigation or the disciplinary action taken by [the managing body of the firm], the complainant will be reminded of the continuing right to file a complaint with the Ontario Human Rights Commission.

PROCEDURE WHERE A PERSON BELIEVES THAT A COLLEAGUE HAS BEEN HARASSED

20. Where a person believes that a colleague has experienced or is experiencing sexual harassment (or retaliation for having brought forward a complaint of sexual harassment) and reports this belief to an Advisor, the Advisor shall meet with the person who is said to have been subjected to sexual harassment and shall then proceed in accordance with subparagraph 19(d).

HARASSMENT BY PERSONS WHO ARE NOT MEMBERS OR EMPLOYEES OF THE FIRM

21. A member or employee of the firm who considers that she or he has been subjected to sexual harassment by a person who is not a member or employee of the firm should seek the advice of an Advisor.

22. The Advisor will take whatever action is necessary to ensure that the firm fulfils its responsibility to support and assist the person subjected to such harassment.

CONCLUSION

23. [Name of firm] has developed this policy because all members and employees of the firm have the right to work in an environment free from sexual harassment. All formal written complaints received under this policy will be thoroughly investigated. Anyone found guilty of sexual harassment may be subject to severe discipline.

CHAPTER 8

Unions and Sexual Harassment

Over the last decade the workforce has been transformed as millions of women have left the home for paid work. For the first time in Canadian history more than 50 per cent of the adult female population was outside the home, an increase of 70 per cent between 1967 and 1977. As a whole, women's membership in unions has also increased dramatically — by 140 per cent between 1972 to 1982 compared with a 50 per cent growth in male membership.[1]

Unions are basically organizations of workers, both men and women. In a broad sense, the goals of the employees could probably be stated as to have security, recognition, self-expression, and job satisfaction. The unions, through their techniques of collective bargaining, arbitration, direct action and political efforts, have sought to further the pursuit of these objectives. Thus, a union is a tool or an instrument by which workers seek to achieve their personal goals.

Unions, in a sense, are social and political institutions which look after the economic and social well-being of their members in and out of the workplace. Unions can have a great influence to bring about change in the unionized working environment. Unions therefore are sometimes called "institutions for change". Apart from wages, the conditions of work at the workplace have always been a priority for unions. Unions have fought courageously and vigorously to improve the conditions of employment and the working environment through the bargaining process and political action. These efforts led to the passage of legislation prohibiting child labour, long hours and poor ventilation, imposing various health and safety standards and factory inspection, etc., and providing benefits such as workers' compensation and unemployment insurance.

Unions are also known to have a genuine concern for the "underdog" — under-privileged and minority groups. The unions believe and act for equality and a fair deal for all workers in the

---

[1] See, "Where the Steelworkers Stand, Summary of Policies Adopted by the Steelworkers of America", Canadian National Policy Conference, Quebec City (May 1983), p. 59.

workplace and within the society. Unions, in principle, are totally opposed to any kind of discrimination, whether it be race, colour, religion or sex, and have pledged to work for the elimination of discrimination from the workplace. In 1970 for example, the eighth Constitutional Convention of the Canadian Labour Congress recognized that the situation called for "renewed emphasis and dedication to the elimination of every form of social injustice" in Canada.

A. UNIONS' ATTITUDE TOWARDS SEXUAL HARASSMENT

If unions have made the elimination of discrimination in the workplace a high priority, should they not be *active* in seeking elimination of sexual harassment from the workplace? Sexual harassment is not only sex discrimination, but it poisons the working environment and threatens the health and well-being of the female employee.

There are some people who believe that unions are lukewarm, if not totally indifferent, to the sensitive issues of sexual harassment. Their fear is based on the reasoning that the unions are dominated by male leaders, who share the same stereotyped views about women as their counterparts in management, and also that women are sexually harassed, not only by supervisors but also by co-workers who are also members of the union. Which side would the union take? Would it protect the victim or the harasser? Are these fears valid?

Unions not only have a social and moral obligation, but also a legal duty to negotiate for a healthy and safe working environment for *all* their members. They also have an implied obligation to protect these rights that are guaranteed by the law of the land. Thus, the fight against discrimination in employment cannot be contracted out of by the unions, even if they so desire. The Supreme Court of Canada in *Ont. Human Rights Commission v. Etobicoke*,[2] stated in no uncertain terms, that the rights and benefits guaranteed to the individual members under the Ontario *Human Rights Code* cannot be waived or varied by unions. The court said:

---

[2] (Ont. 1982), 3 C.H.R.R. D/781.

While this submission is that the condition, should be considered a *bona fide* occupational in my opinion to give it effect would be to per of the provisions of the *Human Rights Code*.

Although the *Code* contains no explicit rest it is nevertheless a public statute and it consti as appears from a reading of the Statute itself a It is clear from the authorities, both in Canad are not competent to contract themselves enactments and that contracts having such effe policy. . . .The *Human Rights Code* has been Province of Ontario for the benefit of the comm members and clearly falls within that catego be waived or varied by private contract; theref effect.[3]

Thus, it is evident that neither car the protection guaranteed by human r union do it on one's behalf. If it were p must be considered basic human righ trade union to do so on an employee's be rights legislation would be seriously *Bell Canada*,[4] the Quebec Superior Co to a settlement for wrongful dismiss not agree to a claim for personal i employee's resistance to sexual ha Although the employee was subsequ wages, through the grievance proc damages for personal injury, such a respect, caused by the sexual harassn

B. UNIONS FACE A CHALLEN

The unions may face the iss different situations:

---

[3] *Ibid.*, at D/785 (paras. 6904-05).
[4] (Que. 1985), 6 C.H.R.R. D/2817 (S.C.).

if the employer takes disciplinary action against the harasser, the union may find itself in the incongruous position of defending the harasser in a grievance against the disciplinary action.

There are concerns in some circles that this type of situation would better be solved within "the four walls" of the union. Some unions, therefore, suggest that the cases involving harassment by co-workers should be redressed internally by the union, under the discipline mechanism of its constitution. Most union constitutions contain a clause which specifies that members shall respect each others' rights. The union can take the position that a member who sexually harasses another member is not upholding the union's constitution. The union then disciplines the harasser (co-worker) within the union structure. The question arises: Would the harasser get a fair trial? It seems obvious that most unions do not like to grieve sexual harassment by co-workers under the collective agreement.

There is a general consensus among union members (including women) that the complaints of sexual harassment by co-workers are best dealt with internally within the union's own structure.[5] However, the adequacy of the unions' present internal structure to handle sexual harassment complaints is seriously questioned. Demands are frequently made that unions amend their constitutions and provide a special mechanism to handle complaints of sexual harassment by co-workers. In 1982, the Ontario Public Service Employees Union (O.P.S.E.U.) amended its constitution and made provision for redressing complaints of sexual harassment by co-workers.[6] However, in 1983, after heated and lengthy debate, a similar resolution was turned down on the convention floor of the Canada Union of Postal Workers (C.U.P.W.).[7]

This, indeed, is a setback. However, it should not lead us to make a hasty conclusion that unions are dragging their feet in providing support to the cause of eliminating sexual harassment. It should not

---

[5] See for example a document entitled *Presentation on the inclusion of sexual harassment within the O.P.S.E.U. Constitution*, presented by the Provincial Women's Committee, for consideration by O.P.S.E.U. Executive Board, April 1982. See also S. Attenborough, *Sexual Harassment at Work* (Ottawa: National Union of Provincial Government Employees, 1981), p. 22.

[6] In June 1982, at the Annual Conference, O.P.S.E.U. finally adopted a constitutional resolution prohibiting sexual harassment. It reads, "Every member in good standing is entitled: (C) To be free from sexual harassment by *another member within the Union* and in the Workplace."

[7] In May 1983, C.U.P.W. at its Annual Convention, held in Ottawa, debated a resolution on sexual harassment to be incorporated in the Union's Constitution. It was voted down by a narrow margin.

be forgotten that trade unions are democratic political institutions, composed of large numbers of people having divergent views. Thus, it is not as easy for a union to change direction or adopt a new policy as it is for an employer. Perhaps it is the democratic process itself that sometimes delays the implementation of good and worthy changes.

The fourth situation is most disturbing for a union. In this situation, a female employee is allegedly sexually harassed by her supervisor, a union official, either paid or elected. The union, in this situation, is in the same position as an employer, whether or not the victim employee is represented by another union. Unions normally hold the employer responsible for establishing and maintaining a safe and healthy working environment free from sexual harassment for its employees. From the victims' point of view, the union is their employer, and therefore, it must accept the same responsibility as other employers are expected to for sexual harassment. This situation normally arises in large unions that are governed or managed not only by elected members, but by a large number of paid employees. That union does not remain a union for its employees, but becomes an employer. The employees of the union are entitled to a safe and healthy environment, free from sexual harassment, in which to work as are their counterparts in government and industry.

Is it too much to expect a union to be a model employer? Rather a union as an employer has an excellent opportunity to set an example of employer-employee relations by establishing clear and effective guidelines against sexual harassment in its own workplace. Action speaks louder than words. If a union's employer-employee relations (its dealings with its own employees) are not covered by its constitution or internal union structures, it should develop a similar policy on sexual harassment to what it expects from other employers in government and industry. If its employees are not covered by a collective agreement, then the union must also develop a fair and equitable complaint procedure for the redress of sexual harassment complaints by its employees.

Unions seem to have either lagged behind or ignored this aspect of the sexual harassment problem. By ignoring or failing to recognize the problem of sexual harassment at their own workplace, unions may invite not only public criticism but also dissatisfaction among a large segment of their own membership. It requires a greater commitment and dedication on the part of the union hierarchy to accept the challenge.

C. LEGAL OBLIGATIONS OF UNIONS

The protection of the equal employment rights of women is not only a social or moral responsibility of unions, but a legal obligation. A labour union is prohibited to discriminate in membership, or in a way that would impair a person's employment or cause, or attempt to cause, an employer to discriminate against an individual. Further, even though the employer controls the terms and conditions of employment, under a human rights statute, a union may be held liable if it attempts to cause discrimination through its own practices. American jurisprudence[8] in this regard is clearer than is Canadian. The courts and tribunals in Canada seem to be reluctant to hold unions responsible for acquiescing in an employer's discriminatory employment practices. In *Hall v. Intl. Firefighters' Association*,[9] two firefighters were forced to retire at age 60, contrary to the *Ontario Human Rights Code*. The collective agreement, between the city and the Firefighters Association, had provided for compulsory retirement at age 60. The complainants brought action against both the employer and the union. The Ontario Board of Inquiry found against the respondent employer but not against the respondent union. The Board observed:

> Both complainants alleged that the Association is also in breach of s. 4(1)(b) and that in addition it is in breach of s. 4(1)(g) and s. 4a(1). *However, I do not find the Association in breach of any of these provisions, because* quite apart from anything that the Association did, the complainants were subject to a compulsory retirement age of 60. In effect, *there is no causal connection between the Association's activities and the complainants' plight.* If the Association had supported the complainants' position perhaps things might have been different, although Mr. DeVaal testified that the Borough had never allowed an employee to work beyond retirement age.

---

[8] D.O. Simon: "Union Liability Under Title VII for Employer Discrimination" (1980), 68 *Georgetown L.J.* 959; see also *Robinson v. Lorilard Corp.*, 444 F. 2d 791 (4th Cir. 1971). In *John v. Goodyear Tire and Rubber Co.*, 491 F. 2d 1354 (5th Cir. 1974), the court also held the union liable in an assessment of back pay because the union was party to the collective bargaining agreement which contained provisions for the discriminatory practices. In *Macklin v. Spector Freight Systems Inc.*, 478 F. 2d 979 (D.C. Cir. 1973), the U.S. Court of Appeals for Washington D.C. held that Title VII of the *Civil Rights Act* imposes an affirmative obligation on a union not to acquiesce in an employer's discrimination. See also *Myers v. Gilman Paper Co.*, 544 F. 2d 837 (5th Cir. 1977); modified on rehearing 556 F. 2d 758 (5th Cir. 1977); cert. denied, 434 U.S. 801 (1977).

[9] (Ont. Bd. of Inquiry, 1977), unreported (Dunlop).

Had the complainants' retirement age been altered by the collective agreement one might have considered it possible that the union was a party to the Borough's breach of the Code, though that conclusion is not obvious nor one that I need reach.

Nor need I consider whether, had the union been responsible in fact for the complainants' plight, it would have been liable under s. 4(1)(g) or 4a(1). [Emphasis added]

The decision of the Board of Inquiry was finally confirmed by the Supreme Court of Canada in *Ont. Human Rights Commission v. Etobicoke*,[10] by holding that "under the Code non-discrimination is the rule of general application and discrimination, where permitted, is the exception." The Supreme Court decision had made no reference to the union's obligation or liability for its acquiescence in a discriminatory practice. Thus, it is not clear whether unions in Canada can be held liable for not negotiating *successfully* to remove discrimination and the effects of past discrimination.

1. Union's Liability

Recent development in the human rights jurisprudence suggests that unions would no more be immune from liability for violation of the *Human Rights Act* and inflicting discrimination in the workplace, even though they may not have directly caused the discriminatory harm to the employee member (victim). The Board of Inquiry have held that human rights statutes prohibit not only direct discrimination but also indirect discrimination. Thus, all those persons (including unions) who may have contributed to the act of discrimination or to a discriminatory effect or result, would be equally liable for the harm caused by the discriminatory conduct, rule or practice.

In 1988, in *Roosma v. Ford Motor Co.*[11] a union argued on a preliminary motion that a trade union could not properly be found to have violated sections 4 and 8 of the Ontario *Human Rights Code, 1981*. Sections 4(1) and 8 of the Code provided:

4(1) Every person has a right to equal treatment with respect to employment without discrimination because of race, ancestry, place of origin, colour,

---

[10] *Supra*, note 2.
[11] (Ont. 1988), 9 C.H.R.R. D/4743 (Mercer); affd (Ont. 1989), 10 C.H.R.R. D/5761 (Div. Ct.).

ethnic origin, citizenship, creed, sex, sexual orientation, age, record of offences, marital status, family status or handicap.

. . .

8. No person shall infringe or do, directly or indirectly, anything that infringes a right under this part.

The Board of Inquiry rejected this argument and concluded that section 8, which was the relevant provision on this issue, could apply to a trade union for the reason expressed as follows:

> There are two features of section 8 which indicate that a trade union may properly be joined as a respondent. The first is that "person" is defined, as counsel noted, to include a trade union under section 45(c) of the *Code*. The second is that an infringement may arise "directly or indirectly". Thus, while issues involving the right to equal treatment with respect to employment might usually be expected to arise "directly" between the employee and the employer, section 8 clearly contemplates them arising at least "indirectly" between employees and other persons, including trade unions.[12]

This decision established an authority for the propositions, first, that a union may properly be named as a respondent in a human rights dispute, and second, that employment discrimination can arise "indirectly" by virtue of the action or inaction of a union.

In *Renaud v. Central Okanagan School District No. 23*,[13] the B.C. Human Rights Council ruled that the union should be held responsible for adverse effect discrimination and for its failure to accommodate the complainant. The complainant in this case, a member of the Seventh Day Adventist Church, was terminated from his employment as a school custodian because of his inability to comply with the shift work requirements for his position. The shift schedule was set out in the collective agreement, and the union refused to allow an alteration of the schedule to accommodate the complainant. In these circumstances, the Council ruled:

> Since the union is equally responsible with the school board for the terms and conditions of the collective agreement (which contains the discriminatory requirement), it would be unjust to so limit the complainant's relief and to order only the school board to bear all the consequences of such discriminatory requirement according to section 17 of the *Act*. . . . It would be a travesty of

---

[12] *Ibid.*, at D/4748 (para. 36712).
[13] (B.C. 1987), 8 C.H.R.R. D/4255 (Verbrugge).

justice to order only one of two persons contravening the Act to cease from doing so only by reason of a possible deficiency in the form of the complaint as opposed to its substance.[14]

The Council ordered that the complaint be amended to include section 9 of the B.C. *Human Rights Act* and ruled that since the collective agreement dictated the complainant's terms of employment, which included the discriminatory terms, and since the union was a party to the collective agreement, it was liable for the violation of the Act.[15]

In the leading case of *Gohm v. Domtar Inc. (No. 4).*,[16] the Ontario Board of Inquiry ruled that a union can be held liable for employment decisions which have the effect of discriminating, even indirectly, against employees. In the *Gohm* case the Board found the union, the Office and Professional Employees International, Loc. 267, also liable for adverse effect discrimination by terminating the employment of the complainant, Ms. Gohm, because of her religion. The Board ordered both the employer and the union, jointly and severally, to pay to the complainant damages for lost wages of just over $74,000.[17]

The complainant, Ms. Irene Gohm, was a Seventh Day Adventist, who followed strict observance of the Sabbath from sundown Friday to sundown Saturday. She was hired by Domtar Inc. in 1981 as a laboratory technician to monitor air and water samples. The complainant had been told during her interview that lab technicians were required to work Saturdays on a rotating basis, but she did not inform the employer of her inability to do so at that time because, as she later admitted, "she thought if she did she would not be offered the position".

The evidence disclosed that the employer's position was that the *complainant could work on Sunday (instead of Saturday) but that she would not be entitled to the overtime provided by the collective agreement.* The union, on the other hand, refused to consent to the complainant working Sunday at the straight time. The union and the employer never did come to any arrangement that would accommodate the complainant. As a result, the complainant was terminated. She did not find work in the area for several years and filed a complaint claiming

---

[14] *Ibid.*, at D/4259 (para. 33442).
[15] The Council ordered the reinstatement of the complainant with $6,250 in lost wages and $1,000 for emotional distress.
[16] (Ont. 1990), 12 C.H.R.R. D/161 (Pentney).
[17] *Ibid.*, at D/182 (para. 142).

discrimination based on the ground of creed contrary to the Ontario *Human Rights Code*.

The Board of Inquiry, chaired by Professor William Pentney, ruled that both the employer and the union were liable for failing to reasonably accommodate the complainant's inability to work on Saturdays. Professor Pentney concluded that liability extended to the union as well as the employer, since it insisted on applying the strict terms of the collective agreement. By refusing to consent to the accommodation of the complainant, the union had participated in the establishment of a discriminatory term or condition of employment contrary to the Ontario *Human Rights Code*. The Board rejected the union's argument that it was the exercise of management rights alone which had led to her termination. The Board stated:

> ... union liability for adverse effect discrimination could arise either directly from the terms of the collective agreement which the Union negotiated and ratified, or indirectly from its participation in the establishment or continuation of the discriminatory term or condition of employment which contributed to the termination of the complainant. In this regard it should be recalled that the *O'Malley* decision was based on the very provision of the *Code* at issue in this case, s. 4, and there the Supreme Court distinguished between "direct" discrimination and "adverse effect" or indirect discrimination. From this I hold that a union may be liable for a breach of s. 4 of the *Code* on the basis that it directly committed, or indirectly contributed to, the adverse effect discrimination arising from the employment rule or situation. I am fortified in this conclusion by the fact that boards of inquiry have long held that the discriminatory consideration need only be one of the factors that motivated the decision, and not the sole factor in the decision .... [A] union may be held accountable even if its actions merely were one factor or element in the creation, maintenance or application of the rule or practice which has a discriminatory adverse effect. In approaching this issue, it should be recalled that the union was intimately involved in the discussions about the complainant's situation during the period in question. It engaged in repeated discussions with the complainant and representatives of the respondent Domtar. The union was not a mere bystander in this sequence of events, it was an active participant.

...

> Counsel for the union submitted that clause 9.05 did not require the Company to schedule Ms. Gohm to work. Rather, the Company did so in exercise of its residual management rights under article 6.01 of the collective agreement, and for this the Union cannot be held liable. The Union also argued that ... it should not be held liable for failing to accede to a modification of the collective agreement when such a modification was not required in order for the company

to accommodate the complainant, or for failing to adequately represent the interests of the complainant in pursuing an accommodation . . . .

In my view, the union's involvement in the maintenance, if not the creation, of this rule through its negotiation of article 9.05 of the collective agreement contributed directly to the imposition of discriminatory terms or conditions of employment on Ms. Gohm, and thus constituted a *prima facie* violation of para. 4(1)(g) of the *Code*.[18]

The Board stated that the union insisted on enforcement of the overtime pay terms of the collective agreement, thereby impeding any reasonable accommodation of the complainant. Professor Pentney pointed out that there was a duty to take "substantial or meaningful steps" to accommodate the complainant, and both the employer and the union had failed to do so. The union failed in its duty to accommodate because it did not offer to negotiate changes to the collective agreement, nor did it make every effort to settle the dispute. Professor Pentney stated:

> . . . I find that the union did not fulfill its responsibility to reasonably accommodate the complainant because it did not specifically offer to negotiate with the company in regard to the changes in the collective agreement which it said were required, nor did it ever specifically offer to agree to these changes in its communications with the complainant or the company. I should add that I realize that neither the company nor the union could unilaterally modify the collective agreement, and so their actions here must be judged according to what action they actually took, what they said or promised to the complainant, and what they discussed as between themselves. On this basis, and based on the findings on the evidence I have made above, I find that the union did not reasonably accommodate the complainant.

. . .

It would not be reasonable to expect a union to go so far as to engage in a strike in order to obtain agreement from the company to an accommodation, but neither is it unreasonable to expect the union to expend substantial and serious efforts to reach an agreement on the matter. In this case, I find that the union did not expend such efforts in relation to the question of amending the collective agreement to permit Ms. Gohm to work on Sunday at straight time. The union's perception that the company was completely unwilling to re-open the collective agreement under any circumstances may have proven accurate, but the fact remains that it never put the question directly to the company in relation to Ms. Gohm's situation, and separate and apart from all

---

[18] *Ibid.*, at D/173-74 (paras. 77, 78, 81, 82).

other considerations, Ms. Gohm made such a request of the union, but I find that the union did not do so, and on this basis I find that in these circumstances the union did not reasonably accommodate the complainant.

This failure is particularly difficult to fathom in view of the evidence of Mr. Eamer, which is confirmed by his notes, that when he spoke with Miss McCabe on October 6, he indicated that the company was prepared to consider the option of Ms. Gohm to work on Sunday at straight time (Exhibit No. 130). This was a clear opportunity for the union to put a specific proposal to the company to amend the collective agreement to permit this, but the evidence shows that this proposition was never advanced by Miss McCabe. Despite her efforts to arrange another accommodation for the complainant on October 9, which indicates that she was sincere in her feeling that Ms. Gohm had been wronged by the company, I find that the actions of Miss McCabe for the union with regard to the amendment of the collective agreement were not adequate to meet the onus on the union to reasonably accommodate the complainant short of undue hardship.

I therefore find that the union has violated para. 4(1)(g) of the Ontario *Human Rights Code*.[19]

The Board ruled that the *Human Rights Code* would impose liability if the *union directly committed or indirectly contributed to* the adverse impact (or indirect) discrimination arising from the employment rule. This decision requires the unions to attempt effectively to negotiate changes to the collective agreement if they are necessary to protect the human rights of the employees. The union would be equally liable if an application of any provision of the collective agreement would cause discrimination in the workplace as prohibited by the human rights law.

The issue of union liability for the discrimination of an employee, in a union setting, was also discussed by the Nova Scotia Board of Inquiry in a mandatory retirement case, *Landry v. Richmond Fisheries Ltd.*[20] However, the Board did not find the union responsible for the discrimination of the complainant. The Board stated:

> The union, to that time, seemed to have the best interests of its members in mind in supporting such a clause, and at the time the collective agreement was signed such a clause was lawful. . . . In my view, there was no action or lack of response that is culpable.[21]

---

[19] *Ibid.*, at D/178 and D/179 (paras. 118 and 120-22).
[20] (N.S. 1991), 13 C.H.R.R. D/4.
[21] *Ibid.*, at D/8 (para. 21).

The decisions in *Renaud* and *Gohm* have clearly established union liability for adverse impact or indirect discrimination. Both these cases involved discrimination on the basis of creed, but there is no reason to doubt that the same principle would be applied to discrimination on other grounds, including sex and sexual harassment.

D. UNION'S DUTY OF FAIR REPRESENTATION

Labour relations legislation in federal and provincial jurisdictions contain provision for a "duty of fair representation" of the employees by a union. For example, the Ontario *Labour Relations Act* provides that "a trade union . . .shall not act in a manner that is *arbitrary, discriminatory or in bad faith* in the representation of any of the employees in the unit, whether or not members of the trade union."[22] This provision requires a union to represent fairly not only union members, but all employees in that bargaining unit. A union's failure to provide fair representation amounts to unfair labour practice on the part of the union. So far there is no reported case making unions accountable for discriminatory practices based on race, religion, sex, etc. However, an employee who feels that his or her union failed to represent him or her fairly has a right to file an unfair labour practice charge against the union to the appropriate labour relations board. However, a union member has no right to sue the union for failure to represent him or her.

A victim of human rights violation has rather limited redress against the union as stated earlier because in some Canadian jurisdictions a trade union is not a legal entity.[23] A union cannot be sued even if it is guilty of a violation of the Human Rights Act. Thus, unions in Canada are less vulnerable to civil action for damages to their members than in the United States. Not only can a victim of discrimination not sue the union for damages but it cannot sue the employer either. His or her only remedy is to file a complaint with an appropriate Human Rights Commission.[24]

The labour movement, both in Canada and in the United States, has vehemently opposed sexual harassment in the workplace. The

---

[22] Ontario *Labour Relations Act*, R.S.O. 1990, c. L.2, s. 69.
[23] See for example the Ontario *Rights of Labour Act*, R.S.O. 1990, c. R.33.
[24] See *Seneca College of Applied Arts and Technology Bd. of Governors v. Bhadauria* (Can. 1981), 2 C.H.R.R. D/468 (S.C.C.).

National Federations in both countries, the A.F.L.-C.I.O. in the United States and the C.L.C. in Canada, have committed themselves to mobilizing all the resources at their disposal to eliminate sexual harassment from the workplace. In Canada, the C.L.C. encouraged lobbying for separate legislation to outlaw harassment.[25] In the United States, the unions seem to be happy with the existing Title VII of the *Civil Rights Act.* They, in fact, are opposed to any amendment to specify prohibition on sexual harassment.[26]

It is suggested that to protect their members from sexual harassment, the unions should develop a comprehensive strategy and plan which may include the following:

1. Negotiating a sexual harassment clause in the collective agreement including grievance procedures and arbitration.
2. Providing support to the victim.
3. Educating members and shop stewards on sexual harassment through seminars and conferences.
4. Encouraging women to participate in union activities.
5. Conducting research and surveys on sexual harassment.
6. Political action — lobbying against sexual harassment alone or with other unions or women's organizations.
7. Co-operating with employers in developing and implementing sexual harassment policy and procedures.
8. Developing their own sexual harassment policy and code of conduct for their members and officers.

E. SEXUAL HARASSMENT CLAUSES IN COLLECTIVE AGREEMENTS

In modern democratic society, collective bargaining plays a vital role in establishing the day to day employer-employee relations. Collective bargaining is defined as a continuing institutional relationship between the employer entity (government or private) and a labour organization (union or association) representing exclusively a defined group of employees concerned with the negotiations, administration, interpretation and enforcement of written agreements covering *joint*

---

[25] See Wilfred List, "CLC takes up cause for women on sexual harassment at work", *The Globe and Mail,* May 7, 1980, p. B6.
[26] The unions in the United States fear that a specific prohibition on sexual harassment may lead to narrower interpretation, which in turn may hurt the women's cause.

understandings as to wages, salaries, rate of pay, hours of work and other *conditions of employment*.

When employer and union negotiate a contract they are reaching a joint understanding on a written statement of policies and procedures under which they must live together for the duration of the agreement. It is a process of living together under the agreement that gives meaning and significance to the written instrument. As Neil Chamberlain and Harry Shulman stressed, the negotiation of a contract is to labour relations what the wedding ceremony is to domestic relations. In their view, "the heart of the collective agreement — indeed, of collective bargaining — is the process of continuous joint consideration and adjustment of plant problems."[27]

Thus, it is the commitment that the parties, the employer and the union, make to implement the joint understanding and thereby improve or modify the conditions of employment. Any change or modification in a collective agreement is not a unilateral action but a joint venture. Normally the unions take credit, and perhaps rightfully, for any change or improvement in the provisions of a collective agreement. As collective bargaining is not a one-way street, any change, addition or deletion in a collective agreement also signifies a recognition by the employer of the fact that a change was called for.

A clause on sexual harassment in a collective agreement could not have been included without pressure from the union. Its presence nevertheless suggests that some employers have finally recognized the seriousness of the problem of sexual harassment on the job. A clause in a collective agreement banning sexual harassment is a serious commitment by the employer to its employees and the union. The employer, on the one hand, assures its employees that their working environment will be free from sexual harassment and, on the other hand, it seeks the co-operation of the union and its employees in the process of eliminating sexual harassment from the workplace.

F. HIGHLIGHTS OF SEXUAL HARASSMENT CLAUSES

Some collective agreements provide a broad-based antidiscrimination" clause and others simply incorporate the provision of

---

[27] H. Shulman and N. Chamberlain, *Cases on Labour Relations Law* (Brooklyn: Foundation Press, 1949).

the Human Rights Code by reference only. Though limited in number, some collective agreements do have a specific clause on sexual harassment. Those clauses normally prohibit sexual harassment of employees by their supervisors and/or co-workers. For example: a collective agreement between Klinic Inc. (Manitoba) and C.U.P.E. Loc. 2348 specifically makes sexual harassment of co-workers a "just cause" for disciplinary action.

> A complaint of sexual harassment made against an employee shall be reported to the employer within five (5) days and *upon investigation shall be cause for disciplinary action to be taken.*

However, a collective agreement between The Place Riel Society and C.U.P.E. Loc. 1975 goes a step further and prohibits sexual harassment even by clients:

> Employees who are being subjected to client harassment will draw this to the attention of the supervisor who will be required to deal with the problem immediately.

The normal grievance procedure, due to the sensitive nature of sexual harassment, has been found ineffective. Thus, the parties have attempted to provide different procedures and special remedies for sexual harassment grievances which may appear to be unusual in ordinary labour-management settings. Some of those provisions include:

1. Confidentiality

> Most of the collective agreements provide that a grievance of sexual harassment shall be processed with strict confidentiality. One contract provides: "Both parties agree that all proceedings and the results thereof will be dealt with in the strictest confidence."[28]
> To keep strict confidentiality another collective agreement provides that "the complainant may elect to be present with or without a union representative, at any meeting where the employer is taking disciplinary action against the harasser."[29]

---

[28] See for example the collective agreement between Klinic Inc. (Manitoba) and C.U.P.E. Loc. 2348 (1983).
[29] *Ibid.*

2. Joint Investigation

Some collective agreements provide for a joint investigation of a harassment complaint by a team composed of the employer and union representatives.[30]

3. Burden of Proof

Some collective agreements provide that "in the case of a complaint of sexual harassment, the onus shall be on the alleged harasser and not on the complainant to disprove the complaint."[31]

4. Harasser to be Transferred and not the Victim

Sexual harassment clauses in collective agreements normally provide that "in a case where sexual harassment may result in the transfer of an employee, it shall be the harasser who is transferred and the victim shall not be transferred against his or her will."[32]

5. Disciplinary Action Against the Harasser

(a) Some collective agreements provide that "the employer undertake to discipline *any person* employed by it who engages in sexual harassment of another employee."[33]
(b) Some collective agreements go a step further and provide that an alleged harasser shall not be entitled to grieve disciplinary action taken by the employer which is consistent with the decision of the Deputy Minister or the panel.[34]

---

[30] See for example the master agreement between The Government of the Province of British Columbia and Government Employees Relations Bureau and British Columbia Government Employees Union (1983).
[31] See for example the collective agreement between Saskatchewan Association of Human Rights and C.U.P.E. Loc. 3012 (1983).
[32] See for example the collective agreement between The Town of Elliot lake and C.U.P.E. Loc. 170 (1983); the collective agreement between the City of Fort St. John and B.C.G.E.U. Loc. 62 (1982); the master agreement between the Province of British Columbia and B.C.G.E.U. (1982); and the collective agreement between Marshall Industries Ltd. and United Steelworkers of America Loc. 4696 (1983).
[33] See for example the collective agreement between the School District No. 44, North Vancouver and C.U.P.E. Loc. 389 (1983).
[34] See for example the master agreement between the Province of British Columbia and B.C.G.E.U. (1982).

6. Leave With Pay to the Victim of Sexual Harassment

One collective agreement provides for seven (7) days' leave with pay to the victim of sexual harassment and three (3) months' leave to a victim of sexual assault.[35]

7. Arbitrator Empowered to Impose a Fine on the Harasser

(a) Some collective agreements in a case of sexual harassment authorize an arbitration board to impose a financial penalty against the harasser. Further, the financial penalty collected from the harasser is to be donated to a named charitable institution.[36]
(b) Some collective agreements provide that "an arbitration board shall have the power to transfer or *discipline any person found guilty* of sexually harassing an employee."[37]
(c) Another collective agreement provides that an "Arbitration Board shall have the power to *transfer, discipline or levy a financial penalty against the harasser and the employer.*"[38]

8. Action for Frivolous Complaints

Collective agreements also provide that where a complaint is determined to be of a frivolous, vindictive or vexatious nature, the employer may take appropriate action. Such action shall only be for just cause and may be grieved pursuant to the collective agreement.[39]

The following clause in the 1991 collective agreement between the B.C. Institute of Technology and B.C.G.E.U. illustrates a different and special arrangement made by the parties for the handling of sexual harassment grievances:

---

[35] See for example the collective agreement between the Canadian Federation of Students and C.U.P.E. Loc. 1281 (1982).
[36] See for example the collective agreement between Fraser Valley Regional Library and C.U.P.E. Loc. 1698 (1983).
[37] See for example, the collective agreement between City of Victoria and C.U.P.E. Loc. 50 (1981).
[38] See for example the collective agreement between the Municipality of Terrace (B.C.) and C.U.P.E. Loc. 2012 (1981).
[39] See for example the master agreement between the Province of British Columbia and B.C.G.E.U. (1982); see also the master agreement between the Government of Manitoba and the Manitoba Government Employees Association (1982).

1.8 Sexual Harassment in the Work Place

(a) The Union and the Employer recognize the right of Employees to work in an environment free from sexual harassment, and the Employer shall take such actions as are necessary respecting an Employee engaging in sexual harassment in the work place.

(b) Sexual harassment means engaging in a course of vexatious comment or conduct of a sexual nature that is known or ought reasonably to be known to be unwelcome and shall include, but not be limited to:

   (1) sexual solicitation or advance or inappropriate touching and sexual assault;

   (2) a reprisal, or threat of reprisal, which might reasonably be perceived as placing a condition of a sexual nature on employment by a person in authority after such sexual solicitation or advance or inappropriate touching is rejected.

(c)

   (1) An Employee who wishes to pursue a concern arising from an alleged sexual harassment may submit a complaint in writing within thirty (30) days of the latest alleged occurrence through the Union directly to the Director, Personnel/Employee Relations. Complaints of this nature shall be treated in strict confidence by both the Union and the Employer.

   (2) An alleged offender shall be given notice of the substance of such a complaint under this clause and shall be given notice of and be entitled to attend, participate in, and be represented at any hearing under this clause.

   (3) The Employer designate and a Union representative shall investigate the complaint and shall submit reports to the Director, Personnel/Employee Relations in writing within thirty (30) days of receipt of the complaint. The Director, Personnel/Employee Relations shall within thirty (30) days of receipt of the reports give such orders as may be necessary to resolve the issue.

   (4) Where the complaint is determined to be of a frivolous, vindictive or vexatious nature, the Employer may take appropriate action. Such action shall only be for just cause and may be grieved pursuant to Article 8.

(5) Pending determination of the complaint, the Director, Personnel/Employee Relations may take interim measures to separate the Employees concerned if deemed necessary

(6) In cases where sexual harassment may result in the transfer of the Employee, where possible it shall be the harasser who is transferred, except that the harassee may be transferred with his/her consent.

(d) Where either party to the proceeding is not satisfied with the Director, Personnel/Employee Relations' response, the complaint will, within thirty (30) days, be put before a panel consisting of a Union representative, an Employer representative, and a mutually agreed upon chairperson, all of whom shall be Institute Employees, and the majority decision will be final and binding. The panel shall have the right to:

(1) dismiss the complaint;

(2) determine the appropriate level of discipline to be applied to the offender, and

(3) make a further order as is necessary to provide a final and conclusive settlement of the complaint.

(e) An alleged offender under this clause shall not be entitled to grieve disciplinary action taken by the Employer which is consistent with the decision of the Director, Personnel/Employee Relations or the panel.

In the absence of a specific clause prohibiting sexual harassment, the arbitrator would be faced with a difficult question, namely, deciding what provision, if any, of the collective agreement had been violated, particularly inasmuch as there was no anti-discrimination clause. As Greenbaum and Fraser pointed out, arbitrators need "enabling legislation" in order to find contractual violations. But what is the arbitrator to rely upon if there is no such clause?[40]

---

[40] M. Greenbaum and B. Fraser, "Sexual Harassment in the Workplace" (1981), 36 *Arbitration Journal* 30 at 37.

Index

ABUS DE DROIT, 208

AD HOC GROUP ON EQUAL RIGHTS FOR WOMEN, 3

ADJUDICATION
Charter of Rights and Freedoms, 168
delays in, 168-179
injunctions, 168
legislative intent, 168
remedies, 170
stay of proceedings, 168

ADVERSE EFFECT RULE
principle, 86

ANGUS REID, 5

ANITA HILL, 5

ARBITRATION
arbitral review, 285
arbitral standards, 299
reasonable person test, 299
employers vicarious liability, 289
grievance by harassers, 290
discharge upheld, 291
disciplinary action, 290
discipline (discharge), 291
penalty quashed, 297
penalty reduced, 295-297
grievance by victims, 286-291
grievance procedure, 285-286
invasion of privacy, 296
policy grievances (union grievances), 287
reinstatement of the harasser, 297
ramifications, 303-305
reaction of female co-workers, 303-305
remedies available, 289

remedies not available, 289
sexual harassment clauses, 290, 305
sexual harassment by managers, 287
sexual harassment by professors, 292, 298
sexual harassment of students, 292
type of harassment
mild, 301-302
severe, 301-302

BOARDS OF INQUIRY
authority to reinstate, 268-270
definition of harassment, 57
educative duty, 271
obligation, 271
philosophy and reasoning, 46, 56
powers, 242-243, 246
remedial powers, 267
scope of discrimination, 33
United States, 16

BURDEN OF PROOF *See also* EVIDENCE
complainant, 41, 129, 130
difficulty, 134
Human Rights Commission, 137
nature of proof, 137-139
prima facie case, 130

CANADA LABOUR CODE
administration, 51
amendments, 316
definition, 20
prohibitions, 50
public policy, 51
purpose, 51
redress mechanism, 51
relevant sections, 51

CANADIAN CHARTER OF RIGHTS AND FREEDOMS, 139
collateral estoppel, 167

CANADIAN CHARTER OF RIGHTS
    AND FREEDOMS, *cont'd*
  contractual rights, 167
  election of remedies theory, 167
  equality rights clause, 240
  relevant sections, 172-173
  res judicata, 167

CANADIAN HUMAN RIGHTS ACT
  amendments, 49
  intent, 39-40
  interpretations
    language, 47
  prohibited conduct, 43
  prohibitions, 43
  purpose, 196
  relevant provisions, 15, 41, 43, 49
  statutory obligations, 195, 200-201

CANADIAN HUMAN RIGHTS
    COMMISSION
  definition, 9-10
  guidelines, 9
  harassment policy, 206, 315, 316
    application, 206
  policy statement, 81
  survey, 5

CANADIAN LABOUR CONGRESS, 367

CEASE AND DESIST ORDER, 272

CIVIL CAUSE OF ACTION, 239

CIVIL RIGHTS ACT
  See UNITED STATES

CLARENCE THOMAS, 5

COERCION
  amounting to sexual harassment, 78
  condition of employment, 78
  definition, 76-77
  elements, 77
  employee-employer relationship, 80
  examples, 77-78
  types, 78

COLLECTIVE AGREEMENT, 157-159
  anti-discrimination clauses, 158
  clauses on sexual harassment, 367-73
  just cause clause, 302

COMMON LAW ON SEXUAL
    HARASSMENT
  evolution, 186
  tort of discrimination, 183, 237-240

COMPLAINANT
  past conduct, 65-68

COMPLAINT PROCEDURE
  availability, 328
  elements, 321
  employer's, 323
  reporting of complaints, 327-328

CONDITIONS OF WORK THEORY, 155

CONFIDENTIALITY, 155

CONSTRUCTIVE DISCHARGE, 34, 155
  arising from harassment, 107-110

CONSTRUCTIVE KNOWLEDGE, 70-73
  burden of proof, 70
  effusive behaviour, 71
  reasonable person, 70-73
  test, 71

CONTRACT LAW
  breach, 229

CORPORATE RESPONSIBILITY
  See EMPLOYER
    RESPONSIBILITY and
    EMPLOYER LIABILITY

CREDIBILITY
  corroborative witnesses, 141

CREDIBILITY, *cont'd*
  preponderance of probabilities, 145
  of witnesses, 140-145

CRIMINAL CODE
  prior proceedings, 164
  remedies, 164
  standard of proof, 164

DAMAGES *See also* REMEDIES
  compensatory, 243-246
    interest on wages, 260-262
    philosophy, 243-246
  delictual, 92
  employment benefits, 251-252
  general, 35, 36
  legislative, 242-243
    Boards of Inquiry, 242, 246
  loss of dignity and humiliation, 248
  loss of job opportunity, 250-251
    common law principles, 250
    criteria for determining, 251
    limitations, 251
    obligation to establish, 250
  monetary, 36-37, 116
    calculating, 247-250
    obligation to mitigate
      rule, 248
  psychological, 36-36, 38

DEFINITION OF SEXUAL
  HARASSMENT
  See SEXUAL HARASSMENT

DELAYS
  community interest, 172-179
    full defense, 174-175
    paramount of rights, 176-178
    remedies, 174-175
    security of the person, 172-173
  defendant, 171
    defense, 171
    full answer, 171
  unreasonable
    criteria for determining, 170-171

DE NOVO
  determination, 163

DEVELOPMENT OF SEXUAL
  HARASSMENT LAW
  Canada, 32-47
  United States, 16-32

DISCIPLINE
  appropriateness, 232, 234
  past practices, 234

DISCRIMINATION
  "atmospheric", 113
  interpretation, 8
  past definition, 14-15
  scope, 15
  by sexual blackmail, 7

DISMISSAL
  Constructive. *See* CONSTRUCTIVE
    DISCHARGE
  contract law, 229
  employment at will doctrine, 228
  job-related consequences, 103-107
  just cause, 103-107, 238, 248
  result of harassment, 35, 105
  tort law, 228, 237, 240
  voluntary
    just cause, 103, 105, 238
    Unemployment Insurance
      Benefits, 281
  wrongful, 103, 228-232, 238

DIVISION OF MINISTRY
  PERSONNEL AND
  EDUCATION (MP & E) OF
  UNITED CHURCH
  survey, 6

DRESS AND GROOMING
  REQUIREMENTS
  amounting to sexual harassment, 89,
    101
  condition of employment, 98, 101
  discriminatory, 99
  test, 101

EMPLOYER
  cost of back pay, 309
  cost implications, 276
  hidden costs, 309
  liability insurance, 316
  obligations, 235
  policies on sexual harassment, 235
    advantages of policies, 320

EMPLOYER LIABILITY, 136, 181-213
  abus de droit theory, 208
  arguments, 181
  bona fide conduct, 105
  common law, 183
  constructive discrimination, 193
  constructive dismissal, 109
  corrective action, 219, 222
  degree of control, 222
  directing mind, 187, 202, 207
  employees, 181
  hostile environment theory, 212
  judicial standards, 194
  non-employees, 181, 218-224
  obiter, 186
  organic theory, 186-190, 202, 207
    conditions, 188
  for poisoned work place, 274
  policies, 105, 186, 198-199, 206
  principle of agency, 211-213
  public policy, 194-198
  quid pro quo, 211
  statutory, 189-190
  strict liability, 182, 193
  vicarious liability, 182, 183-186, 190, 193, 202, 204

EMPLOYER RESPONSIBILITY
  internal complaint procedure, 235-237
    advantages, 236
    disadvantages, 236

EMPLOYMENT AT WILL
  doctrine, 228

EMPLOYMENT RELATIONSHIP, 121
  supervisor and employee, 121
  work environment, 122

EQUAL EMPLOYMENT OPPORTUNITY COMMISSION (United States), 25-27, 57, 316
  definition, 58
  employer liability, 112
  guidelines, 25-27, 319
  purpose, 17
  quality of working environment, 27-32

EQUAL PAY AND OPPORTUNITY COMMISSION (EOC), 4

EVIDENCE
  admissibility, 145
  balance of probabilities, 130
  bona fide occupational qualification, 133
  burden of proof, 27
  conditional proof, 133
    beyond a reasonable doubt, 134
    evidentiary burden, 134
  credibility of witnesses, 140-145
  cross-examination, 146
  error of law, 132
  nature, 137-139
  prima facie, 130
  reverse onus, 130, 137
  standard of reasonable person, 70, 71, 299
  term or condition of employment, 130
  types, 139
    affidavit, 140
    circumstantial, 138
    corroborating, 140
    documentary, 146
    hearsay, 145-147
    misleading, 144
    similar fact, 142, 147-154
  unrelated, 139
  wrongful conduct, 134

Index

FORTUNE 500, 3

FREEDOM FROM DISCRIMINATION DOCTRINE, 239

FREEDOM TO CONTRACT DOCTRINE, 239

GENERAL DAMAGES
 considerations in awarding, 243-250

GRIEVANCE PROCEDURE
 effectiveness, 110
 harasser, 290-291
 ineffectiveness, 369
 victim, 286

GRIEVANCES
 arbitrability, 285-286

HARASSMENT
 characteristics, 122
  examples, 122
 racially motivated, 36

HOSTILE WORK ENVIRONMENT THEORY, 31
 action by employer, 31
 constituting, 31
 damages, 32
 remedial action, 31
 United States, 29

HUMAN RIGHTS CODE
 prohibited conduct, 33
  examples, 33
 prohibited grounds, 33, 34
 violations, 33-34

HUMAN RIGHTS COMMISSIONS
 earlier views, 15-16
 guidelines, 9-10
 mandates, 8, 16
 past definitions, 15-16
 purpose, 15

HUMAN RIGHTS STATUTES
 paramountcy, 166-168
 purpose, 32-33, 243-244

HUMAN RIGHTS TRIBUNALS
 See BOARDS OF INQUIRY

JOB-RELATED CONSEQUENCES
 examples, 102, 110, 111
 hostile and offensive work environment, 123
 negative, 103
 positive, 111
 quid pro quo, 102-103
 resulting from harassment, 102

K-MART CORPORATION, 4

LAW SOCIETY OF UPPER CANADA, 343

LEGAL COSTS, 262-266

LOSS OF EARNINGS
 determination, 251-253

MANITOBA HUMAN RIGHTS ACT
 amendments to, 54
 relevant sections, 50

MASTER AGREEMENT *See* COLLECTIVE AGREEMENT

MICHIGAN EMPLOYMENT SECURITY COMMISSION
 adjudication of claims, 280
 directives, 279-280
 eligibility and qualifications, 280
 relevant sections, 279-280

MISCONDUCT
 guidelines, 280
 Unemployment Insurance Benefits, 281-282

NATIONAL ASSOCIATION FOR FEMALE EXECUTIVES, 4

NATIONAL LAW JOURNAL, 4

NEWFOUNDLAND HUMAN
    RIGHTS CODE
  relevant sections, 49-50

OFFENSIVE WORK
    ENVIRONMENT THEORY, 113,
    123
  amounting to discrimination, 91,93,
    95-96, 122-123
  condition of employment, 112
  different than quid pro quo, 123

ONTARIO HUMAN RIGHTS CODE,
    157
  amendments, 47
  definition, 83-84
  powers of Boards of Inquiry, 48
  relevant sections, 47-48
  scope, 56

ONTARIO HUMAN RIGHTS
    COMMISSION
  discretionary powers of, 162

PENALTIES
  factors to be considered, 331
  nature and types, 331

PERSONNEL FILES
  confidential nature, 329

POISONED WORK ENVIRONMENT
    THEORY, 112-116
  concept, 42, 57
  condition of employment, 115
  cumulative effect, 42, 113
  elements, 114-115
  perpetrators of, 120
  results, 46, 116

PRIMA FACIE CASE
  balance of probabilities, 132-133
  failure to rebut, 42
  onus, 42
  proving, 130-137

PROHIBITED CONDUCT
  examples, 324

PSYCHOLOGICAL DISABILITY
  caused by harassment, 278
  test, 277
  victim to establish, 278

PUNITIVE DAMAGES
  injury to feelings, 258
  jurisdiction of Boards of Inquiry,
    258-260
  purpose, 258-260

QUALITY OF WORK
    ENVIRONMENT
  United States, 27-32

QUEBEC CHARTER OF HUMAN
    RIGHTS AND FREEDOMS
  amendments, 49

QUEBEC STUDY, 5

QUID PRO QUO
  adverse job-related consequences,
    123-125
  concept, 102, 154
  definition, 102
  different than hostile environment,
    123
  economic, 124-125
  harassment by co-workers, 155
  harassment by supervisors, 154
  Tangible Benefits theory, 103

REASONABLE PERSON
  Human Rights Code, 72-73
  poisonous environment, 73
  standard, 72-73

REASONABLE VICTIM
  standard, 72

REDRESS MECHANISM
  appeals, 332
  availability, 328-329

REDRESS MECHANISM, *cont'd*
complaint procedure, 329-330
confidentiality, 329
false accusations, 332
investigation procedure, 330-331
penalties for the harasser, 331
protection against retaliation, 328
remedies for the victim, 331-332
reporting complaints, 327-328

REINSTATEMENT
common law, 268
difficulties, 268-270

REMEDIES *See also* DAMAGES
apology, 270
back pay, 247, 248
cease and desist orders, 273
compensation, 243-248, 254-258
damages for loss of dignity and self-respect, 254-258
law of slander and libel, 229
legal costs, 262-266
prevention, 268-270
punitive, 258-260
special damages, 248-250
unemployment benefits, 252-253
   entitlement, 248
   obligation to establish, 247
welfare benefits, 253-254

RES JUDICATA
application, 156
denial, 160
establishing, 159
estoppel by, 156
grievance and arbitration procedures, 159
grounds, 156
Ontario Labour Relations Act, 157
restrictions under collective agreement, 161

SASKATCHEWAN HUMAN RIGHTS CODE
prohibitions, 38

SEX-BASED HARASSMENT, 116-120
characteristics, 117
co-workers, 117
definition, 116-117
examples, 117
results of, 117, 120

SEX DISCRIMINATION
adverse job differentiation, 122
amounting to harassment, 122
concept, 56
dress and grooming requirements, 98-101
grounds, 45
improper conduct, 45-47
legislative protection, 49
poisoned work environment, 43
scope of prohibition, 56

SEXUAL ANNOYANCE
definition, 10

SEXUAL BEHAVIOUR
banning in the workplace, 311-313
constituting harassment, 7
crude jokes, 89
examples, 13

SEXUAL COERCION
definition, 10
nexus, 10, 27
example, 10

SEXUAL HARASSMENT
behaviour
   amounting to discrimination, 10, 14-16, 32-34, 45-47, 52, 54, 59-60, 62
   by implication, 38
causes of, 55
condition of employment, 10, 14, 36, 62, 73
co-workers, 85, 155, 213-218
   determining, 215-216
   poisoned work environment, 216

SEXUAL HARASSMENT, *cont'd*
  behaviour, *cont'd*
    co-workers, *cont'd*
      quid pro quo, 216
      elements of, 135
      employee's rights, 8
      employer's duty, 214, 219
      examples, 7, 11-13
      non-employees, 325
      not amounting to discrimination, 52, 54
        based on sex appeal, 53-54
      perpetrators of, 120, 136
      prevention, 221-222
      principles, 45
      prohibited conduct, 33-34, 36, 43, 46
        results, 118, 136
        scope, 118
      reasonable person, 72-73
      scope, 1, 11, 10
      supervisors, 62, 84
    characteristics, 3, 10, 62
      cartoons, 12, 96-97
      coerced and forced, 43, 76-80
      crude language, 38-39, 92
        amounting to harassment, 92
        examples, 93
        standard of behaviour, 94
      deliberate/intentional, 85-88
        adverse effects, 86
        intensity and gravity, 86
        intent, 86
        loophole, 85
        motive, 86, 87, 88
        results/effects, 87-88
      dirty jokes
        examples, 9, 11
      gender-based insults, 43
      implicit, 38
      innuendos, 60
      non-verbal, 12
        definition, 12
        examples, 12
      nudity, 96
        effects, 97
        examples, 97
      persistent and repeated, 80-85
        condition of employment, 84
        examples, 82
        frequency, 82
        impact, 83
      physical, 38-39, 43, 60, 61
        examples, 60, 74
      propositioning, 39, 43, 60
      psychological
        examples, 60
      stereotyping, 89
      subtle, 61
      suggestive remarks, 11-12
      taunting, 37
      threats, 39
      unsolicited/unwelcome, 63, 69-70, 73-76
        definition, 63
        voluntary vs unwelcome, 63-64, 73
      verbal, 11-12, 38, 121-122
        standard of reasonableness, 122
  consensual relationships, 73-76
  consequences
    adverse employment consequences, 36-37, 55, 59, 60
    discharge, 81
    emphasis on, 86
    results, 88
  economic, 61, 309-311
  effect on victim, 279, 307
  hidden costs, 309-311
  hostile environment
    characteristics, 84
  implications for employers, 308
  offensive work environment, 30, 37
    atmosphere of discrimination, 30
    grounds for suit, 30
    reprisals *See also* CONSTRUCTIVE DISCHARGE, DISMISSAL

Index

SEXUAL HARASSMENT, *cont'd*
consequences, *cont'd*
  physical, 115
  psychological, 115
  victim, 115, 224-228
  women's groups, 54
  women, 1, 12, 54
definition, 1, 7, 8, 9-10, 14, 61, 122-123
  statutory, 10, 48, 60, 83-84
nature and scope
  condition of employment, 33, 34, 109
  standard of reasonable person, 122
statistics, 2-6

SEXUAL HARASSMENT EDUCATION, 333

SEXUAL HARASSMENT POLICY
application and scope, 325-327
Canada Labour Code, 316
commitment, 320, 321
communication, 333
consensual relations, 326
definition, 319, 321, 323-324
education, 321, 333
effective, 316
employer's philosophy, 321
essential elements, 321-352
example
  City of Toronto, 335-343
  Law Society of Upper Canada, 343-352
explicit policy, 319
false accusation, 332
Human Rights Commission, 315
implementation, 332-334
policy statement, 321-322
prevention
  communication, 320, 321, 333
  education, 333
  a necessity, 307
  training, 333-334

protection of victim, 319, 328
protection of witness, 319, 328
public policy in Canada, 314
purpose, 322-323
redress mechanism, 327-332
  appeals, 332
  appropriate discipline, 317
  availability, 328-329
  complaint procedure, 224, 329-330
  confidentiality, 319, 321, 329
  employee counselling, 312
  internal grievance procedure *See* **COMPLAINT PROCEDURE**
  investigation process, 224, 330-331
  liability insurance, 316
  penalties for the harasser, 331
  preventive action, 317, 320
  preventive program, 319
  remedial action, 317-318
  remedies to the victim, 331-332
reporting of complaints, 327-328
  multiple entry points, 327

SIMILAR FACT EVIDENCE, 147-154
See also **BURDEN OF PROOF**
corporate responsibility, 152
relevant facts, 149
rules for admission, 153-154
standards of admissibility, 153

SOUTHAM NEWS, 5

STEREOTYPING
condition of employment, 89
examples, 89
isolated incidents, 91
objective standard, 90
offensive environment, 89

STRICT LIABILITY *See also* **EMPLOYER LIABILITY**

TANGIBLE BENEFIT THEORY
See QUID PRO QUO

TRANSITIONS IN THE ONTARIO LEGAL PROFESSION, 5

SUPREME COURT OF CANADA
definition, 59
meaning and scope, 60
principles, 60

SURVEYS
B.C. Federation of Labour and Women's Research Centre, 4
Canadian, 4
Canadian Human Rights Commission, 5
by female ministers, 6
United States Merit System Protection Board, 3

UNEMPLOYMENT INSURANCE ACT, 282-283
advantages, 283
entitlement, 283
just cause
definition, 282-283
relevant sections, 282-283

UNEMPLOYMENT INSURANCE BENEFITS
adjudication of claims, 280
eligibility, 279
implications, 280
United States, 279
voluntary termination, 280

UNIONS
attitudes towards sexual harassment, 354-355
collective agreement, 264, 328, 358
Constitutional Convention, 354
constitutions, 357
contracting out, 354
definition, 354
duty to accommodate, 364
duty to eliminate sexual harassment, 367
duty of fair representation, 366-367
grievance procedure, 356
human rights complaints
special mechanisms, 356
implied obligations, 354
indirect discrimination, 360
legal obligations, 359-366
moral obligations, 354
policies on sexual harassment, 358
sexual harassment by co-workers, 356, 357
sexual harassment by union officers, 356
special mechanisms, 356
statistics, 353
unfair labour practices, 366
union liability, 360-366

UNITED STATES
Civil Rights Act, 17
relevant sections, 23
Title VII, 17-25
violation, 209
conciliation, 17
conditions of employment, 24
criminal law, 20
development of law, 16-32
employer liability, 20, 22, 24
criteria for determining, 210
Equal Employment Opportunity Commission Guidelines. See EQUAL EMPLOYMENT OPPORTUNITY COMMISSION
hostile environment theory, 24
Merit System Protection Board, 310
poisoned work environment theory, 210
restricted interpretations, 20
quid pro quo, 210
test in determining harassment, 22
vicarious liability, 210

UNIVERSAL DECLARATION OF
    HUMAN RIGHTS, 2

UNWANTED SEXUAL
    HARASSMENT
  standard of reasonableness, 70-73

VICARIOUS LIABILITY *See also*
    EMPLOYER LIABILITY
  employer, 53
  "in the course of employment"
    definition, 279
  principle, 183-186
  rationale for imposing, 183-186

VICTIMS
  obligations of, 247, 248-249
  reluctance to complain, 127-130
    inviting propositions, 127
  survey, 127-128
    cost, 128-129
    internal redress mechanism, 129
    publicity, 128
    retaliatory defamation suit, 129

WEST PUBLISHING COMPANY, 4

WOMEN
  adverse effects, 127, 307
  entering the workforce
    results, 307-308
  reluctance to complain, 127-129
  studies, 313-314

WOMEN'S ISSUES
  effects of social change, 2

WORKERS' COMPENSATION ACT
  relevant sections, 275, 279
  scope, 275

WORKERS' COMPENSATION
    APPEAL TRIBUNAL, 276
  criteria for determining stress cases,
    277
  examples, 277-278
  standard of evidence, 277

WORKERS' COMPENSATION
    BENEFITS
  award, 274
  poisoned work place environment
    theory, 274
  scope, 273
  test, 273-274
  work-related injury, 273

WORKING WOMEN MAGAZINE, 3

WORKING WOMEN STUDY, 4

WORKING WOMEN UNITED
    INSTITUTE SURVEY, 127

YORK UNIVERSITY'S
    PRESIDENTIAL ADVISORY
    COMMITTEE ON SEXUAL
    HARASSMENT, 58